PROTECTING HUMAN RIGHTS AND BUILDING PEACE IN POST-VIOLENCE SOCIETIES

This book critically examines the relationship between protecting human rights and building peace in post-violence societies. It explores the conditions that must be present, and strategies that should be adopted, for the former to contribute to the latter. The author argues that human rights can aid peacebuilding efforts by helping victims of past violence to articulate their grievance, and by encouraging the state to respond to and provide them with a meaningful remedy. This usually happens either through a process of adjudication, whereby human rights can offer guidance to the judiciary as to the best way to address such grievances, or through the passing and implementation of human rights laws and policies that seek to promote peace. However, this positive relationship between human rights and peace is both qualified and context-specific. Through an interdisciplinary and comparative analysis of four case studies, the book identifies the conditions that can support the effective use of human rights as peacebuilding tools. Developing these, the book recommends a series of strategies that peacebuilders should adopt and rely on.

Volume 25: Human Rights Law in Perspective

Human Rights Law in Perspective

General Editor: Colin Harvey
Professor of Human Rights Law
School of Law
Queen's University Belfast

The language of human rights figures prominently in legal and political debates at the national, regional and international levels. In the UK the Human Rights Act 1998 has generated considerable interest in the law of human rights. It will continue to provoke much debate in the legal community and the search for original insights and new materials will intensify.

The aim of this series is to provide a forum for scholarly reflection on all aspects of the law of human rights. The series will encourage work which engages with the theoretical, comparative and international dimensions of human rights law. The primary aim is to publish over time books which offer an insight into human rights law in its contextual setting. The objective is to promote an understanding of the nature and impact of human rights law. The series is inclusive, in the sense that all perspectives in legal scholarship are welcome. It will incorporate the work of new and established scholars.

Human Rights Law in Perspective is not confined to consideration of the UK. It will strive to reflect comparative, regional and international perspectives. Work which focuses on human rights law in other states will therefore be included in this series. The intention is to offer an inclusive intellectual home for significant scholarly contributions to human rights law.

Recent titles in this series

Governing (Through) Rights
Bal Sokhi-Bulley

Gender Equality in Law: Uncovering the Legacies of Czech State Socialism
Barbara Havelkova

Investment and Human Rights in Armed Conflict: Charting an Elusive Intersection
Daria Davitti

Specifying and Securing a Social Minimum in the Battle Against Poverty
Toomas Kotkas, Ingrid Leijten and Frans Pennings

For the complete list of titles in this series, see 'Human Rights Law in Perspective' link at www.bloomsburyprofessional.com/uk/series/human-rights-law-in-perspective/

Protecting Human Rights and Building Peace in Post-violence Societies

Nasia Hadjigeorgiou

•HART•
OXFORD • LONDON • NEW YORK • NEW DELHI • SYDNEY

HART PUBLISHING

Bloomsbury Publishing Plc

Kemp House, Chawley Park, Cumnor Hill, Oxford, OX2 9PH, UK

1385 Broadway, New York, NY 10018, USA

First published in Great Britain 2020

A catalogue record for this book is available from the British Library.

Library of Congress Cataloging-in-Publication data

Names: Hadjigeorgiou, Nasia, author.

Title: Protecting human rights and building peace in post-violence societies / Nasia Hadjigeorgiou.

Description: Chicago : Hart Publishing, an imprint of Bloomsbury Publishing, 2020. | Series: Human rights law in perspective; volume 25 | Includes bibliographical references and index.

Identifiers: LCCN 2019042248 (print) | LCCN 2019042249 (ebook) | ISBN 9781509923427 (hardback) | ISBN 9781509923434 (Epub)

Subjects: LCSH: Human rights. | Peace-building—Law and legislation. | Peace-building—International cooperation. | Conflict management.

Classification: LCC K3240 .H333 2020 (print) | LCC K3240 (ebook) | DDC 342.08/5—dc23

LC record available at https://lccn.loc.gov/2019042248

LC ebook record available at https://lccn.loc.gov/2019042249

ISBN: HB: 978-1-50992-342-7
ePDF: 978-1-50992-344-1
ePub: 978-1-50992-343-4

Typeset by Compuscript Ltd, Shannon
Printed and bound in Great Britain by CPI Group (UK) Ltd, Croydon CR0 4YY

MIX
Paper from responsible sources
FSC® C013604

To Christoforos and Andreas

Acknowledgements

I NEVER WOULD have thought at the beginning of this process that the writing of a book – what is generally thought to be a lonely endeavour – would result in the accumulation of so much gratitude towards that many people. Since the book started its journey as a doctoral thesis, my first thanks go to the community that pushed and supported me as a PhD student at King's College London. My supervisors, Professors Lorenzo Zucca and Guglielmo Verdirame, gave me the practical tools and confidence to complete the PhD and continue developing my ideas as an early career researcher. Lorenzo in particular, I hope that I am as good a supervisor to my students as you were to me. My PhD examiners – Professors Colm O'Cinneide and Kieran McEvoy – struck the right balance between providing me with meaningful and constructive criticism on the one hand, and encouraging me to pursue the development of the thesis into a book on the other. I would like to especially thank Colm, who has been an inspiration and a mentor since 2008, when I was still an undergraduate student.

Visiting speakers and academics at King's College London over the years have also shaped my thinking, both as a researcher and a young professional. Particularly influential to me were Professors David Kennedy, Allen Buchanan and David Caron. Additional thanks go to Professor Penny Green, Dr Nicola Palmer and (again) Professor Allen Buchanan for reading parts of the PhD thesis and giving me their insightful feedback. Moreover, my funders – the Graduate School of King's College London and the Leventis Foundation – made the PhD journey not only vastly more enjoyable, but in fact, possible in the first place, for which I am immensely grateful. Finally, I will always cherish the community of colleagues and friends that I met during my PhD years: Nikos Skoutaris, Charilaos Nikolaidis, Mathilde Groppo, Ermioni Xanthopoulou, Adrienne Yong, Rachel Seoighe, Angela Sherwood, Arman Sarvarian, Ana Cardenas, Egle Dagilyte, Nikolas Voulgaris, Eleni Papasozomenou, Stefan Mandelbaum, Narutoshi Yoshida, Baskaran Balasingam, Esin Kucuk and Sabrina Gilani.

Following the completion of the PhD, the book continued its journey and found a home in Cyprus, where I was lucky to receive mentorship and support from a humbling number of individuals: Nikolas Kyriakou, Mary-Ann Stavrinidou, Ioanna Demetriou and Maria Kourti from the Law Office of the Republic of Cyprus; Costas Clerides, the Attorney-General of the Republic of Cyprus; Stephanie Laulhé-Shaelou from UCLan Cyprus; and Andreas Kapardis and Aris Constantinides from the University of Cyprus. My colleagues from UCLan Cyprus, both old and new, have been an invaluable source of inspiration and help: Lida Pitsillidou, Natalie Alkiviadou, Klearchos Kyriakides, Nevi

Agapiou, Katerina Kalaitzaki, Demetra Loizou, Despina Christofi, Theodora Theofanous, Sofia Michaelides, Wendy Kennett and Stella Alekou, thank you. During my time in Cyprus, conversations with, and presentations from, several people shaped my research interests, methodology and conclusions. Special mention should be made to Michael Hein, Harry Tzimitras, Achilleas Demetriades, Yaniv Ronzai, Richard Albert and Akis Hadjihambis.

The greatest and most heartfelt thanks go to my family and friends, both in London and Cyprus. Mum, Dad, Demetri, Constantina, what I do and who I am would not have been possible without you.

Finally, Christofore and baby Andrea – you are my all. This book is dedicated to you.

Contents

List of Abbreviations

ANC	African National Congress
Annan Plan	Proposal for the Comprhensive Settlement of the Cyprus Problem
Article 1-1	Article 1 of Protocol No 1 of the European Convention on Human Rights (the right to property)
Article 3-1	Article 3 of Protocol No 1 of the European Convention on Human Rights (the right to vote)
B-BBEE	Broad-Based Black Economic Empowerment (in South Africa)
Belfast Agreement	The Northern Ireland Peace Agreement, Agreement Reached in the Multi-Party Negotiations, signed on 10 April 1998
BiH	Bosnia and Herzegovina
Brahimi Report	Report of the Panel on United Nations Peace Operations
CMP	Committee on Missing Persons (in Cyprus)
CRLR	Commission on Restitution of Land Rights (in South Africa)
Dayton Agreement	General Framework Agreement, signed on 14 December 1995 (for Bosnia and Herzegovina)
ECHR	European Convention on Human Rights
ECNI	Equality Commission of Northern Ireland
ECRI	European Commission against Racism and Intolerance
ECtHR	European Court of Human Rights
EU	European Union
FBiH	Federation of Bosnia and Herzegovina (one of the two entities of Bosnia and Herzegovina)
FETO	Fair Employment and Treatment Order (in Northern Ireland)

GC	Greek Cypriot(s)
HMIC	Her Majesty's Inspectorate of Constabulary (in the UK)
ICTY	International Criminal Tribunal for the Former Yugoslavia
IPC	Immovable Property Commission (in Cyprus)
IRA	Irish Republican Army
NI	Northern Ireland/Northern Irish
OSCE	Organization for Security and Cooperation in Europe
Patten Commission	Independent Commission on Policing for Northern Ireland
PLIP	Property Law Implementation Plan (in Bosnia and Herzegovina)
PRIO	Peace Research Institute Oslo
PSNI	Police Service of Northern Ireland
RoC	Republic of Cyprus
RS	Republika Srpska (one of the two entities in Bosnia and Herzegovina)
SA	South Africa/South African(s)
SFOR	Stabilization Force (in Bosnia and Herzegovina)
TC	Turkish Cypriot(s)
TRC	Truth and Reconciliation Commission (in South Africa)
'TRNC'	'Turkish Republic of Northern Cyprus'
UNFICYP	United Nations Peacekeeping Force in Cyprus
UDHR	Universal Declaration of Human Rights
UNDP	United Nations Development Programme
UNGAR	United Nations General Assembly Resolution
UNHRC	United Nations High Commissioner for Refugees
UNSCR	United Nations Security Council Resolution

Table of Cases

Bosnia and Herzegovina

Cyprus

South Africa

UK

US

European Court of Human Rights

Inter-American Court of Human Rights

International Tribunal for the Former Yugoslavia

Table of Legislation

Cyprus

Bosnia and Herzegovina

South Africa

United Kingdom

International Agreements

United Nations Resolutions

1

Introduction

I. INTRODUCTION

PART OF THE bleak history of the ongoing failed attempts to resolve the Cyprus conflict is an encouraging success story: over the last few years, the Committee of Missing Persons, staffed by Greek Cypriot (GC) and Turkish Cypriot (TC) scientists, has made strides in discovering and identifying the bodies of individuals who had gone missing during the violence of the 1960s and 1970s.[1] This became possible after decades of frustrating stalemate, when the plight of missing persons' families was reconceptualised as a human rights problem affecting, and deserving a response from, both communities on the island.[2] At the same time, the authorities' failure to locate those who disappeared during the apartheid era in South Africa (SA), which was also understood and addressed as a human rights issue, has been described by the country's Truth and Reconciliation Commission (TRC) as 'perhaps the most significant piece of unfinished business' within its mandate.[3] The juxtaposition between these two examples illustrates a tendency among decision makers from very different backgrounds to rely on human rights in order to promote peace in post-violence societies. It also suggests that although the use of human rights as peacebuilding tools can have profound positive effects, this is not an absolute and universal truth.

There is a paradox surrounding our expectations around the protection of human rights: on the one hand, we anticipate that they will provide stability and legitimise the legal and political system within which they operate, and on the other hand, we envisage that they will act as agents of change and be the bearers of necessary social reform.[4] Yet, this paradox has not been translated in equally nuanced expectations about the way in which human rights can be utilised, and the effects they can have, in post-violence societies. Rather, human rights are seen as the 'universally recognised chic language' of writing and implementing peace

[1] For more information on the Committee of Missing Persons, see www.cmp-cyprus.org.

[2] Iosif Kovras, *Grassroots Activism and the Evolution of Transitional Justice: The Families of the Disappeared* (Cambridge, Cambridge University Press, 2017) 154.

[3] TRC, *Report of the Truth and Reconciliation Commission* (Pretoria, TRC, 1998), Volume 6, Section 4, ch 1 [96].

[4] Aileen Kavanagh, 'The Role of a Bill of Rights in Reconstructing Northern Ireland' (2004) 26 *Human Rights Quarterly* 956.

agreements,[5] and utterances that encourage measured expectations about what they can achieve are few and far between.[6] This study challenges the orthodoxy by arguing that human rights can indeed make valuable contributions to peacebuilding efforts, *so long as* the necessary conditions that allow this are in place. Understanding the precise ways in which they can help build peace and identifying the factors that assist in this process are important because these point to practical steps that decision makers can take to enhance their effectiveness in post-violence societies. Thus, clarifying the largely underexplored relationship between protecting human rights and building peace is not (only) an exercise of theoretical importance; rather, if its conclusions are taken seriously and adopted in good faith, they can give rise to a range of strategies that result in the betterment of people's lives around the world.

II. THE CENTRAL QUESTION

References to the peacebuilding potential of human rights are abundantly scattered throughout the literature. The seminal UN report *An Agenda for Peace* confidently declared that 'human rights monitors, electoral officials, refugee and humanitarian aid specialists' – in other words, those professionals who are most directly concerned with the protection of human rights – play a 'central role' in peacebuilding operations.[7] Similarly, the UN High-Level Panel on Threats, Challenges and Change expressed its support for the integration of human rights throughout the work of the UN and encouraged the development of strong domestic human rights institutions, especially in countries emerging from conflict.[8] This faith in human rights was reiterated by UN Secretary-General Kofi Annan when he argued that 'elements of good governance', among them 'monitoring [of] human rights', have received much attention because they 'can promote reconciliation and offer a path for consolidating peace'.[9] This positive relationship has also been explicitly acknowledged by other UN organs, with the General Assembly noting that 'the promotion of a culture of peace [is] based on … respect for human rights'[10] and the Security Council

[5] Christine Bell, *Peace Agreements and Human Rights* (Oxford, Oxford University Press, 2000) 298.

[6] Emily Pia and Thomas Diez, 'Human Rights Discourses and Conflict: Moving Towards Desecuritization' in Raffaele Marchetti and Nathalie Tocci (eds), *Civil Society, Conflicts and the Politicization of Human Rights* (Tokyo, United Nations University Press, 2011).

[7] UN Secretary-General, *An Agenda for Peace: Preventive Diplomacy, Peacemaking and Peace-Keeping: Report of the Secretary-General Pursuant to the Statement Adopted by the Summit Meeting of the Security Council on 31 January 1992*, A/47/277 – S/24111 (New York, United Nations, 1992) [52].

[8] UN Secretary-General's High-Level Panel on Threats Challenges and Change, *A More Secure World: Our Shared Responsibility*, A/59/565 (New York, United Nations, 2004) [284].

[9] Kofi Annan, 'The Quiet Revolution' (1998) 4 *Global Governance* 123, 123.

[10] United Nations General Assembly Resolution 52/13 (15 January 1998), art 2.

stressing 'the urgent need to promote peace and national reconciliation and to foster accountability and respect for human rights', while highlighting 'the key role' that Human Rights Commissions can play in this respect.[11]

Such peacebuilding expectations should be taken with a pinch of salt. Often, the absolute and overreaching, yet vague, language of UN instruments reflects compromises that took place during their drafting process rather than accurate assessments of what human rights can deliver. For this reason, it is not always appropriate to use soundbites from lengthy UN reports and treat them as evidence of simplistic assumptions on behalf of policy makers that protecting human rights necessarily leads to peace. Even so, the history of peacebuilding operations confirms that such statements have, in fact, shaped practices on the ground. Since 1945, which marked the first modern attempts to build peace, and until today, peacebuilding operations have evolved and become much more sophisticated in their objectives and methods. Yet, at no point during this process has the effectiveness of human rights as peacebuilding tools been seriously questioned. The emphasis that was placed on them during the early years is reflected in the establishment of the Nuremberg and Tokyo Tribunals, which were intended to prosecute perpetrators of serious human rights violations.[12] International peacebuilding went into hibernation during the Cold War, but the fall of communism at the end of the twentieth century led to the second stage of its development.[13] Peacebuilding operations during this period – for example, in SA and Latin America – questioned a number of key assumptions, such as whether the use of criminal trials was the best way to promote peace, or whether Truth Commissions, coupled with amnesties, were more appropriate.[14] Yet, paying attention to human rights, either by punishing or being open about their violations, remained among the cornerstones of peacebuilding efforts. The third, and current, stage places even more emphasis on human rights by making them a key tenet of liberal peacebuilding, which since the mid-1990s has been implemented, around the world.[15] This peacebuilding strategy is based

[11] United Nations Security Council Resolution 1270 (22 October 1999), art 17.

[12] Robert Cryer et al, *An Introduction to International Criminal Law and Procedure*, 2nd edn (Cambridge, Cambridge University Press, 2012) 109–19; Darryl Robinson, 'The Identity Crisis of International Criminal Law' (2008) 21 *Leiden Journal of International Law* 952, 958.

[13] Ruti Teitel, 'Transitional Justice Genealogy' (2003) 16 *Harvard Human Rights Journal* 69.

[14] For an excellent literature review of this debate, see Kieran McEvoy and Louise Mallinder, 'Amnesties in Transition: Punishment, Restoration and the Governance of Mercy' (2012) 39 *Journal of Law and Society* 410.

[15] Oliver Richmond, *The Transformation of Peace* (Basingstoke, Palgrave Macmillan, 2006). The literature addressing the limitations of liberal peacebuilding is vast and growing. See, eg, Oliver Richmond, 'A Post-liberal Peace: Eirinism and the Everyday' (2009) 35 *Review of International Studies* 557; Chandra Lekha Sriram, 'Justice as Peace? Liberal Peacebuilding and Strategies of Transnational Justice' (2007) 21 *Global Society* 579; Oliver Ramsbotham, Tom Woodhouse and Hugh Miall, *Contemporary Conflict Resolution: The Prevention, Management and Transformation of Deadly Conflicts* (Cambridge, Polity Press, 2016); Ronald Paris, 'Wilson's Ghost: The Faulty Assumptions of Postconflict Peacebuilding' in Chester Crocker, Fen Osler Hampson and Pamel Aall (eds), *Turbulent Peace: Conflict Resolution versus Democratic Governance: Divergent Paths to Peace?* (Washington DC, United States Institute of Peace Press, 2001); Roger Mac Ginty,

on the premise that the establishment of liberal institutions – among them a democratic and free market, the rule of law and, importantly, the protection of human rights – is all that is needed for the transformation of post-violence societies.

Thus, examples from such societies confirm that there is indeed an almost universal and extensive reliance on human rights as peacebuilding tools. For instance, the post-war Constitution of Bosnia and Herzegovina (BiH) has made the country a member to 16 international human rights agreements,[16] while the SA Final Constitution contains one of the most robust Bills of Rights, with civil, political, economic, social, cultural and group protections.[17] Northern Ireland's (NI) Belfast Agreement often refers to human rights, precisely because any impasse during the negotiations was overcome by resorting to them[18] and many of the peacebuilding initiatives that have been adopted in Cyprus are explicitly based on their protection.[19] Moreover, confidence in the peacebuilding potential of human rights has been echoed by many academics, who are not restrained by the same limitations as diplomats and policy makers. Thus, Parlevliet notes that 'the sustained protection of rights is essential for dealing with conflict constructively',[20] while Barash and Webel,[21] Little[22] and Lederach[23] include human rights protections among their recommended peacebuilding tools. Finally, a literature review by Bonacker et al points to widespread expectations that human rights can help desecuritise conflicts[24] and even Brewer's otherwise

'Indigenous Peace-Making versus the Liberal Peace' (2008) 43 *Cooperation and Conflict* 139; Charles Thiessen, 'Emancipatory Peacebuilding: Critical Responses to (Neo)Liberal Trends' in Thomas Matyok, Jessica Senehi and Sean Byrne (eds), *Critical Issues in Peace and Conflict Studies: Theory, Practice and Pedagogy* (Lanham, MD, Lexington Books, 2011).

[16] Constitution of Bosnia and Herzegovina, Annex 4 of the General Framework Agreement, signed on 14 December 1995, Annex I.

[17] Constitution of the Republic of South Africa (108 of 1996), ss 7–39.

[18] The Northern Ireland Peace Agreement, Agreement Reached in the Multi-Party Negotiations, signed on 10 April 1998 (Belfast Agreement); Bell (n 5) 173.

[19] Nikos Skoutaris, 'Buidling Transitional Justice Mechanisms without a Peace Settlement: A Critical Appraisal of Recent Case Law of the Strasbourg Court on the Cyprus Issue' (2010) 35 *European Law Review* 720.

[20] Michelle Parlevliet, *Bridging the Divide: Exploring the Relationship between Human Rights and Conflict Management* (Cape Town, Centre for Conflict Resolution, March 2002) 20.

[21] David P Barash and Charles P Webel, *Peace and Conflict Studies*, 2nd edn (Thousand Oaks, SAGE Publications, 2009).

[22] David Little, 'Peace, Justice and Religion' in Pierre Allan and Alexis Keller (eds), *What is Just Peace?* (Oxford, Oxford University Press, 2006).

[23] John Paul Lederach, 'Beyond Violence: Building Sustainable Peace' in Arthur Williamson (ed), *Beyond Violence: The Role of Voluntary and Community Action in Building a Sustainable Peace in Northern Ireland* (Belfast, Community Relations Council, 1995).

[24] Thorsten Bonacker et al, 'Human Rights and the (De)Securitization of Conflict' in Marchetti and Tocci (n 6). For additional evidence of this, see Tim Dunne and Nicholas J Wheeler, '"We the Peoples": Contending Discourses of Security in Human Rights Theory and Practice' (2004) 18 *International Relations* 9.

critical analysis of liberal peacebuilding concludes that '[t]he human rights discourse ... is essentially a language of peace'.[25]

Yet, despite such endorsements, relatively little attention has been paid to the specific ways in which human rights can help build peace and the conditions that must be in place for this to happen. Referring to the African context, Widner notes that: 'Because the language of the rule of law is now so much in vogue, observers too often tend to assume that courts can easily promote peace and democratic change in postconflict regimes, without looking closely at the grounds for such optimism.'[26] This tendency is problematic, since it can result in significantly undertheorised expectations. We protect human rights in post-violence societies without having settled on, or even properly discussed, what is the ultimate goal of the intervention, which actors are expected to deliver it, how we envisage this to materialise, whether there are any conditions that must be in place and what are the associated risks with the process.[27] Among the few academics that have adopted a more subtle analysis is Christine Bell, who notes, on the one hand, that the strength of human rights protections and the success of the peacebuilding mission are integrally linked, but warns, on the other hand, of the need to establish strong and effective institutions.[28] Similarly, Marchetti and Tocci argue that whether the human right in question is an individual or a collective one and the way in which it is used in each instance affect its overall peacebuilding potential.[29] The study joins these more critical voices by examining the adjudication, implementation and post-implementation challenges of human rights protection, and identifying the steps that should be taken for these to be addressed.

At the moment, the dominant perception is that any failures of human rights and other liberal tools to promote peace are mainly due to their non-implementation or other exogenous factors, such as underfunding or lack of cooperation between peacebuilders.[30] Disappointing results are never regarded

[25] John D. Brewer, *Peace Processes: A Sociological Approach* (Cambridge, Polity Press, 2010) 48.

[26] Jennifer Widner, 'Courts and Democracy in Postconflict Transitions: A Social Scientist's Perspective on the African Case' (2001) 95 *American Journal of International Law* 64, 64.

[27] Padraig McAuliffe, *Transformative Transitional Justice and the Malleability of Post-conflict States* (Cheltenham, Edward Elgar, 2017) 65.

[28] Bell (n 5) 294.

[29] Raffaele Marchetti and Nathalie Tocci, 'Conflict Society and Human Rights: An Analytical Framework' in Marchetti and Tocci (n 6).

[30] Roland Paris, 'Understanding the "Coordination Problem" in Postwar Statebuilding' in Roland Paris and Timothy D Sisk (eds), *The Dilemmas of Statebuilding: Confronting the Contradictions of Postwar Peace Operations* (London, Routledge, 2009). This is further confirmed by statements from the UN Secretary-General, who identified the problem of peace operations as being an institutional one, with the creation of the Peacebuilding Commission providing one solution (UN Secretary-General, *Address by United Nations Secretary-General Kofi Annan to the Fifty-Sixth Session of the Executive Committee of the High Commissioner's Programme* (Geneva, United Nations, 6 October 2005)).

as the result of human rights being used in an ill-suited way or under conditions that rendered them ineffective. Nevertheless, a belief that 'a bit more human rights can never make things worse' is dangerous because it necessarily 'places blame for whatever goes wrong elsewhere'.[31] As a result, the failures of human rights to build peace tend to be understood as encouragements to keep walking faster in the same direction rather than questioning the correctness of the path that peacebuilding actors are on in the first place. This study proposes a different response: in short, it entertains the possibility that what we ask of human rights in peacebuilding operations might simply be too much.

Undertaking this exercise is essential because continuing to rely on current assumptions can result in several potentially dangerous and counterproductive misconceptions. First, a lack of clarity on how human rights can assist peacebuilding efforts might lead to the inaccurate conclusion that making any human rights policy part of the peacebuilding agenda can have equally positive effects. Second, this can prevent decision makers from assessing whether reliance on human rights is preferable to, or should be supplemented by, the adoption of other peacebuilding strategies. Finally, neglecting to pay close attention to the conditions that make human rights effective peacebuilding tools might lead to the misguided belief that their protection will always result in a positive outcome, irrespective of the context in which they are being implemented. Consequently, this can result in the adoption of uniform strategies with little appreciation of how the peculiarities of each post-violence society should be taken into account. While these dangers might not be an unavoidable eventuality, they become more likely to materialise if the nuanced relationship between human rights and peace is not in the forefront of decision makers' minds.

III. AN ANATOMY OF THE RELATIONSHIP BETWEEN HUMAN RIGHTS AND PEACE

The study clarifies the relationship between human rights and peace by relying both on the development of a theoretical framework and the assessment of hypotheses derived from it through the comparison of human rights-related peacebuilding practices in four post-violence societies. Chapter 2 starts building on the theory by proposing that peacebuilders should be working towards striking a balance between three inter-connected but also potentially conflicting elements. The first, *security*, seeks to both objectively reduce the levels of violence and promote a subjective sense among the population that their physical well-being is no longer under threat. The second, *justice*, involves efforts to address the injustices of the past and ensure that further injustices will not be

[31] David Kennedy, 'The International Human Rights Movement: Part of the Problem?' (2002) 15 *Harvard Human Rights Journal* 101, 124 and 122 respectively.

perpetrated in the future, while the third element, *reconciliation*, aims to build meaningful relationships of cooperation among previously warring parties. As with security, efforts to promote justice and reconciliation should result in institutions that objectively improve people's lives, the effects of which are also experienced and understood as such by the target audience itself. Chapter 3 continues by noting that striking a balance between the three elements of peace does not require the elimination of conflicts among previously warring parties, but ensuring that these conflicts are resolved in a non-violent manner. Human rights can assist peacebuilding efforts by contributing to this conflict resolution process in two ways: on the one hand, they can be used during the adjudication of a conflict in the courtroom and provide guidance to the judge as to the best way to respond to it; on the other hand, they can be given a role during the political process, when activists and concerned citizens frame their arguments in human rights terms and lobby for the enactment and implementation of policies that will respond to a particular conflict. Through these strategies, human rights can give rise to both objective and subjective feelings of security, justice and reconciliation among the population. Their specific peacebuilding contributions depend on a series of factors, which are explored in detail in the three practical chapters that follow.

Chapter 4, which is concerned with the peacebuilding effects of human rights during the adjudication process, argues that these can provide meaningful guidance to judges when they respond to relatively minor, as opposed to fundamental, conflicts. Attempting to resolve fundamental disagreements in the courtroom can result either in a refusal of the judiciary to become involved in the dispute or in the delivery of vague and contradictory judgments that can undermine each of the elements of peace. At the same time, the judiciary's conflict resolution potential also depends on the nature of the court hearing the dispute and, in particular, on whether it is a domestic or an international forum. Finally in terms of adjudication, *when* the disagreement is litigated – specifically, whether a comprehensive peace settlement is in place and the amount of time that has passed since it came into operation – can affect the peacebuilding potential of human rights. Similarly, whether human rights-inspired laws can assist in the conflict resolution process depends on a series of factors and, in particular, on the extent to which they are successfully enforced. Thus, Chapter 5 proposes that the implementation of human rights – and the consequent building of peace – are matters of degree and are shaped by how much political willingness to induce change is present among policymakers. Additionally, the extent of the ability of such laws to influence the conflict resolution process depends on skilful legislative drafting and the presence of enforcement bodies that have the independence, powers, resources and expertise to fulfil their mandate successfully.

Judicial guidance and lobbying for the protection of human rights are useful strategies because they can induce legal and institutional reforms that are necessary for the building of objective peace. However, if the beliefs of the people are also going to be challenged, which will in turn contribute to a subjective sense of peace in the post-violence society, two additional conditions, which are discussed in Chapter 6, must be present. The first is that the protection of human rights must have an impact on the lives of the people in the sense that it results in meaningful socio-economic and psychological changes among the population. Related to this is the second condition, which provides that these changes must not only resolve conflicts as a matter of fact, but should also be understood by their target audience as having this effect. The three sets of conditions, discussed in Chapters 4, 5 and 6, are not exhaustive and cannot guarantee that, when present, the protection of human rights will necessarily result in successful conflict resolution. However, paying attention to them can elucidate the connections between the two concepts and enhance the effectiveness of peacebuilding operations on the ground.

IV. THE METHODOLOGY

This volume explores the relationship between human rights and practice through a comparative analysis of four case studies: BiH, Cyprus, NI and SA. In doing so, it engages in a 'practical reasoning' methodological approach, which 'seeks to derive general conclusions from particular instances and to appreciate a complex reality'.[32] Like a pendulum, it does this by oscillating between theory and practice: it reaches theoretical conclusions through an analysis of specific human rights initiatives in the four case studies, while at the same time, it assesses these initiatives in light of the developing theoretical framework.

A. Defining a Post-violence Society

Post-violence societies are societies that have experienced communal violence, whose effects they are currently recovering from.[33] The definition is concerned with violence emanating from intra-state, rather than inter-state, conflicts because these have been the most common and destructive types of conflicts since the end of the Cold War.[34] Intra-state violence usually results in a higher number of civilian victims and, due to the very close proximity between the combating parties, causes the greatest levels of insecurity among the population.[35]

[32] Tom Gerard Daly, *The Alchemists: Questioning Our Faith in Courts as Democracy-Builders* (Cambridge, Cambridge University Press, 2017) 18.

[33] Brewer (n 25).

[34] Between 1989 and 2003, there were only seven inter-state and 116 intra-state conflicts. See Mikael Eriksson and Peter Wallensteen, 'Armed Conflict, 1989–2003' (2004) 41 *Journal of Peace Research* 625.

[35] Between 1945 and 1999, 20 million deaths took place as a result of intra-state conflicts and three million due to inter-state conflicts. See Sujit Choudhry, 'After the Rights Revolution: Bills of Rights in the Post-conflict State' (2010) 6 *Annual Review of Law and Social Science* 301, 308.

Additionally, this type of violence is linked to a vicious cycle of mistrust that gives rise to unique peacebuilding challenges: the violent conflict intensifies the group divisions that are undermining peace on the one hand, while the securitisation of group identities encourages the continuation or resumption of violence on the other hand. Of course, the distinction between intra-state and inter-state violence is not always clear, with several societies having experienced a combination of the two.[36] While, for instance, the eruption of violence in Cyprus in the 1960s had an intra-state character, in the 1970s this morphed into an inter-state conflict, following Turkey's military invasion of the island.[37] This proviso notwithstanding, the study focuses on examples where the eruption of *communal violence* has affected a *single society* that is currently implementing some form of a *peacebuilding strategy as a response*.

Although violence is always directed at the individual, whether towards his or her person or property, *communal* violence is characterised by attacks that are motivated by the intended victim's membership in a given group. In the four case studies examined here, the violence has been caused by largely unchanging group identities, such as those relating to race, ethnicity, language or religion, rather than, for example, political affiliation, which can more easily fluctuate throughout a person's life. Racial, religious or ethnic groups in post-violence societies are politically organised and have certain demands, usually relating to non-discrimination or greater recognition of their differences. These groups deem such demands to be necessary because they perceive their identities to be distinct and, in many cases, diametrically opposed to each other.[38] This is what Miller calls 'rival nationalities': especially during, or immediately before and after violence has erupted, the groups see themselves as having an antagonistic relationship, partly due to the fact that they define their identity as that which the other is not.[39] Of course, not every society manifests its group divisions violently; examples from the UK/Scotland and Canada/Quebec testify to this. However, where violence does break out, the defining group characteristic becomes the most dominant aspect of a member's identity, groups tend to act cohesively on almost all political issues and, as a result, the conflicts that arise between them are usually zero-sum in nature. Finally, since political threats are not easily distinguished from personal ones, group membership in post-violence societies determines not only who people vote for, but also who they socialise with and marry, who they work with or employ and, ultimately, who they are afraid of and distrust.

[36] Ramsbotham et al (n 15) 313–15.

[37] Harry Anastasiou, *Nationalism, Ethnic Conflict, and the Quest for Peace in Cyprus: Volume One: The Impasse of Ethnonationalism* (Syracuse, Syracuse University Press, 2008) 93–100.

[38] Margaret Moore, 'Globalization, Cosmopolitanism and Minority Nationalism' in Michael Keating and John McGarry (eds), *Minority Nationalism and the Changing International Order* (Oxford, Oxford University Press, 2001) 44.

[39] David Miller, 'Nationality in Divided Societies' in Alain G Gagnon and James Tully (eds), *Multinational Democracies* (Cambridge, Cambridge University Press, 2001) 303.

The label 'post-violence society' is not without its problems, not least the fact that it implies that the signing of a ceasefire agreement, or a comprehensive peace settlement, marks the end of violent hostilities and the creation of a secure society.[40] In fact, it should be acknowledged from the outset that the label 'post-violence' can sometimes be a misnomer, since it is possible for the violent death count to remain high, or even increase, shortly after the official termination of the war.[41] The term is nevertheless useful because it signifies a new state of affairs whereby the previously warring parties commit, albeit often lukewarmly, to resolve their differences in a non-violent manner.

B. Selecting the Four Case Studies

Unlike most comparative works on post-violence societies, which stay within the exclusive ambit of political sciences,[42] this study examines the peacebuilding effect of human rights as *legal* tools. At the same time, it accepts that 'maintaining the disciplinary divide between comparative constitutional law and other closely-related disciplines that study the same set of phenomena does not make sense'.[43] Consequently, it situates the legal analysis of the success or failure of human rights to resolve conflicts within a broader understanding of the prevalent conditions and dynamics in post-violence societies. In light of this, each chapter engages with different disciplines: Chapter 2 relies on peace studies literature, while Chapter 3 draws from conflict resolution, legal, political science and sociological arguments. Chapter 4 focuses on a legal analysis; Chapter 5 on legal and political science literature and Chapter 6 reaches conclusions that are of interest to sociologists. Finally, Chapter 7 brings the different disciplines together and links the arguments made in the previous chapters to peace studies.

In undertaking this interdisciplinary analysis, the study takes heed of Hirschl's insightful critique that legal scholars, of whom this author is one, generally fail to adopt a rigorous methodological approach, thus resulting in undertheorised conclusions and cherry-picking of the most convenient

[40] Pierre du Toit, *South Africa's Brittle Peace: The Problem of Post-settlement Violence* (Basingstoke, Palgrave, 2001).

[41] Geneva Declaration Secretariat, *Global Burden of Armed Violence* (Geneva, Geneva Declaration on Armed Violence and Development, 2008) 49–63.

[42] See, eg, Sumantra Bose, *Contested Lands: Israel-Palestine, Kashmir, Bosnia, Cyprus and Sri Lanka* (Cambridge, MA, Harvard University Press, 2007); Donald Horowitz, *Ethnic Groups in Conflict*, 2nd edn (Berkeley, University of California Press, 1985). Rare examples of legal analysis include Stephen Tierney, *Constitutional Law and National Pluralism* (Oxford, Oxford University Press, 2004); Yash Ghai (ed), *Autonomy and Ethnicity* (Cambridge, Cambridge University Press, 2000); and Bell (n 5).

[43] Ran Hirschl, 'Editorial: From Comparative Constitutional Law to Comparative Constitutional Studies' (2013) 11 *International Journal of Constitutional Law* 1, 11.

case studies.[44] This resonates with criticisms from another direction, namely that the peacebuilding literature overly relies on single case studies that tend to produce lists of 'dos' and 'don'ts', without much explanation of how these were derived beyond descriptive observations of what worked and what did not.[45] In response to these critiques, the four case studies have been carefully selected by taking into account both their similarities and differences. On the one hand, all of them have experienced communal violence, the consequences of which they are still in the process of addressing by adopting liberal peacebuilding strategies with a strong emphasis on human rights. On the other hand, these similar human rights policies have been applied in very different contexts, thus allowing us to assess how such differences impact on their effectiveness as peacebuilding tools. Comparisons between the case studies allow for the drawing of generalisable conclusions and developing a theoretical framework on the relationship between human rights and peace. In turn, such conclusions make the analysis not only relevant to the four post-violence societies that are being compared, but also to other contexts with similar characteristics.[46] This is particularly fruitful in light of the fact that some of these societies may be difficult to research directly, either due to the volatile conditions on the ground or because the need for a swift response after the eruption of violence often makes the carrying out of in-depth research more difficult.

Arguments have been made in the literature that the success of a peacebuilding operation can be affected by the post-violence society's population size,[47] types of divisions,[48] relative size of the groups within it,[49] prevailing socio-economic conditions,[50] the intensity and duration of past violence,[51] the extent of the international peacebuilding intervention[52] and whether there has

[44] Ran Hirschl, 'The Question of Case Selection in Comparative Constitutional Law' (2005) 53 *American Journal of Comparative Law* 125.

[45] Betts Fetherston, 'Peacekeeping, Conflict Resolution and Peacebuilding: A Reconsideration of Theoretical Frameworks' (2000) 7 *International Peacekeeping* 190, 191.

[46] Tood Landman, *Issues & Methods in Comparative Politics: An Introduction* (New York, Routledge, 2000) 10.

[47] Arend Lijphart, *Democracy in Plural Societies: A Comparative Exploration* (New Haven, Yale University Press, 1977) 161.

[48] Stephen Cornell and Douglas Hartmann, *Ethnicity and Race: Making Identities in a Changing World* (Thousand Oaks, Pine Forge Press, 2007); Miller (n 39); Stephan Wolff, 'Conceptualising Conflict Management and Settlement: Perspectives on Successes and Failures in Europe, Africa and Asia' in Ulrich Schneckener and Stephan Wolff (eds), *Managing and Settling Ethnic Conflicts* (London, Hurst & Co Publishers, 2004).

[49] Benjamin Reilly, 'Electoral Systems for Divided Societies' (2002) 13 *Journal of Democracy* 156, 168.

[50] Lijphart (n 47) 161; Davis A James, 'A Formal Interpretation of the Theory of Relative Deprivation' (1959) 22 *Sociometry* 280.

[51] Chaim D Kaufmann, 'When All Else Fails: Ethnic Population Transfers and Partitions in the Twentieth Century' (1998) 23 *International Security* 120.

[52] Michael Barnett and Christoph Zurcher, 'The Peacebuilder's Contract: How External Statebuilding Reinforces Weak Statehood' in Paris and Sisk (eds) (n 30) Timothy D Sisk, 'Pathways of the Political: Electoral Processes after Civil War' in Paris and Sisk (eds) (n 30).

been a signing of a comprehensive peace settlement.[53] The four case studies face commonalities and differences among them in relation to all these factors. For instance, while Cyprus (1.5 million), NI (1.8 million) and BiH (3.5 million) are relatively small, SA has a population of 56 million. Moreover, each differs in terms of the types of divisions it faces, with NI being divided along religious lines (Protestants and Catholics), SA along racial lines (between blacks, whites, coloureds and Indians, but also facing divisions among different tribal groups) and BiH and Cyprus being characterised by ethnic divisions (Bosniacs, Serbs and Croats in BiH and GCs and TCs in Cyprus). The groups also differ in relation to their relative size in their respective societies, as they are fairly equal in NI and (to a lesser extent) BiH, but quite different in Cyprus and SA. Specifically, Protestants and Catholics are divided by a 48:45 population ratio,[54] while Bosniacs, Serbs and Croats make up approximately 43, 31 and 17 per cent of the Bosnian people respectively.[55] Conversely, about 8 in 10 Cypriots are estimated to be GC and 2 in 10 to be TC.[56] In SA, 80 per cent are black; coloured and white people* make up 9 per cent of the population each, and Asians comprise approximately 2 per cent.[57] Finally, groups vary in terms of the relative socio-economic security that each enjoys, since (group) inequality prevails in all four societies.[58]

Further to the background conditions that distinguish each of the case studies, they also differ in terms of the intensity of violence that they have experienced. In Cyprus, the violence erupted during two high-intensity, very short periods between 1963 and 1964 (with violence mostly being targeted towards TCs)

[53] Hanna Lerner, *Making Constitutions in Deeply Divided Societies* (Cambridge, Cambridge University Press, 2011).

[54] Northern Ireland Statistics and Research Agency, *Census 2011: Key Statistics for Northern Ireland* (Belfast, Northern Ireland Statistics and Research Agency, 2012) 3.

[55] 'Ethnic Composition of Bosnia-Herzegovina Population, by Municipalities and Settlements, 1991', Zavod za statistiku Bosne i Hercegovine, Bilten no 234, Sarajevo, 1991, cited in Sabrina P Ramet, *Balkan Babel: The Disintegration of Yugoslavia from the Death of Tito to the Fall of Milosević*, 4th edn (Boulder, Westview Press, 2002) 241. Most of the remaining 9 per cent described itself as 'Yugoslav', a category that is today obsolete.

[56] Department of Statistics and Research, *Census of Population and Agriculture 1960 (Volume III – Demographic Characteristics)* (Nicosia, Department of Statistics and Research, 1963).

* References to the racial groups in South Africa (black, white, coloured and Indian) are included because they reflect the divisions that the apartheid regime was based on; divisions that remain to a large extent relevant, even today. It is for this reason that post-apartheid legislation and government publications also continue relying on them. See, eg, Broad-Based Black Economic Empowerment Act 53 of 2003, s1 and Commission for Employment Equity, *Annual Report 2015–2016* (Pretoria, Department of Labour, 2016).

[57] Statistics South Africa, *Census 2011: Statistical Release (Revised)* (Pretoria, Statistics South Africa, 2012).

[58] In SA, this is a consequence of apartheid policies, which have not been adequately addressed since democratisation; see Mike Cohen, 'South Africa's Racial Income Inequality Persists, Census Shows' *Bloomberg*, 30 October 2012. In Cyprus, this is, at least partly, due to the UN embargo imposed on the (internationally unrecognised) 'Turkish Republic of Northern Cyprus' and, as a result, on the vast majority of TCs; see United Nations Security Council Resolution 541 (18 November 1983), art 7; United Nations Security Council Resolution 550 (11 May 1984), art 3. In NI, this is because of employment discrimination against Catholics that existed during the Troubles; see Edmund A Aunger, 'Religion and Occupational Class in Northern Ireland' (1975) 7 *Economic and Social Review* 1. Finally, for evidence of inequality in BiH, see Marcelo Bisogno and Alberto Chong, 'Poverty and Inequality in Bosnia and Herzegovina after the Civil War' (2002) 30 *World Development* 61.

and 1974 (with the victims being mainly GCs).[59] The two periods resulted in approximately 2,000 missing persons,[60] 6,000 deaths[61] and 200,000 displaced individuals.[62] This was different from the situation in BiH, where the brutally violent conflict raged continuously between 1992 and 1995, producing approximately 100,000 dead[63] and 2.6 million displaced persons, who amounted to more than half of the pre-war population.[64] The conflicts in NI and SA were different still, since the relatively low-intensity violence lasted for decades in both instances. In NI, the Troubles began in 1968 and officially ended following the signing of the Belfast Agreement in 1998, with a total death toll of about 3,500.[65] In SA, the beginning of the conflict is more difficult to pinpoint, since the violent colonial regime gradually morphed into apartheid,[66] until this was abolished in 1993 with the coming into force of the country's Interim (first democratic) Constitution.[67] Celebrations of SA's 'non-violent transition miracle' are largely inaccurate since in the 1980s and early 1990s, approximately 15,000–25,000 South Africans were killed.[68] Indicatively, 3,706 people were killed between 1993 and 1994; 2,434 between 1994 and 1995 and 1,004 between 1995 and 1996,[69] while during March 1994, when the first election campaign was in full swing, 537 deaths were recorded, an average of 17.3 per day.[70]

Additionally, the four case studies differ in terms of the peacebuilding strategies they have adopted since the reduction/stopping of the violence and the extent to which the international community has been involved in these efforts. Comprehensive peace settlements have been signed for BiH, NI and SA (the Dayton Agreement,[71] the Belfast Agreement and the Final Constitution respectively), but a settlement is still elusive in Cyprus, despite the fact that it has been

[59] Paul Sant Cassia, *Bodies of Evidence: Burial, Memory and the Recovery of Missing Persons in Cyprus* (New York, Berghahn Books, 2005) 35 and 52.

[60] Committee on Missing Persons in Cyprus, *Figures and Statistics of Missing Persons up to 31 March 2019* (Nicosia, Committee of Missing Persons, 2019).

[61] Cassia (n 59) 52.

[62] Global IDP Database, *Profile of Internal Displacement: Cyprus* (Geneva, Norwegian Refugee Council/ Global IDP Project, 2003).

[63] Patrick Ball, Ewa Tabeau and Philip Verwimp, *The Bosnian Book of Dead: Assessment of the Database* (Sussex, Households in Conflict Network, 2007).

[64] OSCE Mission to Bosnia and Herzegovina, *Special Report: Musical Chairs: Property Problems in Bosnia and Herzegovina* (Sarajevo, Organisation for Security and Cooperation in Europe, 1996) 45–46.

[65] CAIN Web Service – Conflict and Politics in Northern Ireland: Violence – Statistics and Other Data on Violence, available at www.cain.ulst.ac.uk/issues/violence/cts/fay98.htm#tables.

[66] David Welsh, *The Rise and Fall of Apartheid* (Charlottesville, University of Virginia Press, 2009).

[67] (Interim) Constitution of the Republic of South Africa Act 200 of 1993.

[68] Adrian Guelke, *South Africa in Transition: The Misunderstood Miracle* (London, IB Tauris, 1999) 45.

[69] James L Gibson and Amanda Gouws, *Overcoming Intolerance in South Africa: Experiments in Democratic Persuasion* (Cambridge, Cambridge University Press, 2003) 18.

[70] Welsh (n 66) 535.

[71] General Framework Agreement, signed on 14 December 1995.

a post-violence society for the longest period of time out of the four.[72] Rather, both sides have been respecting a ceasefire since 1974 and have implemented a number of interim or temporary peacebuilding measures until the ongoing negotiations result in the reaching of a comprehensive settlement.[73] The efforts to produce such a settlement are driven forward by the international community, in the form of the UN, which remains actively involved in the negotiations.[74] International participation was also prevalent during the negotiations of the Dayton Agreement, but the US government, which had played a leading role at the time, has taken a step back and has left the EU and Council of Europe to provide guidance and support during the Agreement's implementation phase.[75] Unlike Cyprus and BiH, which have both experienced heavy-handed international intervention, the peacebuilding processes in the other two case studies have been driven by the SA government on the one hand and the devolved institutions of NI and the UK government on the other. However, it should be noted that the difference in the level of international involvement in the various post-violence societies is only a matter of degree, since both NI and SA have received international funding, which is often conditional on following the donors' agenda and implementing their preferred projects.[76]

These characteristics notwithstanding, what is even more important in terms of assessing the peacebuilding potential of human rights are a series of factors that directly relate to the way in which they have been utilised in the post-violence society. The differences and similarities among the four case studies in relation to each of these factors give rise to endless permutations and provide fertile ground for comparative analysis between them. For example, Chapter 5 argues that one of the factors affecting the ability of human rights to resolve conflicts is whether they are implemented by a body with the necessary independence, power, resources and expertise to undertake this task. NI and SA have responded to conflicts relating to discrimination in the workplace through the enactment of substantively similar laws, which are nevertheless enforced by institutions with very different characteristics. While the NI legislation has successfully addressed discrimination in the workplace, the SA law has not had the same effect. This observation can result in a comparison based on what Hirschl has called 'the most similar cases principle', namely an assessment

[72] Michális Stavrou Michael, *Resolving the Cyprus Conflict: Negotiating History* (New York, Palgrave Macmillan, 2009).

[73] UN Secretary-General, *Report of the Secretary-General on the United Nations Operation in Cyprus*, S/2017/20 (New York, United Nations, 9 January 2017).

[74] For a biannual account of the UN's efforts in this respect, see the reports of the Secretary-General, available at https://www.securitycouncilreport.org/un_documents_type/secretary-generals-reports/?ctype=Cyprus&cbtype=cyprus.

[75] For a chronicle of the negotiations, see Richard Holbrooke, *To End a War* (New York, The Modern Library, 1999). For an overview of the EU's actions in BiH, see www.eubih.eu.

[76] Julie Hearn, *Foreign Aid, Democratisation and Civil Society in Africa: A Study of South Africa, Ghana and Uganda* (Brighton, Institute of Development Studies, 1999).

of two human rights strategies that are generally similar, bar one characteristic, yet have resulted in different outcomes.[77] The hypothesis is that the one difference between them – in this case, the characteristics of the implementing body – is causally related to the different outcome.

Conversely, Chapter 6 argues that an effective communication strategy between the peacebuilders and their target audience is instrumental for inducing social and psychological changes within the post-violence society. BiH and SA have each remedied violently displaced individuals in different ways, but they have both neglected to communicate the symbolic importance of these remedies to the victims. In both instances, the provision of a legal remedy has failed to result in meaningful social and psychological changes. This allows for a comparison based on the 'most different cases principle', whereby two cases which are largely dissimilar, but share a common characteristic and result in the same outcome, are examined.[78] Here, the hypothesis is that the similarity (the common failure to adopt a communication strategy) explains the similar outcome (the inability of the remedies to result in social and psychological changes).

V. CONCLUSION

Over the last decade, commentators have assessed the success of peacebuilding operations and have found them wanting. Among the criticisms that have been levelled against existing strategies is the fact that their focus on building institutions and developing the law has not been matched by a concern of how people are affected by, and perceive, these institutions.[79] Consequently, the peace that the liberal recipe gives rise to is 'hollow'[80] and looks more coherent from the outside than the inside.[81] Moreover, current peacebuilding operations have been criticised for adopting excessively uniform policies with little understanding or care that these might not fit the specific contexts of different post-violence societies.[82] A related point is the concern that this, together with the way in which peacebuilding operations are often structured and funded, tends to empower international actors to the detriment of local ones.[83] Finally, allegations have

[77] Hirschl (n 44).
[78] ibid.
[79] Richmond, 'A Post-liberal Peace' (n 15) 569.
[80] Mac Ginty (n 15) 158.
[81] Oliver Richmond, 'UN Peacebuilding Operations and the Dilemma of the Peacebuilding Consensus' (2004) 11 *International Peacekeeping* 83, 91.
[82] Patricia Lundy and Mark McGovern, 'The Role of Community in Participatory Transitional Justice' in Kieran McEvoy and Lorna McGregor (eds), *Transitional Justice from Below: Grassroots Activism and the Struggle for Change* (Oxford, Hart Publishing, 2008).
[83] Severine Autesserre, *Peaceland: Conflict Resolution and the Everyday Politics of International Intervention* (Cambridge, Cambridge University Press, 2014).

been made that the assumptions of liberal peacebuilding, most predominantly the urge to push for democratisation and market liberalisation, have often encouraged rather than successfully reduced violent outbreaks.[84] However, even in the midst of such criticisms, reliance on human rights, as a conflict resolution strategy, has survived unscathed. The need to protect them *in order to build peace* is presented as a matter of common sense, a statement which almost by default does not need to be supported by arguments or empirical evidence. Moreover, while valuable in terms of challenging existing assumptions and practices, these critiques have sometimes been too abstract and negative in their focus, thus failing to identify possible alternative strategies or make constructive suggestions about how such limitations can be addressed.[85] This study seeks to both add to and develop such critiques. On the one hand, it confirms some of the above-mentioned limitations and tailors them specifically to the protection of human rights. It concludes that in a sobering number of instances, human rights could, and should, have done better. On the other hand, it proposes practical recommendations on how best to respond to these limitations. Taking these seriously can make human rights not only popular peacebuilding tools, but also effective ones.

[84] Roland Paris, *At War's End: Building Peace after Civil Conflict* (Cambridge, Cambridge University Press, 2004).

[85] Mac Ginty (n 15) 159. See also Oliver Richmond and Roger Mac Ginty, 'Where Now for the Critique of the Liberal Peace?' (2015) 50 *Cooperation and Conflict* 171.

2

Clarifying the End A Workable Definition of Peace

I. INTRODUCTION

If one's objective is to assess the relationship between human rights and peace, it becomes necessary to understand what is meant by peace in the first place. Existing accounts of the term have tended to be either completely abstract or, conversely, derive their content from peacebuilding practices on the ground. Section II assesses the two methods of defining peace and concludes that neither provides a satisfactory starting point for elucidating the connections between it and human rights. On the one hand, the most popular abstract account, Galtung's definition of positive and negative peace, is promising but ultimately unworkable because of its broad and all-inclusive nature.[1] On the other hand, more practical definitions are also unsatisfactory, since they seem to be guided by nothing more theoretically robust than the urge to reproduce the trappings of already developed and liberal societies.[2]

Considering the limitations of current accounts, section III proposes a new definition of peace which consists of three elements. The first element, *security*, exists when the conditions on the ground prevent a sense of fear from war, internal conflict or serious crime. The second, *justice*, demands that victims and society at large are remedied and confident that the injustices of the past will not be repeated in the future, while the final element, *reconciliation*, requires the creation of meaningful relationships of cooperation – on the personal and political levels – between former enemy parties. Each of these elements requires an objective improvement in the conditions prevailing in the post-violence society, through the establishment of relevant processes and institutions, but also a subjective change in people's perceptions of the conflict and its consequences.

This account of peace is both theoretically and practically informed. It is theoretically sound because it offers arguments in favour of the different elements of peace rather than merely assuming their desirability. Moreover, it

[1] Johan Galtung, 'An Editorial' (1964) 1 *Journal of Peace Research* 1.
[2] Oliver Richmond, *The Transformation of Peace* (Basingstoke, Palgrave Macmillan, 2006).

elaborates on the inter-relationship of the three elements by arguing that in addition to promoting, they can also contradict with each other. It is only when a balance has been struck between them, and maintained for a significant period of time, that peace within the post-violence society has been built. At the same time, the definition can have a practical impact since it is achievable and not all-encompassing. It creates clear objectives that post-violence societies should be working towards and lays the foundations for explaining how different peacebuilding tools, such as human rights, can contribute to their achievement.

II. REJECTING THE CURRENT ACCOUNTS OF PEACE

One way of understanding what is meant by peace is to focus on peacebuilders' efforts within post-violence societies and determine what it is they are working towards. Despite the obvious interest that the peacebuilding literature should have in defining its end objective, there is little agreement among key players about what a successful operation looks like. For example, the 1992–93 peace intervention in Cambodia has variously been described as a 'success', a 'partial success' and a 'failure'.[3] This point is also more generally made when examining in greater detail the UN's definition of peace. McAuliffe asserts that:

> [I]t is clear that the UN's ultimate purpose in all peace missions is what it labels 'sustainable peace' (defined as the capacity of conflict parties to move political or economic struggles from the battlefield and into an institutional framework where disputes can be resolved).[4]

The two most common indicators that this move has been completed and 'sustainable peace' has been achieved are a drop in the level of violence and the organisation of 'free and fair elections', both of which are relatively easy to measure and verify.[5] However, as soon as peacebuilding operations place emphasis on a wider range of objectives, as this section suggests they should, what is meant by 'peace' becomes less clear and subject to greater controversy.

Part of the challenge with the practical literature's definition of peace is that it engages with the term only indirectly by focusing on the methods and tools that are expected to promote it.[6] Thus, starting from the premise that

[3] Michael Lund, *What Kind of Peace is Being Built? Taking Stock of Post-conflict Peacebuilding and Charting Future Directions*, Working Paper No 7 (Ottawa, Peacebuilding and Reconstruction Program Initiative, International Development Research Centre, 2003).

[4] Padraig McAuliffe, *Transformative Transitional Justice and the Malleability of Post-conflict States* (Cheltenham, Edward Elgar, 2017) 27.

[5] George Downs and Stephen J. Stedman, 'Evaluation Issues in Peace Implementation' in Stephen Stedman, Donald Rothchild and Elizabeth Cousens (eds), *Ending Civil Wars: The Implementation of Peace Agreements* (Boulder, Lynne Rienner, 2002).

[6] Laurent Goetschel and Tobias Hagmann, 'Civilian Peacebuilding: Peace by Bureaucratic Means?' (2009) 9 *Conflict, Security and Development* 55, 60; William Maley, 'Introduction: Peace Operations and Their Evaluation' in Daniel Druckman and Paul F Diehl (eds), *Peace Operation Success: A Comparative Analysis* (Leiden, Martinus Nijhoff Publishers, 2013) 7.

'[t]he concept of peace is easy to grasp', *An Agenda for Peace* defines peacebuilding as consisting of 'comprehensive efforts to identify and support structures which will tend to consolidate peace'.[7] Problematically, no explanation is forthcoming about why or how such support structures will, in fact, consolidate peace or what is meant by the term in the first place. Examples of such structures listed in the report include those relating to the disarming of previously warring parties, repatriating refugees, monitoring elections, advancing efforts to protect human rights and reforming and strengthening governmental institutions.[8] The long list of peacebuilding methods also generally comprises building memorialisation sites,[9] establishing Truth Commissions,[10] holding criminal trials[11] and strengthening other 'peace enhancing structures',[12] such as a social free market[13] and an effective and legitimate justice system.[14] Therefore, it appears that while a lot has been written on peacebuilding methods, there has been no debate as to what qualities peace should consist of, leaving peacebuilders with 'no clear idea of what "success" or "failure" actually mean'.[15] Consequently, there is no analysis as to whether, how and the conditions under which these methods connect and contribute to the intended peace outcome.[16]

Despite peacebuilding actors not generally having participated in the definitional debate directly, they seem to have an implied understanding of the term. Richmond traces the development of the international community's efforts to promote peace over the years and concludes that decisions as to which peacebuilding methods are preferred have been affected by unarticulated definitions of the concept.[17] Early peacekeeping operations used to focus on keeping

[7] UN Secretary-General, *An Agenda for Peace: Preventive Diplomacy, Peacemaking and Peace-Keeping: Report of the Secretary-General Pursuant to the Statement Adopted by the Summit Meeting of the Security Council on 31 January 1992*, A/47/277 – S/24111 (New York, United Nations, 1992) [12] and [55] respectively.

[8] ibid.

[9] Brandon Hamber, Liz Ševčenko and Ereshnee Naidu, 'Utopian Dreams or Practical Possibilities? The Challenges of Evaluating the Impact of Memorialization in Societies in Transition' (2010) 4 *International Journal of Transitional Justice* 397.

[10] Priscilla B Hayner, *Unspeakable Truths: Transitional Justice and the Challenge of Truth Commissions* (London, Routledge, 2011).

[11] Diane F Orentlicher, 'Setting Accounts: The Duty to Prosecute Human Rights Violations of a Prior Regime' (1991) 100 *Yale Law Journal* 2537.

[12] Luc Reychler, 'From Conflict to Sustainable Peacebuilding: Concepts and Analytical Tools' in Luc Reychler and Thania Paffenholz (eds), *Peace-Building: A Field Guide* (Boulder, Lynne Rienner, 2001) 13.

[13] Paul Collier et al, *Breaking the Conflict Trap: Civil War and Development Policy* (Washington DC, World Bank and Oxford University Press, 2003).

[14] UN Secretary-General, *The Rule of Law and Transitional Justice in Conflict and Post-conflict Societies*, S/2004/616 (New York, United Nations, 2004) [61].

[15] Keith Krause and Oliver Jütersonke, 'Peace, Security and Development in Post-conflict Environments' (2005) 36 *Security Dialogue* 447, 448.

[16] Alex J. Bellamy, 'The "Next Stage" in Peace Operations Theory?' (2004) 11 *International Peacekeeping* 17; David Mendeloff, 'Truth-Seeking, Truth-Telling, and Postconflict Peacebuilding: Curb the Enthusiasm?' (2004) 6 *International Studies Review* 355.

[17] Richmond (n 2).

combatants separate rather than resolving their differences, because at the time, peace was understood as (just) the absence of violence.[18] Conversely, current peacebuilding operations are premised on the idea that what is needed to build peace are liberal processes, namely democratisation, market liberalisation and the rule of law. Liberal peacebuilding seeks to make post-violence societies 'normal' states by fast-forwarding the processes that liberal societies adopted over the last two or three centuries. It focuses on organising elections, passing laws that will allow the operation of a free market, strengthening the judiciary, developing a working civil service and protecting human rights, expecting that since the trappings of liberalism are there, over time, these societies will adopt liberal behaviours as well.[19] However, conceptualising peace as consisting of institutions rather than values means that the question of what these should achieve, or what the post-violence society should look like at the end of the peacebuilding process, is secondary to the very act of establishing them.[20] Therefore, current implied definitions of peace are inappropriate for the purposes of this study for two reasons: first, despite the fact that they are couched in liberal terms, they pay no (or little) direct attention to the important social and human consequences of peacebuilding.[21] Second, their strong emphasis on institutions and processes, including those promoting the protection of human rights, risks giving rise to circular arguments, if the aim is to examine the relationship between peace and rights in the first place.

An alternative method of deriving a definition of peace would be to focus on more theoretical accounts of the term. Of these, by far the most developed is the one suggested by Johan Galtung.[22] Traditionally, peace had been synonymous with the Latin 'pax', which was understood as the absence of war. However, this account missed the positive characteristics of peace and ignored any further action that had to be taken after the signing of the ceasefire agreement.[23] Galtung's work has been invaluable in making the once controversial, but now widely accepted argument that peace is a more comprehensive concept.[24]

[18] ibid 89–90.

[19] Bethan K Greener, 'Revisiting the Politics of Post-conflict Peacebuilding: Reconciling the Liberal Agenda?' (2011) 23 *Global Change, Peace and Security* 357.

[20] Oliver Richmond, 'The UN and Liberal Peacebuilding: Consensus and Challenges' in John Darby and Roger Mac Ginty (eds), *Contemporary Peacemaking: Conflict, Peace Processes and Post-war Reconstruction*, 2nd edn (New York, Palgrave Macmillan, 2008) 261.

[21] For a more in-depth discussion of this, see ch 6.

[22] Galtung (n 1); Johan Galtung, 'Twenty-Five Years of Peace Research' (1985) 22 *Journal of Peace Research* 141; Johan Galtung, 'Cultural Violence' (1990) 27 *Journal of Peace Research* 291.

[23] Panel on United Nations Peace Operations, *Report of the Panel on United Nations Peace Operations*, A/55/305–S/2000/809 (New York, United Nations, 2000) [3], noting that the absence of war 'can only create a space in which peace can be built' (hereinafter 'Brahimi Report'.)

[24] Contrast, eg, the 1962 accepted definition of peace as a condition of '*more or less lasting suspension of violent modes of rivalry between political units*' (Raymond Aron, *Peace and War: A Theory of International Relations* (London, Weidenfeld & Nicolson, 1962) 151, emphasis in original) with the current definition of peacebuilding as 'building on those foundations [of peace] something that is more than just the absence of war' (Brahimi Report (n 23) [13]).

In addition to the absence of war, what Galtung calls 'negative peace', we should focus on 'positive peace', a term that has developed over time to mean the building of positive relationships between previously warring parties.[25] The fact that part of the definition rests on the elimination of violence makes it intuitively appealing since that is every peacebuilder's primary goal. At the same time, its broader emphasis on positive relations adds sophistication, a characteristic that was missing from wholly negative accounts.

Galtung defined peace as the absence of violence, with violence being present when an individual cannot achieve his full potential due to his surrounding conditions.[26] The most obvious example of violence is physical, or 'direct violence', which is the intentional causing of harm from one person to the other. Clearly, if a person's potential is to live approximately to the age of 80, but he or she is killed during a war when he or she is 25, his or her 'potential realizations' have been limited.[27] Originally, Galtung argued that the absence of direct violence was negative peace, but that a complete theory of peace also required the absence of structural and cultural violence – what he called 'positive peace'.[28] *Structural violence* is caused indirectly if a person limits another's potential simply by doing the job prescribed to him or her by an unfair structure, such as a discriminatory system of government. The third type of violence, *cultural violence*, exists when people use their history, trauma and myths to excuse or justify direct or structural violence.[29] A classic example of this is nationalistic propaganda portraying the 'other' as less than human. Such attitudes are violent both because they are harmful in themselves and because they excuse or justify the other two types of violence, thus making their occurrence even more likely. Through this expanded definition, Galtung persuasively illustrated that peace was absent in societies, which did not suffer from physical violence, yet were only superficially calm.

Galtung's theory is persuasive because it acknowledges that physical violence does not simply start in the absence of underlying problems. This leads to the correct conclusion that merely stopping the killing is in itself not enough, since if such problems remain unaddressed, they will eventually resurface again. Ultimately, however, Galtung's account of peace should be rejected due to its lack of clarity in several of its key assertions, which make its practical application impossible. For instance, Galtung frequently refers to the 'absence of violence' as a necessary condition for peace, but it is unclear whether this requires its reduction or complete elimination.[30] While in 1969 he urged readers to 'imagine

[25] Galtung (n 1).

[26] Johan Galtung, 'Violence, Peace and Peace Research' (1969) 6 *Journal of Peace Research* 167, 168.

[27] ibid.

[28] ibid 183.

[29] Galtung, 'Cultural Violence'.

[30] Galtung (n 1) 2; Galtung (n 26) 167, 168 and 172; Galtung (n 22) 145.

we were able to calculate the losses incurred by the two forms of violence, or the gains that would accrue to mankind if they could be *eliminated*',[31] in 1985 he referred to peace as the '*reduction* of violence'.[32] More recently, Galtung defined negative peace as consisting of 'processes of violence reduction',[33] yet in the same text and almost immediately after, he concluded that: '*Negative peace is the absence of violence of all kinds.*'[34] On the one hand, the choice of the word 'absence' suggests that negative peace requires the complete elimination of violence, something supported by the fact that Galtung does not describe or mention a threshold under which violence has been adequately reduced to make the society a peaceful one. On the other hand, requiring its complete elimination is impossible, since different types of violence can be reduced by using potentially conflicting methods. For instance, while direct violence could theoretically be eradicated by adopting excessively strict criminal laws, this would have been achieved by increasing structural violence, thus undermining Galtung's main thesis that peace should be achieved through peaceful means.[35]

An even greater problem with defining peace as the *absence* of structural and cultural violence is that this is not a positive conception of peace at all, but rather a sophisticated account of negative peace. Responding to this, and although he never explicitly rejected his previous definition of the term, Galtung gradually came to view positive peace as the creation of direct peace, cultural peace and structural peace.[36] Now, negative peace was the absence of all kinds of violence, and positive peace consisted of these more positive values.[37] Yet, this new definition of peace is also ambiguous since it consists of ill-defined concepts, which lack a clear link to peacebuilding measures on the ground. For instance, Galtung argues that positive peace is achieved through 'processes of life enhancement'[38] and, more specifically, a 'culture of peace, confirming and stimulating an equitable economy and an equal polity',[39] without explaining what each of these phrases means.[40] He simply states that the field of 'equity of the economy' is theoretically and practically very underdeveloped, with the

[31] Galtung (n 26) 182, emphasis in original. The reference to 'two forms of violence' is because he only introduced the concept of cultural violence later, in 1990.

[32] Galtung (n 22) 151, emphasis added.

[33] Johan Galtung, *Peace by Peaceful Means: Peace and Conflict, Development and Civilization* (London, SAGE Publications, 1996) 30.

[34] ibid 31, emphasis in original.

[35] Johan Galtung, 'Introduction: Peace by Peaceful Conflict Transformation – the Transcend Approach' in Charles Webel and Johan Galtung (eds), *The Handbook of Peace and Conflict Studies* (London, Routledge, 2007) 22.

[36] The articles in which Galtung originally developed his theory were still cited in Johan Galtung, 'Peace, Positive and Negative' in Daniel J Christie (ed), *The Encyclopedia of Peace Psychology* (Chichester, Wiley-Blackwell, 2012).

[37] Galtung (n 33) 32.

[38] ibid 30.

[39] Galtung (n 36) 759.

[40] Kjell Eide, 'Note on Galtung's Concept of "Violence"' (1971) 8 *Journal of Peace Research* 71, 71; Peter Lawler, *A Question of Values: Johan Galtung's Peace Research* (Boulder, Lynne Rienner, 1995).

International Covenant on Economic Social and Cultural Rights being a step towards its achievement, and that 'equality of the polity' is where democracy and human rights enter, not only within countries, but also among them.[41] However, the broadness and vagueness of these definitions leave the reader wondering what exactly needs to be done to promote positive peace on the ground. Moreover, it is unclear how these positive values can be achieved and how they connect to peace exactly. For example, Galtung states that direct positive peace consists of 'verbal and physical kindness', the epitome of which is love, 'a union of bodies, minds and spirits'.[42] However, arguably such feelings are impossible among strangers generally, let alone between enemy groups in post-violence societies. Similarly, he associates structural positive peace with values such as integration, solidarity and participation, and cultural positive peace with democracy, human rights, peace education and peace journalism.[43] Again, though, he does not explain how these general principles can be promoted by peacebuilding measures on the ground and in what way exactly. Therefore, it seems that despite Galtung's assertions that peace should 'refer to something attainable and also in fact attained, not to something utopian', his is mainly an idealistic account, with little application in practice.[44]

Galtung's is the most popular theoretical definition of peace, but not the only one. Yet, these alternative definitions also suffer from a range of limitations. For instance, the literature now consists of references to stable,[45] (self-)sustainable,[46] just,[47] liberal[48] and real peace.[49] Often, such labels are presented as being self-explanatory, since neither the adjective that describes peace in each instance nor the term 'peace' itself is defined further. Reading between the lines, this literature suggests that the term 'peace' on its own implies the absence of war or violence, while the prefix adjective is an add-on of a desirable characteristic that this non-violent state of affairs should also possess. For instance, Allan distinguishes between different levels of peace by arguing that 'stable peace' defines a situation where the probability of war is not entertained by the people; 'just peace' exists when all parties are satisfied because their relations are regulated in a legitimate way; and (borrowing from Galtung)

[41] Galtung (n 35) 32 fns 2 and 3.

[42] ibid 32.

[43] ibid.

[44] Galtung (n 26) 185.

[45] Kenneth Ewart Boulding, *Stable Peace* (Austin, University of Texas Press, 1978).

[46] Francesco Strazzari, 'Between "Messy Aftermath" and "Frozen Conflicts": Chimeras and Realities of Sustainable Peace' (2008) 2 *Human Security Perspectives* 45.

[47] Pierre Allan and Alexis Keller (eds), *What is Just Peace?* (Oxford, Oxford University Press, 2006).

[48] This is currently the most popular characterisation of peace. Despite the fact that the UN does not explicitly characterise the peace it is working towards as 'liberal', this is suggested by the peacebuilding methods it has been adopting. See Roland Paris, *At War's End: Building Peace after Civil Conflict* (Cambridge, Cambridge University Press, 2004); Richmond (n 2); Daniel Philpott and Gerard F Powers (eds), *Strategies of Peace: Transforming Conflict in a Violent World* (Oxford, Oxford University Press, 2010).

[49] Richard Nixon, *Real Peace* (London, Sidgwick & Jackson, 1983).

'positive peace' is established when structural violence is absent.[50] However, such definitions are problematic for three distinct reasons: first, the idea of security (encapsulated in stable peace) and justice (captured in the other two terms) should be considered inherent characteristics of the concept rather than add-ons that might or might not accompany peace.[51] Second, prefacing the term with an adjective does not solve the problem of a lack of a definition, but simply shifts attention from one term that is difficult to define to two. Thus, the Brahimi Report interchangeably refers to 'stable' and 'sustainable' peace,[52] but does not clarify what characteristics each 'type' of peace should possess, which peacebuilding strategies have been successful in promoting one or both of them, and how. Finally, references to 'just peace' prioritise the elements of justice and security over reconciliation, presumably because of an assumption that this follows naturally when the first two have been established. However, as the tripartite definition proposed in the next section suggests, this assumption is faulty, since reconciliation might be promoted by security and justice, but can also contradict them.

III. FORGING A NEW DEFINITION OF PEACE

As a result of the limitations of current definitions of peace, a new account of the concept, which relies on striking a balance between security, justice and reconciliation, is proposed instead. The notion that peace consists of different elements is not necessarily novel, with Baillet and Larsen, for instance, referring to different 'Components of Peace'.[53] However, these components quickly dissolve into a long list of good things that the authors would like to see in any society – such as the elimination of inequality, exclusion and poverty, education on human rights, fundamental freedoms, non-violent dispute resolution and the protection of the environment – without an explanation on how each links to peace. Conversely, the choices of security, justice and reconciliation as elements of peace are based on both theoretical insights and experiences from peacebuilding practice. Thus, the importance of security has been highlighted in the literature on disarmament[54] and police reform,[55] and has also

[50] Pierre Allan, 'Measuring International Ethics: A Moral Scale of War, Peace, Justice and Global Care' in Allan and Keller (n 47).

[51] Yossi Beilin, 'Just Peace: A Dangerous Objective' in Allan and Keller (n 47).

[52] Brahimi Report (n 23) [87] and [22] respectively.

[53] Cecillia Marcela Baillet and Kjetil Mujezinovic Larsen, 'Introduction' in Cecillia Marcela Baillet and Kjetil Mujezinovic Larsen (eds), *Promoting Peace through International Law* (Oxford, Oxford University Press, 2015) 9–10.

[54] Joanna Spear, 'Disarmament and Demobilisation' in Stedman, Rothschild and Cousens (eds) (n 5).

[55] Charles T Call and William Stanley, 'Civilian Security' in Stedman, Rothschild and Cousens (eds) (n 5).

been acknowledged by Boulding, who argues that 'stable peace is a situation in which the probability of war is so small that it does not really enter the calculations of the people involved'.[56] At the same time, its significance is illustrated in practice through the passing of international treaties, such as the Convention on the Prohibition of the Use, Stockpiling, Production and Transfer of Anti-Personnel Mines and on their Destruction, and the attention that the reform of the security sector has received by peacebuilders in various post-violence societies.[57]

The second element of peace is also frequently perceived as being key in the literature, with numerous authors having attempted to define what is meant by (transitional) justice in post-violence contexts.[58] The justification behind such attempts has generally been that 'the absence of justice is often the primary reason for the absence of peace'.[59] In practice, the emphasis on justice has been reflected through the creation of the International Criminal Court,[60] the development of tools for the remedying of displaced people[61] and the attention paid to reforming domestic judicial systems.[62] Finally, the third element of peace, reconciliation, is considered increasingly important and has produced vibrant debates on how truth commissions[63] and other reconciliation-promoting methods, such as peace education[64] and peace journalism,[65] can be utilised in post-violence societies. The growing literature on reconciliation also includes analysis of related theoretical concepts, such as trust,[66] forgiveness,[67] empathy and the rehumanisation of the enemy.[68] The significance of this

[56] Boulding (n 45) 13.

[57] Thomas Muehlmann, 'International Policing in Bosnia and Herzegovina: The Issue of Behavioural Reforms Lagging Behind Structural Reforms, Including the Issue of Reengaging the Political Elite in a New System' (2007) 16 *European Security* 357.

[58] The definition of transitional justice is discussed in section III.B below.

[59] Michelle Parlevliet, *Bridging the Divide: Exploring the Relationship between Human Rights and Conflict Management*, Track Two Occasional Paper (Cape Town, Centre for Conflict Resolution, March 2002) 11; Rama Mani, *Beyond Retribution: Seeking Justice in the Shadows of War* (Cambridge, Polity Press, 2002) 5.

[60] The preamble of the Statute of the International Criminal Court refers to the need to 'guarantee lasting respect for and the enforcement of international justice'.

[61] UN Sub-Commission on the Promotion and Protection of Human Rights, *Housing and Property Restitution in the Context of the Return of Refugees and Internally Displaced Persons*, E/CN4/Sub2/2005/17 (Geneva, United Nations, 28 June 2005), which makes several references to the principle of restorative justice.

[62] UN Secretary-General (n 14) [61].

[63] Hayner (n 10).

[64] Hamber, Ševčenko and Naidu (n 9).

[65] Lisa J Laplante and Kelly Phenicie, 'Media, Trials and Truth Commissions: "Mediating" Reconciliation in Peru's Transitional Justice Process' (2010) 4 *International Journal of Transitional Justice* 207.

[66] Trudy Govier and Wilhelm Verwoerd, 'Trust and the Problem of National Reconciliation' (2002) 32 *Philosophy of the Social Sciences* 178.

[67] Russell Daye, *Political Forgiveness: Lessons from South Africa* (Maryknoll, Orbis Books, 2004).

[68] Jodi Halpern and Harvey M Weinstein, 'Empathy and Rehumanization after Mass Violence' in Eric Stover and Harvey M Weinstein (eds), *My Neighbor, My Enemy: Justice and Community in the Aftermath of Mass Atrocity* (Cambridge, Cambridge University Press, 2004).

element of peace has been acknowledged by the UN Secretary-General, who noted as early as 1995 that 'international intervention must extend beyond military and humanitarian tasks and must include the promotion of national reconciliation'.[69]

The elements' importance is also confirmed when they are compared to Galtung's three types of violence. Although the two definitions of peace are different, there is a clear connection between security and the absence of direct violence, justice and the absence of structural violence, and reconciliation and the absence of cultural violence. These connections notwithstanding, the proposed definition's main distinguishing feature from Galtung's is that it creates space for the positive qualities that a peaceful society must possess, while simultaneously remaining achievable. For example, security varies from the absence of direct violence because its promotion requires the taking of additional steps, such as effective disarmament of ex-combatants and the proper training of the police. Similarly, justice is a different concept from the absence of structural violence because it also imposes positive, but realistic obligations on the state: remedying past injustices and ensuring that they are not repeated in the future. Finally, a post-violence society is not reconciled simply because negative feelings against other groups are not uttered out loud (the absence of cultural violence). Reconciliation, which involves building positive relationships between people, requires cooperation among ex-enemy groups, which does not occur naturally even when cultural violence is eliminated. Nevertheless, while the three elements are broader than negative peace, they also avoid the lack of clarity and utopian character of Galtung's positive account.

The tripartite definition is also different from the implied understanding of liberal peace. The premise of liberal peacebuilding is that peace has been built in a post-violence society upon the establishment of liberal institutions, laws and procedures.[70] To the extent that perceptions, feelings or reactions of the local population are considered, it is expected that these will become more peace-friendly as a direct consequence of creating the liberal structures.[71] Conversely, the tripartite definition is based on a more nuanced understanding of what is required to build peace, by focusing equally on an objective *and* a subjective sense of the concept.[72] The term 'objective' does not necessarily imply that every outside observer has exactly the same view of what a peaceful society should look like. Rather, it derives from the belief that outsiders, who are not as

[69] UN Secretary-General, *Supplement to an Agenda for Peace*, A/50/60 – S/1995/1 (New York, United Nations, 1995) [13].

[70] Oliver Richmond, 'A Post-liberal Peace: Eirinism and the Everyday' (2009) 35 *Review of International Studies* 557, 565.

[71] Goetschel and Hagmann (n 6).

[72] A similar point has been made in Pierre Allan and Alexis Keller, 'The Concept of Just Peace, or Achieving Peace through Recognition, Renouncement and Rule' in Allan and Keller (n 47), where it was argued that justice encapsulates substantive, procedural and emotional conceptions of the term.

familiar with the intricate dynamics of a post-violence society, are more likely to pay closer attention to laws, processes and institutions, the establishment of which is observable and can be confirmed as a matter of fact. Conversely, for insiders, the relationships between individuals, or groups, are more important than the existence of the structures themselves. As a result, they are more likely to pay attention to subjective peace, meaning that they will assess the success of peacebuilding operations, not only by focusing on the launching of specific initiatives, but also on how these are experienced by, and affect themselves and the people around them, which is a more subjective exercise. There is a risk that a definition of peace that solely emphasises people's perceptions makes subjectivity a way of circumventing material change (by just fooling people into feeling better rather than bringing about tangible improvements) or psychologising a conflict that has its roots in injustices. At the same time, a definition that is exclusively focused on observable and measurable change ill-advisedly removes the human experience from the equation. It is only by placing emphasis on both that the Skylla and Charybdis can be avoided.[73]

Although attention has been paid to security, justice and reconciliation both in the theoretical literature and when designing peacebuilding mechanisms in practice, there has not been a concerted effort to examine how the three elements connect to create peaceful societies.[74] However, understanding one element independently from the other two and discussing which strategies can promote each of them in isolation is unsatisfactory because it ignores key links between the elements themselves and between them and peace. Security, justice and reconciliation are distinct, and different methods and tools are available to peacebuilders for their achievement. Nonetheless, they are also connected in that the promotion of one could make the achievement of the others more likely. Thus, as the situation in a post-violence society becomes more secure, justice becomes easier to administer, since judicial decisions can be based on merit rather than be influenced by the power of the parties.[75] This was the case in BiH, where shortly after the war, the domestic judiciary was reluctant to find that the dominant ethnic group in each entity was still acting in a discriminatory manner against the members of the other two.[76] Conversely, 20 years later, and with the possibility of returning back to violence being a more distant one, judges

[73] A similar argument is made in John Burton, *Resolving Deep-Rooted Conflict: A Handbook* (Lanham, University Press of America, 1987) 47.

[74] For an exception to this, and although he uses slightly different terminology, see Brandon Hamber, *Dealing with Painful Memories and Violent Pasts: Towards a Framework for Contextual Understanding* (Berghof Handbook Dialogue Series No 11, Berlin, Berghof Foundation, 2015) 12.

[75] Organisation for Security and Co-operation in Europe, *Security Sector Governance and Reform: Guidelines for OSCE Staff* (Vienna, OSCE, 2016) 16.

[76] Sheri P Rosenberg, 'Equality after Genocide: Jurisprudence of the Legal Institutions Established in Dayton's Bosnia' in Dina Francesca Haynes (ed), *Deconstructing the Reconstruction: Human Rights and the Rule of Law in Postwar Bosnia and Herzegovina* (Farnham, Ashgate, 2008).

have become more willing to decide legal cases neutrally.[77] At the same time, the promotion of justice by, for example, prosecuting past offenders contributes to greater security as it removes potentially dangerous actors from society and positions of authority.[78] Similarly, justice and reconciliation are also connected because remedying past injustices and ensuring that they will not be repeated in the future results in a more hospitable climate for reconciliation.[79] Equally important is the positive relationship between that and security because only if people can leave the fear of the conflict behind them can they start trusting and cooperating with one another.[80] Finally, this relationship also works in the opposite direction, since the improvement in the cooperation among members of previously warring parties and the consequent creation of a peace dividend make it less likely that they will be interested in resuming the violence and therefore promotes security.

While these positive connections between the different elements should be made explicit, the definition of peace also rests on the possible tension between them, hence the need to balance them against each other.[81] For instance, justice might demand that all perpetrators are punished for their actions, which could in turn result in increased tension between the previously warring parties and even lead to renewed violence.[82] Similarly, trials, which by their nature produce clear winners and losers, can also damage reconciliation efforts.[83] As a result, several post-violence societies have adopted strategies that limit the accountability of past offenders in the name of reconciliation.[84] The need to find an equilibrium between the elements of peace has also been recognised by the UN,

[77] Compare the BiH Constitutional Court cases *U-5/98 (3rd Partial Opinion)* (BiH Constitutional Court, 1 July 2000) with *U-44/01* (BiH Constitutional Court, 27 February 2004).

[78] Kathryn Sikkink, *The Justice Cascade: How Human Rights Prosecutions are Changing World Politics* (New York, Norton & Company, 2011) 184.

[79] Jemima Garcia-Godos, 'It's about Trust: Transitional Justice and Accountability in the Search for Peace' in Baillet and Larsen (eds) (n 53).

[80] Marie Smyth, 'The Human Consequences of Armed Conflict: Constructing "Victimhood" in the Context of Northern Ireland's Troubles' in Marcus Cox, Adrian Guelke and Fiona Stephen (eds), *A Farewell to Arms? From 'Long War' to Long Peace in Northern Ireland* (Manchester, Manchester University Press, 2000) 132. This is further supported by the Brahimi Report, which states that a 'relatively less dangerous environment … is a fairly forgiving one' (Brahimi Report (n 23) [12]).

[81] This tension is particularly apparent in the early stages of the peacebuilding process when the previously warring groups are least willing to depart from their positions on a given issue and compromise with each other. The consequences of this phenomenon are discussed in more detail in ch 4.

[82] This was acknowledged by the SA Constitutional Court in *The Azarian Peoples Organisation (AZAPO) and Others v The President of the Republic of South Africa* (CCT 17/96) (SA Constitutional Court, 25 July 1996) [31], when it stated that if 'human rights criminals … are treated too harshly – or if the net of punishment is cast too widely – there may be a backlash that plays into their hands'.

[83] Michael Ignatieff, 'Articles of Faith' (1996) 5 *Index of Censorship* 110.

[84] This has been the approach adopted both by the TRC in SA and by the Republic of Cyprus (RoC) in relation to missing persons. For background information on both cases, see Iosif Kovras, *Grassroots Activism and the Evolution of Transitional Justice: The Families of the Disappeared* (Cambridge, Cambridge University Press, 2017).

which argued that: 'At times, the goals of justice and reconciliation compete with each other. Each society needs to form a view about how to strike the right balance between them.'[85]

Due to the possible tension between the three elements, absolute security, justice and reconciliation are unattainable and unnecessary for peace to be built. Instead, all three must meet a certain threshold and, after that is satisfied, they should be balanced against each other so that the maximum of each can be achieved without undermining the other elements.[86] It is always hard to abstractly define how much of each element is enough, but, upon inspection, it is possible to determine whether a given society is sufficiently secure, just or reconciled based on the situation on the ground. When the balance between the three elements has been struck, the longer it is maintained, the more peaceful that society becomes for two reasons.[87] First, peace itself increases the resilience of a peaceful society. Although soon after the war the parties might feel they can benefit more if they continue fighting, the longer peace persists, the more likely they are to want to continue enjoying the benefits conferred by it, to which they are now accustomed.[88] Second, peace becomes more durable because, over time, the society in question will have successfully resolved a number of divisive conflicts, thus making it easier to address any subsequent ones.[89]

The tripartite definition results in a dynamic conception of peace. It acknowledges that peace is not a state of bliss, but exists in a society where a balance between the three elements is constantly negotiated. This balancing exercise and its implementation in practice are aided by the fact that the definition draws a clear connecting line between peace, its elements and the peacebuilding measures that promote them. Where the different elements contradict, difficult decisions will still have to be made, but at least they will be made transparently. At the same time, the specific balance that must be struck between the elements changes, depending on the context of each post-violence society and the timing at which the tension arises. This is in line with the widely accepted view, at least on paper, that we should resist the tendency to adopt virtually identical peacebuilding strategies in vastly different post-violence contexts.[90] Rather, we should have a clear understanding of what is meant by the different elements and, based

[85] UN Secretary-General, 'Press Release, Secretary General Expresses Hope for New Security Council Commitment to Place Justice, Rule of Law at Heart of Efforts to Rebuild War-Tort Countries', SG/SM/8892 (New York, United Nations, 2003), available at www.unis.unvienna.org/unis/pressrels/2003/sgsm8892.html.

[86] For the argument that peace is a matter of degree, rather than an either/or value, see Allan (n 50).

[87] Boulding (n 45) 62.

[88] On the importance of the 'peace dividend', see UNDP, *Governance for Peace: Securing the Social Contract* (New York, United Nations Development Programme, 2012) 12.

[89] Galtung (n 35).

[90] Roger Mac Ginty, 'Indigenous Peace-Making versus the Liberal Peace' (2008) 43 *Cooperation and Conflict* 139; UN Secretary-General (n 14) [14]–[16].

on this, devise a coherent strategy on how they can be promoted, bearing in mind each society's unique characteristics.

A. Security as the First Element of Peace

The first element within the proposed definition of peace is security, which exists when the conditions on the ground prevent fear from war, internal conflict or serious crime. Security from physical threats is essential to any definition of peace because people's first concern during and after the eruption of violence is their physical well-being. As Doyle and Sambanis put it: 'The first step is security. A secure environment is the *sine qua non* of the new beginning of peace.'[91] Illustrative of this is the case of Cyprus, where mass-scale violence has not broken out on the island in the last 45 years. Despite the relatively secure conditions, more than 70 per cent of GCs and TCs believe that security should be the 'highest priority item' during the peace negotiations.[92] In addition to a subjectively perceived sense of insecurity, as in the case of Cyprus, it is possible that a society is experiencing real violence, even after the signing of a ceasefire or a comprehensive peace settlement.[93] This might be because the previously warring parties do not have a genuine willingness to stop the hostilities, spoilers are trying to reignite war for their own interests, or networks and structures associated with the war economy have remained in place.[94] Lack of security, whether objective or subjective, makes it impossible for people to plan their future and put the conflict behind them due to concerns that any attempts to do so will be undermined by more violence. A society that operates under such constant threats is always in a state of emergency and, until these are dismissed, cannot be entirely peaceful.

Until the end of the Cold War, the clear answer to whom security was for was the state, since an assumption existed that if the state was secure, so were its subjects.[95] This traditional understanding of the concept was rightly challenged in a 1994 United Nations Development Programme (UNDP) Report, which argued in favour of a new 'human security' ideal that focused on individuals

[91] Michael W Doyle and Nicholas Sambanis, *Making War and Building Peace* (Princeton, Princeton University Press, 2006) 338.

[92] Alexandros Lordos and Erol Kaymak, *Public Opinion and the Property Issue: Quantitative Findings*, Cyprus 2015: Research and Dialogue for a Sustainable Future (Cyprus, Interpeace, 2010).

[93] Maria Schuld, 'The Prevalence of Violence in Post-conflict Societies: A Case Study of KwaZulu-Natal, South Africa' (2013) 8 *Journal of Peacebuilding and Development* 60; Jonny Byrne and Neil Jarman, 'Ten Years after Patten: Young People and Policing in Northern Ireland' (2011) 43 *Youth & Society* 433.

[94] Geneva Declaration Secretariat, *Global Burden of Armed Violence* (Geneva, Geneva Declaration on Armed Violence and Development, 2008) 49.

[95] Barbara von Tigerstrom, *Human Security and International Law: Prospects and Problems* (Oxford, Hart Publishing, 2007) 9.

instead of states.[96] The report rejected the traditional approach, since threats to people's security come not only from other states, but also from non-state actors or the state itself. Making the state more secure and powerful does not always result in the increased protection of the people and can even have the reverse effect. The human security definition is particularly important when defining security as one of the elements of peace in post-violence societies, where the state was at least, until recently, trying to protect only some of its citizens and was turning against the rest.[97] Thus, a necessary element for peace is the security of all the individuals residing in the state, irrespective of their group membership or connections with the government.

Perhaps the question that has generated the most debate in the security literature concerns the types of threats people must be protected from. The UNDP Report adopted an excessively broad approach, arguing that the notion of security is 'all-encompassing' and that 'most' of the threats that fall under this heading can be grouped into seven categories: (i) economic security (freedom from poverty); (ii) food security (physical and economic access to food); (iii) health security; (iv) environmental security; (v) personal security (physical safety); (vi) community security (survival of traditional cultures and ethnic groups); and (vii) political security (enjoyment of civil and political rights).[98] The Report states that the categories are inter-connected since a threat to one type can influence all forms of human security.[99] However, such a broad definition is problematic because the causes of, and ways to deal with, physical threats are very different from those concerning other dangers. The only reason for including different types of threats under the single concept of security was to send the message that governments should prioritise other policy areas, aside from physical security, as well. Nevertheless, the very broadness of the term defeats this purpose because by prioritising everything, we are prioritising nothing.[100] Furthermore, an all-inclusive definition of security suggests that there are no limits to the concept's expansion, illustrated by the fact that despite the UNDP's broad definition, scholars have suggested additional threats that should be dealt with under the security label. For example, Reed and Tehranian also argue for the protection of psychological security (involving conditions establishing respectful, loving and humane interpersonal relations) and communication security (concerning freedom of, and balance in, information flows).[101] However, 'the broad vision of human security is ultimately nothing more than

[96] UNDP, *Human Development Report: Annual Report* (New York, United Nations Development Programme, 1994).

[97] OSCE (n 75) 53.

[98] UNDP (n 96) 24.

[99] ibid, 33.

[100] Keith Krause, 'The Key to a Powerful Agenda, if Properly Delimited' (2004) 35 *Security Dialogue* 367.

[101] Laura Reed and Majid Tehranian, 'Evolving Security Regimes' in Majid Tehranian (ed), *Worlds Apart: Human Security and Global Governance* (London, IB Tauris, 1999).

a shopping list … At a certain point, human security becomes a loose synonym for "bad things that can happen"', thus losing its useful purpose as a single concept.[102]

Instead, a narrower definition of human security, which focuses on protecting people only from physical threats, should be adopted. Such threats could be the result of war, internal conflict or serious crime such as gang violence, which tends to increase after the war has ended.[103] Physical security should be singled out from the seven UNDP categories because, first, it is the one most directly related to post-violence contexts and, second, a narrower definition of the term makes it more useful in practice. The importance of physical security was highlighted by the UNDP itself, which stated that: 'Perhaps no other aspect of human security is so vital for people as their security from physical violence.'[104] Furthermore, the broad nature of the UNDP's definition was even criticised by Canada, one of the most enthusiastic supporters of the concept of human security, for undermining the importance of threats relating to violent conflict.[105] An all-inclusive definition could imply that physical security is almost easy to guarantee, especially when compared to categories such as environmental or health security, which are not completely within human control. In contrast, a narrow definition allows policy makers to clearly identify the issues that must be dealt with in order for security to be achieved and to connect them with peacebuilding policies on the ground. This leads to the next question, namely, the type of policies that should be adopted in post-violence societies in order to promote security.

Security might be undermined because perpetrators of human rights violations remain unpunished after the end of the conflict,[106] by the high crime rates in the post-violence society[107] or due to a popular belief that the enemy may still pose a threat.[108] As a result, different societies are likely to respond to their lack of security in different ways,[109] but they should all adopt measures that target and address these challenges directly rather than expect that related peacebuilding initiatives, such as strengthening the judiciary, will be sufficient.[110] Dilemmas as to what these measures should look like arise both in the short and medium term after the violence has ceased. A short-term security

[102] Krause (n 100) 367.

[103] Call and Stanley (n 55); Independent Commission on Policing for Northern Ireland, *A New Beginning: Policing in Northern Ireland* (Belfast, Northern Ireland Office, 1999) [13.6] (hereinafter 'Patten Report').

[104] UNDP (n 96) 30.

[105] Department of Foreign Affairs and International Trade, *Human Security: Safety for People in a Changing World* (Ottawa, Government of Canada, 1999) 2.

[106] International Crisis Group, *Bosnia's Stalled Police Reform: No Progress, No EU*, Europe Report N°164 (Sarajevo/Brussels, International Crisis Group, 2005) 2–4.

[107] Call and Stanley (n 55).

[108] Daniel Bar-Tal, 'From Intractable Conflict through Conflict Resolution to Reconciliation: Psychological Analysis' (2000) 21 *Political Psychology* 351, 354.

[109] OSCE (n 75) 74.

[110] Geneva Declaration Secretariat (n 94) 64.

dilemma concerns the process and timing of disarmament; this is a delicate decision because, on the one hand, ex-combatants should be disarmed early on to make people feel safe. On the other hand, disarmament should not take place too soon because ex-fighters might be afraid that they are losing their power with nothing in return, thus being encouraged to act as spoilers.[111] The stakes are high since, if the process fails, citizens may suffer from 'microinsecurity', where individuals fear that they will be the victims of crimes perpetrated by former soldiers, or 'macroinsecurity', which is the fear that the state might be overthrown by insurrection.[112] Equally important are medium-term security dilemmas, such as the reform of the police.[113] A legitimate and properly working police force can promote security in an objective sense by reducing crime rates in the country, but also subjectively, since it affects the public's confidence in the state's ability to preserve the social order.[114] At the same time, and pointing to the inter-connectedness between the elements of peace, a well-organised and legitimate effort to reform the police could have a positive effect on reconciliation. For instance, the Patten Commission in NI was tasked with making recommendations for the reform of the then Royal Ulster Constabulary and therefore promoting security, but during the course of public meetings that it organised, it also heard personal stories from victims of police violence that would usually have been told to a TRC.[115]

The final question that should be asked with regard to security relates to the mechanics of the proposed definition of peace and is concerned with how much security is necessary in a given society and at what cost. It is wrong to assume that little security is really no security; rather, security is a matter of degree and peacebuilders should be concerned with how much of it is enough.[116] This is because security has a cost, not only in financial terms – an important factor in post-violence societies – but also in terms of potentially undermining justice and reconciliation. A minimum level of security is needed, but how much is desirable beyond that depends on how much already exists. So, if people are, and feel, relatively secure, peacebuilders might prefer to focus their resources on something else, even if investing in security could have increased it a little more.[117] Therefore, optimum security is achieved when physical safety exists to the greatest degree that is practically possible, without compromising justice and reconciliation.

[111] Spear (n 54).

[112] Paul Collier, 'Demobilization and Insecurity: A Study in the Economics of the Transitions from War to Peace' (1994) 6 *Journal of International Development* 349.

[113] Brice Dickson, 'Policing and Human Rights after the Conflict' in Cox, Guelke and Stephen (n 80).

[114] Graham Ellison, Nathan W Pino and Peter Shirlow, 'Assessing the Determinants of Public Confidence in the Police: A Case Study of a Post-conflict Community in Northern Ireland' (2010) 13 *Criminology and Criminal Justice* 552.

[115] Independent Commission on Policing for Northern Ireland, *Patten Report* [1.19].

[116] David Baldwin, 'The Concept of Security' (1997) 23 *Review of International Studies* 5.

[117] ibid.

B. Justice as the Second Element of Peace

Justice, the second element of peace, is understood as remedying past injustices that were caused before or during the eruption of violence and ensuring that they will not be repeated in the future. Although the post-violence justice described here is connected to the more general definition of justice in liberal societies, the two differ in significant ways. For instance, issues such as access to courts and social equity are relevant to both types of societies, but post-violence justice is primarily concerned with them to the extent that they have to do with the remedying of past, or preventing of future, injustices. Additionally, justice-promoting institutions in post-violence societies often deal with issues that are not so widespread in mostly liberal contexts, such as remedying large numbers of displaced people. As time passes, the concerns of post-violence justice become less important and are replaced by those of ordinary justice;[118] however, here we are only concerned with the former.

Justice in post-violence societies has been deemed important since the early inception of peacebuilding, with practically every human rights treaty stressing in its preamble the need for 'peace and justice in the world'.[119] These two concepts have been connected in the literature in two ways. First, communal violence is usually fuelled by feelings of injustice. Leaving such injustices unremedied and allowing them to continue after the violence has ended sends people the message that nothing has changed.[120] This, in turn, is likely to result in frustration and eventually even more violence, until the victims of the injustice obtain what they believe they are entitled to.[121] It is for this reason that justice requires not only the existence of objectively observable institutions dealing with past grievances, but also that the public subjectively believes that these have been addressed. Second, the promotion of justice legitimises the peace agreement and the new state of affairs by distinguishing the actions of the new regime from the illegitimate acts caused during the violence.[122] The impact of justice on legitimacy was highlighted by Boulding, who argued that a:

> [S]ystem of peace which is perceived by increasing numbers of its participants to have elements of injustice will be subject to increasing strain … The sense of injustice ultimately erodes the whole legitimacy of the system and it collapses.[123]

[118] Eric Posner and Adrian Vermeule, 'Transitional Justice as Ordinary Justice' (2004) 117 *Harvard Law Review* 761.

[119] This phrase is repeated in the preamble of the Universal Declaration of Human Rights, the International Covenant on Civil and Political Rights, the International Covenant on Economic Social and Cultural Rights and the European Convention on Human Rights.

[120] Parlevliet (n 59).

[121] Connie Peck, *Sustainable Peace: The Role of the UN and Regional Organizations in Preventing Conflict* (Lanham, Rowman & Littlefield, 1998).

[122] Christine Bell, *Peace Agreements and Human Rights* (Oxford, Oxford University Press, 2000) 294; Nigel Biggar, 'Making Peace or Doing Justice: Must We Choose?' in Nigel Biggar (ed), *Burying the Past: Making Peace and Doing Justice after Civil Conflict* (Washington DC, Georgetown University Press, 2003).

[123] Boulding (n 45) 70–71.

However, in addition to the positive connections between justice and peace in the literature, arguments have also been made that the two are incompatible with each other. In 1996 and shortly after the Dayton Agreement ending the war in BiH had been signed, an influential and anonymous article was written by one of the people involved in the negotiations.[124] Outlining what has become known as the 'peace v justice' debate, it argued that the international community's insistence on the protection of human rights (what it called 'justice') undermined the likelihood of peace being achieved, since it delayed the conclusion of the peace settlement between the parties.[125] Nonetheless, although the anonymous article referred to 'peace' and 'justice', it did not use the two terms in the same way as they are being understood here. By 'peace', the author essentially meant the stopping of hostilities, which resembles the definition of security, while by 'justice', he or she was referring to the protection of human rights. Essentially, he or she was arguing that insistence on full compliance with human rights in a post-violence context might undermine security, an argument that is explored in more detail in subsequent chapters. In any case, the proposed definition of peace, which is based on the idea that the elements might contradict each other, confirms the broader point made in the 'peace v justice' literature, namely that the promotion of justice is not always conductive to peacebuilding efforts.[126] Rather, justice-promoting measures might contradict security or reconciliation considerations, and therefore the broader objectives of peace. However, this is not to say that justice cannot also make important positive contributions to peacebuilding objectives.

Perhaps the clearest indication of the importance of justice for peace is the rich and growing literature on transitional justice. Despite the important lessons that can be learned from this literature, the term 'transitional justice' will not be used here, as it relies on three assumptions that are best reconsidered. The first is the belief that transitional justice can be promoted through, and therefore emphasis must be placed on, addressing violent crimes rather than other types of injustices.[127] This bias has resulted in a consistent lack of attention to violations of socio-economic rights, thus providing a skewed understanding of justice in post-violence societies.[128] This is particularly

[124] Anonymous, 'Human Rights in Peace Negotiations' (1996) 18 *Human Rights Quarterly* 249.

[125] For greater analysis of the 'peace v justice' debate, see Cecilia Albin, 'Peace vs Justice – and Beyond' in Jacob Kremenyuk, Victor Bercovitch and William Zartman (eds), *The SAGE Handbook of Conflict Resolution* (London, SAGE Publications, 2008); Chandra Lekha Sriram, *Confronting Past Human Rights Violations: Justice vs Peace in Times of Transition* (New York, Frank Cass, 2004).

[126] Ronald Paris, 'Wilson's Ghost: The Faulty Assumptions of Postconflict Peacebuilding' in Chester Crocker, Fen Osler Hampson and Pamel Aall (eds), *Turbulent Peace: Conflict Resolution Versus Democratic Governance: Divergent Paths to Peace?* (Washington DC, United States Institute of Peace Press, 2001).

[127] Sheri P Rosenberg, 'Promoting Equality after Genocide' (2008) 16 *Tulane Journal of International and Comparative Law* 329.

[128] Recent literature has tried to bridge this gap by focusing on 'transformative' rather than 'transitional' justice in post-violence contexts. However, this trend 'should not be exaggerated – transitional justice still remains legalistic in orientation and rooted in a civil and political rights-based framework at a policy level' (McAuliffe (n 4) 4).

problematic because providing reparations for victims for past violent crimes is likely to have a lesser impact in terms of building peace in contexts where poverty and social inequalities persist.[129] Conversely, the current definition considers not only retributive, but also distributive justice that is often equally important, yet neglected, in the aftermath of violence.[130] At the same time, it favours a retributive conception of justice over a restorative conception because the latter, with its focus on rehabilitating the offenders and mending their relationship with victims and the society at large, is encapsulated within the element of reconciliation.[131]

The second assumption that merits reconsideration is the belief that transitional justice has been delivered when the relevant institutions have been set up.[132] In contrast, post-violence justice considers institution-building as an important first step, but as ultimately incapable of exhausting its demands. In addition to the establishment and strengthening of liberal institutions, post-violence justice focuses on the experiences and perceptions of victims, perpetrators and members of society at large. This suggests that in one sense at least, post-violence justice is broader than traditional conceptions of transitional justice, since it envisions addressing injustices through a range of tools, some of which are institution-focused and others of which are people-centred. Examples of the former involve trials, vetting and reparation programmes, while instances of the latter could be the issuing of apologies from the state for past unjust policies or actions[133] and the provision of better educational, housing and economic opportunities to the groups that suffered from injustices.[134]

At the same time, the definition of post-violence justice is also narrower than that of its transitional counterpart, which points to the last set of assumptions that must be reconsidered. Illustrative of this is Teitel's account, which contends that the main purpose of transitional justice is to assist in the change from a less to a more liberal society through a 'collective public ritual', irrespective of that ritual's content.[135] Transitional justice can consist of both 'amnesties and punishment [which] are two sides of the same coin: [they are] legal rites that visibly and forcefully demonstrate the change in sovereignty that makes for political transition'.[136] However, this definition lacks even minimum justice

[129] Hamber (n 74) 13.
[130] Mani (n 59).
[131] Daniel Philpott, 'An Ethic of Political Reconciliation' (2009) 23 *Ethics and International Affairs* 389.
[132] Chandra Lekha Sriram, 'Justice as Peace? Liberal Peacebuilding and Strategies of Transnational Justice' (2007) 21 *Global Society* 579.
[133] Patricia Lundy and Bill Rolston, 'Redress for Past Harms? Official Apologies in Northern Ireland' (2016) 20 *International Journal of Human Rights* 104.
[134] Nevin T Aiken, 'Learning to Live Together: Transitional Justice and Intergroup Reconciliation in Northern Ireland' (2010) 4 *International Journal of Transitional Justice* 166. Such measures were also recommended by the TRC in SA (TRC, *Report of the Truth and Reconciliation Commission* (Pretoria, TRC, 1998), vol 5, ch 5 [78], [102], [107]–[108] and [113]).
[135] Ruti Teitel, *Transitional Justice* (Oxford, Oxford University Press, 2000) 49.
[136] ibid 59.

criteria; ultimately anything can be part of transitional justice as long as it signifies change in some way. This broad but shallow definition is problematic as it compromises justice for the sake of transition; yet, such a compromise should be viewed with suspicion, not least because of the lack of a general agreement as to what it is we are (and should be) transitioning towards.

Transitional justice has been broadened to such an extent that it has even been used in contexts that are not undergoing a peacebuilding process at all.[137] While this might be seen as a welcome transplantation of justice considerations to different settings, the increased elasticity of the concept risks degenerating it into amorphousness.[138] An additional limitation of such a broad definition is that if everything that helps in the transition is part of transitional justice, it leaves little or no content for the other two elements of peace. This is not only troublesome because it is descriptively inaccurate, but also because by classifying all peacebuilding strategies as instances of transitional justice, one is left unable to decide between them when these conflict with each other. For example, some argue that transitional justice may require the forgiveness rather than the punishment of war criminals,[139] while others counter that only by punishing the perpetrators can society move forward.[140] Yet, by conceptualising both alternatives as 'transitional justice', a choice between them becomes arbitrary. Conversely, a narrower definition of post-violence justice as the remedying of past injustices provides a clear answer to this dilemma by offering reasons for the punishment of criminals. Perpetrators, whether of violent crimes or discriminatory policies, must be identified – and ideally punished – because it would preserve a sense of injustice if they did not pay for their crimes.[141] While amnesties acknowledge the existence of perpetrators (since for an amnesty to be given, a crime must have been committed), this acknowledgement might be perceived as empty and thus unable to appeal to the people's sense of justice.[142] This is not to argue that amnesties are never appropriate in post-violence contexts; they might be necessary to appease a still-powerful and armed opposition (thus promoting security) or because forgiving the perpetrators might be the best way to achieve reconciliation.[143] Yet, in such cases, amnesties are used not because of justice's demands, but despite them, as promoting security or reconciliation is considered more pressing in the circumstances.

[137] Stephen Winter, *Transitional Justice in Established Democracies: A Political Theory* (Basingstoke, Palgrave Macmillan, 2014).

[138] Tom Gerard Daly, *The Alchemists: Questioning Our Faith in Courts as Democracy-Builders* (Cambridge, Cambridge University Press, 2017) 48.

[139] Kieran McEvoy and Louise Mallinder, 'Amnesties in Transition: Punishment, Restoration and the Governance of Mercy' (2012) 39 *Journal of Law and Society* 410.

[140] Orentlicher (n 11).

[141] Sikkink (n 78).

[142] Mahmood Mamdani, 'Amnesty or Impunity? A Preliminary Critique of the Report of the Truth and Reconciliation Commission of South Africa (TRC)' (2002) 32 *Diacritics* 32.

[143] *The Azarian Peoples Organisation (AZAPO) and Others* (n 82) [9] and [20].

Since injustices vary from society to society, there is a need to adopt context-specific justice-promoting measures. While, for instance, BiH's violent war might require a focus on retributive justice, the fact that the conflict in NI was fuelled by socio-economic inequalities puts additional emphasis on distributive considerations.[144] Such differences notwithstanding, undoing injustices always requires that attention is paid to both the perpetrators and victims. Efforts to identify and punish the perpetrators are important, but remedying victims to the greatest possible extent for the harm they have suffered is also necessary. Of course, 'victims' do not form a single homogeneous category of people with the same justice preferences and needs.[145] Rather, these preferences change, depending on the specific injustice that different victims have been subjected to. If the injustice is in the form of physical harm or discrimination, it might be necessary to provide monetary or in-kind compensation. Alternatively, if it concerns forced displacement, remedying it might require that the victim either receives restitution of his or her property, or is fairly compensated for it. Moreover, victims often claim that an equally important way of promoting justice is the issuing of an apology from the state or perpetrators for their unjust conduct.[146] Finally, in addition to providing personalised remedies to individual victims, justice can also require the adoption of more holistic measures. Take, for instance, post-apartheid SA, where decades-long discriminatory practices affected all areas of life for millions of people. One way of addressing this injustice and reducing the socio-economic gap that has been created as a result is to adopt countrywide policies that provide better educational, housing and economic opportunities to the disadvantaged communities.[147]

The need to pay close attention to victims and perpetrators suggests that peacebuilders should have a nuanced understanding of who falls in each category and what is entailed through membership in such a group. Rather simplistic depictions of post-violence societies falsely distinguish between 'noble victims' and diametrically opposed 'nefarious victimisers', without acknowledging that someone might, in fact, meet the definitions for both.[148] At the same time, victims tend to be presented as innocent and helpless, which in turn creates political advantages for them.[149] In particular, the 'victim' label makes it easier

[144] Colin Harvey, 'Power-Sharing, Communal Contestation, and Equality: Affirmative Action, Identity and Conflict in Northern Ireland' in Gomez Edmund Terence and Premdas Ralph (eds), *Affirmative Action, Ethnicity and Conflict* (London, Routdledge, 2013) 158.

[145] Tristan Anne Borer, 'A Taxonomy of Victims and Perpetrators: Human Rights and Reconciliation in South Africa' (2003) 25 *Human Rights Quarterly* 1088.

[146] Anna Bohlin, 'A Price on the Past: Cash Compensation in South African Land Restitution' (2004) 38 *Canadian Journal of African Studies* 672.

[147] Bernadette Atuahene, 'From Reparation to Restoration: Moving Beyond Restoring Property Rights to Restoring Political and Economic Visibility' (2007) 60 *Southern Methodist University Law Review* 1419, 1446.

[148] Mark J Osiel, 'Ever Again: Legal Remembrance of Administrative Massacre' (1995–96) 144 *University of Pennsylvania Law Review* 463, 556.

[149] Nicky Rousseau and Madeleine Fullard, 'Accounting and Reconciling in the Balance Sheet of the South African Truth and Reconciliation Commission' (2009) 4 *Journal of Multicultural Discourses* 123, 129.

for a group to attract sympathy and support, while portraying any attacks perpetrated by its members as actions of self-defence and therefore legitimate.[150] Concurrently, the label of 'perpetrator' should also be used with caution, since it can group together actors with ranging levels of culpability.[151] Thus, effective peacebuilding strategies must take these considerations into account and ensure that oversimplifications about the status of different parties are avoided.

Finally, because of the balancing exercise that takes place between the three elements of peace, the requirements of justice are often not fully respected in post-violence societies. Practical difficulties, such as the passage of time,[152] the unreliability of evidence[153] and the large numbers of victims and/or perpetrators,[154] also suggest that the injustices of the past will not be remedied completely.[155] Furthermore, the emphasis the definition places on people's experiences and expectations, rather than just the establishment of institutions, makes it unlikely that perfect justice will be achieved in the eyes of the victims. Illustrative of this is the reaction of Munira Subašić, leader of the Mothers of the Enclaves of Srebrenica and Žepa in BiH, following General Krstić's conviction by the International Criminal Tribunal for the Former Yugoslavia (ICTY).[156] Disappointed, she announced that she did not think that justice had been served because Krstić, at the time an old man, had been sentenced to a 46-year prison term, instead of receiving life imprisonment.[157] In light of these challenges, peacebuilders are advised that what is important is that post-violence justice is present to a satisfactory, rather than full, extent.[158]

C. Reconciliation as the Third Element of Peace

The third element of peace is reconciliation and, like the other two, its definition has been contested; there are, for example, disagreements as to whether it involves personal or political reconciliation and whether it should be understood

[150] Smyth (n 80) 132.

[151] Borer (n 145).

[152] Anneke Smit, *The Property Rights of Refugees and Internally Displaced Persons: Beyond Restitution* (London, Routledge, 2012) 170.

[153] *Varnava and Others v Turkey*, App No 16064/90 (ECtHR, 18 September 2009) [61], noting: 'With the lapse of time, memories of witnesses fade, witnesses may die or become untraceable, evidence deteriorates or ceases to exist, and the prospects that any effective investigation can be undertaken will increasingly diminish; and the Court's own examination and judgment may be deprived of meaningfulness and effectiveness.'

[154] Teitel (n 135) 36.

[155] Mark Freeman, *Truth Commissions and Procedural Fairness* (New York, Cambridge University Press, 2006).

[156] *Krstić* (IT-98-33) (ICTY, 2 August 2001).

[157] Sikkink (n 78) 25–26.

[158] For a cautionary warning to avoid judging attempts to promote justice against the ideal standard, see ibid 165.

as a process or an outcome.[159] This section defines reconciliation in terms of both the outcome it is intended to promote and the methods used to achieve this. It argues that the end result of this process should be meaningful cooperation between members of different groups on a personal *and* political level. Willingness to cooperate on a personal level is likely to encourage political cooperation because whether political parties representing different communities are prepared to work together at least partly depends on the attitudes of their members. On the other hand, political cooperation promotes good personal relations, since these are more likely to be undermined by politicians who encourage inter-group animosity to win easy votes.[160] The outcome of meaningful personal and political cooperation is achieved when a certain process is followed. Specifically, people must start trusting, which in turn requires that they no longer dehumanise each other.

The trust and rehumanisation of the enemy that are necessary steps for reconciliation can be promoted by removing the hurdles that prevent former enemies from being perceived as people.[161] During the period of violence, negative stereotyping, propaganda against and fear of the other side usually make people view members of the opposing group as less than human.[162] The fact that members of the other group could be feeling scared of, victimised by or ashamed of the actions of their fellow group members, or that all sides caused atrocities during a war is completely lost on most people.[163] For instance, when interviewed, members of different ethnic groups in BiH expressed feelings that they were the biggest victims of the conflict and that while atrocities had been carried out by all sides, the ones committed by other groups were premeditated, while those involving their own people were simply individual excesses.[164] As negative stereotyping of the other becomes more common, the individuality of the stereotyped group's members is lost and their dehumanisation becomes easier.[165] Such stereotyping, portraying whole groups of people as less than human,

[159] Daniel Bar-Tal and Gemma Bennink, 'The Nature of Reconciliation as an Outcome and as a Process' in Yaacov Bar-Siman-Tov (ed), *From Conflict Resolution to Reconciliation* (Oxford, Oxford University Press, 2004).

[160] Clare Magill, Alan Smith and Brandon Hamber, *The Role of Education in Reconciliation: The Perspectives of Children and Young People in Bosnia and Herzegovina and Northern Ireland* (Ulster, Special EU Programmes Body, University of Ulster, 2009) 3.

[161] Arie Nadler, 'Reconciliation: Instrumental and Socioemotional Aspects' in Christie (ed) (n 36).

[162] Bar-Tal (n 108) 354.

[163] Marko Milanovic, 'Establishing the Facts about Mass Atrocities: Accounting for the Failure of the ICTY to Persuade Target Audiences' (2016) 47 *Georgetown Journal of International Law* 1321.

[164] Dinka Corkalo et al, 'Neighbors Again? Intercommunity Relations after Ethnic Cleansing' in Stover and Weinstein (n 68).

[165] Halpern and Weinstein (n 68). Also, for a discussion of how simplifying stereotypes and zero-sum conceptualisations of identities characterise post-violence societies, see Marlene C Fiol and Edward J O'Connor, 'Managing Intractable Identity Conflicts' in Christie (ed) (n 36).

predatory and unreasonable in their personal and political relationships, is the biggest hurdle to meaningful cooperation and it is this that reconciliation methods should attempt to address.

Two important distinctions should be made when clarifying the meaning of reconciliation. The first is between meaningful cooperation and inter-group harmony, with the former being a much more modest aim than the arguably utopian goal of achieving the latter.[166] As Govier and Verwoerd put it, a 'realistic goal in contexts of reconciliation is not total harmony; nor is it a state of blissfully enduring unity'.[167] In order for harmony to exist, there must be compatibility of the groups' needs and interests, but competitive politics in post-violence societies operate by highlighting precisely this lack of compatibility.[168] Moreover, had such compatibility existed, it is unlikely that the society would have resorted to violence in the first place. Separate groups, characterised by distinct identities, needs and interests, do not have to be assimilated in order for reconciliation to be achieved. Reconciliation does not require the elimination of differences, but the ability to live with these differences through cooperation.[169] This cooperation can be attained when there is an adequate amount of trust, a confident expectation that one will act in a manner which will not take advantage of the other's vulnerability.[170]

The second distinction that must be made is between meaningful cooperation and mere co-existence among members of the previously warring parties. If people are living next to each other without communicating, cooperating or having common goals, wishing that they did not have to mingle with the other group at all, there is no real reconciliation.[171] It is just a brief pause before the racist perceptions of each group resurface and potentially even reignite the violence. If the UN is right that post-violence societies need a 'society wide system of values … to put a premium on peace, to desire peace, to seek peace and to stand for peace', then reconciliation must mean more than simple co-existence.[172] However, rejecting this minimalist definition does not mean

166 For a definition of reconciliation as inter-group harmony, see Yaacov Bar-Siman-Tov, 'Dialectics between Stable Peace and Reconciliation' in Bar-Siman-Tov (n 159), where he argues that reconciliation involves 'transforming the relations between rival sides from hostility and resentment to friendly and harmonious relations'.

167 Govier and Verwoerd (n 66) 185.

168 Peter Harris and Ben Reilly, *Democracy and Deep-Rooted Conflict: Options for Negotiators* (Stockholm, International Institute for Democracy and Electoral Assistance, 1998) 17–18.

169 Halpern and Weinstein (n 68).

170 Govier and Verwoerd (n 66).

171 Carlos E Sluzki, 'The Process toward Reconciliation' in Antonia Chayes and Martha Minow (eds), *Imagine Coexistence: Restoring Humanity after Violent Conflict* (San Francisco, Jossey-Bass, 2003).

172 UN Department of Public Information, *Prospects for Peace in the Middle East: An Israeli-Palestinian Dialogue: Proceedings of the United Nations Department of Public Information's International Encounter for European Journalists on the Question of Palestine* (New York, United Nations, 1992).

that meaningful cooperation necessarily stems from the altruistic goals of loving one's enemy. It could result from the simple understanding that unless the members of the previously warring groups reconcile, the alternative will be catastrophic for all of them.[173]

An argument could be made that the definition of reconciliation as the meaningful cooperation between different groups is too ambitious; a better (and more achievable) alternative is to focus instead on the need to respect the rights of others.[174] In every society, whether it is a post-violence one or not, there are disagreements about what should be the preferred course of action in relation to different political conflicts. Unless structured debates can take place and ultimately lead to a negotiated outcome, these political conflicts can paralyse the country.[175] Conceptualising reconciliation as the need to respect the rights of others helps address this danger because it provides a discourse and vocabulary through which such debates can take place. Additionally, explicitly linking reconciliation with human rights allays suspicions that have been raised in some post-violence societies that talk of reconciliation as, in fact, an attempt to silence the weaker party. This has, for instance, been the case in NI, where nationalists argue that the agenda for reconciliation and improvement of community relations is promoted by clouding the political nature of the conflict, the long-term inequality that has fuelled the violence and the role of the state in maintaining this.[176] Conversely, if reconciliation was understood as the protection of human rights, such challenges would be overcome, since these are precisely the issues that human rights are designed to address.

Arguably, however, this understanding of reconciliation is too restrictive because it ignores the fact that not every political conflict can be understood as a human rights dilemma.[177] Moreover, in the likely scenario where the parties are not in agreement as to what each competing right entails, expressing the political conflict in rights terms only rephrases, rather than resolves, the problem. A third consideration is that while the protection of human rights might indeed promote reconciliation, the two might also be seen as antithetical to, or at least not always compatible with, each other, since the former is about challenging governments and reforming the law, while the latter focuses on relationship-building among individuals.[178] Finally, this definition should be avoided because

[173] Charles Villa-Vicencio, 'Reconciliation' in Charles Villa-Vicencio and Erik Doxtader (eds), *Pieces of the Puzzle: Keywords on Reconciliation and Transitional Justice* (Cape Town, Institute of Justice and Reconciliation, 2004).

[174] Lesley McEvoy, Kieran McEvoy and Kirsten McConnachie, 'Reconciliation as a Dirty Word: Conflict, Community Relations and Education in Northern Ireland' (2006) 60 *Journal of International Affairs* 81.

[175] Harris and Reilly (n 168) 19.

[176] McEvoy, McEvoy and McConnachie (n 174).

[177] Nasia Hadjigeorgiou, 'Conflict Resolution in Post-violence Societies: Some Guidance for the Judiciary' (ICON·S 2017 Conference on 'Courts, Powers, Public Law', Copenhagen, July 2017).

[178] Maggie Beirne and Colin Knox, 'Reconciliation and Human Rights in Northern Ireland: A False Dichotomy?' (2014) 6 *Journal of Human Rights Practice* 26.

of its unsuitability in answering the question at hand: since our objective is to clarify the relationship between rights and peace (and consequently between rights and reconciliation), any analysis becomes circular if reconciliation itself is defined as the respect of other people's rights.

Thus, reconciliation is best understood as having been achieved when hostile feelings are slowly transformed into a tendency to not dehumanise the members of other groups and then into the development of trust and willingness to cooperate. Even in the most favourable conditions, this takes years to complete; reconciliation does not occur naturally – it needs effort and time and is rarely the result of a linear process.[179] While positive attitudes between individuals from different groups might develop in the workplace, social pressures might prevent them from materialising in their personal lives.[180] Further, such positive attitudes might increase or decrease depending on a number of external factors, such as economic crises or spoilers.[181] Consequently, a number of reconciliation-promoting methods, both bottom-up and top-down and spanning different periods of time, have to be used. Each method has its strengths and weaknesses and might work with some people, but not others, so a combined effort is preferable. The blend of methods that should be used depends on factors such as the specific challenges faced within the post-violence society, the resources available and the cultures of the groups involved.[182]

Common examples of reconciliation-promoting mechanisms are Truth Commissions and communication workshops. Truth Commissions, like the one that was established in SA, can help build reconciliation by providing evidence about the atrocities that took place during the period of violence and eliminating some of the myths that were circulated before and during its occurrence.[183] Such myths, an outcome of negative stereotyping, include suggestions that only one side was the perpetrator of crimes or that every member of that group enthusiastically endorsed the violations. On the other hand, communication workshops can lead to reconciliation by encouraging participants to listen to the other's story in order to appreciate that he or she is not the monster that he or she is portrayed to be.[184] Understanding a person's motives for acting in a specific way or making a particular demand makes it more likely that this will be accepted as reasonable and, as a result, encourages compromise between the

[179] Hamber (n 74) 7–8; Bar-Tal and Bennink (n 159); Beirne and Knox (n 178).

[180] Jennifer Todd et al, 'Does Being Protestant Matter? Protestants, Minorities and the Remaking of Ethno-religious Identity after the Good Friday Agreement' (2009) 11 *National Identities* 87.

[181] Joachim J Savelsberg and Ryan D King, 'Law and Collective Memory' (2007) 3 *Annual Review of Law and Social Science* 189, 191.

[182] See, Oliver Ramsbotham, Tom Woodhouse and Hugh Miall, *Contemporary Conflict Resolution: The Prevention, Management and Transformation of Deadly Conflicts* (Cambridge, Polity Press, 2016) 287, arguing that 'the scope for reconciliation – and the different ways by which it can be achieved – varies greatly from culture to culture'. See also Bar-Tal and Bennink (n 159).

[183] Ignatieff (n 83).

[184] Harry Anastasiou, 'Communication across Conflict Lines: The Case of Ethnically Divided Cyprus' (2002) 39 *Journal of Peace Research* 581.

different parties.[185] When in place, these mechanisms promote reconciliation in the eyes of an outside observer and start promoting subjective feelings of reconciliation as well. However, the development of sufficient levels of trust in order to allow meaningful cooperation is a unique journey for each person and, almost always, spans beyond the completion of the work of formal institutions.

IV. CONCLUSION

This chapter started from the premise that any robust analysis of the relationship between peace and human rights requires that the two terms are defined. Focusing on the first of the two terms, it argued that current definitions are either extrapolated from peacebuilding practice or derived from a wholly abstract analysis. Both suffer from significant shortcomings. Since neither of the two accounts of peace provides a satisfactory foundation for answering the question at hand, a new definition, consisting of the elements of security, justice and reconciliation, was proposed. An advantage of this definition is that it draws a clear line connecting the different elements of peace and the tools that should be used to achieve them. The definition does not make decisions about what peacebuilding tools should be used, when and in what way easy to reach; however, it does make them more transparent. Relying on this definition, the following chapter turns to human rights as one example of peacebuilding tools and argues that under the right conditions, their protection can indeed contribute to both an objectively observable and a subjectively perceived sense of peace in the post-violence society.

[185] ibid.

3

The Means and the End Connected

A Framework for the Relationship between Human Rights and Peace

I. INTRODUCTION

IF THE END objective of peacebuilding processes should be to strike a balance between considerations of security, justice and reconciliation, one means through which this can be achieved is the protection of human rights. Human rights, as defined in section II, are concerned with the *legal* protection of values on both the domestic and the international plane. Such protection could involve the adjudication of human rights cases in national or international courts, or the enactment and enforcement of human rights laws or policies by state officials or international peacebuilders. This definition relies on a fairly limited understanding of human rights as legal rights and does not take into account, for example, the ways in which their moral counterparts can inform school curriculums[1] or contribute to the psychological support provided by victim groups.[2] Yet, it is considered appropriate for elucidating the relationship between human rights and peace in practice, because it reflects the way in which they have been understood and utilised by peacebuilders themselves. Section III proceeds to argue that despite the existence of references in the literature to instances when the protection of human rights contributed to security, justice or reconciliation, these are usually merely examples or intuitions of a positive relationship between them and peace. Instead, what is needed is a comprehensive framework that explains how human rights protection relates to the building of peaceful relationships, in a way that can shape practices on the ground.

This framework centres around the process of conflict resolution. Conflicts, section IV maintains, are incompatibilities of positions on any given subject

[1] Michalinos Zembylas et al, 'Human Rights and the Ethno-Nationalist Problematic through the Eyes of Greek-Cypriot Teachers' (2016) 11 *Education Citizenship and Social Justice* 19.

[2] Brandon Hamber, *Dealing with Painful Memories and Violent Pasts: Towards a Framework for Contextual Understanding* (Berghof Handbook Dialogue Series No 11, Berlin, Berghof Foundation, 2015).

matter and, as such, they are natural and frequently occurring phenomena in all democracies. When they remain unaddressed, they can become dangerous, while their successful resolution can result in the promotion of security, justice and reconciliation. Bearing in mind that conflicts are complex phenomena with personal, social and structural dimensions, the adoption of strategies that address all of these is necessary. Thus, the extent to which human rights are effective peacebuilding tools depends on their ability to respond to such diverse demands of the conflict resolution process. Section V argues that human rights can have this effect in two ways: on the one hand, their adjudication in a court of law can provide guidance as to the best ways to address incompatibilities of positions; on the other hand, they can inspire the adoption, and push for the implementation, of laws and policies that are designed to address such conflicts. Combined, these strategies can induce legal and institutional reforms imperative for the building of objective peace, while also contributing to the promotion of socio-economic and psychological changes necessary for developing subjective feelings of security, justice and reconciliation. Yet, the contributions that human rights can make to the conflict resolution process are neither automatic nor unqualified; for them to materialise, peacebuilders must ensure that certain conditions are in place. Consequently, the main advantage of the proposed framework is that it elucidates the specific ways in which human rights can help build peace and the conditions that must be present for this to happen, so that peacebuilders can strategically target their efforts and resources accordingly.

II. DEFINING THE MEANS

Human rights have been the subject of an impressive number of academic debates that seek to define, justify and explain their content.[3] Yet, when the Brahimi Report states that 'the human rights component of a peace operation is indeed critical to effective peace-building', but offers no definition of 'human rights', it creates the misleading impression that there is a consensus as to what this means.[4] Addressing this limitation, the study proposes a working definition of the term. This is not intended to offer 'the best philosophical account of human rights' or even suggest that such an account exists.[5] Moreover, it does not seek to convince the reader that any alternative understanding of the term is wrong, or produce an exhaustive list of the characteristics that human rights

[3] Guglielmo Verdirame, 'Human Rights in Legal and Political Theory' in Nigel Rodley and Scott Sheeran (eds), *Routledge Handbook of International Human Rights Law* (Abingdon, Routledge, 2013).

[4] Panel on United Nations Peace Operations, *Report of the Panel on United Nations Peace Operations*, A/55/305–S/2000/809 (New York, United Nations, 2000) [41] (hereinafter 'Brahimi Report'.)

[5] James Griffin, 'Discrepancies between the Best Philosophical Account of Human Rights and the International Law of Human Rights' (2001) 101 *Proceedings of the Aristotelian Society,* New Series 1.

generally possess. Rather, it clarifies what peacebuilders themselves imply when they refer to 'human rights'. It argues, in particular, that when they discuss and work towards their protection, peacebuilders have in mind institutions and mechanisms that safeguard *legal* human rights. While this definition might be criticised as being too narrow or artificially restricted, an alternative account that also focused on the protection of moral human rights would have achieved definitional inclusion to the detriment of accuracy as to how the term is understood and used in practice.

Statements emphasising the importance of 'the human rights component of a peace operation', like the ones found in the Brahimi Report, leave unclear whether they refer to the protection of moral or legal human rights.[6] At the same time, philosophical accounts vary widely on whether these are one and the same thing,[7] or completely disconnected from each other.[8] Arguably, a distinction between the two should be maintained since each has a different scope and content, gives rise to distinct remedies and contributes to peacebuilding efforts in varying ways.[9] A moral right is created when there are sufficient moral interests to something, which are not undermined by other conflicting considerations.[10] Only if a legal institution decided that this moral right should also be legally protected and enforceable would this turn into a legal right as well.[11] The justifications for the existence of a moral right usually play a role in the decision to create an equivalent legal right, but additional factors are also relevant.[12] The most important of these factors concerns the appropriateness of legal institutions, such as the judiciary, to decide certain issues and points to the fact that not every moral right should also be converted into a legal one. Thus, a moral right might protect important interests, which should, nevertheless, not be the concern of the law, because legal institutions are not always well-suited to deal with morality's demands. In Buchanan's words, '[j]ustifying assertions about the existence of certain moral rights is one thing; justifying an institutionalized system … to realize them is quite another'.[13] An additional difference between moral and legal rights is that the two result in different types of remedies. Not converting a moral right into a legal one does not mean that no right exists; it simply suggests that any recourse for a failure of the duty-bearer to comply with

[6] For the argument that human rights extend beyond the legal realm, see Jeremy Waldron, 'The Role of Rights in Practical Reasoning: "Rights" versus "Needs"' (2000) 4 *Journal of Ethics* 115, 116.

[7] Griffin (n 5).

[8] Allen Buchanan, *The Heart of Human Rights* (New York, Oxford University Press, 2014).

[9] On the importance of maintaining a distinction between moral and legal rights, see Neil MacCormick, 'Children's Rights: A Test-Case for Theories of Right' in Neil MacCormick (ed), *Legal Right and Social Democracy: Essays in Legal and Political Philosophy* (Oxford, Oxford University Press, 1984).

[10] Allen Buchanan, *Human Rights, Legitimacy, and the Use of Force* (Oxford, Oxford University Press, 2010).

[11] Joseph Raz, 'Legal Rights' (1984) 4 *Oxford Journal of Legal Studies* 1, 14.

[12] Joseph Raz, 'Rights and Individual Well-Being' (1992) 5 *Ratio Juris* 127, 140.

[13] Buchanan (n 8) 51.

his or her obligations rests in morality rather than legal sanctions.[14] Thus, the violation of moral rights will result in the social condemnation of the perpetrator, while that of legal rights will also have legal consequences.

The different characteristics of moral and legal rights mean that they tend to be used in distinct ways by various actors. On the one hand, moral rights are usually relied on by politicians as a way of lending popular support to their policies, or by international peacebuilders when they want to provide added legitimacy to their practices or general presence in the post-violence society.[15] Moral human rights are also valuable peacebuilding tools when they are used by teachers or civil society organisations to educate the public at large of the values that they give effect to.[16] On the other hand, legal human rights are tools usually used in more formal processes of domestic or international institutions. The most common example of such institutions are courts, but other bodies can also be responsible for ensuring that legal human rights are respected, protected and fulfilled. These bodies could be part of the executive[17] or the legislature,[18] might be created on an ad hoc basis by international peacebuilders with temporary powers to act within the post-violence society,[19] or could be specialised administrative[20] or quasi-judicial institutions[21] that were formed to implement specific human rights-inspired legislation. When peacebuilders rely on human rights in the context of these institutions, they do so with particular objectives in mind, such as giving effect to a specific policy or implementing a particular law.

[14] John Skorupski, 'Human Rights' in Samantha Beeson and John Tasioulas (eds), *The Philosophy of International Law* (Oxford, Oxford University Press, 2010).

[15] Kevin Boyle, 'Linking Human Rights and Other Goals' in John Morison, Kieran McEvoy and Gordon Anthony (eds), *Judges, Transition, and Human Rights* (Oxford, Oxford University Press, 2007).

[16] Betty A Reardon, 'Human Rights as Education for Peace' in George J Andreopoulos and Richard Pierre Claude (eds), *Human Rights Education for the Twenty-First Century* (Philadelphia, University of Pennsylvania Press, 1997); Owen M Fiss, 'Human Rights as Social Ideals' in Carla Hesse and Robert Post (eds), *Human Rights in Political Transitions: Gettysburg to Bosnia* (New York, Zone Books, 1999).

[17] See, eg, the Ministry of Human Rights and Refugees in BiH, available at www.vijeceministara.gov.ba/ministarstva/ljudska_prava_i_izbjeglice/default.aspx?id=120&langTag=en-US. Also, the Office of the Custodian, responsible for the protection of TC properties, is part of the Ministry of Interior of the Republic of Cyprus (Nasia Hadjigeorgiou, 'Case Note on *Kazali and Others v Cyprus*' (2013) 2 *Cyprus Human Rights Law Review* 103.)

[18] See, eg, the Joint Committee on Human Rights in the UK; see Courtney Hillebrecht, 'Implementing International Human Rights Law at Home: Domestic Politics and the European Court of Human Rights' (2012) 13 *Human Rights Review* 279.

[19] See, eg, the Office of High Representative in BiH; Richard Caplan, 'Who Guards the Guardians? International Accountability in Bosnia' in David Chandler (ed), *Peace without Politics? Ten Years of International State Building in Bosnia* (London, Taylor & Francis, 2006).

[20] See, eg, the Immovable Property Commission in Cyprus (Nasia Hadjigeorgiou, 'Remedying Displacement in Frozen Conflicts: Lessons from the Case of Cyprus' (2016) 18 *Cambridge Yearbook of European Legal Studies* 152) and the Missing Persons Task Team in SA (Jay D Aronson, 'The Strengths and Limitations of South Africa's Search for Apartheid-Era Missing Persons' (2011) 5 *International Journal of Transitional Justice* 262).

[21] See, eg, the TRC in SA (TRC, *Report of the Truth and Reconciliation Commission* (Pretoria, TRC, 1998), vol 1, ch 6 [63]).

A right, like the right to life or equality, might have both a moral and a legal facet, meaning that it can be used both for rhetorical or educational purposes, and in legal institutions. At the same time, it is possible that a right only has a moral facet in the sense that references to it have a moral punch, but it is not in itself legally enforceable. A case in point is the right to peace itself. Scholars have been discussing the human right to peace and its content for decades, a debate that has also been picked up by UN General Assembly.[22] This has resulted in the passing of the Declaration on the Preparation of Societies for Life in Peace, which recognised that peace 'is mankind's paramount value',[23] and the Declaration of the Right of Peoples to Peace, which reaffirmed the existence of the right and asserted that 'the maintenance of a peaceful life for peoples is the sacred duty of each state'.[24] Further, references to the right to peace have re-emerged, since 2012, within the UN Human Rights Council due to the initiative of a non-governmental organisation, the Spanish Society for International Human Rights Law.[25] Nevertheless, arguments that the right to peace also has a legal content or is legally enforceable remain largely underexplored and unpersuasive.[26] While a political argument along the lines of the General Assembly resolutions can be made for the existence of a moral right to peace, it is unclear how it would ever be used in a court of law, since fundamental questions, such as the identities of the right-holder and the duty-bearer, and the legal obligations that the right gives rise to, remain unanswered.

There are therefore good reasons why legal and moral human rights should remain separate; key among them is the need to distinguish between those rights that can appropriately be protected by legal or quasi-legal institutions and those that are better left in the moral realm. This distinction is not only theoretically persuasive, but also practically important for the conclusions of the book, which are only concerned with the relationship between peace and the protection of *legal* human rights. The choice to limit the analysis in this manner reflects the way peacebuilders themselves have understood the tools they have at their disposal. When UN reports refer to 'human rights', they do not explicitly restrict themselves to their legal protection. Nevertheless, the examples they offer of how human rights can contribute to peace always seem to focus on their legal, rather

[22] Jim Ife, 'Human Rights and Peace' in Charles Webel and Johan Galtung (eds), *The Handbook of Peace and Conflict Studies* (London, Routledge, 2007); Abdul Aziz Said and Charles O. Lerche, 'Peace as a Human Right: Toward an Integrated Understanding' in Julie Mertus and Jeffrey W Helsing (eds), *Human Rights and Conflict: Exploring the Links between Rights, Law and Peacebuilding* (Washington DC, United States Institute of Peace Press, 2006).

[23] UN General Assembly Resolution 33/73 (15 December 1978), preamble.

[24] UN General Assembly Resolution 39/11 (12 November 1984), preamble.

[25] Cecilia Marcela Bailliet, 'Normative Foundation of the International Law of Peace' in Cecillia Marcela Baillet and Kjetil Mujezinovic Larsen (eds), *Promoting Peace through International Law* (Oxford, Oxford University Press, 2015).

[26] Jack Donnelly, 'Peace as a Human Right: Commentary' in Mertus and Helsing (n 22).

than moral, facet.[27] Thus, *An Agenda for Peace* refers to the need to 'identify and support structures which will tend to consolidate peace' and uses the monitoring of elections and the protection of human rights as examples.[28] Further, the Brahimi Report recommends that the Office of the High Commissioner for Human Rights increases its peacebuilding efforts by creating 'model databases for human rights field work'.[29] Finally, the UN Secretary-General has noted that: 'The establishment of independent national human rights commissions is one complementary strategy that has shown promise for helping to restore … peaceful dispute resolution.'[30] Nowhere in these key UN documents are there signs of moral human rights being perceived as instrumental peacebuilding tools.

This emphasis on legal human rights is also reflected in peacebuilding operations within post-violence societies themselves. While, for example, there has been a growing literature on the importance of moral rights in relation to peace education,[31] and even some small-scale grassroots attempts to apply the theoretical findings in practice,[32] most peacebuilding strategies are still focused on the contributions of legal rights.[33] Thus, considerable attention and resources have been invested in the reform of the judiciary, the development of the rule of law and the creation of legal remedies for past injustices.[34] This is not surprising: moral rights are not as intellectually disciplined or clear in their content as their legal counterparts. This renders them susceptible to abuse by politically partisan groups seeking to undermine the peace process, a danger that peacebuilders are, understandably, keen to avoid.[35] Conversely, legal rights are preferred among

[27] eg, Teitel defines transitional justice, to which human rights give effect, as the 'conception of justice associated with periods of political change, characterized by *legal* responses to confront the wrongdoings of repressive predecessor regimes' (Ruti Teitel, 'Transitional Justice Genealogy' (2003) 16 *Harvard Human Rights Journal* 69, 69, emphasis added). See also UN Secretary-General, *The Rule of Law and Transitional Justice in Conflict and Post-conflict Societies*, S/2004/616 (New York, United Nations, 2004) [7].

[28] UN Secretary-General, *An Agenda for Peace: Preventive Diplomacy, Peacemaking and Peace-Keeping: Report of the Secretary-General Pursuant to the Statement Adopted by the Summit Meeting of the Security Council on 31 January 1992*, A/47/277 – S/24111 (New York, United Nations, 1992) [55]. The emphasis on structures is also apparent in UN Secretary-General (n 27) [2].

[29] Brahimi Report (n 4) [244]; see also [324] for a similar comment.

[30] UN Secretary-General (n 27) [31].

[31] Lesley McEvoy and Laura Lundy, '"In the Small Places": Education and Human Rights Culture in Conflict-Affected Societies' in Morison, McEvoy and Anthony (eds) (n 15).

[32] Sara Clarke-Habibi, 'Transforming Worldviews: The Case of Education for Peace in Bosnia and Herzegovina' (2005) 3 *Journal of Transformative Education* 33.

[33] UN Secretary-General (n 27) [34]–[36]; Kjetil Mujezinovic Larsen, 'United Nations Peace Operations and International Law: What Kind of Law Promotes What Kind of Peace?' in Baillet and Larsen (n 25).

[34] Patricia Lundy and Mark McGovern, 'The Role of Community in Participatory Transitional Justice' in Kieran McEvoy and Lorna McGregor (eds), *Transitional Justice from Below: Grassroots Activism and the Struggle for Change* (Oxford, Hart Publishing, 2008) 99.

[35] For an example of how the moral right to return was abused by Bosnian politicians to undermine the repatriation of displaced persons, see section V in ch 5.

peacebuilders because they are more in line with their liberal agenda and its focus on the reform of laws and institutions.[36] Finally, legal tools are more readily relied on because they are easier to deploy and utilise than moral human rights and their impact is simpler to measure, assess and fund.[37]

Since the objective is to devise a framework that describes how human rights relate to peacebuilding efforts in practice, the preferences of those who utilise them are important. It is for this reason that the ensuing analysis will also not be dealing with the impact of socio-economic rights in peacebuilding efforts. While such rights can provide the impetus for the development of socio-economic reform policies necessary for peace,[38] they have not attracted much attention from peacebuilders themselves.[39] Thus, UN reports often refer to the development of democratic institutions,[40] the elimination of discrimination among ethnic groups[41] and responses to past violence,[42] all of which relate to the protection of civil and political rights, but there is little mention of the right to food, housing or education, beyond the general push to transform post-violence societies into liberal economies.[43] Furthermore, the specific contributions that socio-economic rights can make to peace, the considerations of who should use them and in what way in order to induce such reforms, and the conditions that must be present for these to materialise arguably differ from those relating to civil and political rights. An assessment of their potential peacebuilding effects is therefore crucial, but it is not an exercise that can be undertaken here. This is not to suggest that socio-economic reforms remain exclusively outside the focus of the book. In fact, several of the rights that are explored, such as the right to property or freedom from discrimination (especially in the workplace), are directly connected to such reforms. However, the analysis will only be focusing on those rather than also exploring the (albeit potentially fruitful) relationship between them and the protection of a category of rights that has remained largely ignored by peacebuilders themselves.

The proposed framework is also only concerned with individual rather than group rights, but for different reasons. Although the peacebuilding

[36] Bethan K Greener, 'Revisiting the Politics of Post-conflict Peacebuilding: Reconciling the Liberal Agenda?' (2011) 23 *Global Change, Peace and Security* 357.

[37] Kerry Rittich, 'Governing by Measuring: The Millennium Development Goals in Global Governance' in Ruth Buchanan and Peer Zumbansen (eds), *Law in Transition: Human Rights, Development and Transitional Justice* (Oxford, Hart Publishing, 2016).

[38] Makau W Mutua, 'The Transformation of Africa: A Critique of Rights in Transitional Justice' in Buchanan and Zumbansen ((n 37) 96.

[39] Lorna McGregor, 'International Law as a "Tiered Process": Transitional Justice at the Local, National and International Level' in McEvoy and McGregor (n 34) 59.

[40] UN Secretary-General (n 28) [59].

[41] UN Secretary-General (n 27) [4].

[42] ibid [44].

[43] For an analysis of the connection between current peacebuilding practices and the strengthening of the free market, see Paul Collier and et al, *Breaking the Conflict Trap: Civil War and Development Policy* (Washington DC, World Bank and Oxford University Press, 2003).

contributions[44] and even the very existence[45] of group rights are still being debated in the literature, peacebuilding reports and practice have already acknowledged them as important conflict resolution tools. For instance, *An Agenda for Peace* calls for a 'a deeper understanding and respect for the rights of minorities', which will contribute to a greater stability of states.[46] At the same time, the UN has supported peace agreements, such as the Annan Plan that was put to a referendum in Cyprus in 2004, which heavily relied on group rights, such as the veto power of ethnic groups in political decisions[47] and the provision of ethnic quotas on the number of people that would be allowed to reside in a given geographical area within the post-violence society.[48] Nevertheless, the specific contributions that group rights can make to peacebuilding efforts differ from those of individual rights and should be explored separately. Moreover, while potentially beneficial to promoting a sense of security among previously warring parties,[49] the possibility of abuse of group rights is much higher than that of their individual counterparts and merits specific attention that cannot be devoted here.[50] Finally, judges have already recognised that individual and group rights may conflict with each other, thus making it dangerous to place the two under the umbrella term of 'human rights'.[51]

III. THE MEANS AND THE END UNCONNECTED

Human rights can indeed make positive contributions to each of the elements of peace. For instance, especially in contexts where the police force was perceived as having played a role in the continuation of the violence by favouring one community over the other, its reform can send the message that things are changing and can help promote security.[52] While not every aspect of police reform

[44] John Packer, 'On the Content of Minority Rights' in Juha Räikkä (ed), *Do We Need Minority Rights? Conceptual Issues* (The Hague, Martinus Nijhoff Publishers, 1996).

[45] Marlies Galenkamp, 'The Rationale of Minority Rights: Wishes Rather than Needs?' in Räikkä (ed) (n 44).

[46] UN Secretary-General (n 28) [81] and [18].

[47] United Nations, *Proposal for the Comprhensive Settlement of the Cyprus Problem* (New York, United Nations, 2004), art 5(2)(b) (hereinafter 'Annan Plan').

[48] ibid art 3(5) and (6).

[49] John McGarry and Brendan O'Leary, 'Consociation and its Critics: Northern Ireland after the Belfast Agreement' in Sujit Choudhry (ed), *Constitutional Design for Divided Societies: Integration or Accommodation?* (Oxford, Oxford University Press, 2008).

[50] Avigail Eisenberg, 'Identity and Liberal Politics: The Problem of Minorities within Minorities' in Avigail Eisenberg and Jeff Spinner-Halev (eds), *Minorities within Minorities: Equality, Rights and Diversity* (Cambridge, Cambridge University Press, 2005).

[51] See, eg, *Sejdić and Finci v Bosnia and Herzegovina* App No 27996/06 (ECtHR, 22 December 2009).

[52] Brice Dickson, 'Policing and Human Rights after the Conflict' in Marcus Cox, Adrian Guelke and Fiona Stephen (eds), *A Farewell to Arms? From 'Long War' to Long Peace in Northern Ireland* (Manchester, Manchester University Press, 2006) 114.

is connected to human rights, they can provide clear guidance on the types of changes that should be adopted in order to make this process both more effective and legitimate in the eyes of the people.[53] Thus, when the Patten Commission in NI was asked to make recommendations for the reform of the – then – Royal Ulster Constabulary, it gave a prominence to human rights that even human rights activists had not dared predict.[54] For instance, it recommended the introduction of 'a comprehensive programme of action to focus policing in NI on a human rights-based approach';[55] the adoption of a new Code of Ethics, integrating the European Convention on Human Rights (ECHR) into police practice;[56] and the hiring of a human rights legal expert in the police legal services.[57] Moreover, it suggested that the performance of the police service with regard to human rights be closely monitored by the new Policing Board,[58] a body that would include at least one member with a human rights background.[59]

An additional peacebuilding contribution of human rights concerns the way in which they can inform policies intended to remedy those who have suffered from past injustices. For instance, the right to property is directly associated with the remedying of displaced people,[60] while the right to life has provided useful guidance on the procedural requirements that the authorities should comply with, when investigating conflict-related deaths[61] or disappearances.[62] By inspiring and shaping such remedies, human rights can empower victims and create a sense, both among them and the general population at large, that the injustices of the past are being overcome.[63] Similarly, a key assumption of peacebuilding strategies such as Truth Commissions and even criminal trials is that '[i]t is essential for reconciliation to have the parties agree on the historical responsibility of human rights abuses'.[64] Finally, it has been argued that ideas that are popularly associated with human rights, such as dignity and respect of

[53] Organisation for Security and Cooperation in Europe, *Security Sector Governance and Reform: Guidelines for OSCE Staff* (Vienna, OSCE, 2016) 14.

[54] Dickson (n 52) 107.

[55] Independent Commission on Policing for Northern Ireland, *A New Beginning: Policing in Northern Ireland* (Belfast, Northern Ireland Office, 1999) [4.6] (hereinafter 'Patten Report'.)

[56] ibid [4.8].

[57] ibid [4.11].

[58] ibid [4.12].

[59] ibid [6.12].

[60] UN Sub-Commission on the Promotion and Protection of Human Rights, *Housing and Property Restitution in the Context of the Return of Refugees and Internally Displaced Persons*, E/CN4/Sub2/2005/17 (Geneva, United Nations, 28 June 2005) (hereinafter 'Pinheiro Principles'.) As a practical example, see the Property Law Implementation Plan in BiH (Charles Philpott, 'Though the Dog is Dead, the Pig Must Be Killed: Finishing with Property Restitution to Bosnia Herzegovina's IDPs and Refugees' (2005) 18 *Journal of Refugee Studies* 1).

[61] *McKerr v United Kingdom* App No 28883/95 (ECtHR, 4 May 2001).

[62] *Varnava and Others v Turkey* App No 16064/90 (ECtHR, 18 September 2009).

[63] Idit Kostiner, 'Evaluating Legality: Toward a Cultural Approach to the Study of Law and Social Change' (2003) 37 *Law and Society Review* 323.

[64] Nadim N Rouhana, 'Identity and Power in the Reconciliation of National Conflict' in Alice H Eagly, Reuben M Baron and Lee V Hamilton (eds), *The Social Psychology of Group Identity and Social Conflict* (Washington DC, American Psychological Association, 2004) 179.

the person, could promote reconciliation.[65] When the reasoning of legal institutions is influenced by, and refers to, such principles, the expectation is that this could encourage people to live by them, therefore enhance feelings of rehumanisation and trust.[66]

While these accurately describe contributions that human rights can make to peacebuilding efforts, the first two, relating to the reform of the police and the remedying of specific injustices, merely offer examples of the positive relationship between human rights and security, and human rights and justice respectively. At the same time, the expectation that the 'truth' about human rights violations, or merely the use of human rights language by a legal institution, can contribute to feelings of reconciliation, is only an intuition. On the one hand, it has been argued that truth and reconciliation are not necessarily compatible objectives and that efforts to promote the former can, in fact, undermine the latter.[67] On the other, rarely is empirical evidence presented that the public is familiar with human rights initiatives, or likely to change its perceptions of the conflict because human rights language has been used as part of the legal process.[68] Such examples and intuitions of the positive relationship between peace and human rights are not necessarily wrong or factually incorrect. However, they do lack analytical robustness and therefore, should not be used to draw lessons about the relationship between the two concepts more generally. In McAuliffe's words:

> Even the most basic or generic theory of change in the transformative transitional justice literature would explicitly outline a link between a transitional justice intervention, a change process and ultimate goals, the input needs, the actors involved, internal or external risks, obstacles to success and potential knock-on effects. Such thinking, however, has rarely been present in a literature that assumes better insight, participatory ethics or broader articulation of … rights have an inherent potency to transform structures and behaviours.[69]

Briefly, expectations about the peacebuilding potential of human rights have been justified in the literature in two ways. The first is based on the idea that

[65] Bertrand Ramcharan, 'Human Rights and Human Security' (2004) 3 *Disarmament Forum* 39, 45.

[66] For the use of such principles in legal decisions, see *August v Electoral Commission* (CCT 8/99) (SA Constitutional Court, 1 April 1999) [17], where Sachs J states that: 'The vote of each and every citizen is a badge of dignity and of personhood.' For the argument that judicial decisions can contribute to reconciliation, see James L Gibson and Amanda Gouws, *Overcoming Intolerance in South Africa: Experiments in Democratic Persuasion* (Cambridge, Cambridge University Press, 2003).

[67] David Mendeloff, 'Truth-Seeking, Truth-Telling, and Postconflict Peacebuilding: Curb the Enthusiasm?' (2004) 6 *International Studies Review* 355.

[68] Gerarld N Rosenberg, 'The Irrelevant Court: The Supreme Court's Inability to Influence Popular Beliefs about Equality (or Anything Else)' in Neal Devins and Dave Douglas (eds), *Redefining Equality* (Oxford, Oxford University Press, 1998).

[69] Padraig McAuliffe, *Transformative Transitional Justice and the Malleability of Post-conflict States* (Cheltenham, Edward Elgar, 2017) 65.

the failure to protect human rights is likely to result in an eruption of violence. This justification is mentioned in the Brahimi Report and *An Agenda for Peace*, which argue for the protection of human rights as an effective conflict prevention method.[70] Nevertheless, there is, at most, *some* evidence that violations of civil and political rights, or of economic rights coupled with discrimination, are *among the factors* that can promote violence; uprisings are not necessary and unavoidable consequences of all human rights violations.[71] Moreover, even in cases where violence does erupt, it does not follow that protecting human rights can stop the fighting after it has already broken out. And even if it did, stopping violence is not synonymous with building peace; rather, a secure environment is just the first step in achieving the overall objective.[72] This leads to the second justification for their protection, namely, that if human rights violations caused the eruption of violence, safeguarding those rights can undo that and build peace. Thus, *An Agenda for Peace* states that 'the sources of war are pervasive and deep' and to address them, we must enhance our respect for human rights.[73] However, large-scale human rights violations can cause deep personal, psychological, cultural, social, economic and political rifts.[74] Protecting human rights might successfully address each of these problems to different degrees. Yet, the *Agenda* does not provide any further explanation about the extent to which these problems can be resolved through the protection of human rights, how or why. It is this gap in our understanding of the relationship between the two concepts that the book seeks to address.

IV. RESOLVING CONFLICTS AND BUILDING PEACE

The framework that will be used to explore the relationship between human rights and peace relies on the idea of conflict resolution, thus making it necessary to define what is meant by 'conflict' in the first place. A conflict can be

[70] Brahimi Report (n 4) [29]; UN Secretary-General (n 28) [18].

[71] Oskar N Thoms and James Ron, 'Do Human Rights Violations Cause Internal Conflict?' (2007) 29 *Human Rights Quarterly* 674; Kjersti Skarstad, 'Human Rights Violations and Conflict Risk: A Theoretical and Empirical Assessment' in Baillet and Larsen (n 25).

[72] NI provides evidence that security, and in particular a militarised approach towards it, is not enough to promote peace. Thus: 'Long before the conflict was brought to an end, it was officially acknowledged (and under a Conservative Party administration) that religious and political discrimination in employment should be challenged' (Colin Harvey, 'Power-Sharing, Communal Contestation, and Equality: Affirmative Action, Identity and Conflict in Northern Ireland' in Gomez Edmund Terence and Premdas Ralph (eds), *Affirmative Action, Ethnicity and Conflict* (London, Routdledge, 2013) 158).

[73] UN Secretary-General (n 28) [5].

[74] Michelle Parlevliet, *Rethinking Conflict Transformation from a Human Rights Perspective* (Berghof Handbook Dialogue Series No 9, Berlin, Berghof Research Centre for Constructive Conflict Management, 2009).

understood both as a violent dispute and, more generally, as an 'incompatibility of goals'[75] or an 'incompatibility of positions'.[76] The former of the two definitions should be rejected for the purposes of this analysis because it focuses too narrowly on a specific manifestation of a dispute and loses sight of the reasons why it became violent, and what can be done to address it.[77] Conversely, the latter is much more suitable because its broad nature includes both violent and non-violent disagreements and offers a good starting point for a comprehensive theory that encapsulates a range of peacebuilding dilemmas. If conflicts are understood as incompatibilities of positions, it becomes clear that they are a universal feature of all human societies,[78] 'an intrinsic and inevitable aspect of social change',[79] and a necessary part of life in all healthy democratic states that accept and encourage divergence of opinion.[80] It is for this reason that the book adopts the term 'post-violence' rather than 'post-conflict' since there can be no society that is completely devoid of conflict. Moreover, a distinction between constructive and destructive conflicts, like the one made by Deutsch, is both unhelpful and factually misleading.[81] What is problematic is not the existence of specific types of conflicts per se, but the failure to respond to them in the appropriate way. If they are addressed constructively, they can act as the impetus for society's development and progress.[82] It is only when they are ignored and allowed to fester that disillusionment among the population can result in their more negative manifestations, including violence.[83]

References to conflicts are sometimes understood as alluding to *behaviour and actions* that create objectively observable tension among the parties.[84] Alternatively, other commentators have emphasised their expressive or perceived

[75] Johan Galtung, 'Introduction: Peace by Peaceful Conflict Transformation – the Transcend Approach' in Charles Webel and Johan Galtung (eds), *The Handbook of Peace and Conflict Studies* (London, Routledge, 2007).

[76] Jacob Kremenyuk, Victor Bercovitch and William Zartman, 'Introduction: The Nature of Conflict and Conflict Resolution' in Jacob Kremenyuk, Victor Bercovitch and William Zartman (eds), *The SAGE Handbook of Conflict Resolution* (London, SAGE Publications, 2008) 3.

[77] John Paul Lederach, *Preparing for Peace: Conflict Transformation across Cultures* (Syracuse, Syracuse University Press, 1995) 16.

[78] Benjamin Reilly, *Democracy in Divided Societies: Electoral Engineering for Conflict Management* (Cambridge, Cambridge University Press, 2001) 5.

[79] Oliver Ramsbotham, Tom Woodhouse and Hugh Miall, *Contemporary Conflict Resolution: The Prevention, Management and Transformation of Deadly Conflicts* (Cambridge, Polity Press, 2016) 17.

[80] Kremenyuk, Bercovitch and Zartman, 'Introduction' (n 76) 3.

[81] Morton Deutsch, 'A Theory of Cooperation and Conflict' (1949) 2 *Human Relations* 149; Morton Deutsch, *The Resolution of Conflict: Constructive and Destructive Processes* (New Haven, Yale University Press, 1973).

[82] Lederach (n 77) 16; Thorsten Bonacker et al, 'Human Rights and the (De)Securitization of Conflict' in Raffaele Marchetti and Nathalie Tocci (eds), *Civil Society, Conflicts and the Politicization of Human Rights* (Tokyo, United Nations University Press, 2001) 15.

[83] William Zartman, 'Dynamics and Constraints in Negotiations in Internal Conflicts' in William Zartman (ed), *Elusive Peace: Negotiating an End to Civil Wars* (Washington DC, Brookings Institution, 1995); John Burton, *Conflict Resolution and Prevention* (Basingstoke, Macmillan, 1990).

[84] Deutsch, *The Resolution of Conflict* (n 81).

nature, with conflicts arising whenever the parties *believe* they have incompatible objectives.[85] Thus, in contrast to Deutsch's argument that a conflict arises 'whenever incompatible actions occur',[86] Bar-Tal contents that:

> [A] conflict becomes reality for society members only when a particular situation is identified as conflictive by them … From the psychological perspective of conflict analysis, outbreaks of conflicts are dependent on the appearance of particular perceptions, beliefs, attitudes and motivations, all of which must change for conflict resolution to occur.[87]

Differently to these positions, a conflict is defined here as an 'empirical phenomenon'[88] *and* 'a psychological state of affairs',[89] thus suggesting that the ideal way of responding to it is by addressing the challenges that emerge at both levels. Examples of conflicts include disagreements as to the best strategy for reforming the police, the remedies that should be provided to the displaced, or the types of powers that must be afforded to institutions investigating the fate of missing persons. When such disagreements are publicly articulated and manifest as empirical phenomena, a failure of the parties to adopt strategies that respond to them (such as agreeing on a specific plan for the reform of the police or on a policy for remedying victims) is apparent to an outside observer and objectively undermines security, justice and reconciliation. Conversely, conflicts as psychological states of affairs may arise before their manifestation as empirical phenomena, at the same time as this manifestation, or could linger even after the objectively observable disagreement has been resolved through the adoption of a formal process. Thus, if the examples above are also seen as psychological incompatibilities of positions, the conflicts will be resolved in this respect when the general public experiences and appreciates the benefits of a reformed police, the victims feel remedied for their forced displacement and satisfied with the outcome of the investigations concerning the missing persons. These positive changes in the beliefs and attitudes of the public are likely to aid the peacebuilding process by improving subjective perceptions about the extent to which security, justice and reconciliation are present in the post-violence society.

This more complex understanding of the nature of conflict was identified early on by authors such as Johan Galtung, who argued that the 'contradiction' at the heart of the dispute can manifest as a 'behaviour', an 'attitude' or both.[90] Thus, a contradiction could be 'real', resulting in a conflict at the manifest level,

[85] Louis Kriesbert, *Social Conflict* (Englewood Cliffs, Prentice Hall, 1982) 17.

[86] Deutsch, *The Resolution of Conflict* (n 81) 10.

[87] Daniel Bar-Tal, 'From Intractable Conflict through Conflict Resolution to Reconciliation: Psychological Analysis' (2000) 21 *Political Psychology* 351, 351–52.

[88] Raymond Mack and Richard Snyder, 'The Analysis of Social Conflict: Toward an Overview and Synthesis' (1957) 1 *Journal of Conflict Resolution* 212.

[89] Kenneth Ewart Boulding, *Stable Peace* (Austin, University of Texas Press, 1978) 5.

[90] Johan Galtung, *Peace by Peaceful Means: Peace and Conflict, Development and Civilization* (London, SAGE Publications, 1996) 89.

or 'perceived', arising as a dispute at the latent level.[91] The terminology adopted by Galtung, and the distinction between real and perceived conflicts, should not be taken to mean that the former is somehow more difficult to resolve than the latter. Rather, in order for a conflict to be successfully resolved, it is almost always necessary to respond to it on both the manifest and the latent level, with each posing different but equally challenging demands. Appreciating the importance of each level is imperative because negative behaviours can result in negative attitudes and vice versa, thus perpetuating a vicious cycle of unresolved conflict. In addition to Galtung, this view has been supported by peacebuilders such as Jean-Paul Lederach,[92] John Brewer[93] and Herbert Kelman,[94] who have argued that a sustainable and effective response to conflict requires not only that actions and institutions are reformed, but also that attention is paid to the internal dynamics of the society as well.

Having defined the term 'conflict', it now becomes necessary to clarify what is meant by 'addressing' or 'responding' to such a phenomenon and how this links to the ultimate goal of building peace. Over the years, different terms have been used to describe this process, with 'conflict management', 'conflict resolution' and 'conflict transformation' being among the most popular ones. Rather confusingly, each of these terms has been defined in different ways by various authors and has generally emphasised distinct aspects of, and responses to, the conflict. Bearing in mind the caveat that terminology has evolved with the changing understandings of practitioners,[95] it is generally agreed that the three terms differ in terms of the timeframe within which they operate (with conflict management having the shortest-term and conflict transformation the longest-term goals) and the depth of the intervention they endorse.[96] Thus, conflict management is usually concerned with the limitation or containment of violence,[97] conflict resolution with addressing underlying incompatibilities and accepting the existence of distinct goals from each party,[98] and conflict transformation with the reconstruction of the social realities that led to the eruption of violence in the first place.[99]

[91] ibid.

[92] Lederach (n 77) 16.

[93] John D Brewer, *Peace Processes: A Sociological Approach* (Cambridge, Polity Press, 2010) 19.

[94] Herbert Kelman, *International Behaviour: A Social Psychological Analysis* (New York, Holt, Rinehart & Winston, 1965).

[95] Lederach (n 77) 16.

[96] ibid.

[97] William Zartman, 'Towards the Resolution of International Conflicts' in William Zartman and Lewis Rasmussen (eds), *Peacemaking in International Conflict: Methods & Techniques*, 2nd edn (Washington DC, United States Institute of Peace Press, 2007) ii.

[98] Peter Wallensteen, *Understanding Conflict Resolution: War, Peace and the Global System* (London, SAGE Publications, 2002).

[99] John Paul Lederach, *The Little Book of Conflict Transformation* (New York, Good Books, 2003); Veronique Dudouet, *Transitions from Violence to Peace: Revisiting Analysis and Intervention in Conflict Tranformation* (Berghof Handbook Dialogue Series No 15, Berlin, Berghof Research Centre, 2006).

Advocating passionately in favour of adopting the term 'conflict transformation', Lederach contends that the other two labels should be avoided because of negative connotations that each is associated with.[100] On the one hand, he maintains, conflict resolution impliedly portrays conflicts as negative phenomena that must be decisively addressed and left behind, thus ignoring the fact that incompatibilities of positions are always present, but merely change in terms of how they are manifested and perceived over time. On the other, while the term conflict management could reflect a more nuanced understanding of conflict, its focus has historically been unacceptably narrow, emphasising only the ceasing of violence and should therefore also be rejected. However, perhaps most problematically in relation to both is what Lederach perceives as their undue attention to society's institutions rather than the need to address the conflict at a much deeper level and attempt to shape – or transform – people's beliefs so that they can sustainably move beyond the incompatibility in question. Nevertheless, while the attention it pays to social and psychological changes is indeed an advantage of conflict transformation, the term's all-encompassing focus clouds the fact that even less comprehensive responses, such as the adjudication of a dispute or the implementation of a single law, can help positively address an ongoing conflict.

Paradoxically, the heated debate about which label should be adopted ignores the observation that over time, authors have used different terms to describe the same thing, sometimes even rendering them indistinguishable from each other. Thus, Lederach's definition of conflict transformation as 'centred and rooted in the quality of … social, political, economic and cultural relationships'[101] is not materially different from the definition of conflict resolution provided by Ramsbotham et al as 'the deep-rooted sources of conflict [being] addressed and transformed. This suggests that behaviour is no longer violent, attitudes are no longer hostile and the structure of the conflict has been changed'.[102] Similar to these is Burton's definition of 'conflict provention', which refers to the structural changes that must take place and the fostering of conditions that create cooperative relationships within a society.[103] This comparison warns against the caricature of different terms and suggests that what matters is the content rather than the label of each process. In light of this, addressing or responding to incompatibilities of positions will be referred to as 'conflict resolution', since it is the most widely used term.[104] This will encompass all the steps needed to respond to conflicts as both empirical phenomena and psychological states of affairs.

[100] Lederach (n 77) 16–17.

[101] John Paul Lederach, 'Conflict Transformation: Beyond Intractability' in Guy Burgess and Heidi Burgess (eds), *Conflict Information Consortium* (Boulder, University of Colorado Press, 2003).

[102] Ramsbotham, Woodhouse and Miall (n 79) 34–35.

[103] John Burton, *Conflict: Resolution and Provention* (New York, St Martin's Press, 1990) 3.

[104] Ramsbotham, Woodhouse and Miall (n 79) 16.

If the process of conflict resolution is successful, its outcome will be the building of a peaceful – in other words, secure, just and reconciled – post-violence society. The connection between conflict resolution on the one hand and the building of peace on the other has been made by a number of authors,[105] but was most explicitly articulated by Ramsbotham et al when asserting that: 'Defining what peacebuilding is, what peacebuilders seek to achieve, and how they pursue peacebuilding raises fundamental questions about the nature of conflict resolution and its relationship to the peace that it wants to build.'[106] This connection is further supported when one looks at the whole process in reverse. The longer a conflict within a state remains unresolved, the more likely are the people to feel disillusioned, frustrated or threatened by the existing circumstances.[107] Consequently, especially in ethnically or racially divided societies, where almost all disagreements are perceived in terms of the whole group's interests, failure to resolve a conflict entails a very apparent and collective loss of legitimacy.[108] The more divisive the conflict, the higher the stakes and the greater the loss of legitimacy; when this is combined with the frustration of the people, it can lead to the eruption of violence and undermine security.[109] Similarly, if a conflict concerns disagreements as to whether past atrocities should be remedied, or differences on the best way to do this, leaving it unresolved can have detrimental effects on feelings of justice. Thus, what security and justice require is the successful resolution of these conflicts.[110] At the same time, successful conflict resolution can also promote reconciliation in the post-violence society.[111] Even when festering conflicts do not result in the eruption of violence, they require the parties to constantly defend their positions from the verbal attacks of those who hold an incompatible view.[112] This constant position of being in defence leaves the parties in limbo and makes it more difficult for them to focus on the building of common ground. Conversely, successful conflict resolution makes the parties

[105] See, eg, Betts Fetherston, 'Peacekeeping, Conflict Resolution and Peacebuilding: A Reconsideration of Theoretical Frameworks' (2000) 7 *International Peacekeeping* 190, 192, who argues that 'peacekeeping has not for the most part facilitated the establishment of long-term sustainable peace – it has not created, in other words, space for conflict resolution'.

[106] Ramsbotham, Woodhouse and Miall (n 79) 271.

[107] Boulding (n 89) 70–71; Galtung (n 75) 15.

[108] Michelle Parlevliet, *Bridging the Divide: Exploring the Relationship between Human Rights and Conflict Management* (Track Two Occasional Paper, Cape Town, Centre for Conflict Resolution, March 2002).

[109] Zartman (n 83); John Burton, *Conflict: Resolution and Prevention* (London, Macmillan, 1990).

[110] Galtung (n 75).

[111] Ramsbotham, Woodhouse and Miall (n 79) 286, noting that 'reconciliation ... can be seen as the ultimate goal of conflict resolution'. However, this is different from Lederach's argument that peacebuilding, conflict resolution and reconciliation are identical since, as explained in ch 2, the building of peace also requires the promotion of security and justice, which might contradict with the objective of reconciliation (John Paul Lederach, *Building Peace: Sustainable Reconciliation in Divided Societies* (Washington DC, United States Institute of Peace Press, 1997).

[112] Bar-Tal (n 87).

less defensive and eventually encourages them to enter into meaningful relationships of cooperation with each other.

In a nutshell, therefore, the peacebuilding and conflict resolution processes are synonymous terms, with their end objective being the striking of a balance between security, justice and reconciliation. The two processes consist of the adoption of a range of peacebuilding strategies, among them the protection of human rights. Different strategies can respond to various conflicts to different extents and the more comprehensive this response, the more sustainable and better balanced will be the promotion of the three elements. Conversely, a failure to successfully resolve a conflict can undermine peace, especially if incompatibilities of positions are understood as impacting on the parties' identities and very survival.[113] In cases where the incompatibility is a manifest one, with the conflict presenting itself as an empirical phenomenon, a failure to resolve it can have an objective and observable detrimental effect on peace. In instances where the contradiction is a latent one, a psychological state of affairs that affects people's perceptions and beliefs, unsuccessful conflict resolution will undermine subjective feelings of security, justice and reconciliation.

Since in most instances, a conflict is both an empirical phenomenon and a psychological state of affairs, a successful peacebuilding strategy is one that resolves a conflict both objectively and in the eyes of those who are affected by it. In this sense, successful conflict resolution implies action that responds to the dispute as a matter of fact *and* ensures that the people themselves do not perceive it as being ongoing. This observation is important because it (partly) departs from assumptions in the mainstream literature that a conflict can be successfully resolved merely by establishing the relevant procedures and institutions.[114] Such strategies, which Brewer calls 'political peace processes', are effective in introducing institutional and legal reforms that are necessary for the resolution of conflicts as empirical phenomena and the building of objective peace. However, at the same time, they are, on their own, insufficient peacebuilding tools and must be adopted alongside additional 'social peace processes'.[115] These processes, which aim to 'make a difference to the lives of ordinary people who are struggling with the aftermath of conflict', are concerned with social and psychological reform and are necessary in order to resolve conflicts as psychological states of affairs and promote subjective peace.[116] The attention that should be paid to social peace processes as a method of conflict resolution is not meant to take away from the importance of institutional and legal reform,

[113] Stephan Wolff, 'Conceptualising Conflict Management and Settlement: Perspectives on Successes and Failures in Europe, Africa and Asia' in Ulrich Schneckener and Stephan Wolff (eds), *Managing and Settling Ethnic Conflicts* (London, Hurst & Co, 2004).

[114] See, eg, UN Secretary-General (n 27) [6].

[115] Brewer (n 93) 46.

[116] John D Brewer, 'The Public Value of the Sociology of Peace Processes' (Innovation and Engagement Public Lecture Series, Cardiff University, 2 December 2014).

which remains an imperative peacebuilding step. Rather, as the preceding analysis suggests, political and social peace processes are symbiotic, with one being unable to develop sufficiently when the other is ignored.[117]

V. HUMAN RIGHTS AS TOOLS IN THE CONFLICT RESOLUTION PROCESS

A. An Overview of the Different Human Rights Strategies

The connection between conflict resolution and human rights was recognised in the Universal Declaration of Human Rights, which states in its preamble that 'it is essential if man [*sic*] is not to be compelled to have recourse, as a last resort, to rebellion against tyranny and oppression, that human rights should be protected'. Despite this early acknowledgement, by the early 1990s, it was widely believed that conflict resolution and the protection of human rights were antithetical to each other, since the two had different objectives, used distinct conceptual tools and were practised by various actors.[118] Over the last decade, both academic writings and UN reports have reverted to the traditional understanding of the relationship, with human rights being considered an essential tool for the resolution of conflict and building of peace.[119] However, having gone a full circle, the exact way in which the two connect and the conditions that must be in place for the former to lead to the latter have not been explored in detail. This section argues that legal human rights can be used in two different types of forums and in each instance, and subject to conditions, they can make specific and distinct contributions to conflict resolution.

Divisive conflicts should ideally be resolved during the negotiations of the peace agreement, when human rights can provide guidance on the best available option to the parties.[120] An added advantage of relying on human rights at this preliminary stage is that 'the language of law imbues the new order with legitimacy and authority' and creates a clear break from the violent past.[121] However,

[117] Brewer (n 93) 37.

[118] See, eg, Alan Keenan, 'Building a Democratic Middle Ground: Professional Civil Society and the Politics of Human Rights in Sri Lanka's Peace Process' in Mertus and Helsing (n 22); Pauline Baker, 'Conflict Resolution versus Democratic Governance: Divergent Paths to Peace?' in Chester Crocker, Fen Osler Hampson and Pamela Aall (eds), *Managing Global Chaos: Sources of and Responses to International Conflict* (Washington DC, United States Institute of Peace, 1996); Pearson Nherere and Ansah-Koi Kumi, 'Human Rights and Conflict Resolution' in Pearson Nherere et al (eds), *Issues in Third World Conflict Resolution* (Uppsala, Uppsala University Press, 1990); Anonymous, 'Human Rights in Peace Negotiations' (1996) 18 *Human Rights Quarterly* 249.

[119] Parlevliet (n 74); Mertus and Helsing (n 22).

[120] Christine Bell, 'Human Rights, Peace Agreements and Conflict Resolution: Negotiating Justice in Northern Ireland' in Mertus and Helsing (n 22); Bar-Tal (n 87) 361.

[121] Ruti Teitel, *Transitional Justice* (Oxford, Oxford University Press, 2000) 220. This symbolic rejection of the past was highlighted by the SA Constitutional Court when it noted in *S v Makwanyane* (CCT 3/94) (SA Constitutional Court, 6 June 1995) [262] that: 'The South African

because of their often intractable nature, negotiators have sometimes preferred to sidestep rather than resolve conflicts and have resorted to either using vague terms that can be interpreted in different ways[122] or have avoided any references to particularly divisive disagreements altogether.[123] Such strategies, while effective in getting the parties to reach an agreement, simply push the need to resolve conflicts to a later point in time. When these re-emerge, or new conflicts appear that had not been originally foreseen by the drafters, human rights can contribute to their resolution in two distinct ways: on the one hand, they can be relied on by the parties and judiciary during the adjudication of the conflict and, on the other hand, they can be used by the legislature, executive or international peacebuilders when they are drafting and implementing peacebuilding policies. In both instances, human rights provide victims of the conflict with a vocabulary that allows them to express their grievances and empowers them to demand that they are acknowledged and addressed.[124] When these claims are communicated in human rights terms, they are particularly likely to be heard and responded to because of the legitimacy attached to them and stigma that is associated with their violations.[125] Depending on the subject matter of the conflict, state responses to human rights violations, in the form of revised legislation or the establishment of institutions, can address conflicts as empirical phenomena and promote one or more of the objective elements of peace. At the same time, the successful implementation of these initiatives in a way that has an impact on the lives of the people, responds to conflicts as psychological states of affairs and can eventually lead to subjective feelings of security, justice and reconciliation.

Take, for example, the conflict that existed in NI about whether the police adequately investigated a series of Republican deaths that had taken place between 1968 and 1998 or whether they had in fact colluded with the suspected murderers.[126] Those complaining of inadequate state investigations articulated their grievance in human rights terms and thus obtained access to the European Court of Human Rights (ECtHR), which in turn found in their favour.[127]

Constitution … represents a decisive break from and a ringing rejection of, that part of the past which is disgracefully racist, authoritarian, insular, and repressive and a vigorous identification of and commitment to a democratic, universalist, caring and aspirationally egalitarian ethos, expressly articulated in the Constitution. The contrast between the past which it repudiates and the future to which it seeks to commit the nation is stark and dramatic.'

[122] Hanna Lerner, *Making Constitutions in Deeply Divided Societies* (Cambridge, Cambridge University Press, 2011).

[123] Christine Bell, 'Dealing with the Past in Northern Ireland' (2003) 26 *Fordham International Law Journal* 1095.

[124] James Sweeney, 'Restorative Justice and Transitional Justice at the ECHR' (2012) 12 *International Criminal Law Review* 313, 336.

[125] Michael Ignatieff, 'Human Rights' in Hesse and Post (eds) (n 16).

[126] Paul Magean and Martin O'Brien, 'From the Margins to the Mainstream: Human Rights and the Good Friday Agreement' (1998–99) 22 *Fordham International Law Journal* 1499, 1509.

[127] *McKerr v United Kingdom* (n 61).

This, coupled with the lobbying of policy makers that had been taking place domestically, which also relied on human rights argumentation, resulted in the adoption of a 'package of measures' by the UK government that was designed to respond to this grievance.[128] Among the measures was the establishment of the Historical Enquiries Team (HET), which was responsible for re-examining the deaths, thus potentially leading to arrests (security) and assisting 'in bringing a measure of resolution to those families of victims' (justice) 'in a way that commands the confidence of the wider community' (reconciliation).[129] Hence, the resolution of the conflict through the use of human rights and the consequent establishment of the HET contributed to an objective sense of peace. At the same time, to the extent that the HET undertook its tasks successfully, it also had a positive impact on subjective feelings of security, justice and reconciliation.[130]

While this and subsequent chapters tend to discuss the two ways in which legal human rights can be used (that is, in the courtroom and through the lobbying of policy makers) separately, it should be noted from the outset that the two strategies are interconnected to, rather than mutually exclusive from, each other. On the one hand, enacting a peacebuilding policy in the legislature might have been triggered by the adjudication of a dispute in a court of law. On the other hand, applicants may take a case to court if they feel that an existing peacebuilding policy that was enacted by the legislature does not sufficiently comply with human rights standards. The joint use of both strategies to address a single issue is illustrated, in addition to the HET example above, through the actions of family members of missing persons, who relied on existing human rights instruments, such as the Inter-American Convention on Human Rights, in court, while at the same time, lobbying governments to adopt a new legal instrument that was tailored to their specific needs (which eventually resulted in the International Convention for the Protection of All Persons from Enforced Disappearance).[131] Thus, drafting and implementing human rights-inspired legislation and relying on human rights adjudication are two strategies that often go hand in hand.[132] Having acknowledged this, the following subsections divide, for ease of reference, the contributions of human rights as peacebuilding tools into three parts – when they inspire the drafting, and push for the implementation, of policies that respond to conflicts as empirical phenomena; when they are being used in the adjudication of such phenomena; and when both strategies induce social and psychological changes necessary for the promotion of subjective feelings of peace (in other words, when they resolve conflicts as psychological states of affairs). In each case, human rights can contribute to peacebuilding

[128] HMIC, *Inspection of the Police Service of Northern Ireland Historical Enquiries Team* (London, Her Majesty's Inspectorate of Constabulary, 2013) 7.

[129] These are found in the HET Operational Guide [2.1], quoted in ibid 7.

[130] For a greater analysis of the HET's impact on building subjective peace, see section IV in ch 6.

[131] Iosif Kovras, *Grassroots Activism and the Evolution of Transitional Justice: The Families of the Disappeared* (Cambridge, Cambridge University Press, 2017) 113–14.

[132] Hamber (n 2) 12.

efforts subject to certain conditions. The overall framework connecting peace and human rights, together with a summary of these conditions, is summarised in the figure below.

Figure 3.1 An overview of the relationship between peace and human rights

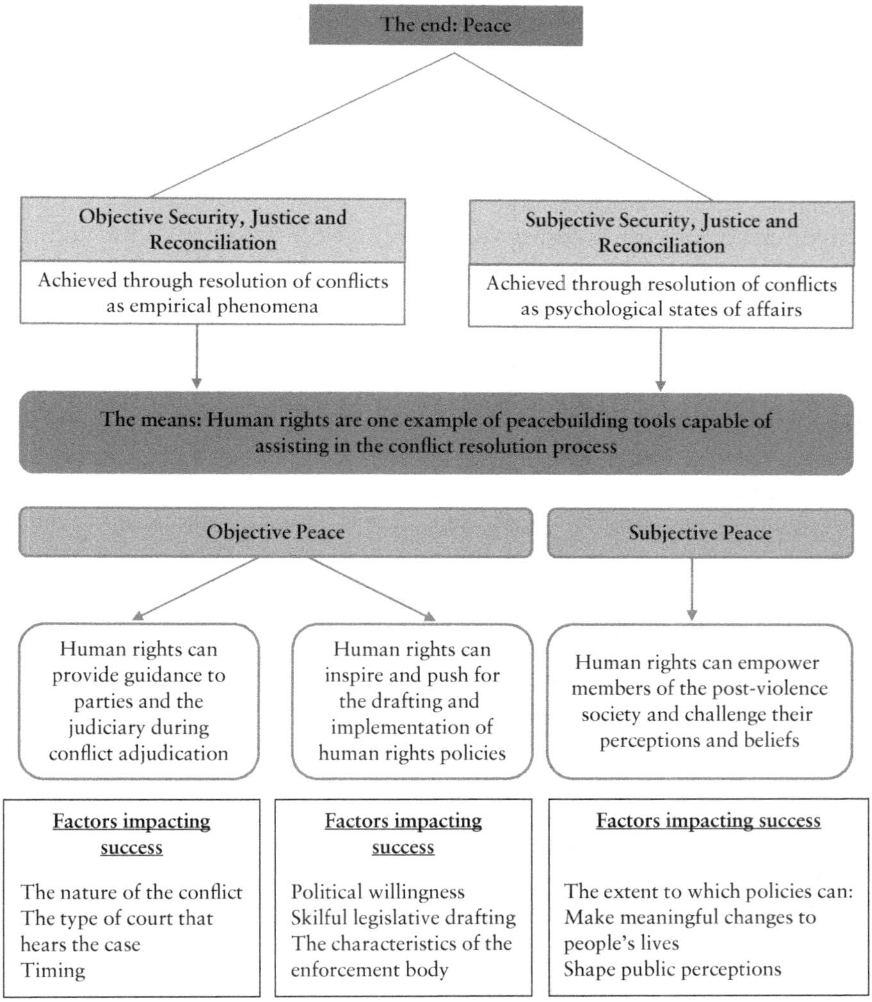

Before elaborating on the specific ways in which human rights can help resolve conflicts, it is worth questioning whether it is desirable, or indeed even possible, to measure their impact in terms of building peace in the first place. On the one hand, there are good reasons for undertaking such an exercise. As the role of human rights activists has shifted from identifying violations to offering solutions for them, it has become necessary to assess whether these solutions achieve what they promised.[133] Further, with the development of related disciplines and organisations with similar socially responsible agendas, human rights are no longer the only game in town.[134] This makes it necessary to measure their impact in order to reach informed decisions about whether their protection is indeed the most efficient way to achieve the desired result. However, at the same time, activists have cited concerns that measuring the impact of human rights could result in an overemphasis in numbers, thus encouraging organisations or states to set the bar too low in order to appear successful.[135] Moreover, they have justifiably been worried about the reliability of results, since it is often difficult to assess causality and prove that it is the adoption of a human rights initiative that led to the positive social change attributable to it.[136] Finally, an in-principle disagreement with measuring the impact of human rights work has also been expressed because some policies should always be on actors' and funders' agendas, whether or not they actually result in significant social changes in the short to medium term.[137]

The framework proposed in this study draws inspiration from both schools of thought. It accepts that if human rights are going to be used as tools to achieve a social objective – in this case, peace – it becomes necessary to determine whether they are indeed up to the task. This is especially so because they are not the only tools in the peacebuilding toolkit, thus reinforcing the need to justify reliance on them rather than any other strategy. Concurrently, the framework seeks to respond to the concerns of human rights activists. It avoids the danger of setting the bar of success too low by defining from the outset what peacebuilders should be striving to achieve. This definition, which relies on both an objective and a subjective understanding of peace, acknowledges that 'success' in peacebuilding contexts should not be measured exclusively, or even primarily, in terms of the number of human rights cases litigated before a court or laws passed by the legislature. Further, recognising that the challenges with regard to proving causality are real, the framework does not rely on a rigid assessment of whether a single case or legislative provision has had a positive impact. Rather, it is satisfied with reaching conclusions about more general trends and broad conditions that must be in place in order for human rights to undertake their task successfully. Finally, the framework avoids the stifling of innovation among human rights activists through three caveats: first, what is meant by the promotion of

[133] Paul Gready, 'Reasons to Be Cautious about Evidence and Evaluation: Rights-Based Approaches to Development and the Emerging Culture of Evaluation' (2009) 1 *Journal of Human Rights Practice* 380, 382.

[134] ibid.

[135] Ian Gorvin, 'Producing the Evidence that Human Rights Advocacy Works: First Steps Towards Systematized Evaluation at Human Rights Watch' (2009) 1 *Journal of Human Rights Practice* 477, 481.

[136] Yasmine Ergas, 'Human Rights Impact: Developing an Agenda for Interdisciplinary, International Research' (2009) 1 *Journal of Human Rights Practice* 459.

[137] Robert Archer, "Introduction to the Special Issue: Where is the Evidence?" (2009) 1 *Journal of Human Rights Practice* 333.

each of the three elements of peace differs from context to context. Second, whether a human rights initiative has been 'successful' in promoting peace also depends on the timing of the assessment, making a difference, for example, if the impact of the strategy was measured immediately after it was adopted or at a much later point in time.[138] And, third, the definition of success as consisting of a balance between security, justice and reconciliation should encourage human rights actors to identify their priorities and choose to focus on different elements during various stages of their work. Thus, while situating itself within a literature that does not take the success of human rights as a given,[139] this study also accepts that a detached and non-context-specific audit of the impact of human rights is equally problematic.

B. Resolving Conflicts by Lobbying for the Implementation of Human Rights

Following the conclusion of a peace agreement, lingering conflicts are best resolved by the legislature, which is institutionally and democratically best-equipped to undertake this task.[140] Since such conflicts are by their nature divisive and attempts to address them will likely result in controversies, any debates relating to them should ideally take place in a forum, whose members are accountable to, and representative of the competing interests of, the public.[141] Moreover, the procedures of the legislature, as opposed to the judiciary, encourage more successful conflict resolution in five different ways. First, by transparently balancing different considerations, the legislature can avoid a winner-takes-all situation, which in turn alleviates some of the conflicts' zero-sum characteristics and makes them less intractable.[142] Second, unlike courts, which necessarily decide issues in an ad hoc manner, the legislature can look at a conflict in its entirety and situate any proposed solutions within a broader context.[143] This is important not only in terms of the outcome that will ultimately emerge from this process, but also for determining how much it will cost and ensuring that resources are made available to follow it through.[144]

[138] See Hamber (n 2) 7, arguing that peacebuilding is a context-dependent, lifelong process that changes with time.

[139] David Kennedy, 'The International Human Rights Movement: Part of the Problem?' (2002) 15 *Harvard Human Rights Journal* 101.

[140] Ulrich Schneckener, 'Making Power-Sharing Work: Lessons from Successes and Failures in Ethnic Conflict Regulation' (2002) 39 *Journal of Peace Research* 203, 223.

[141] Richard Bellamy, 'The Democratic Qualities of Courts: A Critical Analysis of Three Arguments' (2013) 49 *Representation* 333; Luc B Tremblay, 'The Legitimacy of Judicial Review: The Limits of Dialogue between Courts and Legislatures' (2005) 3 *International Journal of Constitutional Law* 617; Jeremy Waldron, 'Judges as Moral Reasoners' (2009) 7 *International Journal of Constitutional Law* 2.

[142] Lon Fuller, 'The Forms and Limits of Adjudication' (1978–79) 92 *Harvard Law Review* 353.

[143] Marc Galanter, 'Why the "Haves" Come out Ahead: Speculations on the Limits of Legal Change' (1974) 9 *Law and Society Review* 95, 136–37.

[144] ibid 150.

Third, contrary to courts that tend to rule on cases as these are presented to them by the applicants, the legislature can decide whether to prioritise divisive conflicts or let them simmer down, thus determining the best timing for its intervention. Fourth, the legislature, more so than the judiciary, possesses the mechanisms to ensure the successful implementation of the peacebuilding policy. On the one hand, it has the power to establish the necessary institutions and processes that will be responsible for the smooth enforcement of the law.[145] On the other hand, it can autonomously monitor the implementation of a given policy and intervene when it considers necessary, either by changing substantive provisions of the law or tweaking the procedures that relate to it.[146] Finally, because legislative decisions are generally more visible than those of courts,[147] elected bodies are likely to contribute to conflict resolution not only through legal and institutional reforms, but also by challenging personal and social perceptions of the conflict, thus promoting the elements of peace on a more subjective level as well.

Since legislative interventions can contribute to conflict resolution, using human rights as part of this process is beneficial in several ways. At first instance, they can help set governmental agendas and encourage the passing of peace-friendly legislation by enabling victims to identify as bearers of rights and demand that these are protected.[148] Zemans refers to this contribution as 'the educative role of law', which has the ability to 'change the citizenry's perception of their interests'.[149] More broadly, human rights can help people reimagine their relationship with the state and transform them from disempowered and passive individuals into active citizens. Additionally, human rights provide victims with the tools to lobby the legislature by increasing the strength, clarity, visibility and legitimacy of their claims.[150] In cases where the legislature has already decided to respond to the conflict, human rights can provide guidance as to the considerations that should be kept in mind during this process. Finally, rights set benchmarks against which the performance of the state can be assessed, thus providing further incentives for it to improve. This becomes possible because the international legitimacy of human rights reassures individuals

[145] Philip Leach and Alice Donald, *Parliaments and the European Court of Human Rights* (Oxford, Oxford University Press, 2016), especially ch 3.

[146] For example, this is the role played by the Joint Committee of Human Rights, consisting of members of Parliament, in the UK. For more information, see www.parliament.uk/business/committees/committees-a-z/joint-select/human-rights-committee/role.

[147] Rosenberg (n 68).

[148] Thomas Risse and Kathryn Sikkink, 'The Socialisation of International Human Rights Norms and Domestic Practices: Introduction' in Thomas Risse, Kathryn Sikkink and Stephen Ropp (eds), *The Power of Human Rights: International Norms and Domestic Change* (Cambridge, Cambridge University Press, 1999); Emilia J Powell and Staton K Jeffrey, 'Domestic Judicial Institutions and Human Rights Treaty Violation' (2009) 53 *International Studies Quarterly* 149.

[149] Frances Kahn Zemans, 'Legal Mobilization: The Neglected Role of the Law in the Political System' (1983) 77 *American Political Science Review* 690, 697.

[150] Beth Simmons, *Mobilizing for Human Rights: International Law in Domestic Politics* (Cambridge, Cambridge University Press, 2009) 149.

that their demands are not unreasonable and encourages them to mobilise and expect governmental action to address them.[151] These considerations should not be taken to suggest that human rights guarantee the adoption of peace-friendly legislation.[152] Human rights 'alter politics; they do not cause miracles. They supplement, and interact with, domestic political and legal institutions; they do not replace them'.[153] However, the way in which they do this, and the pressures and incentives they create, make it more likely that policy makers will be responsive to the demands of those who use them for lobbying and who, through their protection, seek to promote security, justice and reconciliation.

Even if successful lobbying results in the passing of human rights-inspired laws, it does not necessarily follow that these will be implemented or that peace will be built. Rather, in order for this causal relationship to develop, three conditions must be in place in the post-violence society. The first and most widely acknowledged condition is that there must exist political will to implement the law; if this is absent, it is likely that the law will never be implemented or will be enforced in a way that does not contribute to peacebuilding efforts. The second condition is that the law must be drafted in such a way that its implementation will, in fact, contribute to objective security, justice or reconciliation. Finally, it is necessary that the institution that has been tasked with implementing the legislation has the capacity, resources, independence and expertise to achieve this. In the event that the implementation of a human rights-inspired law does not have the expected results, it is important that peacebuilders are able to assess which of the three conditions is absent in order to tailor their responses accordingly. Thus, threatening the government of a post-violence society with sanctions is understandable in cases where there is political unwillingness to implement a law, but is likely be a counterproductive strategy if non-enforcement is due to lack of resources or expertise within the body responsible for its implementation. The contributions that human rights can make when encouraging the implementation of peace-friendly legislation, conditions that must be in place for this to happen and steps that should be adopted in the absence of these conditions are discussed in more detail in Chapter 5.

C. Resolving Conflicts through Human Rights Adjudication

Despite arguments for favouring the resolution of conflicts by the legislature, increasingly over the last 20 years, such processes have also played out in the courtroom.[154] One reason for this is that post-violence societies are undergoing

[151] ibid 147.
[152] Parlevliet (n 74) 14.
[153] Simmons (n 150) 15.
[154] Ran Hirschl, *Towards Juristocracy: The Origins and Consequences of the New Constitutionalism* (Cambridge, MA, Harvard University Press, 2004); Stephen Tierney, *Constitutional Law and National Pluralism* (Oxford, Oxford University Press, 2004) viii; Erik G Jensen, 'The Rule of

significant political changes.[155] When these give rise to divisive disagreements, political elites might be unwilling or unable to reach a compromise.[156] If, as a result, the political branches of the state are paralysed, the task of decision making falls on the shoulders of other institutions, such as the judiciary.[157] For instance, the SA Constitutional Court played the role of the tiebreaker in perhaps the most divisive conflict in the country's history when it was asked to certify under section 71(2) of the SA Interim Constitution whether the Final Constitution complied with Constitutional Principles that the political parties had agreed to during the negotiations leading to the end of apartheid.[158] It was the resolution of this conflict that cemented the beginning of democracy and, through the certification of the Final Constitution, promoted objective peace in the country. Despite the unusually high level of judicial intervention, the Court's success in contributing to peacebuilding efforts has led academics to propose the adoption of the certification process in other post-violence societies as well.[159]

The unwillingness of political elites to resolve conflicts during times of transition is often institutionalised in societies that have adopted consociational systems of government.[160] Consociationalism is a system of power-sharing among political elites that is, in principle, intended to ensure cooperation between different ethnic or racial groups.[161] However, the characteristics of consociational systems, and in particular their tendency to give to representatives of different groups the veto power, often result in the stagnation of the political process and an inability to reach decisions.[162] While advocates of consociationalism had originally failed to appreciate the significance of a strong judiciary, the need to address and avoid these political dead ends has made

Law and Judicial Reform: The Political Economy of Diverse Institutional Patterns and Reformers' Responses' in Erik G Jensen and Thomas C Heller (eds), *Beyond Common Knowledge: Empirical Approaches to the Rule of Law* (Stanford, Stanford University Press, 2003).

155 David Robertson, *The Judge as Political Theorist: Contemporary Constitutional Review* (Princeton, Princeton University Press, 2010) 28.

156 Carlo Guarnieri and Patrizia Pederzoli, *The Power of Judges: A Comparative Study of Courts and Democracy* (Oxford, Oxford University Press, 2002).

157 John Ferejohn, 'Judicializing Politics, Politicizing Law' (2002) 65 *Law and Contemporary Problems* 41, 55.

158 *Certification of the Constitution of the Republic of South Africa* (CCT 23/96) (SA Constitutional Court, 6 September 1996) and *Certification of the Amended Text of the Constitution of the Republic of South Africa* (CCT 37/96) (SA Constitutional Court, 4 December 1996).

159 Neophytos Loizides, *Designing Peace: Cyprus and Institutional Innovations in Divided Societies* (Philadelphia, University of Pennsylvania Press, 2015) 145–48.

160 Jurisdictions that have, over the years, adopted consociational arrangements include Belgium, the Netherlands, Switzerland, South Tyrol, Cyprus, BiH, the Former Yugoslav Republic of Macedonia, NI, Lebanon, the Netherlands Antilles, SA (between 1993 and1996) and Iraq. See Christopher McCrudden and Brendan O'Leary, 'Courts and Consociations, or How Human Rights Courts May De-stabilise Power-Sharing Settlements' (2013) 24 *European Journal of International Law* 477, 480.

161 Arend Lijphart, *Democracy in Plural Societies: A Comparative Exploration* (New Haven, Yale University Press, 1977).

162 David Wippman, 'Practical and Legal Constraints on Internal Power-Sharing' in David Wippman (ed), *International Law and Ethnic Conflict* (Ithaca, Cornell University Press, 1998).

courts in societies that have adopted consociational structures among the most relied-upon institutions.[163] Thus, Article IV(3)(f) of the Constitution of BiH provides that the power to veto legislation can be used by delegates of each of the country's three main ethnic groups when the relevant law has been 'declared to be destructive of a vital interest of the Bosniac, Croat, or Serb people'. If the delegates of each of the other two groups disagree with the use of the veto power, the dispute is resolved by the Constitutional Court. Such disagreements revolve around the most divisive conflicts in the country – hence the reason they attracted the use of the veto in the first place – yet it is the unelected judiciary that is expected to resolve them.[164] While there has been some criticism of judicial intervention in consociational structures,[165] other commentators have identified and applauded the potential of courts to resolve divisive conflicts.[166]

An additional explanation for the increase in the resolution of conflicts through adjudication concerns the fact that since the early 1990s, post-violence societies have tended to adopt a model of constitutional democracy that yields considerable power to the judiciary.[167] The most popular method of empowering judges has been the adoption of constitutionally entrenched Bills of Rights, which applicants have used, often with the judiciary's blessing, as a vehicle for bringing lingering conflicts to the courtroom and demanding their adjudication.[168] To be sure, when adjudicating conflicts, courts do not necessarily have to rely on human rights.[169] Nevertheless, they often use this strategy because of their broad and permissive language, which allows lawyers and judges to structure their arguments in legal terms, even when these are more directly related to political disagreements.[170] Judges, in an attempt to maintain their mantle of neutrality and not appear partisan, have generally been less willing to engage directly with political arguments made by the parties.[171] Conversely, where such arguments are presented through the lens of human rights, courts have been

[163] McCrudden and O'Leary (n 159); Richard H Pildes, 'Ethnic Identity and Democratic Institutions: A Dynamic Perspective' in Choudhry (ed) (n 49) (BiH Constitutional Court, 28 April 2004) [27] adopts this reasoning before attempting to resolve a fundamental conflict on the use of veto powers.

[164] A similar provision was included in the Annan Plan ((n 47) [6(3)]).

[165] McCrudden and O'Leary (n 160).

[166] Samuel Issacharoff and Richard H Pildes, 'Politics as Markets: Partisan Lockups of the Democratic Process' (1998) 50 *Stanford Law Review* 643.

[167] Sujit Choudhry, 'After the Rights Revolution: Bills of Rights in the Post-conflict State' (2010) 6 *Annual Review of Law and Social Science* 301.

[168] ibid.

[169] Gordon Anthony, 'Judicial Review in Northern Ireland – A Guide to the "Real" Devolution Issues' (2009) 14 *Judicial Review* 230.

[170] Hirschl (n 154).

[171] See, eg, the SA Constitutional Court's claims in *United Democratic Movement v President of the Republic of South Africa and Others (No 2)* (CCT 23/02) (SA Constitutional Court, 4 October 2002) [11].

more willing to entertain them.[172] This is partly due to the judiciary's constitutional obligation to uphold human rights, even when it might have politically controversial consequences.[173] It is also because of the view that while judges are ill-suited to deal with political arguments,[174] they are particularly well-placed to decide on the interpretation of human rights.[175] Especially in cases concerning divisive conflicts, judges have an interest in presenting their judgments as reflections of deeper political values, such as human rights, in order to lend them more legitimacy and acceptance by the public and political actors that are affected by them.[176] Finally, the increasing reliance on human rights arguments when resolving divisive conflicts is not only a characteristic of the domestic judiciary, but has (more controversially) also been practised by international human rights courts.[177] In turn, the institutional dialogue that takes place between national and international actors fuels the tendency to rely on human rights on the domestic level to an even greater extent.[178]

Resolving disputes in an institutionalised setting, like a court, not only promotes justice but also lessens the chance that the different parties will resort to violence and therefore enhances security.[179] The main contribution of human rights in this respect is that they can provide guidance to the parties and judges on the best ways to address conflicts. On the one hand, the broad language of human rights suggests that they will often be unable to pinpoint the one 'correct' answer, or most appropriate response, to a given dilemma.[180] On the other hand, a joint agreement by the parties that they will respect human rights at least excludes as possibilities those responses to the conflict that are not compatible with them. This creates a framework for the parties to operate

[172] Ferejohn (n 156).

[173] Fuller (n 141).

[174] Waldron (n 140); John Morison and Marie Lynch, 'Litigating the Agreement: Towards a New Judicial Constitutionalism for the UK from Northern Ireland' in Morison, McEvoy and Anthony (eds) (n 15).

[175] Joseph Raz, *The Morality of Freedom* (Oxford, Oxford University Press, 1986) 259–62.

[176] For an analysis of how essentially political disputes were fought out in a legal forum in NI, 'not least because of the moral punch that human rights and legal rhetoric can deliver', see Christopher McCrudden, 'Consociationalism, Equality and Minorities in the Northern Ireland Bill of Rights Debate: The Role of the OSCE High Commissioner on National Minorities' in Morison, McEvoy and Anthony (eds) (n 15) 353. For a detailed illustration of this practice by the SA Constitutional Court, see Theunis Roux, *The Politics of Principle: The First South African Constitutional Court 1995–2005* (Cambridge, Cambridge University Press, 2013) 238–48.

[177] Christopher McCrudden, 'Common Law of Human Rights? Transitional Judicial Conversations on Constitutional Rights' (2000) 20 *Oxford Journal of Legal Studies* 499.

[178] Tom Gerard Daly, *The Alchemists: Questioning Our Faith in Courts as Democracy-Builders* (Cambridge, Cambridge University Press, 2017).

[179] Jennifer Widner, 'Constitution Writing in Post-conflict Settings: An Overview' (2008) 49 *William and Mary Law Review* 1513.

[180] Ayla Gürel and Kudret Özersay, *The Politics of Property in Cyprus: Conflicting Appeals to 'Bizonality' and 'Human Rights' by the Two Cypriot Communities*, 3/2006 (Nicosia, PRIO Cyprus Centre, 2006).

in, limits their choices to a range of more moderate and legitimate options, and makes it easier for them to settle on one as their preferred compromise.[181] For example, although different post-violence societies have remedied victims of forced displacement in various ways, all of them started from the premise that the right to property should be respected. The right identified a range of acceptable responses to displacement – restitution, monetary or in-kind compensation and exchange of properties – while at the same time excluding the possibility of leaving the victims without a remedy altogether.[182] Further, and although adjudication remains expensive, in ideal circumstances, access to courts gives 'a flavour of equality' to the conflict resolution process because it allows even those who do not have the resources to achieve legislative amendments by mobilising the masses to make changes to rules they consider unjust.[183]

In addition to providing guidance to the judges and making the conflict resolution process more accessible, the use of human rights in the courtroom also has a communicative effect.[184] Ideally, it sends the message that things are changing and signals a new, more legitimate state of affairs that deserves the support of the people.[185] This was the argument made by the SA Constitutional Court in *Doctors for Life International*, in which a group of citizens complained that they had not been consulted before the passing of legislation that directly affected their interests.[186] The complaint, which was couched in human rights terms, led the Court to invalidate the law and order that a consultation procedure take place before this was debated again. In its reasoning, it explicitly contrasted the democratic SA that the applicants were living in to the apartheid, human rights-violating regime that they had left behind.[187] Finally, as long as human rights language is being used accurately and prudently, it can help rein in public expectations about what can be done to resolve a conflict and therefore avoid or limit disappointments and frustration about the state's subsequent response.[188] By shaping the perceptions of the public about what a compromise to a given disagreement will look like, human rights can pre-empt or contain conflicts as

[181] Aileen Kavanagh, 'The Role of a Bill of Rights in Reconstructing Northern Ireland' (2004) 26 *Human Rights Quarterly* 956, 973 and 980.

[182] Rhodri C Williams and Ayla Gürel, *The European Court of Human Rights and the Cyprus Property Issue: Charting a Way Forward*, 1/2011 (Nicosia, PRIO Cyprus Centre, 2011).

[183] Galanter (n 142) 135. For a similar argument, see Teitel (n 121) 23, where she argues that: 'Access to constitutional courts through litigation enables a form of participation in the creation of democracy since over time, access to the courts could enable popular input into constitutional interpretation.'

[184] Padraig McAuliffe, 'Transitional Justice and the Rule of Law: The Perfect Couple or Awkward Bedfellows?' (2010) 2 *Hague Journal on the Rule of Law* 110.

[185] Teitel (n 121) 220.

[186] *Doctors for Life International v Speaker of the National Assembly and Others* (CCT 12/05) (SA Constitutional Court, 17 August 2006).

[187] ibid [112].

[188] Jennifer Widner, 'Courts and Democracy in Postconflict Transitions: A Social Scientist's Perspective on the African Case' (2001) 95 *American Journal of International Law* 64.

psychological states of affairs and therefore contribute to the subjective aspect of the peacebuilding process.

As with human rights-inspired legislation, the effectiveness of human rights adjudication as a peacebuilding tool depends on a range of conditions. The first is that the conflict that will be adjudicated must somehow relate to, and its resolution must promote, at least one of the elements of peace. Thus, in ideal scenarios, when a court decides a case with peacebuilding implications, it should expressly acknowledge the effect this is likely to have on security, justice and reconciliation. This will not only help structure the court's reasoning and therefore make the judgment more persuasive, but will also enhance its transparency. Illustrative of this is the *AZAPO* case in which the SA Constitutional Court expressly acknowledged that granting amnesties to perpetrators of crimes committed during apartheid might undermine feelings of justice among the population on the one hand, but it promoted security and reconciliation on the other.[189] By spelling out the reasons that shaped its decision, the Court sent the message that it took into account and balanced, rather than ignored, considerations that were important to the parties. A similar approach was adopted by the UK House of Lords when it was called to adjudicate the conflict of whether new elections should take place in NI in light of the parties' long delay in choosing the First Minister and Deputy First Minister.[190] The majority of the Court's judges expressly relied on the argument that the NI Act 1998 should be interpreted in a way that gave effect to the objectives of the Belfast Agreement, particularly the achievement of 'reconciliation, tolerance and mutual trust' and 'the protection and vindication of the human rights of all'.[191] In making this argument, Lord Bingham directly linked these objectives to the peacebuilding process and stressed that deciding the case in a different manner 'would have precluded the possibility of negotiation and compromise'.[192]

Since the main reason for using human rights in the courtroom is that they provide guidance as to the best way to resolve conflicts, the remaining conditions for their effective use as peacebuilding tools centre around this idea. Thus, whether courts are able to offer such guidance depends on the type of conflict that is being adjudicated, the type of court that hears the case and the timing of the whole process. Chapter 4, which discusses these conditions in greater detail, argues that a distinction should be made between fundamental and minor conflicts in a post-violence society, with the former being more intractable and harder to resolve than the latter. While festering fundamental conflicts are

[189] *The Azarian Peoples Organisation (AZAPO) and Others v the President of the Republic of South Africa* (CCT 17/96) (SA Constitutional Court, 25 July 1996). For a discussion of the case, see Hirschl (n 154) 192.

[190] *Robinson v Secretary of State for Northern Ireland and Others* [2002] UKHL 32. For a discussion of the case, see Jenna Marie Sapiano, 'Courting Peace: Judicial Review and Peace Jurisprudence' (2017) 6 *Global Constitutionalism* 131.

[191] *Robinson* (n 190) [2] (per Lord Bingham).

[192] ibid [14] (per Lord Bingham).

more likely to have detrimental consequences for peace, the heightened levels of controversy that surround them make it less likely that the courts will be able, or willing, to contribute to their successful resolution. Even when the judiciary becomes involved in the adjudication of fundamental conflicts, the guidance it can provide to the parties is such, that it will most probably not be conductive the promotion of security, justice and reconciliation. Additionally, for a human rights case to offer guidance for the resolution of a conflict, it must be delivered by a body that has the legitimacy to do so.[193] The important differences between domestic and international courts, relating to the perceived neutrality and expertise of their members, affect the extent of the intervention, and the consequent peacebuilding potential, that each can make. This is not to argue that domestic courts are better suited than international ones to becoming involved in the adjudication of divisive conflicts or vice versa; rather, the strengths and weaknesses of each body suggest that these should be considered carefully and parties should choose strategically, to the extent that they can, which court they will resort to in each instance. The final factor affecting the judiciary's ability to provide guidance for conflict resolution concerns the timing of the case and, in particular, the passage of time since the ending of the violence and the signing of the peace agreement. Specifically, the passage of time makes courts more willing to intervene in cases where a comprehensive peace agreement has been reached, but can have the opposite effect where this is absent.

D. Resolving Conflicts as Psychological States of Affairs

The *Report of the Secretary-General on the Rule of Law and Transitional Justice* confidently declares that:

> [T]he consolidation of peace in the immediate post-conflict period, as well as the maintenance of peace in the long term, cannot be achieved unless the population is confident that redress for grievances can be obtained through legitimate structures for the peaceful settlement of disputes and the fair administration of justice.[194]

This statement, which reflects a common belief among peacebuilders, assumes that there is a positive causal connection between the establishment of 'legitimate structures' (including human rights institutions) and the resolution of conflicts as psychological states of affairs. Yet, the belief, which Scheingold has aptly called the 'myth of rights', is misguided because it is not the case that reliance on (human rights) structures automatically translates into social and psychological changes that are necessary for the building of subjective peace.[195]

193 Fuller (n 142).

194 UN Secretary-General (n 27) [2].

195 Stuart A Scheingold, *The Politics of Rights: Lawyers, Public Policy, and Political Change*, 2nd edn (Ann Arbor, University of Michigan Press, 2004).

While the two might be connected, their relationship is more complex than this, as suggested by the fact that legal change on its own has often failed to translate into the social objectives of peacebuilders.[196] Exactly the opposite view to the UN's is expressed by Brewer, who argues that liberal instruments, chief among them human rights, exclusively affect 'political peace processes'.[197] Their use, he maintains, distracts peacebuilders from the task of promoting social and psychological changes that can only be induced through the empowerment of civil society organisations. With respect, this also lacks persuasiveness since it confuses the (legal) nature of human rights with the possible effect they might have, assuming that their only contribution can be in the form of amending the law, reforming procedures and strengthening government institutions. While civil society actors, such as churches, trade unions, universities, businesses, charities, journalists and educators, clearly have a massively important role to play in 'social peace processes', it is not clear why courts and other state institutions that rely on legal human rights should be excluded from this effort.

This section argues that, under the right conditions, human rights can help resolve conflicts as psychological states of affairs and therefore promote subjective feelings of peace. On the one hand, as explained above, human rights provide the vocabulary to parties to express their grievances and push for the resolution of a conflict. In addition to mobilising state institutions into action, the very act of empowering victims by giving them a voice, and the public acknowledgement of their grievance by an official body when this voice is heard, can contribute to psychological and social changes.[198] Moreover, human rights can assist in the conflict resolution process by challenging perceptions and dominant narratives that portray one group's identity as diametrically opposed to that of the other.[199] Reliance on human rights by different groups within a society can highlight the common concerns and fears of their members and, consequently, counter ideas of unavoidably conflicting interests between them. An example of this was the foundation of the NI's Women Coalition, the members of which, Protestant and Catholic alike, worked towards ensuring the protection of human rights in the Belfast Agreement.[200] Similarly, their common experiences following the disappearance of their family members has challenged perceptions of conflicting interests among GC and TC victims.[201] Thus, while human rights cannot construct new identities, they can soften the edges of existing ones and

[196] Jensen (n 154).

[197] Brewer (n 93).

[198] Tina Rosenberg, *The Haunted Land: Facing Europe's Ghosts after Communism* (London, Vintage, 1996) xviii, stating that victims can only 'truly heal' when 'their dignity and suffering have been officially acknowledged'.

[199] Scheingold (n 195) 8.

[200] Magean and O'Brien (n 126).

[201] Kovras (n 131) 162.

start making space for peacebuilding measures that more explicitly focus on reconciliation.[202] Finally, human rights can contribute to peacebuilding efforts by providing remedies that have a social or economic impact on the living conditions of the population. If administered correctly, such remedies can affect the public's beliefs and perceptions of the conflict and its aftermath, and ultimately promote subjective feelings of peace.

In order for human rights to contribute to peacebuilding efforts in this way, two conditions, which are discussed in more detail in Chapter 6, must be present. First, it is necessary that they actually deliver on their promises by making real improvements to people's lives rather than appearing as successes only on paper. If this does not happen, the frustration and disillusionment of the public will compound feelings of insecurity, injustice and lack of reconciliation. This suggests that peacebuilders must acknowledge both the strengths and limitations of human rights in inducing social and psychological change, and, where necessary, supplement them with additional conflict resolution mechanisms. Second, people must *perceive* human rights-inspired initiatives as, in fact, contributing to the promotion of peace. As Brewer aptly put it: 'Good governance has to work and be *seen* to work.'[203] It is little use deciding human rights cases or enacting human rights policies intended to promote peace with the best intentions if the public does not see them in this light. Such responses might be commendable, particularly by outsiders, for taking steps to resolve the conflict as an empirical phenomenon, but are unlikely to successfully address the conflict as a psychological state of affairs.[204] Although these conditions are rather vague, when they are taken seriously, they give rise to two specific recommendations that can enhance the subjective peacebuilding potential of human rights. First, they propose that the composition of peacebuilding teams be reconsidered and shifted along two axes: from international to domestic actors on the one hand and from lawyers to other types of professionals on the other. Second, human rights initiatives must be accompanied by a communication strategy with the direct objective of encouraging social and psychological change among the victims and the population at large. This strategy should be comprehensive in that it will be concerned not only with the content of the message that peacebuilders want to convey, but also with the way in which this is disseminated. Additionally, it should result in a two-way communication, which sends messages to the target audience *and also* transmits information in the opposite direction, from the public back to the peacebuilders.

[202] Hamber (n 2) 5. See also Nasia Hadjigeorgiou 'Promoting Reconciliation and Protecting Human Rights: An Underexplored Relationship' in Kalliopi Chainoglou, Barry Collins, Michael Phillips and John Strawson (eds), *Injustice, Memory and Faith in Human Rights* (London, Routledge, 2017) 106.

[203] Brewer (n 93) 37.

[204] Oliver Richmond, 'The UN and Liberal Peacebuilding: Consensus and Challenges' in John Darby and Roger Mac Ginty (eds), *Contemporary Peacemaking: Conflict, Peace Processes and Post-war Reconstruction*, 2nd edn (New York, Palgrave Macmillan, 2008) 261.

These conditions are not only important because they help induce subjective feelings of peace, but also because they are likely to encourage human rights mobilisation (whether through lobbying or the courtroom) and contribute to the resolution of conflicts as empirical phenomena as well. Being aware of the peacebuilding effects of human rights can push even more applicants to turn to the courts and demand that a conflict is resolved.[205] Moreover, this potentially contributes to the more effective mobilisation of the masses, and the creation of additional incentives on the legislature to adopt peacebuilding policies that address the applicants' grievances more holistically.[206] Thus, the use of human rights as a conflict resolution strategy results in a virtuous cycle, whereby subjective feelings of peace make it more likely that both objective and subjective security, justice and reconciliation are further promoted.

VI. CONCLUSION

This chapter has outlined a framework that explains the reasons and ways in which the protection of human rights can contribute to the building of peaceful relationships. It argued that the balancing of security, justice and reconciliation takes place through the continuous successful resolution of conflicts that divide the post-violence society. Human rights, as one of many peacebuilding tools, provide mechanisms that assist in this process. On the one hand, their adjudication can provide guidance on how best to resolve such conflicts, while on the other hand, they can mobilise policy makers into action and push for the drafting and implementation of human rights-inspired laws that will address such incompatibilities of positions. The resolution of conflicts through this dual strategy can contribute in different ways to both an objective and a subjective sense of each of the three elements of peace.

However, while this framework confirms that there is a positive relationship between peace and human rights, it also makes it contingent on several factors. Human rights adjudication is most likely to provide the necessary guidance to resolve conflicts when courts are called to respond to relatively minor rather than fundamental disagreements; when the strengths and weaknesses of domestic and international courts have been weighted against each other and peacebuilders have targeted the best-suited institution in each case; and when the timing of adjudicating this conflict is right. Equally, the effective adoption and implementation of peacebuilding policies does not follow automatically from reliance on human rights; rather, it depends on the drafting quality of the law in question, the existence of political willingness among policy makers to promote the law's

[205] Kate Clark, *War Reparations and Litigations: The Case of Bosnia*, International Litigation Series No 1 (Amsterdam, Nuhanovic Foundation Center for War Reparations, 2014) 55.

[206] Tilman Blumenstock, 'Legal Protection of the Missing and Their Relatives: The Example of Bosnia and Herzegovina' (2006) 19 *Leiden Journal of International Law* 773, 774.

peacebuilding objectives, and the independence, power, expertise and resources of the implementing body. If these conditions are present, human rights are likely to result in legal and institutional reforms that are necessary to promote objective peace. At the same time, and subject to a different set of conditions, they can help induce social and psychological changes that are imperative for the promotion of subjective feelings of security, justice and reconciliation. Specifically, human rights can have this effect when they make a real and meaningful impact on the lives of the people within the post-violence society and are also perceived by the target audience as having this effect.

4

Promoting Objective Peace through Human Rights Adjudication

I. INTRODUCTION

IF RESOLVING CONFLICTS is necessary for the promotion of security, justice and reconciliation, one way in which human rights can contribute to the building of peace is by offering guidance to the judiciary as to the best way of doing this. The chapter is concerned with how using human rights in the courtroom can contribute to the resolution of conflicts as empirical phenomena and the promotion of objective peace. It argues that the extent and quality of the guidance provided by the courts, and therefore the effectiveness of human rights as peacebuilding tools, depend on three factors. The first relates to the nature and intractability of the conflict in question and, in particular, whether it is a fundamental or minor one. On the one hand, courts are more reluctant to decide disputes concerning fundamental conflicts and, on the other hand, even in cases where they do get involved, the reasoning and guidance they provide are not always persuasive or conductive to peace. As a result, human rights adjudication can contribute to conflict resolution, but mostly in cases that have to do with minor disagreements as opposed to more fundamental ones.

The second factor affecting the peacebuilding potential of human rights has to do with the type of court that adjudicates the dispute, since domestic and international bodies differ in terms of the sources of their legitimacy, the likelihood that their judgments will be enforced and the types of documents that each can interpret. An assessment of these differences suggests that the best peacebuilding strategy is not to favour one type of court over the other, but to be aware of the strengths and limitations of each, and use them accordingly. More specifically, international courts often pave the way for conflict resolution, with their domestic counterparts utilising that first judgment to make the provision of a remedy, and the promotion of each of the elements of peace, more accessible to the masses within the post-violence society. The final factor that affects the extent to which human rights adjudication can contribute to conflict resolution is the amount of time that has passed since the stopping of the violence and whether this ceasefire has also been followed by the signing of a comprehensive peace settlement. While in the absence of a peace agreement, the passage of time makes the judiciary more reluctant to adjudicate a conflict, the longer the time since the reaching of a comprehensive settlement between the parties, the more likely are the courts to intervene. Identifying these factors is important because they can provide practical guidance to peacebuilders on the strategies they should adopt in order to ensure that conflicts are resolved as effectively as possible.

II. THE NATURE OF THE CONFLICT BEING ADJUDICATED

This section argues that the extent to which human rights adjudication can provide adequate guidance for conflict resolution and the building of peace depends on the nature of the conflict at hand. In particular, it makes a distinction between fundamental and minor conflicts, and argues that human rights can act as effective peacebuilding tools in the adjudication of the latter, but not the former. Since courts are well suited to address minor conflicts, such as disagreements about the interpretation of a statutory provision, they regularly undertake this task and do so successfully. Conversely, the intractable nature of fundamental conflicts results either in an unwillingness on behalf of the judiciary to adjudicate them or in the provision of guidance that is somehow deficient. Thus, even in cases where courts find cases concerning fundamental conflicts to be admissible, their judgments might be contradictory, fail to address the key issue at the heart of the disagreement or give guidance that is too broad or vague to be meaningful. This observation is significant because it is the mishandling and festering of fundamental conflicts, rather than of more minor disagreements, that most negatively impacts peacebuilding efforts.

A. Distinguishing between Fundamental and Minor Conflicts

A fundamental conflict is one where the parties disagree over issues of value, while a minor one is concerned with disagreements over competing interests.[1] In the former case, the parties experience an incompatibility of positions in terms of what they want to achieve, while in the latter, an in-principle agreement is in place, with the conflict focusing on the means through which the end will materialise.[2] Thus, in post-violence societies, fundamental conflicts tend

[1] Albert O Hirschman, 'Social Conflicts as Pillars of Democratic Market Society' (1994) 22 *Political Theory* 203.

[2] Jacob Kremenyuk, Victor Bercovitch and William Zartman, 'Introduction: The Nature of Conflict and Conflict Resolution' in Jacob Kremenyuk, Victor Bercovitch and William Zartman (eds), *The SAGE Handbook of Conflict Resolution* (London, SAGE Publications, 2008) 6. A superficially similar distinction is made by Aubert, who differentiates between 'consensual' conflicts over interests (where the disputants want the same thing) and 'dissensual' conflicts over values (where they want something different); see Vilhelm Aubert, 'Competition and Dissensus: Two Types of Conflict and of Conflict Resolution' (1963) 7 *Journal of Conflict Resolution* 26. However, he reaches very different conclusions about how each type of conflict can be resolved, so his terminology will not be adopted here.

to arise because the parties have competing visions of the state or how best to deal with the past, which are often completely at odds with each other.[3] More minor conflicts, on the other hand, emerge when the groups have settled on the basic characteristics and structure of a state or on the most suitable ways of addressing past injustices, but are in disagreement on how best to implement their common vision. Fundamental conflicts have been described as 'either/or' or zero-sum, with a 'win' by one party, necessarily being perceived as a 'loss' by the other.[4] This is in contrast to minor conflicts, which can more readily result in a compromise solution, since they are perceived as having less serious implications for the parties' identity survival.[5] Thus, Scheingold is right that:

> [W]hen the stakes are high, conflict is likely to be the most intense and the loser's will to resist likely to be at its strongest. The stakes are probably highest when the rights at issue are inelastic – that is, when victory is directly and totally at the expense of the loser.[6]

Often, fundamental conflicts are so intractable, precisely because the parties disagree on how a balance between the different elements of peace will be struck. For instance, the major disagreement between GCs and TCs as to how best to remedy persons who were displaced during the periods of violence on the island stems from the fact that the former prioritise justice considerations, while the latter are more concerned with security.[7] Whether a conflict is fundamental or minor is often a matter of degree, and depends on the attention it has received in the society in question, the willingness of the different parties to negotiate and any other external factors that might hinder or encourage the reaching of a compromise solution. Generally, however, the more fundamental the conflict, the more likely it is that its lingering presence or mishandling will detrimentally affect peacebuilding efforts. Specifically, if major disagreements remain unresolved, especially for long periods of time, this signifies a significant gap between the views of the parties, which in turn makes the promotion of reconciliation more difficult. In extreme cases, where the parties feel that this gap cannot be overcome, security might also be undermined, either because of the resumption of violence (which results in a lack of objective security) or due to fears among the population that this might happen (thus affecting feelings of subjective security).

While lingering fundamental conflicts are more detrimental to peace, they are also more difficult to resolve through human rights adjudication due to

[3] Hanna Lerner, *Making Constitutions in Deeply Divided Societies* (Cambridge, Cambridge University Press, 2011).

[4] Donald Horowitz, *Ethnic Groups in Conflict*, 2nd edn (Berkeley, University of California Press, 1985) 176.

[5] Hirschman (n 1).

[6] Stuart A Scheingold, *The Politics of Rights: Lawyers, Public Policy, and Political Change*, 2nd edn (Ann Arbor, University of Michigan Press, 2004) 128–29.

[7] For a greater analysis of this, see section II.C below.

three reasons. The first concerns the institutional limitations of the courts when becoming involved in these kinds of disputes. Since major conflicts are complex, controversial and divisive, it is better that they are resolved by the democratically elected and legitimate bodies of the country rather than judges.[8] While a conflict might involve three or four parties, the judiciary can only resolve disputes between two sides and, especially in adversarial systems, exclusively depends on the information each party provides to it.[9] Conversely, the legislature has access to more sources of information and is institutionally and procedurally better-equipped to balance the competing interests of many different stakeholders. Second, as the ensuing examples suggest, fundamental conflicts often concern the very nature of the state or affect the interests of communities and collectives; human rights, with their focus on the individual, cannot adequately capture these considerations and offer guidance for their resolution.[10] The final reason why human rights adjudication best (or only) addresses *some* types of conflicts concerns the remedies that courts can deliver.[11] Although minor conflicts are usually resolved through a statutory re-interpretation, a suggestion for a legislative amendment or change in procedures, addressing fundamental conflicts might require the overhaul of a policy, a complete departure from current operations or even the redefinition of the character of the state. Courts are simply unable to deliver decisions with such wide-ranging implications.

B. Outlining the Disparate Approach to Conflict Adjudication

As a result of the factors outlined above, courts have adopted very different approaches when adjudicating minor and fundamental conflicts. In particular, while the adjudication of the former is considered routine, the judiciary often tries to avoid giving any guidance relating to the resolution of the latter, most notably by finding the case inadmissible. Evidence of the judiciary's disparate approach is offered by contrasting two Cypriot right to vote cases heard by the ECtHR, namely *Aziz v Cyprus*[12] and its follow-up case *Erel and Damdelen v Cyprus*.[13] To understand the claims of the parties in the two cases, some background on the complex development of the Cypriot electoral provisions

[8] Jeremy Waldron, 'Judges as Moral Reasoners' (2009) 7 *International Journal of Constitutional Law* 2.

[9] Lon Fuller, 'The Forms and Limits of Adjudication' (1978–79) 92 *Harvard Law Review* 353.

[10] Makau W Mutua, 'The Transformation of Africa: A Critique of Rights in Transitional Justice' in Ruth Buchanan and Peer Zumbansen (eds), *Law in Transition: Human Rights, Development and Transitional Justice* (Oxford, Hart Publishing, 2016) 92.

[11] Marc Galanter, 'Why the "Haves" Come out Ahead: Speculations on the Limits of Legal Change' (1974) 9 *Law and Society Review* 95, 136–37.

[12] *Aziz v Cyprus* App No 69949/01 (ECtHR, 22 September 2004).

[13] *Ali Erel and Mustafa Damdelen v Cyprus* App No 39973/07 (ECtHR, 30 April 2007).

is necessary. The 1960 Republic of Cyprus (RoC or Republic) Constitution provided for executive and legislative elections through two electoral registers – one for GCs and the other for TCs. GCs would vote for 70 per cent of the legislature and the President, while TCs would decide on the composition of 30 per cent of the legislature and the Vice-President.[14] When the TCs withdrew from government in 1963, all their positions remained vacant, thus making the Republic's operation according to the Constitution impossible.[15] In response to this situation, the Supreme Court of Cyprus decided that the doctrine of necessity could be used to interpret the Constitution in such a way so as to allow for the state's continued existence.[16] As a result, the Republic has, since then, been operating with decision-making bodies consisting only of GCs, who are, according to the Constitution, only elected through the GC electoral register. This, coupled with the continuing requirement that TC voters should be registered in their own electoral catalogue, wholly prevented them from exercising their right to vote. In practical terms, since the Turkish invasion of 1974, this has been a problem for a few hundred TCs who have chosen to continue residing in the areas under the control of the RoC and have not moved to the unrecognised 'Turkish Republic of Northern Cyprus' ('TRNC').[17]

Over the years, the GC electoral register came to include those foreigners who had become naturalised, but not TCs. Mr Aziz challenged this situation, arguing that since the Republic had for all intents and purposes a single electoral register, TCs permanently residing in RoC-controlled areas should be included in it as well. The Supreme Court rejected the argument, finding that what prevented TCs from voting was not the law, but the TC community's unilateral decision to abandon their positions in the Republic.[18] The case reached the ECtHR, where this argument was, unsurprisingly, dismissed: the 40-year disenfranchisement of TCs permanently living in the RoC-controlled areas was a violation of Articles 3 of Protocol No 1 (Article 3-1, right to vote) and 14 (freedom from discrimination) of the Convention.[19] Thus, reliance on human rights forced the parties to transform their political positions into legal arguments and paved the way for

[14] Constitution of the RoC, signed on 16 August 1960, art 1 (for the executive) and art 72 (for the legislature).

[15] Nasia Hadjigeorgiou and Nikolas Kyriakou, 'Entrenching Hegemony in Cyprus: The Doctrine of Necessity and the Principle of Bi-communality' in Yaniv Roznai and Richard Albert (eds), *Constitutionalism under Extreme Conditions: Law, Emergency, Exception* (New York, Springer, forthcoming).

[16] *The Attorney-General of the Republic v Mustafa Ibrahim and Others* (1964) CLR 195 (CA) (RoC Supreme Court, 10 November 1964).

[17] The 'TRNC' is the part of the island of Cyprus that is under Turkish occupation and therefore is not under the effective control of the Republic. It declared its independence in 1983, but has not been recognised by any state other than Turkey, in accordance with United Nations Security Council Resolution 544 (15 December 1983).

[18] *Ibrahim Aziz v Ministry of the Interior* (Case No 369/2001) (RoC Supreme Court, 23 May 2001).

[19] *Aziz* (n 12) [38]. Note that the case dealt only with TCs permanently living in the areas controlled by the Republic rather than with TCs generally.

the resolution of the conflict. The question was no longer about which community was to blame for what happened in 1963, but about whether any individual should remain disenfranchised solely on the grounds of their ethnicity. In turn, this change in the terms of reference allowed the Court to resolve the conflict by adopting a reasoning that was politically neutral, objectively persuasive and conductive to a sense of justice.[20] The judgment was swiftly implemented: the applicant and other TCs in a similar position are now included in the Republic's single electoral register, are allowed to vote in all elections and be voted in all elections except the presidential election.[21] Encouraged by the applicant's success in *Aziz*, a group of TCs challenged the electoral law again, arguing that Article 3-1 required not only that they are allowed to vote in the RoC, but also that they are entitled to a separate electoral register through which they could vote for 30 per cent of the legislature and the Vice-President in accordance with the Constitution.[22] This time, referring to Cyprus' wide margin of appreciation, the ECtHR declared the case inadmissible.

The ECtHR adopted radically different approaches in the two cases: the challenge in *Aziz* was not only found to be admissible but also successful, while that in *Erel* was swiftly dismissed as manifestly ill-founded. An explanation for this is that while the two cases seemingly dealt with a same issue, the demands of the applicants were much more at odds with the position of the RoC in *Erel* than in *Aziz*. In other words, while the conflict in *Aziz* was a relatively minor one, the one in *Erel* was of a more fundamental nature. The challenge of the state's structures in *Erel* was based on the belief that Cypriots should not vote as individual citizens, but rather as members of ethnic groups (hence the need for separate electoral registers). This fundamentally contrasted with the GC understanding of the purpose of the state, thus giving rise to a zero-sum, intractable conflict.[23] Conversely, the applicants in *Aziz* agreed with the RoC that individuals should enjoy voting rights because of their status as citizens rather than due to their ethnic group membership. They were merely asking that their ethnic background did not cloud this agreement and affect the rights they should enjoy.

It is therefore not surprising that the ECtHR adopted varying approaches in the two cases. The applicants in *Erel* essentially asked an international court to compel the RoC to fundamentally change its democratic structures: increase the number of Members of Parliament, re-introduce the position of

[20] Ibrahim Aziz, *Ibrahim Aziz v Republic of Cyprus*, Series of Lectures 'The People behind Judicial Decisions' (Nicosia, University of Cyprus, 26 November 2016).

[21] The Law Concerning the Right to Vote and Be Elected of the Members of the Turkish Community that Permanently Reside in the Unoccupied Areas of the Republic of 2006 (2(I)/2006).

[22] *Erel and Damdelen* (n 13).

[23] On the GC positions with regard to minority rights, see UN Secretary-General, *Report of the Secretary-General on His Mission of Good Offices in Cyprus*, S/2003/398 (New York, United Nations, 1 April 2003) [19].

the Vice-President and create another electoral register.[24] However, a country's democratic structures are deeply affected by a 'wealth of differences, inter alia, in historical development, cultural diversity and political thought'.[25] It is not the place of an international court to set uniform standards on this issue, something that was acknowledged by the ECtHR in *Erel* when it referred to each state's 'considerable latitude in establishing constitutional rules'.[26] Ultimately, resolving such divisive conflicts requires considerably more intervention and guidance than an international court can legitimately engage in.[27] Nevertheless, even a domestic court is likely to have exercised similar judicial restraint. The issue at hand goes to the heart of a state's relationship with its citizens and concerns a question that should be publicly debated and decided not by judges, but by democratically elected and accountable politicians, or even the public itself through a referendum.[28] In any case, the judiciary – domestic or international – can only interpret human rights within a given matrix. It can protect an individual's interests in a specific context, not build the structure of a society from scratch, which is what the applicants in *Erel* sought to achieve.[29] As Scheingold aptly put it:

> Courts can be of some use in [adjudicating conflicts] that apply principally to government agencies and which turn mainly on procedural matters and issues of due process. However, the deeper that it is necessary to penetrate into society, the more undependable courts become.[30]

This disparate approach to the handling of fundamental and minor conflicts is not only a characteristic of the European Court. Rather, it has been manifested in the case law of domestic courts as well, with the SA Constitutional Court acting as a peacebuilding agent when adjudicating minor conflicts, and the judiciary of BiH failing to do so when asked to resolve fundamental conflicts.

[24] Such a conflict tends to be among 'the most testing and intransigent of the challenges because it concerns the fundamental question over which all major political conflicts are in the end waged – who rules?' (Oliver Ramsbotham, Tom Woodhouse and Hugh Miall, *Contemporary Conflict Resolution: The Prevention, Management and Transformation of Deadly Conflicts* (Cambridge, Polity Press, 2016) 257).

[25] *Hirst v United Kingdom (No 2)* App No 74025/01 (ECtHR, 6 October 2005) [61].

[26] *Erel and Damdelen* (n 13).

[27] Andreas Follesdal, 'Much Ado about Nothing? International Judicial Review of Human Rights in Well Functioning Democracies' in Andreas Follesdal, Johan Karlsson Schaffer and Geir Ulfstein (eds), *The Legitimacy of International Human Rights Regimes* (Cambridge, Cambridge University Press, 2014).

[28] Richard Bellamy, 'The Democratic Qualities of Courts: A Critical Analysis of Three Arguments' (2013) 49 *Representation* 333. For the argument that neither domestic nor international courts are well-suited to address such divisive conflicts, see Christopher McCrudden and Brendan O'Leary, 'Courts and Consociations, or How Human Rights Courts May De-stabilise Power-Sharing Settlement' (2013) 24 *European Journal of International Law* 477, 492.

[29] Galanter (n 11) 137, noting that 'courts cannot address problems by devising new regulatory or administrative machinery (and have no taxing and spending powers to support it); courts are limited to solutions compatible with the existing institutional framework'.

[30] Scheingold (n 6) 130.

Arguably, the distinction in the types of conflicts the courts in the two countries were asked to adjudicate, and the response of the judiciary in each, is not accidental. The SA judiciary was able to contribute to peacebuilding efforts because the conflicts it was faced with were minor ones, and it was therefore well-equipped to resolve them. In turn, this had become possible because most fundamental disagreements had already been addressed during the negotiations leading to the adoption of the Interim and Final Constitutions.[31] Conversely, the Dayton negotiations for BiH had been less effective in resolving such disagreements, which were then left to be handled by domestic institutions, including the judiciary.[32] An example of a fundamental conflict in BiH arose when the Human Rights Chamber, a hybrid court that had temporarily been established by the Dayton Agreement, was asked to address the systemic and country-wide problem of discrimination in the workplace.[33] During the war in BiH, people of the 'wrong' ethnic group[34] were either fired or provisionally put on waiting lists for employment, with the promise that they would return to their jobs after the war.[35] When this promise did not materialise, thus resulting in ethnically homogenous workplaces, applicants sought to challenge the state of affairs as discriminatory. On many occasions, judges found cases relating to this fundamental conflict inadmissible by reasoning that they did not have jurisdiction, since the dismissal or placing of the applicant on the waiting list had taken place during the war and before the establishment of the judicial body that was hearing the dispute.[36]

Conversely, the SA Constitutional Court has been both more willing to adjudicate and more successful in resolving the (minor) conflicts it has been faced with. One example of this is *New National Party v Government of South Africa*, a case concerning a minor disagreement as to what documents could be used for identification purposes during the country's second democratic elections.[37] According to the Electoral Act No 73 of 1998, acceptable forms of ID only included documents published under the Identification Acts No 72 of 1986

[31] Adrian Guelke, 'South Africa: The Long View on Political Transition' (2009) 15 *Nationalism & Ethnic Politics* 417.

[32] Gro Nystuen, *Achieving Peace or Protecting Human Rights? Conflicts between Norms Regarding Ethnic Discrimination in the Dayton Peace Agreement* (Leiden, Martinus Nijhoff Publishers, 2005).

[33] The Human Rights Chamber was made up of seven domestic and seven international judges, and ceased operating on 31 December 2003. For more information, see General Framework Agreement for Peace in BiH, signed on 14 December 1995, Annex 6, Chapter 2, Part C.

[34] In other words, those who were in the minority ethnic group in the part of the country in which they were living.

[35] For a description of this practice, see *Zahirović v Bosnia and Herzegovina and Federation of Bosnia and Herzegovina* (CH/97/67) (Human Rights Chamber, 8 July 1999) [1].

[36] Sheri P Rosenberg, 'Promoting Equality after Genocide' (2008) 16 *Tulane Journal of International and Comparative Law* 329, 371.

[37] *New National Party v Government of South Africa* (CCT 9/99) (SA Constitutional Court, 13 April 1999).

and No 68 of 1997 or the Electoral Act itself. This left about 10 per cent of the population unable to vote and resulted in a challenge of the legislation as being incompatible with the right to political participation, protected under section 19 of the Constitution. Essentially, the case was about determining the rationale of the law in question and assessing whether its provisions reasonably limited section 19. No other body was better suited to carry out this task than the judiciary, which explains the Constitutional Court's success in resolving the conflict. Delivering a well-reasoned judgment, the majority held that practically speaking, the new identification documents were necessary because the 10 per cent of the population who had older forms of ID could have been in possession of one of seven different documents, thus considerably confusing the situation at the poll.[38] Moreover, the 1997 Electoral Act had been passed long enough before the elections, leaving those who wanted to vote six months within which to apply for the necessary document.[39] Finally, the Court considered the symbolic value of the older documents, which had been issued during apartheid and reflected the race of the person in possession of them. They were a reminder of SA's shameful past, which was personally offensive to many people and inappropriate for signalling the beginning of democracy in the country.[40] Thus, by relying on the right to political participation, the Court decisively resolved the conflict and offered a clear set of arguments as to why the use of specific forms of ID was necessary in the post-apartheid era. In doing that, it stressed that it was no longer acceptable to rely on racially discriminatory documents and contributed to a sense of justice and reconciliation in the country.[41]

The SA Constitutional Court further promoted peacebuilding efforts when it addressed minor conflicts concerning forced displacement by relying on the right to property.[42] The right under section 25 of the SA Constitution prima facie protects not the original owner, but the secondary occupier of the property (that is, the person who acquired the property under apartheid law). While starting from the premise that the current occupant is protected from the arbitrary deprivation of his or her property,[43] the right also allows its expropriation for public interest purposes.[44] '[T]he nation's commitment to land reform', which was considered necessary due to the forced displacement practices carried out

[38] ibid [33].
[39] ibid [40].
[40] ibid [35].
[41] ibid [19]–[20].
[42] Whether a conflict is fundamental or minor does not depend on the specific right it relates to, but on how conflicting the demands between the parties are and its consequent intractability. It is therefore possible that a conflict relating to the right to property in Cyprus is fundamental, while one framed in the same terms in SA is a minor one.
[43] SA Constitution, s 25(1).
[44] ibid s 25(2).

during apartheid, is explicitly mentioned as such an interest.[45] Section 25(7) makes specific reference to the remedying of apartheid injustices when it states that:

> A person or *community* dispossessed of property after 19 June 1913 *as a result of* past *racially discriminatory laws or practices* is entitled, to the extent provided by an Act of Parliament, either to restitution of that property or to equitable redress. (Emphasis added)

It is the interpretation of this subsection that has resulted in several minor conflicts, which the Constitutional Court has been called to adjudicate. In particular, there have been disagreements about what is the exact meaning of the phrases 'community', 'as a result of' and 'racially discriminatory laws or practices', all of which affect the number of people labelled as victims and who are entitled to a remedy. In turn, the provision of a remedy, especially in light of the vast socio-economic differences in the country[46] and the psychological significance of this issue for black SAs,[47] is likely to influence the promotion of justice and reconciliation.[48] Finally, arguments have been made that unless forced displacement in SA is effectively remedied, 'the tinderbox of historical land injustice may, with the right spark, ignite in a critical political conflagration engulfing the entire country', thus undermining security.[49] Therefore, the resolution of these conflicts has a direct impact on each of the elements of peace.

In relation to the first disagreement, the Court adopted a broad interpretation of the term 'community' as 'a sufficiently cohesive group of persons', with 'some element of commonality between the claiming community and the community as it was at the point of dispossession'.[50] It acknowledged that this definition is relatively easy to satisfy, but justified its decision by pointing to the fact that the displacement, and the consequent scattering of the people, did not only have adverse economic consequences for them, but also weakened the bonds holding the community together in the first place.[51] A similarly broad interpretation was given to the phrase 'as a result of': the Court pointed out that apartheid laws allowing land dispossession were a labyrinth of different

[45] ibid s 25(4).

[46] In 2011, SA had the highest Gini coefficient, indicating socio-economic inequality, in the world (Gini Index, World Bank estimate, www.indexmundi.com/facts/indicators/SI.POV.GINI/rankings).

[47] James L Gibson, *Overcoming Historical Injustices: Land Reconciliation in South Africa* (Cambridge, Cambridge University Press, 2009) 40.

[48] Bernadette Atuahene, 'Paying for the Past: Redressing the Legacy of Land Dispossession in South Africa' (2011) 45 *Law and Society Review* 955.

[49] Gibson (n 47) 218.

[50] *Department of Land Affairs and Others v Goedgelegen Tropical Fruits (PTY) Ltd* (CCT 69/06) (SA Constitutional Court, 6 June 2007) [39].

[51] ibid [42].

statutes preventing non-whites from owning land and that 'often the cause of historical dispossession of land rights will not lie in an isolated moment in time or a single act'.[52] Consequently, the phrase 'as a result of' was held to mean 'as a consequence of' rather than 'solely as a consequence of'.[53] White landowners might have terminated the tenancy rights of the displaced community for commercial reasons, but this only became possible due to, and was therefore a result of, the matrix of racially discriminatory laws that existed in the country at the time. The judiciary adopted a broad interpretation of these phrases by considering the declared purpose of the law, namely to offer redress to as many victims of the violation of the right as possible.[54]

Finally, the right to property provided guidance on and helped the Court resolve the conflict about the meaning of the phrase 'racially discriminatory laws and practices'. This became an issue in *Alexkor v Richtersveld Community*, in which the appellant, Alexkor, argued that the Richtersveld Community should not be entitled to a remedy because it was removed from its land not by one of the statutes directly forcing black displacement, but by the Precious Stones Act No 44 of 1927.[55] The Court, rejecting the argument, started its analysis by referring to the need 'to provide redress to those individuals and communities who were dispossessed of their land rights'.[56] It pointed out that while the motive of the Precious Stones Act might not have been racially discriminatory, its consequences were, because it made a distinction between registered owners of the land and those who had indigenous law ownership. Registered owners were allowed to continue having access to the land and share its mineral wealth with the government; conversely, indigenous law owners were simply excluded from the land when the government exploited their resources without compensating them in any way.[57] Bearing in mind that indigenous law ownership was the main way in which black communities held land in SA and that these rights were not recognised or protected by the law, the legislation was inherently racially discriminatory through its consequences, even though it did not seek to achieve 'the (then) ideal of spatial apartheid'.[58] As in the other cases addressing minor conflicts, the Court was both willing and able to resolve the disagreement by adopting familiar strategies of statutory interpretation. Its reliance on human rights arguments supported and further legitimised the reasoning and outcome of the decision, and made positive contributions towards peacebuilding efforts in the country.

[52] ibid [66].
[53] ibid [69].
[54] ibid [42].
[55] *Alexkor Ltd and Another v the Richtersveld Community and Others* (CCT 19/03) (SA Constitutional Court, 14 October 2003).
[56] ibid [98].
[57] ibid [89].
[58] ibid [97].

C. The Dangers of Resolving Fundamental Conflicts in the Courtroom

The examples discussed so far have been concerned with situations where the judiciary's lack of guidance stemmed from its unwillingness to become involved in the resolution of the fundamental conflict in the first place. Nevertheless, even on those rare occasions that a court addresses a fundamental conflict directly, the guidance it provides for its resolution is still likely to be deficient. Donald and Mottershaw are right in arguing that: 'The impact of a legal decision may depend upon the extent to which it clearly articulates a discrete principle with broad potential application.'[59] Simply put, in cases of fundamental conflicts, courts find it very difficult to articulate such discrete principles in a way that balances the considerations of security, justice and reconciliation. Perhaps the clearest illustration of this stems from an analysis of the Cypriot right to property cases, in which the ECtHR dealt with the divisive question of how best to remedy forced displacement. The right to property is protected under Article 23 and section 36 of the RoC and 'TRNC' Constitutions respectively, and is also safeguarded by Article 1 of Protocol No 1 (Article 1-1) of the European Convention. Rather exceptionally, GC applications relating to this issue had, until recently, been decided by the ECtHR directly, without being subject to the requirement of exhausting domestic remedies, because the 'TRNC' law offered no remedy at all for the violation of the rights of GCs to property.[60]

The first right to property case concerning the Cypriot conflict to reach the ECtHR was *Loizidou v Turkey*, where the Court found a violation of Article 1-1.[61] The (GC) applicant owned a house in the occupied part of Cyprus and argued that the presence of Turkish troops, and the fact that they prevented her from accessing and enjoying it, violated her right to property.[62] The majority of the Court agreed, finding that Turkey was in effective control of the northern part of Cyprus and therefore was responsible for any violations that were taking place there.[63] Conversely, the minority in *Loizidou* expressed serious reservations about whether the ECtHR should become involved in the adjudication of such a zero-sum conflict. Judge Jambreg, for example, pointed out that:

> The 'political nature' of the present case is in my view rather related to the place of the courts in general, and of the Strasbourg mechanism in particular, in the scheme of the division and separation of powers. There, the courts have a different role to play, than, eg the legislative and executive bodies. Courts are adjudicating in individual and concrete cases according to prescribed legal standards. They are ill-equipped

[59] Alice Donald and Elizabeth Mottershaw, 'Evaluating the Impact of Human Rights Litigation on Policy and Practice: A Case Study of the UK' (2009) 1 *Journal of Human Rights Practice* 339, 356.

[60] For an analysis of this argument, see *Demopoulos and Others v Turkey* App No 46113/99 (ECtHR, 1 March 2010) [50]–[129].

[61] *Loizidou v Turkey (Merits)* App No 15318/89 (ECtHR, 18 December 1996).

[62] ibid [58].

[63] ibid [64].

> to deal with large-scale and complex issues which as a rule call for normative action and legal reform.[64]

Echoing these concerns, Judge Pettiti noted that:

> [T]he whole problem of the two communities … has more to do with politics and diplomacy than with European judicial scrutiny based on the isolated case of Mrs Loizidou and her rights under Protocol No 1.[65]

Confirming the minority's concerns, over the years approximately 1,400 cases with similar facts flooded the European Court, which kept reaffirming the majority's decision in *Loizidou*.[66] This state of affairs, with the Court almost mechanically finding a violation of Article 1-1, changed in *Demopoulos v Turkey*, a case with essentially identical facts to *Loizidou*. In *Demopoulos*, Turkey accepted responsibility for the violation of GC property rights and sought to offer a remedy by establishing the Immovable Property Commission (IPC). The Court examined the IPC's power to offer restitution, compensation or exchange of properties to the applicants and declared that it provided effective legal remedies, which barred further legal action from GC applicants to the ECtHR.[67] As a result, applicants who are currently seeking a remedy for the violation of their property rights must apply to the IPC and only after exhausting all legal remedies within the 'TRNC' can they apply to the ECtHR.[68] Thus, *Demopoulos* brings the Cyprus cases into line with other decisions of the ECtHR on forced displacement, in which the Court has altogether avoided the adjudication of such zero-sum conflicts.[69]

[64] ibid, Dissenting Opinion by Judge Jambreg [7].

[65] ibid, Dissenting Opinion by Judge Pettiti. Similar concerns have also been raised in the literature; see, eg, Thomas Allen, 'Restitution and Transitional Justice in the European Court of Human Rights' (2007) 13 *Columbia Journal of European Law* 1, 27.

[66] Nikos Skoutaris, 'Building Transitional Justice Mechanisms without a Peace Settlement: A Critical Appraisal of Recent Case Law of the Strasbourg Court on the Cyprus Issue' (2010) 35 *European Law Review* 720, 725.

[67] *Demopoulos* (n 60) [114]–[119].

[68] Nasia Hadjigeorgiou, 'Remedying Displacement in Frozen Conflicts: Lessons from the Case of Cyprus' (2016) 18 *Cambridge Yearbook of European Legal Studies* 152; Nasia Hadjigeorgiou, 'Joannou v Turkey: An Important Legal Development and a Missed Opportunity' (2018) 2 *European Human Rights Law Review* 168.

[69] Tom Allen and Benedict Douglas, 'Closing the Door on Restitution: The European Court of Human Rights' in Antoine Buyse and Michael Hamilton (eds), *Transitional Jurisprudence and the ECHR: Justice, Politics and Rights* (Cambridge, Cambridge University Press, 2011). Further confirming the position that the Court's decision to adjudicate a fundamental conflict in *Loizidou* was exceptional is a comparison between it and *Blecić v Croatia* App No 59532/00 (ECtHR, 8 March 2006). *Blecić* concerned Croatian laws that allowed the domestic judiciary to terminate specially protected tenancies during the war, on the ground that the tenants had been absent for more than six months without good reason. The applicant argued that the termination violated her right to property, but the Grand Chamber found the case inadmissible. In stark contrast to *Loizidou*, the Court declined to consider the broader context in which this dispute occurred, and its reasoning does not disclose the slightest hint that terminations of this type were often part of a larger campaign of ethnic cleansing. For an analysis of the judgment, see Allen, (n 65) 14–15.

Loizidou is one of the rare instances in which the ECtHR allowed itself to become involved in the resolution of a fundamental disagreement. It is also an illustration of the dangers, in terms of undermining peace, that can materialise when this has not been done successfully. Arguably, despite the ECtHR's assessment that the Cyprus problem 'should have been resolved by all parties assuming full responsibility for finding a solution on a political level', its case law on the right to property has in fact hindered the successful outcome of the negotiations.[70] One of the major hurdles to reaching a comprehensive peace settlement is the dispute between the two sides as to what the right to property requires. On the one hand, GCs consider the 1974 Turkish invasion of the island to be the root of the displacement problem. Their preferred remedy is restitution, since this will take them back to the pre-1974 situation as much as possible and promote justice.[71] On the other hand, most TCs see the events of 1974 not as an illegal invasion, but as a necessary intervention for the protection of their endangered ethnic identity from the GC majority.[72] They consider the current state of affairs, with the two populations largely segregated and therefore unable to undermine each other's sense of security, as the best alternative. They argue that GCs should recognise the realities on the ground and accept that the only realistic remedies to the displacement problem are compensation and exchange of properties.[73] These different remedies envisioned by the two communities are not the result of different interpretations of the law; rather, they stem from diametrically opposed visions of what a peaceful Cyprus should look like, thus explaining the unwillingness of the two sides to compromise their positions.

The ECtHR's involvement in the adjudication of this fundamental conflict has done little to bridge these positions and promote a successful outcome in the negotiations. On the contrary, it has hardened the respective positions of the parties since each has selectively read the Court's case law as only confirming its own point of view. For instance, after *Loizidou* had been decided in the applicant's favour, many GCs assumed that the ECtHR had confirmed their long-standing position that all displaced persons should return to their homes and that nothing short of restitution of *all* properties could satisfy the European Court's standards.[74] The Court had insisted that it 'does not consider

[70] *Demopoulos* (n 60) [85].

[71] UN Secretary-General, *Report of the Secretary-General on His Mission of Good Offices in Cyprus* (1 April 2003) [107].

[72] The 'TRNC' Constitution makes reference in its preamble to 'bitter experiences [the TC people] had undergone until the year 1974 when the Peace Operation, which was carried out by the Heroic Turkish Armed Forces by virtue of the Motherland's natural, historical and legal right of guarantorship emanating from Agreements, provided to the Turkish Cypriots the means of living in peace, security and liberty'.

[73] Ayla Gürel and Kudret Özersay, *The Politics of Property in Cyprus: Conflicting Appeals to 'Bizonality' and 'Human Rights' by the Two Cypriot Communities*, 3/2006 (Nicosia, PRIO Cyprus Centre, 2006).

[74] Elena Katselli-Proukaki, 'The Right of Displaced Persons to Property and to Return Home after Demopoulos' (2014) 14 *Human Rights Law Review* 701.

it necessary, let alone desirable … to elaborate a general theory concerning the lawfulness of legislative and administrative acts of the "TRNC"'.[75] Despite this, most GCs have understood *Loizidou* to mean that the property issue is a matter of rectifying an illegal situation, a task that can only be achieved through full compliance with international law.[76] This has, in turn, resulted in an unwillingness among the majority of GCs to approve of a solution that does not allow restitution in the majority of cases.[77] On the other hand, the *Demopoulos* line of cases has also created very few incentives for TCs to resolve the conflict. In *Xenides-Arestis v Turkey*, a case that preceded *Demopoulos* and in which it was held for the first time that the IPC could in principle be an effective domestic remedy, the Court pointed out that the possibility of restitution should exist for the applicants.[78] Nevertheless, it was subsequently stated in *Demopoulos* that it is within the discretion of each state what remedy it will provide, since 'property is a material commodity which can be valued and compensated for in monetary terms'.[79] As a result of *Demopoulos*, almost all the cases that have been decided by the IPC so far have been settled through compensation.[80] However, if the IPC provides the opportunity to the 'TRNC' to resolve the overwhelming majority of claims through *its* preferred remedy, this removes any incentive from the TC side to negotiate an agreement, which is likely to require the return of considerable areas of land back to GCs.[81]

Thus, the ECtHR's handling of this fundamental conflict has undermined the possibility of reaching a comprehensive peace settlement.[82] In turn, this has had detrimental consequences on each of the elements of peace: while there has been no serious violence in Cyprus since the 1974 Turkish invasion, there are still thousands of Turkish troops stationed there, which Turkey uses as a threat against the RoC in order to influence its decisions on issues of national importance.[83] In addition to undermining security, the ongoing, unsuccessful

[75] *Loizidou* (n 61) [45].

[76] Loukis G Loucaides, 'Is the European Court of Human Rights Still a Principled Court of Human Rights after the *Demopoulos* Case?' (2011) 24 *Leiden Journal of International Law* 435.

[77] Alexandros Lordos and Erol Kaymak, *Public Opinion and the Property Issue: Quantitative Findings,* Cyprus 2015: Research and Dialogue for a Sustainable Future (Cyprus, Interpeace, 2010) 7.

[78] *Xenides-Arestis v Turkey* App No 46347/99 (ECtHR, 14 March 2005).

[79] *Demopoulos* (n 60) [115].

[80] Presidency of Immovable Property Commission, *Monthly Bulletin* (Nicosia, Immovable Property Commission, April 2019), available at www.tamk.gov.ct.tr/dokuman/istatistik_nisan19ing.pdf.

[81] For an outline of what it is being proposed with regard to the remedying of refugees and the return of properties in a comprehensive peace settlement, see UN Secretary-General, *Report of the Secretary-General on His Mission of Good Offices in Cyprus* (1 April 2003) [109]–[111].

[82] This is despite the fact that the ECtHR addressed this concern directly and held that 'it was not persuaded by the argument that it would undermine political discussions concerning the Cyprus problem' (*Loizidou v Turkey (Article 50)* App No 15318/89 (28 July 1998) [26]).

[83] The UN Secretary-General has described 'the northern part of the island [as] one of the most highly militarized areas in the world in terms of the ratio between numbers of troops and civilian population' (UN Secretary-General, *Report of the UN Secretary-General to the Security Council on the UN Operation in Cyprus,* S/1994/680 (New York, United Nations, 7 June 1994) [28]). As an example of Turkish interference with RoC national security issues, see the threats that if Cyprus continues

negotiations keep reminding Cypriots of both communities that the injustices of the 1960s and 1970s continue until today and that a solution to the problem will be a compromise where their preferred form of justice will not be fully protected. Finally, the current status quo also undermines reconciliation since each side portrays the other as making maximalist demands and being solely to blame for the lack of a peace agreement.[84] The unsuccessful resolution of this conflict has also had indirect negative consequences for peace; it has created conditions for nationalist rhetoric to flourish, demonised the idea of inter-ethnic cooperation and contributed to electoral disillusionment, none of which helps promote the three elements.[85]

The judiciary's inability to provide guidance that meaningfully contributes to the resolution of fundamental conflicts, even when it does become involved in their adjudication, is also evident from the handling of the BiH workplace discrimination cases briefly mentioned in the previous section. While the BiH Human Rights Chamber has found many such cases to be inadmissible, on other occasions it has overcome the *rationae temporis* argument[86] by referring to the existence of a continuous violation, since the applicants have remained unremedied until after the conclusion of the war and the establishment of the new Dayton institutions.[87] However, the lack of a consistent approach and the resulting contradictory case law has done little to encourage a universal strategy of non-discrimination in the workplace and promote a sense of justice among the victims.[88]

Moreover, the Human Rights Chamber's failure to offer guidance for the resolution of the conflict has also been compounded by its unwillingness to

with natural gas exploitation, 'Turkey will absolutely retaliate' (Statement by the Turkish Deputy Prime Minister, cited in Ayla Gürel, Fiona Mullen and Harry Tzimitras, *The Cyprus Hydrocarbons Issue: Context, Positions and Future Scenarios*, 1/2013 (Nicosia, PRIO Cyprus Centre, 2012) 62). Such threats continue to be made today.

[84] See, eg, the UN Secretary-General Special Adviser in Cyprus, encouraging the parties to avoid the 'blame game' following (yet another) collapse of the negotiations: 'Not the Time for "Blame Game," Urges UN Special Advisor on Cyprus' (18 July 2017), available at www.un.org/apps/news/story.asp?NewsID=57209#.Wf7R8baQ3BI.

[85] For an overview of the political state of affairs in the two communities and the impact of this on their willingness to reach a political compromise and promote reconciliation, see Maria Ioannou, Giorgos Filippou and Alexandros Lordos, 'The Cyprus Score: Finding New Ways to Resolve a Frozen Conflict' in Tabitha Morgan (ed), *Predicting Peace: The Social Cohesion and Reconciliation Index as a Tool for Conflict Transformation*, 2nd edn (Cyprus, UNDP-Action for Cooperation and Trust, 2015).

[86] In other words, the argument that it does not have temporal jurisdiction because the violations of human rights took place before it had been established.

[87] See, eg, *Zahirović* (n 35); *Rajić v the Federation of Bosnia and Herzegovina* (CH/97/50) (Human Rights Chamber, 8 April 2000); *Mitrović v Federation of Bosnia and Herzegovina* (CH/98/948) (Human Rights Chamber, 6 September 2002).

[88] For a statistical analysis of the levels of social cohesion, reconciliation and political integration in BiH, see Maria Ioannou, Nicolas Jarraud and Alexandros Lordos, 'The Bosnia Score: Measuring Peace in a Multi-ethnic Society' in Morgan (ed) (n 82).

address what is at the heart of this fundamental disagreement by refusing to find a violation of the right to non-discrimination in cases where it had already found the violation of another right.[89] An illustration of this is the case of *Zahirović v BiH and Federation of BiH*, in which a Bosniac bus conductor had been put on the employment waiting list during the war.[90] By the end of the war, a number of Croats had been hired by the state company, with the applicant remaining, without good reason, still without a job. Evidence was presented in court that this was just one example of a pattern of discrimination against Bosniacs, which the Croat-controlled authorities – including the local judiciary – in the area in question had left largely unchallenged.[91] This state of affairs, the applicant contended, constituted discrimination in his enjoyment of his right to work, and since he had been unable to challenge it in court, a violation of the right to fair trial and of a separate count of freedom from discrimination. The Human Rights Chamber, finding a violation of freedom from discrimination in the workplace and the right to fair trial,[92] held that it was unnecessary to examine the question of discrimination by the judiciary separately.[93] Yet, this unwillingness to find an additional violation is regrettable because the judiciary's discriminatory practices were part of a well-thought-out strategy to continue pursuing the ethnic cleansing objectives of the war through other means.[94] By stopping itself from identifying the root of the problem and acknowledging that the violation of the right to fair trial was itself a consequence of discrimination, the Court indirectly endorsed the continuation of this practice and undermined each of the elements of peace.

The discriminatory practices that the Human Rights Chamber failed to condemn are but one example of the continuing ethnic cleansing policies that exist in BiH. Bosnians are being treated differently on grounds of religion and ethnicity in almost all areas of life, including the provision of housing,[95] social services[96] and education.[97] Such discriminatory policies have significant

[89] This approach reflects the ECtHR's methodology in freedom from discrimination cases, especially in the 1990s; since then, its methodology has become more protective of the right. See Bernadette Rainey, Elizabeth Wicks and Clare Ovey, *Jacobs, White and Ovey: The European Convention on Human Rights*, 6th edn (Oxford, Oxford University Press, 2014) 572–73.

[90] *Zahirović* (n 35).

[91] ibid [137]. Similarly, in *D.M. v the Federation of Bosnia and Herzegovina* (CH/98/756) (Human Rights Chamber, 12 May 1999) [73], which was also concerned with discrimination in Canton 10, the Chamber noted that even 'the respondent party … conceded that there [was] "a problem" in the Court system in Canton 10 "in respect of both efficiency and independence".'

[92] *Zahirović* (n 35) [130] and [139] respectively.

[93] ibid [140].

[94] Rosenberg (n 36) 363.

[95] European Commission against Racism and Intolerance, *ECRI Report on Bosnia and Herzegovina (Fifth Monitoring Cycle)*, CRI(2017)2 (Strasbourg, Council of Europe, 6 December 2016) [61].

[96] ibid [63].

[97] ibid [54]–[55].

detrimental effects on peacebuilding efforts, and the judges' inability to fully challenge them has further compromised attempts to promote justice and reconciliation.[98] At the same time, and especially in the short term, it has undermined feelings of security among members of the 'wrong' ethnic group in different parts of the country. For instance, making reference to discriminatory practices, such as racist crimes and the use of hate speech that go unpunished by the authorities, the European Commission against Racism and Intolerance (ECRI) argued that these have resulted in feelings of insecurity among minority returnees.[99] While a finding of discrimination by the judiciary would not have automatically addressed these problems, it would have sent out the message that such practices are no longer acceptable.

D. The Lessons to Draw

The mixed performance of human rights adjudication as a conflict resolution strategy points to three practical recommendations for peacebuilders. First, since it is an ill-suited mechanism for resolving fundamental conflicts, efforts should be made to ensure that these are addressed during the political negotiations leading to the peace agreement.[100] Adopting strategies such as constructive ambiguity, which gloss over disagreements during the negotiating stages and leave them to be handled later on, might indeed assist in the conclusion of the agreement.[101] They should nevertheless be avoided because they achieve this by shifting the task of addressing fundamental conflicts to a later point in time, when political momentum for their resolution might have been lost. In turn, this often pushes peacebuilders to turn to the judiciary, a temptation that, as the preceding analysis suggests, should be avoided.

Related to this is the second practical recommendation, namely that when faced with fundamental conflicts, peacebuilders should always push so that they are resolved by the legislature rather than adjudicated in the courts. The judiciary may have the advantage of being more insulated from the political process and the power relations that push or hinder change, but it is also less well-equipped to introduce institutional changes, re-allocate resources or ensure effective implementation of its decisions.[102] Therefore, in cases concerning fundamental conflicts, the courts might be able to confer the applicant a temporary advantage, but they are usually unable to decisively resolve the disagreement and promote peace. As a result, a more effective use of peacebuilding resources

[98] ibid [53].
[99] ibid [14] and [19].
[100] For the argument that in divided societies there should be political or 'softer' conflict resolution mechanisms than the judicial ones, see Ulrich Schneckener, 'Making Power-Sharing Work: Lessons from Successes and Failures in Ethnic Conflict Regulation' (2002) 39 *Journal of Peace Research* 203.
[101] Lerner (n 3).
[102] Galanter (n 11) 150.

in such cases would be to focus on lobbying for legislative action rather than rallying behind lawyers. Often, of course, the adjudication of a fundamental conflict is beyond the control of peacebuilders, since the case may be brought to court by an individual applicant. However, even in such cases, peacebuilders may be able to influence individual cases by deciding whether to make submissions as third parties. For example, while GC property cases to the ECtHR were initiated by individuals, in many of them, the applicants received support from the RoC government, which acted as an intervening party in their favour.[103] If the conclusions of this section are taken seriously, the RoC should rethink this strategy and focus its efforts on reaching a political compromise instead.

The final recommendation stemming from this analysis is that since courts can help resolve minor conflicts, they should be strengthened in order to achieve this more effectively. Efforts to empower the institutions that are likely to adjudicate such disputes have started being made in BiH, where, since 2012, the authorities estimate that around 50 per cent of relevant prosecutors and judges have received training on hate crimes and discrimination.[104] While this is a step in the right direction, ideally, similar schemes should have been initiated much earlier during the peacebuilding process. Moreover, increased knowledge of the law is ultimately unhelpful if the judiciary that applies it remains relatively inaccessible to individual applicants. Factors that affect the accessibility of legal institutions include, inter alia, their geographical location,[105] the financial cost involved in the application,[106] any personal risk that the applicant is adopting by resorting to them[107] and the extent to which an individual can navigate the process on his own, instead of relying on a lawyer.[108] Thus, especially when being repeatedly faced with the manifestation of the same minor conflict, peacebuilders should consider changes in the structures and rules of procedures of courts that are likely to hear such disputes. These changes should take into account the fact that, as a general rule, minor conflicts are likely to be brought to court by 'one-shooters' – people with little or no experience of the judicial process – against more experienced 'repeat players'.[109] As a result, proposals could envision the establishment of specialised courts, or even alternative dispute resolution

[103] Nasia Hadjigeorgiou, 'A One-Sided Coin: A Critical Analysis of the Legal Accounts of the Cypriot Conflicts' in Berber Bevernage and Nico Wouters (eds), *The Palgrave Handbook of State-Sponsored History after 1945* (London, Palgrave Macmillan, 2018).

[104] European Commission against Racism and Intolerance (n 95) [46].

[105] Graeme Simpson, Edin Hodžić and Louis Bickford, *Looking Back, Looking Forward: Promoting Dialogue through Truth-Seeking in Bosnia and Herzegovina* (Sarajevo, United Nations Development Programme, 2012) 80.

[106] Peter van der Auweraert, *Reparations for Wartime Victims in the Former Yugoslavia: In Search of the Way Forward* (Geneva, International Organization for Migration, 2013) 15.

[107] *Xenides-Arestis* (n 78) section 3(b)(iii).

[108] Anton Kok, 'The Promotion of Equality and Prevention of Unfair Discrimination Act 4 of 2000: Proposals for Legislative Reform' (2008) 24 *South African Journal on Human Rights* 445.

[109] Galanter (n 11) 169–70.

mechanisms, such as Ombudspersons.[110] These tend to operate using simpler procedures and evidentiary rules, which make them more readily available to the applicants and result in quicker access to justice.[111] Furthermore, they are likely to encourage the accumulation of knowledge and expertise among their judges or members, which will in turn produce better reasoned and more consistent decisions.

Equally important as the establishment of these institutions is the requirement that they operate within an applicant-friendly framework, which will encourage the swift resolution of minor conflicts. The detrimental consequences to peace-building efforts when this consideration is ignored are illustrated through an assessment of the mechanics of the Employment Equity Act No 55 of 1998, which prohibits direct or indirect discrimination against an employee in SA.[112] Responsible for implementing its provisions are the Commission of Conciliation, Mediation and Arbitration and the Labour Courts. The Act provides that in order for a complaint to be heard by a Labour Court, the alleged victim must first make an attempt to resolve the dispute within the company that employs him or her and be able to provide proof that he or she has taken such steps.[113] This is in itself a barrier to adjudication, since applicants are likely to be hesitant to raise their complaints internally if they have already faced indifference or hostility by the very employers they are complaining against. If the dispute is not resolved through this initial step, the applicant has six months from the time the alleged discrimination has taken place to submit his or her complaint to the Commission,[114] and only after conciliation has failed can the dispute be referred to a Labour Court.[115] This long process, which remains the same irrespective of how serious the alleged discrimination or urgent its response is, arguably discourages potential victims from voicing their grievances and undermines feelings of justice.[116]

Even when individual applicants have reached the Labour Court, they can face additional challenges since hiring a lawyer and going through a cumbersome legal process might be too onerous for them, both economically and psychologically.[117] One method of addressing this would be to allow for class

[110] Sharon Gilad, 'Why the Haves Do Not Necessarily Come out Ahead in Informal Dispute Resolution' (2010) 32 *Law and Policy* 283.

[111] Beth Gaze and Rosemary Hunter, 'Access to Justice for Discrimination Complaints: Courts and Legal Representation' (2009) 32 *University of New South Wales Law Journal* 699.

[112] Employment Equity Act No 55 of 1998, s 6.

[113] ibid s 10(4)(b).

[114] ibid s 10(2).

[115] ibid s 10(6)(a).

[116] Andries Bezuidenhout et al, *Tracking Progress on the Implementation and Impact of the Employment Equity Act since its Inception*, Research Consortium: Human Science Research Council, Development Policy Research Unit, Sociology of Work Unit (Johannesburg, Research Commissioned by Department of Labour South Africa, 2008) 17.

[117] Jean R Sternlight, 'In Search of the Best Procedure for Enforcing Employment Discrimination Laws: A Comparative Analysis' (2004) 78 *Tulane Law Review* 1401, 1475.

action lawsuits, which are also more effective than individual applications in dealing with entrenched systems of discrimination, but this is not a possibility that is permitted by the Act.[118] Alternative responses include making legal aid available, and therefore empowering applicants to hire a lawyer, or allowing representation or other forms of assistance by an institutional player, such as an Equality Commission. These strategies can contribute to the more effective adjudication of disputes, since both lawyers and mandated institutions are 'repeat players', who can guide the applicants around the pitfalls of the process. Finally, the remedy that a specialised body can award is important because it signals to potential applicants whether it is worth trying to adjudicate a minor conflict in the first place. Problematically in this regard, the Employment Equity Act creates a complete exemption from liability in cases where employers did what was 'reasonably practicable to eliminate' the discrimination in question.[119] In the majority of cases, instead of disciplining the discriminatory conduct, employers respond to victims' complaints merely by compensating them, a practice that the Labour Court has considered adequate.[120] This is irrespective of the fact that monetary awards are arguably insufficient ways of remedying the loss of a person's dignity and esteem, and especially when these are very small, it is also questionable whether they deter future discriminatory practices.[121] Thus, in order for human rights adjudication to become an effective peacebuilding strategy, consideration must be paid to the structure and powers given to courts, as well as the institutions that can supplement their work.

III. THE TYPE OF COURT ADJUDICATING THE CONFLICT

A. Exploring the Differences between Domestic and International Courts

Peacebuilding reports refer to the need to protect human rights in post-violence societies, but they do not often clarify whether by that, they mean domestic or international protection.[122] Practice on the ground is also mixed: peace agreements are usually accompanied by accession to an array of international human rights treaties, while at the same time, there is an increased focus on the strengthening and professionalisation of the domestic judiciary.[123]

[118] Bezuidenhout et al (n 116) 18.

[119] Employment Equity Act, s 60.

[120] Emma Fergus and Debbie Collier, 'Equality at Work: The Role of the Judiciary in Promoting Transformation' (2014) 30 *South African Journal on Human Rights* 484.

[121] ibid.

[122] See, eg, the generally worded expectation in Panel on United Nations Peace Operations, *Report of the Panel on United Nations Peace Operations*, A/55/305–S/2000/809 (New York, United Nations, 2000) [41] that 'the human rights component of a peace operation is indeed critical to effective peace-building'.

[123] For example, while the Dayton Agreement makes BiH a member of 16 international human rights agreements (BiH Constitution (General Framework Agreement, signed on 14 December 1995, Annex 4), Annex I), there has also been increased attention on the reform of the domestic judiciary

Yet, a comparison of the different characteristics of domestic and international (human rights) courts suggests that each can make distinct peacebuilding contributions and can be utilised in different ways.[124] This section argues that in addition to the nature of the conflict, what also affects its successful resolution are the relevant actors, the interests they (are perceived to) serve and the characteristics each possesses. In light of this, the analysis focuses on three features of domestic and international courts: first, the fact that they derive their legitimacy from different sources; second, the varying likelihood that the decisions of each will be enforced; and, third, that they are tasked with interpreting different documents. These differences should not be taken to mean that domestic courts are somehow better peacebuilding institutions than their international counterparts or vice versa; rather, they point to the conclusion that the combined use of both types of courts is the most effective peacebuilding strategy.

The first difference between the two types of courts concerns the legitimacy that each enjoys.[125] While arguments have been made that 'legitimacy talk' mainly serves attempts to mask state power and its abuse,[126] it should be taken seriously because it can impact the ability of courts to provide guidance that parties will pay attention to when resolving divisive disputes. Both domestic and international courts struggle with the adjudication of fundamental conflicts because of their democratic deficit, which renders them less legitimate and well-suited to respond to intractable disagreements. However, in addition to this common feature, the two types of courts also have different characteristics, which further impact on the legitimacy that each enjoys. On the one hand, when international courts interpret human rights provisions, they derive their legitimacy from the notion that they are detached from the conflicts dividing the post-violence society and are therefore more likely to act as neutral decision makers.[127] On the other hand, the legitimacy of domestic judges stems from

(European Commission, *Instrument for Pre-accession Assistance (IPA II) 2014–2020 – Bosnia and Herzegovina: Enhanced Justice Sector and Cooperation in Rule of Law* (Brussels, European Commission, 2014)).

[124] On the argument that a clear distinction should be made between domestic and international human rights, see Charles R Beitz, *The Idea of Human Rights* (Oxford, Oxford University Press, 2009); Cole M Wade, 'Mind the Gap: State Capacity and Implementation of Human Rights Treaties' (2015) 69 *International Organization* 405.

[125] For a discussion of the 'multi-dimensional' and complex character of notions of legitimacy, see David Beetham, *The Legitimation of Power* (London, Macmillan, 1991).

[126] Marti Koskenniemi, 'Legitimacy, Rights and Ideology: Notes towards a Critique of the New Moral Internationalism' (2003) 7 *Associations* 349.

[127] Philip Leach and Alice Donald, *Parliaments and the European Court of Human Rights* (Oxford, Oxford University Press, 2016) 132; Severine Autesserre, *Peaceland: Conflict Resolution and the Everyday Politics of International Intervention* (Cambridge, Cambridge University Press, 2014) 65; Lorna McGregor, 'International Law as a "Tiered Process": Transitional Justice at the Local, National and International Level' in Kieran McEvoy and Lorna McGregor (eds), *Transitional Justice from Below: Grassroots Activism and the Struggle for Change* (Oxford, Hart Publishing, 2008) 53.

their familiarity with the context of the society in question and ability to appreciate nuances that might be missed by international observers.[128] As a result, and unlike international human rights judgments that might operate as more blunt peacebuilding tools, decisions of domestic courts are expected to be more in tune with the sensitivities of the people who will be affected by them.[129]

Notably, neither of these two sources of legitimacy is without its drawbacks. In the case of domestic judges, their insiders' detailed knowledge might be compromised by biases, preventing them from deciding a case in an impartial manner. Of course, in theory, both domestic and international courts are expected to be neutral arbiters,[130] but the danger that they will be influenced by non-legal considerations, especially when adjudicating fundamental conflicts, remains.[131] It is presumably because of this risk that peace agreements often include ethnic quotas in the composition of apex courts;[132] had domestic judges always managed to detach themselves from their own unconscious biases, such a safeguard would simply not be necessary. An illustration of the detrimental peacebuilding effects of this danger is provided by contrasting two missing persons cases heard by the RoC judiciary, with one concerning a GC and the other a TC victim. On the facts of the first case, *Vasiliou*, the applicants' (GC) relative had not returned from the war in 1974 and since there was no evidence of his death, he was included by the RoC in the list of missing persons.[133] Following private investigations that took place in 1999, it transpired that the applicants' relative had been buried in 1974 in an unidentified grave in the area under the control of the RoC by state officials. The first instance court held that since the RoC had access to information and witnesses concerning this case, it had an obligation to investigate the death, which it had not fulfilled. While the case was dismissed on appeal, finding in favour of the government, the appellate court found the case admissible and reasoned that the RoC had an obligation towards the applicant, which it had discharged sufficiently in light of the chaotic conditions that existed at the time.[134]

[128] Andreas Follesdal, 'The Legitimacy Deficits of the Human Rights Judiciary: Elements and Implications of a Normative Theory' (2013) 14 *Theoretical Inquiries in Law* 339; Christopher McCrudden and Brendan O'Leary, *Courts and Consociations: Human Rights Versus Power-Sharing* (Oxford, Oxford University Press, 2013) 42.

[129] James Sweeney, 'Restorative Justice and Transitional Justice at the ECHR' (2012) 12 *International Criminal Law Review* 313, 337; Chandra Lekha Sriram, 'Post-conflict Justice and Hybridity in Peacebuilding: Resistance or Cooptation?' in Oliver P Richmond and Audra Mitchell (eds), *Hybrid Forms of Peace: From Everyday Agency to Post-liberalism* (Basingstoke, Palgrave Macmillan, 2016) 62–63.

[130] Mutua (n 10) 100.

[131] John AG Griffith, *The Politics of the Judiciary*, 5th edn (London, Fontana Press, 1997) 290.

[132] See, eg, BiH Constitution, art VI(1); (Draft) Comprehensive Settlement of the Cyprus Problem (Annan Plan, 31 March 2004), art 36(1).

[133] *Republic of Cyprus v Vasos Vasiliou* (Civil Appeal No 381/2010) (RoC Supreme Court, 26 May 2015).

[134] ibid.

In the second case, the applicants, this time of TC origin, also argued that the RoC had a responsibility to investigate the disappearance of their family members, which had taken place in 1963 in an area that was at the time (and remains today) under the control of the Republic.[135] Adopting a completely different reasoning from *Vasiliou*, the Supreme Court accepted as a defence to the alleged violation of the procedural right to life, the doctrine of an 'act of government'. According to this novel defence, the question of missing persons constitutes one of the many aspects of the 'Cyprus problem', an issue of political nature which falls within the exclusive competence of the executive. Since the RoC President was already involved in political negotiations concerning the Cyprus issue, which also related to the fate of missing persons, the Court held that it should not become involved in the resolution of the conflict. A combined reading of the two cases suggests that the only distinguishing factor between them was the ethnicity of the victims. In every other respect, the cases were manifestations of the same conflict, namely whether a government has the responsibility to investigate disappearances of missing persons that have taken place within its territory. The most likely explanation for the conflicting reasoning of the domestic judiciary – finding in one case that the Republic was under a duty to comply with its human rights obligations and in the other that it was not – is the unconscious bias of the (exclusively GC) bench.[136] Through their position of power, the domestic judges, whether strategically or inadvertently, adopted diametrically different approaches in the two cases, thus undermining all three elements of peace in the process.

Conversely, the more detached position of international court judges avoids the danger of unconscious bias on their behalf, but gives rise to other 'lack of legitimacy' concerns. Key among them is that this very detachment makes them even more distant from the citizens whose rights they are adjudicating and therefore more likely to misunderstand the domestic context when delivering their judgments.[137] Such detachment also means that international courts might be speaking to the respondent state, while also being aware that other interested parties are paying attention to their deliberations. Because of this, they might be less willing to defer to the particularities of one post-violence society, lest they encourage the loosening of human rights standards elsewhere in the future.[138] Such incentives for delivering ambitious human rights judgments notwithstanding, it is worth remembering that international courts derive their legitimacy from the fact that they apply treaties, which states have signed and are parties to.

[135] *Özalp Behiç v Republic of Cyprus* (Case No 589/2006) (RoC Supreme Court, 29 May 2008).

[136] The Cypriot judiciary offers a good case study for this since, following the TC withdrawal from government in the 1960s, it is composed exclusively by GC members (Georgios M. Pikis, *Constitutionalism – Human Rights – Separation of Powers: The Cyprus Precedent* (Leiden, Martinus Nijhoff Publishers, 2006) 28).

[137] Follesdal (n 27); McGregor (n 127) 50.

[138] Tom Gerard Daly, *The Alchemists: Questioning Our Faith in Courts as Democracy-Builders* (Cambridge, Cambridge University Press, 2017) 167.

Yet, a creative interpretation of these treaties can be criticised as an intervention into the state's sovereignty that has not been consented to.[139] This makes international courts easy targets of attacks by local opinion leaders, which further compromise their legitimacy. Such attacks usually present international judgments as outside interference with national matters, which, as the UN Security Council recognised, makes them 'frequently politicised' and likely to be 'used for propaganda purposes' by spoilers.[140]

The second difference between domestic and international courts relates to the enforceability of their judgments, with those of the former being more likely to result in implementation than the latter.[141] The reason for this stems from the truism that domestic institutions generally operate within much better-developed structures than international institutions.[142] Moreover, although sanctions are in principle available to international bodies as a way of inducing enforcement, political and diplomatic considerations often make them unavailable or ineffective in practice.[143] To the extent that human rights cases are implemented because of popular pressure within the post-violence society, international judgments are again likely to be at a disadvantage because they may be less well known to the public and therefore not as likely to generate sufficient interest and traction to push politicians into action.[144] Finally, since the legitimacy of a court affects the extent to which the parties are likely to comply with its rulings, international courts, especially when delivering 'creative' judgments, might suffer from lower compliance rates than their domestic counterparts.[145] An alternative view is that these factors are more likely to result in partial compliance with international human rights judgments rather than no implementation at all.[146] Thus, the state might unduly delay the enforcement of the decision, comply with the individual but not general measures required by the judgment, or offer a response that only partly addresses the human rights

[139] Follesdal (n 27).

[140] UN Security Council, *Report of the International Tribunal for the Prosecution of Persons Responsible for Serious Violations of International Humanitarian Law Committed in the Territory of the Former Yugoslavia since 1991*, S/1999/846 (New York, United Nations, 25 August 1999) [148].

[141] Dia Anagnostou and Alina Mungiu-Pippidi, 'Domestic Implementation of Human Rights Judgments in Europe: Legal Infrastructure and Government Effectiveness Matter' (2014) 25 *European Journal of International Law* 205.

[142] Open Society Justice Initiative, *From Rights to Remedies: Structures and Strategies for Implementing International Human Rights Decisions* (New York, Open Society Foundation, 2013) 75.

[143] Committee on Legal Affairs and Human Rights, *Draft Resolution on the Implementation of Judgments of the European Court of Human Rights*, Doc 13864 (Strasbourg, Parliamentary Assembly of the Council of Europe, 9 September 2015) [15] and [48].

[144] Follesdal (n 27).

[145] ibid.

[146] Darren Hawkins and Wade Jacoby, 'Partial Compliance: A Comparison of the European and Inter-American Courts of Human Rights' (2010) 6 *Journal of International Law and International Relations* 35.

violation.[147] Yet, as the next chapter explores in more detail, even if not outright ignoring a court's decision, partial compliance can still have detrimental peace-building effects.

The final difference between domestic and international courts explored here concerns the documents that each is interpreting. While domestic courts interpret national legislation and their respective constitutions, international human rights bodies are limited to their constituent documents.[148] Differences in the wording of similar provisions among these might result in diverse interpretations and a varied ability among courts to resolve the conflicts they are called upon to adjudicate. An illustration of this is the differentiation between the right to vote protected under Article 3-1 of the European Convention, which only safeguards the exercise of the right 'in the choice of the legislature', and section 19 of the SA Constitution, which is more broadly worded. In addition to protecting the right to vote and stand for public office (section 19(2) and (3)), it also refers to every citizen's freedom 'to make political choices', which extend beyond the electoral period. Thus, section 19(1) includes three non-exhaustive examples of protected political choices, namely the rights to form a political party, participate in the activities of a political party, and campaign for a political party or cause. This difference in wording suggests that the ECtHR can deal with a narrower range of arguments than the SA judiciary, which can affect the reasoning of each court and its consequent ability to resolve related disagreements.

Further to potentially applying to a wider range of cases, constitutions are more likely to provide greater inspiration to the judiciary for the resolution of conflicts than international human rights treaties. This is because, in addition to bills of rights, constitutions also often include references to other principles that judges can rely on in order to inform their reasoning.[149] This was, for instance, the approach adopted by the BiH Constitutional Court when it was asked to resolve a conflict about whether the Croatian caucus in the Parliamentary Assembly was right to block a contentious law through the use of the veto power.[150] In answering this question, the Court bolstered its analysis by relying on Article I(2) of the Constitution, which provides that BiH shall be a 'democratic state'. This use of a constitutional principle, which relates to but is broader than the right to vote, allowed the Court to define the term and offer more meaningful guidance as to when parties were entitled to make use of the veto power. Thus, the Court reasoned that a 'democratic state' should protect group rights, but should also be a functional one, hence urging the parties to be frugal in the use of the veto

[147] ibid.

[148] Tom Gerard Daly, 'The Alchemists: Courts as Democracy-Builders in Contemporary Thought' (2017) 6 *Global Constitutionalism* 101; Daly (n 138) 162–63.

[149] For a detailed argument of how this is happening, see Nasia Hadjigeorgiou, 'Conflict Resolution in Post-violence Societies: Some Guidance for the Judiciary', ICON·S 2017 Conference on 'Courts, Powers, Public Law', Copenhagen, July 2017.

[150] *U-8/04* (BiH Constitutional Court, 25 June 2004); *U-10/05* (BiH Constitutional Court, 22 July 2005).

power, a nuanced conclusion that an international court would have been less capable of reaching.

Combined, these reasons suggest that international courts will be less likely to provide detailed guidelines for conflict resolution compared to domestic ones. This is supported by doctrines adopted by the ECtHR, such as the margin of appreciation, which is used when the circumstances of the case are somehow unique or the right in question has varying interpretations in different Member States.[151] Thus, the European Court has ruled that a wide margin will be afforded when 'there is no consensus within the member states of the Council of Europe, either as to the relative importance of the interest at stake or as to the best means of protecting it'.[152] Moreover, acknowledging the importance of being sensitive to the context of each society, the Court has held that '[b]y reason of their direct and continuous contact with the vital forces of their countries, state authorities are in principle in a better position than the international judge to give an opinion' on certain controversial issues.[153] However, despite such declarations, the Court has, in fact, stepped in and adjudicated conflicts that domestic courts have refused to address. Perhaps the most striking example of this is the case of *Sejdić and Finci v BiH*, discussed in section IV.B below, which dealt with the fundamental conflict of ethnically discriminatory electoral provisions in the BiH Constitution.[154] Similar complaints to those in *Sejdić* had been made in two previous cases that the BiH Constitutional Court had found inadmissible.[155] In a third case, the Constitutional Court ruled the case admissible, but refused to find a violation, with one judge explicitly requesting the ECtHR to intervene.[156]

Thus, *in principle* domestic courts seem to be better equipped to resolve divisive conflicts than international courts: they are less likely to be criticised as illegitimate when delivering a controversial decision, their judgments generally enjoy higher implementation rates and they have more tools at their disposal that will help them imaginatively address the conflict. However, *in practice*, their susceptibility to political pressures at home, whether these are explicit or exerted in less direct ways, might undermine both their willingness to adjudicate such disagreements and the quality of the guidance they provide when they undertake the task. This results in the following paradox: while domestic courts could offer guidance for the resolution of conflicts, in fact the road is often paved by international judgments. This is not to argue that the domestic judiciary is not an effective peacebuilding actor, since it often continues the conflict

[151] David Harris et al, *Harris, Boyle and Warbrick: Law of the European Convention on Human Rights*, 3rd edn (Oxford, Oxford University Press, 2014) 14–17.

[152] *Evans v United Kingdom* App No 6339/05 (ECtHR, 10 April 2007) [77].

[153] *Handyside v United Kingdom* App No 5493/72 (ECtHR, 7 December 1976) [48].

[154] *Sejdić and Finci v Bosnia and Herzegovina* App No 27996/06 (ECtHR, 22 December 2009).

[155] *U-5/04* (BiH Constitutional Court, 27 January 2006); *U-13/05* (BiH Constitutional Court, 29 September 2006).

[156] *AP-2678/06* (BiH Constitutional Court, 26 May 2006), Separate Concurring Opinion of Judge Feldman [5].

resolution process by engaging in strategic citation of the international judgment and therefore legitimising, and garnering support for, its own case law.[157] In turn, through their follow-up decisions, domestic judges can make remedies more accessible to the parties and provide more sustained guidance for the resolution of the conflict. This suggests that it is the combined use of both types of courts, rather than the favouring of one over the other, that is likely to promote security, justice and reconciliation to the greatest possible extent.[158]

B. Assessing the Combined Use of Domestic and International Human Rights Courts

Perhaps the best illustration of the success of combining the strengths of both domestic and international courts can be observed through a series of right to life cases relating to the NI conflict. Of the 3,600 people who had died during the Troubles, approximately 10 per cent were killed by the police or the army, yet only 33 members of the security forces have been prosecuted in relation to these deaths and just four have been convicted.[159] As the numbers suggest, attempts by the victims' families to find justice through domestic institutions have been largely ineffective and, at times, counterproductive. For instance, in a 1982 incident, three police officers of a specially trained mobile support unit of the Royal Ulster Constabulary fired 109 rounds at a car ridden by Gervaise McKerr, Eugene Toman and Sean Burns, all three of whom were unarmed, and killed them. At the conclusion of the murder trial, Lord Justice Gibson, who was sitting without a jury, found the defendants not guilty and noted the following:

> I want to make clear that having heard the entire Crown case exposed in open court I regard each of the accused as absolutely blameless in this matter. I consider that in fairness to them, that finding also ought to be recorded together with my commendation for their courage and determination in bringing the three deceased men to justice, in this case to the final court of justice.[160]

This deferential approach of the domestic judiciary to the executive in issues that were concerned with the NI conflict was in no way exceptional. Stephen Livingstone, examining 13 House of Lords cases decided between 1969 and 1993, concluded that the Law Lords had consistently failed to consider human

[157] Johanna Kalb, 'The Judicial Role in New Democracies: A Strategic Account of Comparative Citation' (2013) 38 *Yale Journal of International Law* 423.

[158] Leach and Donald (n 127) 134; Eyal Benvenisti and Alon Harel, 'Embracing the Tension between National and International Human Rights Law: The Case for Discordant Parity' (2017) 15 *International Journal of Constitutional Law* 36. A similar conclusion is reached by Daly (n 138) 284 in relation to the ability of courts to contribute to the democratisation process of post-authoritarian regimes.

[159] Brice Dickson, 'The House of Lords and the Northern Ireland Conflict – A Sequel' (2006) 69 *Modern Law Review* 383, 388.

[160] Quoted in *McKerr v United Kingdom* App No 28883/95 (ECtHR, 4 May 2001) [19].

rights arguments in their reasoning and had therefore ruled themselves out of playing a constructive role in the resolution of conflicts relating to NI.[161] In light of this, victims turned to the ECtHR and argued that the deficient responses to conflict-related deaths by the UK authorities constituted violations of the procedural obligation under the right to life (Article 2 of the Convention). Upholding the applicants' complaints, the European Court held in *Jordan*,[162] *McKerr*,[163] *Kelly*[164] and *Shanaghan v United Kingdom*[165] that the domestic authorities' practices were indeed problematic because, among other things, the police officers investigating the incidents were not sufficiently independent from the officers implicated in them; there was a lack of public scrutiny and provision of information to the victims' families concerning the investigation; the inquest procedure did not allow for any verdict or findings which might have helped secure a criminal prosecution; and there were undue delays in the completion of the investigations.[166] These findings by the ECtHR were symbolically important because they confirmed allegations in an international and highly visible forum that agents of the UK government were not always acting as neutral parties to the conflict.[167] At the same time, the cases had practical significance because they provided clear guidance on what the UK needed to do in order to improve its investigative practices. Thus, by acknowledging the grievances of the victims and providing direction on how these should be addressed, the Court promoted feelings of justice and began the reconciliation-building process.

Nonetheless, had the adjudication of the conflict stopped when the ECtHR delivered its judgment, its peacebuilding impact would have been relatively limited, since most victims lack the time and resources to go through this procedure.[168] What made the Court's recommendations applicable to a broader range of interested parties, and pushed for the implementation of changes that would result in the effective investigation of these deaths, was the fact that its rulings were utilised by the domestic judiciary.[169] Although the adoption of ECtHR case law by domestic courts has not been conducive to the promotion of justice at each step of the way, over time British judges have moved in the right

[161] Stephen Livingstone, 'The House of Lords and the Northern Ireland Conflict' (1994) 57 *Modern Law Review* 333.

[162] *Jordan v United Kingdom* App No 24746/94 (ECtHR, 4 May 2001).

[163] *McKerr* (n 160).

[164] *Kelly v United Kingdom* App No 30054/96 (ECtHR, 4 May 2001).

[165] *Shanaghan v United Kingdom* App No 37715/97 (ECtHR, 4 April 2001).

[166] *Jordan* (n 162) [142] and [144]; *McKerr* (n 160) [157]–[158]; *Kelly* (n 164) [136] and [138]; *Shanaghan* (n 165) [122].

[167] Christine Bell and Johanna Keenan, 'Lost on the Way Home? The Right to Life in Northern Ireland' (2005) 32 *Journal of Law and Society* 68, 88.

[168] As an indication, McKerr died in 1982 and the ECtHR's decision was delivered in 2001. The Court awarded the applicant, who had also received legal aid from the Council of Europe, an additional £25,000 for costs and expenses; *McKerr* (n 160) [185]. See also Galanter (n 11) 93, arguing that the impact of judgments of 'peak' courts is not always felt by the people on the ground.

[169] Bell and Keenan (n 167) 75.

direction. For instance, the Coroners Act (NI) 1959 provides that the purpose of an inquest is to set forth the identity of the deceased and ascertain 'how, when and where he [*sic*] came to his death'.[170] Problematically, this had been interpreted to mean 'by what means' the death took place rather than 'in what broad circumstances', which left family members with very little information about what had caused their loved one's death.[171] After the ECtHR decisions, the House of Lords dubiously held in (a domestic case also called) *McKerr* that although there was a right to an effective investigation of deaths that had occurred before 2000 under the European Convention, this right did not exist under the Human Rights Act 1998.[172] The decision meant that the restrictive interpretation of the Coroners Act was maintained and those who wanted to complain about ineffective investigations of deaths that had taken place during the Troubles could only do so by resorting to the European Court.

Despite this originally restrictive interpretation of the law, which perpetuated a lack of information and undermined feelings of justice, as time passed, judges started laying the foundations for developing a more peace-friendly jurisprudence. Thus, the House of Lords ruled in *Middleton*, a (non-conflict-related) case concerning the investigation of a suicide in prison that had taken place before 2000, that an inquest verdict which only focused on the means through which someone died was not compatible with Article 2.[173] Problematically, the two domestic cases – *McKerr* and *Middleton* – resulted in an unsustainable state of affairs: both were delivered on the same day and were concerned with the state's procedural obligations under Article 2. Yet, one held that there was a duty to investigate a death under the Human Rights Act and the other held that no such obligation existed. In practice, this meant that family members could be given information about their loved ones' death, except when the death was somehow connected to the NI conflict. Recognising the problems this created, three years later in *Jordan*, the House of Lords relaxed the strict *McKerr* approach and held that although juries in inquests had to deliver a verdict of 'lawful' or 'unlawful death', nothing prevented them from interpreting their mandate more broadly.[174] Finally, in 2011, the UK Supreme Court completely abandoned the originally restrictive approach and held that the procedural obligations under Article 2 of the Human Rights Act should directly apply to conflict-related deaths as well.[175]

[170] Coroners Act (Northern Ireland) 1959, s 31(1).

[171] *R v HM Coroner for North Humberside and Scunthorpe ex parte Jamieson* [1995] QB 1.

[172] *McKerr* [2004] 1 WLR 807. This is part of a long saga of *McKerr* cases and was decided after the ECtHR delivered *McKerr v UK* (n 160).

[173] *R (on the Application of Middleton) v West Somerset Coroner* [2004] UKHL 10.

[174] Marny Requa and Gordon Anthony, 'Coroners, Controversial Deaths and Northern Ireland's Past Conflict' [2008] *Public Law* 443, 450; Marny Requa, 'Keeping up with Strasbourg: Article 2 Obligations and Northern Ireland's Pending Inquests' [2012] *Public Law* 610.

[175] *Re McCaughey's Application* [2011] UKSC 20.

A negative reading of this line of cases would see the domestic courts as simply following – with much delay and in a very roundabout way – the European Court's guidance and would suggest that the former have not been effective peacebuilding actors. In fact, domestic judges have arguably done a lot more than that. Although the House of Lords was initially reluctant to adopt a human rights-friendly approach, over time, it developed the ECtHR's jurisprudence by applying it in less controversial cases (such as those relating to deaths in custody) and gradually expanded its interpretation to cover conflict-related deaths.[176] Moreover, as the years passed, domestic courts addressed with renewed vigour the problematic practices that had been identified by the ECtHR and pushed for the reform of the investigation process in novel ways that had not been flagged up by the European Court. For instance, domestic case law has held that inquests should be prompt,[177] secured the granting of legal aid to families[178] and ensured that adequate document disclosure takes place during the investigations.[179] Additionally, in cases where the inquest had been concluded before the domestic judiciary revised its position, applicants have instigated proceedings to compel the Secretary of State to initiate a new investigation[180] and challenged decisions of the Director of Public Prosecutions to not prosecute suspects and/or refuse to give reasons for this decision.[181] Most of these are not issues that were directly addressed by the ECtHR, but are nevertheless important in ensuring that the conflicts concerning deaths during the Troubles are resolved in a way that promotes justice to the greatest possible extent.

Therefore, it was the *combined use* of domestic and international courts that led to the development of this jurisprudence, which in turn pushed for greater transparency and accountability of the state's actions. On the one hand, had it not been for the ECtHR, the first difficult step of finding the original violation would arguably not have been taken. This is supported by the fact that when the House of Lords had been asked in another conflict-related case whether there was a right to have a solicitor present when someone was being interviewed by the police, it held that no such right existed.[182] Part of the Law Lords' reasoning was based on the argument that the ECtHR had not yet held that Article 6 of the Convention, relating to the right to fair trial, encompasses such an obligation. Similarly, in the right to life cases, it is unlikely that the domestic courts would have adopted a progressive attitude towards investigating past injustices had the European Court not taken the first step in this direction. On the other hand, the gradual adoption of the ECtHR's case law by the domestic judiciary

[176] See, eg, *R (Amin) v Secretary of State for the Home Department* [2004] 1 AC 653.
[177] *Jordan, Re Application for Judicial Review* [2002] NICA 27.
[178] *Jordan, Re Application for Judicial Review* [2003] NICA 30.
[179] *Wright* [2003] NIQB 17.
[180] *McKerr* (n 172).
[181] *Jordan, Re Application for Judicial Review* [2003] NICA 54.
[182] *R v Chief Constable of the Royal Ulster Constabulary ex parte Begley and Mcwilliams* [1997] 1 WLR 1475.

had its own distinct advantages, such as the fact that it developed this guidance further, helped build momentum for its implementation by the relevant authorities and brought the provision of remedies closer to home. However, calling for better teamwork between the two levels of courts, which is what is being proposed here, is a strategy that requires peacebuilders to focus not only on judges, but other actors as well. Thus, secondments, exchanges, meetings, conferences and joint associations for the staff of domestic and international courts are likely to assist in this process.[183]

IV. THE IMPACT OF TIMING ON THE SUCCESSFUL ADJUDICATION OF THE CONFLICT

While academics have identified courts as potential peacebuilding actors, and therefore appreciated their abilities to resolve conflicts,[184] little, if anything, has been written on *when* judicial intervention should take place in order to be most effective.[185] This section argues that it makes a difference if the conflict is being adjudicated before or after the signing of a comprehensive peace agreement and how much time has passed since the stopping of the violence. In instances where a comprehensive peace agreement has been signed, the passage of time encourages judicial involvement in the resolution of a dispute. Conversely, where time passes in the absence of a peace settlement, judges are less likely to become involved.

A. The Passage of Time in the Absence of a Comprehensive Peace Agreement

It is not a coincidence that in the analysis in this chapter, Cyprus offers examples where conflict adjudication had the most disappointing results in the promotion of each of the elements of peace. GCs and TCs are still divided over fundamental conflicts, which, as section II explained, are more difficult to resolve than minor disagreements. This section argues that the *passage of time* since the outbreak of the violence on the island, coupled with the failure of the parties to negotiate a comprehensive peace settlement in the meantime, offers an additional reason why the adjudication of conflicts has not had positive peacebuilding effects.

[183] Daly (n 138) 285.

[184] Jenna Marie Sapiano, 'Courting Peace: Judicial Review and Peace Jurisprudence' (2017) 6 *Global Constitutionalism* 131.

[185] For brief mentions of this factor, see Thorsten Bonacker et al, 'Human Rights and the (De) Securitization of Conflict' in Raffaele Marchetti and Nathalie Tocci (eds), *Civil Society, Conflicts and the Politicization of Human Rights* (Tokyo, United Nations University Press, 2001) 40; Jenna Marie Sapiano, 'Courting Peace: Peace Constitutions and Jurisprudence' (PhD thesis, University of St Andrews, 2017). The insulation of the judiciary from a divisive conflict because of the time that passes between its manifestation and adjudication has also been explored in Alexander M Bickel, *The Least Dangerous Branch* (New Haven, Yale University Press, 1986) 25 and ch 4.

Thus, while courts are in any case ill-suited to resolve zero-sum disagreements, the phenomenon is even more heightened when these linger and remain unaddressed for years in the absence of a comprehensive peace settlement.

Illustrative of this is the ECtHR decision of *Varnava v Turkey*, a 2009 case in which a group of GC applicants complained about the lack of an effective investigation following the disappearance of their family members during the 1974 Turkish invasion.[186] They argued that since the missing persons had been last seen either in the custody of Turkish troops or in areas under the effective control of the Turkish army, it was the respondent state's obligation to provide information on what happened to them or, if it did not have it, to carry out investigations to this end.[187] Endorsing the applicants' argument, the ECtHR held that Turkey's inaction resulted in a violation of the procedural aspect of the right to life of the missing persons and a separate violation of their families' freedom from inhuman treatment.[188] However, while the Court ultimately found in favour of the applicants, confirming its earlier decision in *Cyprus v Turkey*,[189] it adopted a reasoning that prevented any other relatives of Cypriot missing persons from launching their complaints, thus signalling its clear reluctance to become further involved in the adjudication of this conflict. Starting from the controversial premise that even cases of continuous violations have a time limit after which they are not admissible, it reasoned that applicants cannot wait indefinitely before applying to Strasbourg.[190] In such cases, it continued, the burden of proof shifts to the applicants, who have to show that they undertook efforts to receive information about their relatives' whereabouts and, if this was not forthcoming, introduced their application to the ECtHR without undue delay.[191] Applying these principles to the Cypriot context, the Court held that family members should have realised by the end of 1990 that attempts to investigate their relatives' disappearances were not underway and brought their cases to the Court. The applications of those who did not meet this retrospective deadline, who in practice were all potential applicants except the ones in *Varnava* itself, were rejected as inadmissible.[192]

The lack of investigations concerning the fate of missing persons has given rise to fundamental conflicts that go to the heart of the Cyprus problem.[193] The parties disagree as to whether investigations should take place, who should be responsible for these and who should be considered a victim for the purposes of

[186] *Varnava and Others v Turkey* App No 16064/90 (ECtHR, 18 September 2009).
[187] ibid [175].
[188] ibid [191] and [201]. Like in the Cypriot right to property cases before *Demopoulos*, the total absence of an effective remedy gave the applicants direct access to the ECtHR without having to go through the domestic courts first.
[189] *Cyprus v Turkey* App No 25781/94 (ECtHR, 10 May 2001).
[190] *Varnava* (n 186) [161].
[191] ibid [166].
[192] ibid [170].
[193] Paul Sant Cassia, *Bodies of Evidence: Burial, Memory and the Recovery of Missing Persons in Cyprus* (New York, Berghahn Books, 2005) 23–24 and 79.

this exercise.[194] While the ECtHR's unwillingness to adjudicate this zero-sum dispute is therefore understandable, its reasoning in reaching this conclusion is less than persuasive and ultimately detrimental to peacebuilding efforts. The main justification for the Court's 1990 time limit was that the UN Committee on Missing Persons (CMP), a bicommunal body tasked with locating the remains of these individuals, had been established in and remained largely inactive since 1981.[195] By 1990, therefore, it should have been obvious that the CMP had not resulted in effective investigations and the applicants should have already launched their complaints to the ECtHR. Yet, when the Strasbourg Court had previously referred to the CMP in *Cyprus v Turkey*, it had explicitly stated that the CMP could not in itself provide an effective investigation.[196] While the obligation to investigate the disappearances rested with Turkey, the CMP had been established by the UN, was staffed by GCs and TCs, and was primarily funded by the EU.[197] Moreover, the Committee's role was to locate and identify anonymous graves and return the remains of those who had been exhumed to their families.[198] Although this was an important task, it did not exhaust Turkey's obligation to investigate the disappearances more generally and could not be used to exonerate it from its obligations.

Yet, by relying so heavily on the CMP's (lack of) performance and finding future cases inadmissible on this basis, this is precisely what the Court did in *Varnava*.[199] When it adopted this reasoning, it sent a rather confused message as to what actions should be taken, and by whom, in order to resolve the conflict of missing persons. As a result, the case is likely to have undermined a sense of justice among their relatives, since it denied them the opportunity to be remedied by the respondent state simply on the ground that some steps had already been taken in this direction by third parties. Finally, contrary to the Court's assessment that by 1990 it should have become obvious to the applicants that no additional steps would be taken towards their relatives' recovery, in 1997 the leaders of the two communities adopted a common statement in which they agreed to share information about the burial sites of missing persons, and in 2004, the CMP resumed its long-delayed work.[200] Since then, the CMP has located, identified and returned to the families the remains of 569 out of 1,508 GCs and 184 out of 493 missing TCs.[201] These concrete results that are

[194] *Cyprus v Turkey* (n 189) [134].
[195] *Varnava* (n 186) [168].
[196] *Cyprus v Turkey* (n 189) [135].
[197] Committee on Missing Persons in Cyprus – Donors, available at www.cmp-cyprus.org/content/donors.
[198] *Cyprus v Turkey* (n 189) [16] and [27].
[199] Nikolas Kyriakou, 'Enforced Disappearances in Cyprus: Problems and Prospects of the Case Law of the European Court of Human Rights' (2011) 2 *European Human Rights Law Review* 190, 195.
[200] ibid.
[201] Committee on Missing Persons in Cyprus – Facts and Figures, available at www.cmp-cyprus.org/content/facts-and-figures.

currently being produced by the CMP confirm the arbitrariness of the Court's 1990 deadline and further highlight the lack of persuasiveness of its decision. Most importantly in terms of assessing the case's peacebuilding potential, these positive results in terms of locating the missing appear to have materialised *despite* rather than *because of* the Court's decision in *Varnava*. Assuming that the ECtHR's decision 'transformed the normative framework within which Turkey acted'[202] simply because the Court found a violation oversimplifies and misleads as to the effect of the case.

One could make the argument that *Varnava* simply provides evidence of the fact that the ECtHR was reluctant to adjudicate a fundamental conflict rather than illustrating the Court's unwillingness to become involved because of the passage of time. However, a more in-depth reading of the case confirms that as time passes, the judiciary does, in fact, become less likely to adjudicate such disputes. The importance of the passage of time in *Varnava* was expressly acknowledged by the Court when it noted that:

> In a complex disappearance situation such as the present, arising in a situation of international conflict, where it is alleged that there is a complete absence of any investigation or meaningful contact with the authorities, it may be expected that the relatives bring the case within, at most, several years of the incident.[203]

The increasing reluctance of the Court to adjudicate long-running fundamental conflicts also becomes apparent through its right to property case law in relation to Cyprus. The majority of the judges in *Loizidou* found in 1995 that the applicant's displacement from her property more than 20 years earlier did not stop the finding of a violation. Conversely, when the issue was revisited in 2010, the Court unanimously declared that the secondary occupiers eventually form their own bonds with the properties in question, thus making it 'arbitrary and injudicious'[204] if it did not take into account 'the attenuation over time between the holding of title and the possession and use of the property'.[205] The Court's reasoning, while deeply unpopular among GCs,[206] is not completely unreasonable: some TC secondary occupiers have been living in the GC properties in question for 45 years and they, many of them not having been born during the war, consider these properties their own homes.[207] The decision is nevertheless

[202] Iosif Kovras, *Grassroots Activism and the Evolution of Transitional Justice: The Families of the Disappeared* (Cambridge, Cambridge University Press, 2017) 167.

[203] *Varnava* (n 186) [165].

[204] *Demopoulos* (n 60) [116].

[205] ibid [113].

[206] See, eg, Loucaides (n 76); Katselli-Proukaki (n 74).

[207] Ayla Gürel, Mete Hatay and Christalla Yakinthou, *Displacement in Cyprus: Consequences of Civil and Military Strife: An Overview of Events and Perceptions*, 2012/5 (Nicosia, PRIO Cyprus Centre, 2012) 10. The argument that restitution should be limited in cases of passage of time has also been made in the theoretical literature. See, eg, Jeremy Waldron, 'Redressing Historic Injustice' (2005) 52 *University of Toronto Law Journal* 135; Tyler Cowen, 'How Far Back Should We Go? Why Restitution Should Be Small' in Jon Elster (ed), *Retribution and Reparation in the Transition to Democracy* (Cambridge, Cambridge University Press, 2006).

problematic because, like *Varnava*, it sends the message to Turkey that all it has to do in order to legitimise past injustices is to wait.[208]

The passage of time does not diminish the need to respond to an injustice that has taken place. Providing an adequate remedy helps the victims be re-introduced to the social, political and economic life of the country, a necessary condition for each of the elements of peace.[209] At the same time, a decisive response by the state addresses not only the harm that has been done to the victims, but also the harm done to the legal system itself, and makes a break from the oppressive past.[210] Yet, despite these good reasons for resolving lingering conflicts, the judiciary's unwillingness to become involved in them, which increases when time passes and no peace agreement has been signed, is not surprising. When being asked to adjudicate these disagreements, the ECtHR finds itself in an impossible situation. It has to do justice to the individual applicant, while acknowledging that the case before it is only a small part of a political puzzle that is constantly changing as the negotiations progress.[211] The best strategy it can adopt is decide the case in a way that will benefit the applicant, while also pushing the political players to take action and resolve the conflict in a more comprehensive manner. In fact, the Court expressly outlined this strategy in *Loizidou*[212] and expressed its disappointment that the parties had not found a solution on the political level in *Demopoulos*.[213] As even more time passes, yet its proposed strategy continues to be ignored, the judges are left between a rock and a hard place: they will either find new cases inadmissible, as the ECtHR did in *Varnava*, thus distancing themselves from the adjudication of the conflict, or they will settle for a largely unsatisfactory remedy provided by the respondent state, as the Court did in *Demopoulos*.[214] Both responses are likely to undermine feelings of justice and suggest that the passage of time in societies that have not signed a comprehensive peace agreement will bring even more clearly to the fore the limitations of the judiciary in resolving fundamental conflicts.

B. The Passage of Time since the Signing of the Peace Agreement

Conversely, where a comprehensive peace settlement has already been signed, the more time passes, the more willing the judiciary becomes to adopt an activist

[208] Costas Paraskeva and Eleni Meleagrou, 'Homes from the Past: An Expiration Date for the Right to Respect for Home under Article 8 of the European Convention on Human Rights' (2012–13) VII *Annuaire International des Droits de l'homme* 845; Kyriakou (n 199) 196.

[209] Wouter Veraart, 'Redressing the Past with an Eye to the Future: The Impact of the Passage of Time on Property Rights Restitution in Post-apartheid South-Africa' (2009) 27 *Netherlands Quarterly of Human Rights* 45, 48.

[210] ibid.

[211] The Court expressly acknowledged this difficulty in *Demopoulos* (n 60) [85].

[212] *Loizidou* (n 61) [6].

[213] *Demopoulos* (n 60) [83]–[85].

[214] On the deficiencies of the remedies endorsed in *Demopoulos*, see section IV in ch 6.

stance when asked to resolve a conflict. This is, first, because the passage of time helps transform the agreement from a political document that cannot be interfered with into a legal source that should be interpreted, often creatively, by judges.[215] Second, as time passes, conflicts appear that had not been foreseen during the negotiating stage; if politicians are unwilling to address these, it often falls to the judiciary to take action. And, finally, the repetitive adjudication of a conflict can lead to the development of judicial reasoning and the consequent adoption of a gradually more activist approach by judges. This is particularly so with newly established domestic courts, which, with the passage of time, become more likely to find their footing and deliver more confident judgments. However, the greater judicial willingness to adjudicate conflicts does not necessarily translate into more successful peacebuilding outcomes. Rather, whether this will also result in better guidance towards conflict resolution and, in turn, help promote security, justice or reconciliation at least partly depends on the two previously discussed factors, namely the nature of the conflicts and the types of courts that adjudicate them.

A comprehensive peace agreement requires fine balancing between the demands and interests of the different sides to the conflict and is the result of delicate negotiations by politicians, members of civil society and the international community.[216] As a result, the judiciary is likely to hesitate to intervene in such arrangements and risk upsetting this balance,[217] especially if these have been approved directly by the public in a referendum.[218] The fresher the memory of the political process that gave rise to the peace agreement, the less likely judges are to want to interfere with its outcome. Conversely, the longer the interval between the original agreement and the Court's action, the greater the legitimacy in its intervention and adjudication of the conflict.[219] Simply put, the more time has passed, the more willing the judges become to see the settlement as a legal document (rather than a fragile political compromise) and therefore interpret it accordingly. This dilemma of whether to construe the peace agreement as a political or a legal act went to the heart of a divided House of Lords judgment in *Re Northern Ireland Human Rights Commission*.[220] Here, the judges had to

[215] For the argument that a peace agreement is both a legal and a political document, see Sapiano (n 185) 1. On the multifaceted nature of a peace agreement, see Colm Campbell, Fionnuala Ni Aolain and Colin Harvey, 'The Frontiers of Legal Analysis: Reframing the Transition in Northern Ireland' (2003) 66 *Modern Law Review* 317.

[216] Christine Bell, *Negotiating Justice? Human Rights and Peace Agreements* (Geneva, International Council of Human Rights Policy, 2006).

[217] John Morison and Marie Lynch, 'Litigating the Agreement: Towards a New Judicial Constitutionalism for the UK from Northern Ireland' in John Morison, Kieran McEvoy and Gordon Anthony (eds), *Judges, Transition and Human Rights* (Oxford, Oxford University Press, 2007).

[218] McCrudden and O'Leary (n 28) 499.

[219] Richard H Pildes, 'Ethnic Identity and Democratic Institutions: A Dynamic Perspective' in Sujit Choudhry (ed), *Constitutional Design for Divided Societies: Integration or Accommodation?* (Oxford, Oxford University Press, 2008) 197.

[220] *R (on the Application of Northern Ireland Human Rights Commission) v Greater Belfast Coroner* [2002] UKHL 25.

decide whether the Commission had the power to intervene as a third party in judicial proceedings concerning human rights, even though it was not expressly allowed to do so by the NI Act 1998, which had set it up. Therefore, the essence of the disagreement concerned the question of whether the judiciary could interpret the NI Act, and the Belfast Agreement that this gave effect to, and potentially in the process create powers, rights or duties that their drafters had not intended or foreseen. The lower courts that had heard the case, and the minority of the House of Lords, argued that the 'Belfast Agreement was an intensely political act', which called for a restrictive interpretation because:

> Matters which might easily be thought to be reasonable for inclusion in the Belfast Agreement may well not have been included for some political reason not apparent subsequently to lawyers who have not been privy to what occurred.[221]

Conversely, and with 'almost a whiff of exasperation', the majority held that although the Act did not expressly give the Commission this power, it created an implied one.[222] Since it was the work of the courts to interpret human rights legislation, any guidance by the Commission in the exercise of this duty would be valuable.[223] Thus, several years after the signing of the Belfast Agreement, the majority of the House of Lords adopted a reasoning that viewed the NI Act as a statute that required interpretation, in a way that may not have been possible a few years before.

The second factor explaining the increased willingness of courts to resolve conflicts concerns the fact that with the passage of time, new disagreements might arise that the drafters of the peace agreement either had not foreseen or had not realised the full magnitude of.[224] Especially if the political leaders are unwilling or unable to address these new disputes through the political process, it might be that the judiciary, with its 'relative insulation' from politics,[225] finds that it has a responsibility to intervene.[226] Illustrative of this phenomenon is *Sejdić and Finci v BiH*, *Zornić v BiH*[227] and *Pilav v BiH*,[228] in which the ECtHR explicitly cited the passage of time as a reason that contributed to its finding of a violation.[229] In order to understand the claims of the parties and controversy of the disputes in each of these cases, some knowledge of the complex BiH Constitution is necessary. The Constitution establishes a federal government and two entities – the Federation of BiH and the Republika Srpska – and divides all political power equally between the three Constituent Peoples (the Bosniacs, Serbs and Croats). The House of Peoples (the upper chamber

[221] ibid [66].
[222] Dickson (n 159) 410.
[223] *R (on the Application of Northern Ireland Human Rights Commission)* (n 220) [21].
[224] Sapiano (n 184).
[225] Galanter (n 11) 150.
[226] Pildes (n 219).
[227] *Zornić v Bosnia and Herzegovina* App No 3681/06 (ECtHR, 15 July 2014).
[228] *Pilav v Bosnia and Herzegovina* App No 41939/07 (ECtHR, 9 June 2016).
[229] *Sejdić* (n 154) [45]–[47]; *Zornić* (n 227) [43]; *Pilav* (n 228) [47].

of the Legislative Assembly) consists of five Serbs from the Republika and five Bosniacs and five Croats from the Federation, while two-thirds of the members of the House of Representatives (the lower chamber) come from the Federation and a third from the Republika.[230] Similarly, the Presidency is made up of three members, one from each constituent people, with the proviso that the Serb representative comes from the Republika and the Bosniac and Croat representatives come from the Federation.[231]

Necessary as this protection of the ethnic groups was deemed to be for the ending of the war and the promotion of security, it has resulted in two major problems in terms of human rights protection. The first is that it purposively excludes the citizens of BiH who do not identify as members of one of the three constituent groups, referred to in the Constitution as 'Others', from exercising their right to be elected in one of these positions. This was the complaint in both *Sejdić* and *Zornić*, with the applicants in the former being excluded because of their Jewish and Roma identities, and the applicant in the latter being unable to run for office because she did not wish to declare an affiliation with one of the Constituent People. The second problem is that the Constitution prevents members of Constituent Peoples living in the 'wrong' entity – that is, Bosniacs and Croats living in the Republika and Serbs living in the Federation – from running for elections.[232] This was the complaint of the applicant in *Pilav*, a Bosniac who was excluded from running for office as long as he continued residing in the Republika Srpska. This state of affairs, the ECtHR held in *Sejdić* and confirmed in the other two cases, results in violations of the right to vote and freedom from discrimination.[233]

In reaching this conclusion, the Court rejected the argument that ethnic group protections and the consequent disenfranchisement of the applicants were necessary to maintain peace and security in the country. In particular, it held that while this was a legitimate aim, one that was especially important considering BiH's history, it could not justify the restriction of human rights indefinitely. While in the early stages following the signing of the Dayton Agreement, the Court might have been willing to accept that the limitation of certain rights was necessary, this argument became harder to accept as more time passed. The Court's explanation in *Zornić* is worth quoting in full:

> [W]hen the impugned constitutional provisions were put in place a very fragile ceasefire was in effect on the ground [... with its] provisions [being] designed to end a brutal conflict marked by genocide and 'ethnic cleansing' ... However, now, more

[230] BiH Constitution, art IV.
[231] ibid art V.
[232] This second consequence of the ethnocentric provisions also negatively affects the relocation of refugees to their pre-war properties, thus indirectly compromising the right to property as well. See Ayaki Ito, 'Politicisation of Minority Return in Bosnia-Herzegovina: The First Five Years Examined' (2001) 13 *International Journal of Refugee Law* 98, 118.
[233] *Sejdić* (n 154) [50] and [56].

> than eighteen years after the end of the tragic conflict, there could no longer be any reason for the maintenance of the contested constitutional provisions. The Court expects that democratic arrangements will be made without further delay. In view of the need to ensure effective political democracy, the Court considers that the time has come for a political system which will provide every citizen of Bosnia and Herzegovina with the right to stand for elections.[234]

Support for the Court's position that the passage of time made judicial intervention even more pressing was provided by the fact that the decision had been preceded by three failed attempts to negotiate the amendment of the Constitution.[235] This can be perceived as evidence of unwillingness on behalf of the politicians to resolve the fundamental conflict, which in turn legitimised the ECtHR's decision to intervene and provide additional incentives for action through the finding of a violation. Further, during the period between the signing of the Dayton Agreement and the Court's decisions, several international bodies, such as the Venice Commission, had examined the Constitution's provisions, deemed them to be problematic and suggested alternatives that were in line with human rights.[236] This preparatory work that took place over two decades, and on which the Court relied heavily in all three cases, increased the judges' confidence, both in adjudicating the conflict and finding that the BiH Constitution was in violation of the European Convention.

The analysis here should not be taken to suggest that the passage of time made the Court's decisions 'good' ones or that the guidance it provided when delivering its judgments necessarily contributed to peacebuilding efforts. It merely proposes that as time passes, the judiciary becomes more likely to adjudicate the conflict in question; whether this will also promote peace depends on the ability of the judiciary to address the conflict at hand.[237] In this case, since the conflict was a fundamental one, the Court's interventions have arguably not been very constructive. In fact, the rulings in *Sejdić*, *Zornić* and *Pilav*, which essentially ask the parties to return to the negotiating table and amend the BiH Constitution, risk undermining the fragile settlement that prevents the eruption of violence in the country.[238] In all three cases, the respondent government had argued that the ethnic quotas in the Constitution were necessary to end 'one of the most destructive conflicts in recent European history' and were therefore

[234] *Zornić* (n 227) [43].

[235] International Crisis Group, *Bosnia's Gordian Knot: Constitutional Reform*, Europe Briefing N° 68 (Sarajevo/Instabul/Brussels, International Crisis Group, 2012) 2–3.

[236] Reference is made to these documents in *Sejdić* (n 154) [17] and [21]–[23].

[237] The ECtHR's judgment has been criticised as being too interventionist (McCrudden and O'Leary (n 128)), but little attention has been paid to the fact that if the Constitutional Court had found a violation, it would indirectly be delegitimising itself, as its composition is determined using the same formula. See Daly (n 138) 275.

[238] In his dissenting judgment in *Sejdić*, Judge Bonello noted: '[O]ne cannot possibly disagree with the almost platitudinous Preamble to the Convention that human rights "are the foundation of peace in the world". Sure they are. But what of exceptionally perverse situations in which the enforcement of human rights could be the trigger for war rather than the conveyor of peace?'.

paramount to 'the establishment of peace and dialogue between the three main ethnic groups'.[239] Implying that the passage of time since the end of the hostilities made the maintenance of peace and dialogue a less pressing aim, the ECtHR rejected this argument.[240] However, what is missing from the judgments is an explanation as to *why* the ethnic protections were necessary in the first place.[241] Since this was not clear, the Court's subsequent argument – namely that the passage of time made this protection less essential – became even more difficult to support. The absence of a persuasive reasoning could send the message that BiH elites should amend the Constitution simply because the ECtHR said so rather than because there are good reasons for it, and reduces the possibility that its adjudication will contribute to the resolution of this fundamental conflict.[242]

The final factor that explains the judiciary's willingness to adjudicate conflicts when some time has passed since the signing of the peace agreement concerns the phenomenon of repetitive litigation. It is not unlikely that over a period of a few years, usually domestic courts will be asked to adjudicate the same or a similar dispute more than once. In such instances, when courts are given several opportunities to respond to the conflict, they tend to take into account the effects of their first decision, develop their reasoning and provide more constructive guidance in subsequent ones. Domestic judges, who after all are members of the society that is being affected by the conflict, are particularly likely to adopt this approach if their original decision has not been received favourably by academics, members of civil society or the public at large.[243] This analysis rejects the characterisation of the judge as a 'social eunuch', someone who is completely detached from the consequences of the judgments he or she delivers.[244] It also creates room for the possibility that newly established courts, which are often set up as part of the peacebuilding process, might need some time to determine their relationship with the other branches of government, deliver judgments that potentially go against the preferences of political elites and develop case law that empowers them to provide guidance for the resolution

[239] *Sejdić* (n 154) [34]; *Zornić* (n 227) [24]; *Pilav* (n 228) [31].

[240] *Sejdić* (n 154) [22] and [48]; *Zornić* (n 227) [43]; *Pilav* (n 228) [46].

[241] In fact, one could argue that these constitutional provisions were to the detriment of rather than necessary for peace and security in the country. See Nystuen (n 32) 252.

[242] Even a cursory reading of the BiH press shows that the concern seems to be a lack of compliance with Europe's demands rather than the improvement of the democratic structures per se. See, eg, Elvira M Jukic, 'EU "Losing Patience with Bosnia", Official Says' *Balkan Insight*, 4 February 2013; Elvira M Jukic, 'EU Censures Bosnia for Missing Reform Deadline' *Balkan Insight*, 4 September 2012.

[243] Barry Friedman, 'Mediated Popular Constitutionalism' (2003) 101 *Michigan Law Review* 2595. For the argument that judges 'perform' for imagined audiences, like other judges, legal professionals and legal academics, and are likely to shape their decisions when addressing these audiences, see Kieran McEvoy and Alex Schwartz, 'Judges, Conflict and the Past' (2015) 42 *Journal of Law and Society* 528; and, more generally, Lawrence Baum, *Judges and Their Audiences: A Perspective on Judicial Behavior* (Princeton, Princeton University Press, 2006).

[244] Griffith (n 131) 290.

of divisive conflicts.[245] This is especially so in contexts where domestic judges need, and receive, additional human rights training, or when they start engaging in an institutional dialogue with international human rights bodies, such as the ECtHR.[246]

The peacebuilding effects of the continuous litigation of a single dispute over several years are illustrated through the developing jurisprudence of the UK House of Lords with regard to the obligation to investigate deaths that had taken place in NI during the Troubles. As the analysis in the preceding section suggests, while the Court originally adopted a restrictive interpretation of the applicability of the Human Rights Act, it completely reversed its approach over a seven-year period, when it delivered four judgments on this issue. During this time, academics questioned the persuasiveness of the first decision, applauded the judicial change of direction in the second and urged for further clarity following the third.[247] As a result of this evolving case law, today, UK authorities have clear guidance about the steps they must take in order to ensure that a conflict-related death has been duly investigated. In turn, compliance with the Court's decisions promotes accountability and is a step towards ensuring that the injustices of the past will be addressed.

Another example of the peacebuilding effects of continuously litigating a conflict over time arises through the case law of the BiH Constitutional Court, when it was asked to judicially review the decisions of the High Representative, who is responsible for overseeing the implementation of the Dayton Agreement.[248] Despite being staffed by unelected international officials, the Office of the High Representative has been given a wide range of powers, including the power to pass legislation and fire civil servants.[249] Problematically, especially in light of the fact that the international community's objective was to build a democratic BiH, the High Representative remains completely unaccountable for

[245] Theunis Roux, *The Politics of Principle: The First South African Constitutional Court 1995–2005* (Cambridge, Cambridge University Press, 2013). For evidence that peace agreements often result in the creation of new constitutional courts, see Donald L Horowitz, 'Constitutional Courts: A Primer for Decision Makers' (2006) 17 *Journal of Democracy* 125, 126; and for an argument that constitutional courts tend to be more activist than supreme courts that hear a broader range of cases, see Victor Ferrers Comella, 'The Consequences of Centralizing Constitutional Review in a Special Court: Some Thoughts on Judicial Activism' (2003–04) 82 *Texas Law Review* 1705.

[246] On the institutional dialogue between domestic and international bodies, see Daly (n 138) 174–75.

[247] Requa and Anthony (n 174).

[248] For additional information on the Office of the High Representative, see General Framework Agreement for Peace in Bosnia and Herzegovina, Annex 10; and see the analysis in section V of ch 5. See also Roland Kostić, 'Shadow Peacebuilders and Diplomatic Counterinsurgencies: Informal Networks, Knowledge Production and the Art of Policy-Shaping' (2017) 11 *Journal of Intervention and Statebuilding* 120.

[249] Office of the High Representative, *Peace Implementation Council Bonn Conclusions: Bosnia and Herzegovina 1998: Self-Sustaining Structures* (Sarajevo, Office of the High Representative, 10 December 1997).

any of his decisions or actions.[250] The BiH Constitutional Court had originally developed a wholly deferential approach that found any challenges to the High Representative's decisions as inadmissible, thus perpetuating this unacceptable state of affairs.[251] Over time, however, it revised its approach and held that the inability to judicially review the decisions of the High Representative constituted a violation of the right to an effective remedy under Article 13 of the European Convention.[252] In turn, this pronouncement of the Court sent the message that BiH was slowly and gradually moving away from the extraordinary state of affairs of being ruled by an unaccountable international official and increased a sense of justice among those who were directly affected by his decisions.

The three factors that have been outlined above suggest that the passage of time in cases where a comprehensive peace settlement has already been reached is likely to encourage the judiciary to adopt an activist approach. Whether the Court's reasoning can also provide useful guidance for the resolution of the conflict depends not only on the passage of time itself, but on other factors as well, such as whether the disagreement is a fundamental or a minor one and if the body hearing the dispute is a domestic or an international court. Thus, the ECtHR's reasoning in the BiH voting cases has been unable to promote peace for the simple reason that the Court attempted to resolve a (fundamental) conflict that it was ill-suited to deal with. Conversely, the House of Lords' judgment in *Re Northern Ireland Human Rights Commission* was both persuasive and relatively uncontroversial because the case was concerned with a minor conflict that merely required the interpretation of a statute rather than the taking of a political stance on a divisive issue. This is also the case with the BiH Constitutional Court decisions on the High Representative; they might have been ill-received by the High Representative himself,[253] but they were open-and-shut-cases in terms of applying established ECtHR case law to the uncontested facts on the ground.

V. CONCLUSION

This chapter has been concerned with the question of whether the adjudication of human rights can contribute to conflict resolution and, consequently, to peacebuilding efforts. It has argued that the success, or otherwise, of the

[250] Richard Caplan, 'Who Guards the Guardians? International Accountability in Bosnia' in David Chandler (ed), *Peace without Politics? Ten Years of International State Building in Bosnia* (London, Taylor & Francis, 2006).

[251] *U-9/00* (BiH Constitutional Court, 3 November 2000); *U-25/00* (BiH Constitutional Court, 23 March 2001); *AP-777/04* (BiH Constitutional Court, 30 June 2004).

[252] *AP-953/05* (BiH Constitutional Court, 8 July 2006).

[253] Office of the High Representative, *Order on the Implementation of the Decision of the Constitutional Court of Bosnia and Herzegovina in the Appeal of Milorad Bilbija et al, No AP-953/05*, Doc 37/07 (Sarajevo, Office of the High Representative, 23 March 2007).

judiciary to resolve conflicts depends on three factors: the type of conflict that is being adjudicated; whether the court reaching the decision is a domestic or an international one; and the signing of, and amount of time that has passed since, the comprehensive peace agreement. When these factors are taken seriously, they point to practical lessons that peacebuilders can adopt so that human rights adjudication can more effectively lead to the building of peace. In particular, since fundamental conflicts are best resolved through a political process, peacebuilders should focus their efforts and resources on lobbying and encouraging politicians to reach a mutually agreed compromise. This lesson becomes even more pressing in cases where a fundamental conflict remains unresolved for a long period of time. If there is a comprehensive peace agreement in place, the court will be more willing to intervene, which in cases of fundamental conflicts like the ones adjudicated in *Sejdić*, *Zornić* and *Pilav* risks destabilising the post-violence society. At the same time, in the absence of a peace agreement, even a refusal to become further involved, as was the case in *Demopoulos* and *Varnava*, can result in confusing guidance for the resolution of the conflict and undermine a sense of justice among the applicants and others in a similar position.

Conversely, since courts are well-suited in adjudicating and successfully resolving minor disagreements, peacebuilders should adopt steps that strengthen domestic bodies, which are likely to hear the bulk of these cases. For instance, training should be provided to judges and lawyers, with emphasis on lower instance courts; class action suits should be allowed and alternative dispute resolution mechanisms should be considered; legal aid must be made available to applicants; and domestic institutions should adopt procedures and evidentiary rules that make them as accessible as possible to individuals in post-violence societies. Finally, while domestic courts are likely to decide most cases that are concerned with minor conflicts, international courts generally lead the way in adjudicating test cases relating to more controversial or divisive disputes. Thus, if peacebuilders have decided that the best way to resolve a conflict is through human rights adjudication, they are advised to continue pursuing this strategy all the way to the ECtHR, or potentially another international human rights body available to them, rather than give up after a negative response to their complaint from the domestic courts.

5

Promoting Objective Peace through Human Rights Implementation

I. INTRODUCTION

IMPLEMENTING HUMAN RIGHTS – whether these are in the form of judicial decisions or laws – can help resolve conflicts and promote peacebuilding efforts in post-violence societies.[1] For example, protecting the rights to property and life can have a real and positive impact on building objective peace by remedying war victims and promoting justice and reconciliation[2] or by investigating past crimes and enhancing security.[3] In addition to the specific contributions that the protection of each right can make, depending on the conflict it responds to, a post-violence society that regularly complies with its human rights obligations is likely to have a more promising peacebuilding trajectory for a number of other reasons. First, the strict implementation of human rights leaves less discretion to nationalist politicians or civil servants and makes it more difficult for them to act as spoilers to this process.[4] Second, following the signing of a peace agreement, which often refers to human rights, people expect to see a real change in their lives.[5] The enforcement of human rights promises sends a clear message that such a change will materialise and increases

[1] Christine Bell, *Peace Agreements and Human Rights* (Oxford, Oxford University Press, 2000) 298.

[2] UN Secretary-General, *The Rule of Law and Transitional Justice in Conflict and Post-conflict Societies,* S/2004/616 (New York, United Nations, 2004) [7]; UN Secretary-General's High-Level Panel on Threats Challenges and Change, *A More Secure World: Our Shared Responsibility,* A/59/565 (New York, United Nations, 2004) [284].

[3] Hurst Hannum, 'Human Rights in Conflict Resolution: The Role of the Office of High Commissioner for Human Rights in UN Peacemaking and Peacebuilding' (2006) 28 *Human Rights Quarterly* 36; Christine Bell, 'Human Rights, Peace Agreements and Conflict Resolution: Negotiating Justice in Northern Ireland' in Julie Mertus and Jeffrey W Helsing (eds), *Human Rights and Conflict: Exploring the Links between Rights, Law and Peacebuilding* (Washington DC, United States Institute of Peace Press, 2006).

[4] Alan Keenan, 'Building a Democratic Middle Ground: Professional Civil Society and the Politics of Human Rights in Sri Lanka's Peace Process' in Mertus and Helsing (n 3) 472.

[5] Erik G Jensen, 'Justice and the Rule of Law' in Charles T. Call (ed), *Building States to Build Peace* (Boulder, Lynne Rienner, 2008); Kieran McEvoy, 'Beyond Legalism: Towards a Thicker Understanding of Transitional Justice' (2007) 34 *Journal of Law and Society* 411, 426.

the public's confidence in, and legitimises, the new state of affairs.[6] Third, the continuous implementation of human rights decisions and policies is likely to result in a virtuous cycle, whereby the introduction of one peacebuilding strategy can make it easier to introduce additional ones.[7] Finally, respecting human rights promotes a sense of security among the population by showing that the executive's power is not exercised arbitrarily and is less likely to be abused in the future.[8]

At the same time, however, the best-known limitation of human rights is that they often remain unenforced and therefore are effective only on paper.[9] This general critique also affects the extent to which they can contribute to conflict resolution efforts in post-violence societies, with Putnam, for instance, arguing that peacebuilders should avoid 'human rights cheerleading' and start working towards their enforcement on the ground.[10] The most frequently cited explanation for this limitation of human rights is the fact that 'the vast majority of states lack the requisite political will to effect transformative transitions'.[11] This chapter argues that peacebuilders are right in considering political willingness to implement human rights as an important condition for the success of peacebuilding operations.[12] Yet, overly focusing on this conclusion can result in crude peacebuilding strategies, like giving excessive legislative and enforcement powers to international officials in an attempt to circumvent the challenges posed by local spoilers. Instead, peacebuilders should nuance their understanding of the relationship between human rights implementation and the building of peace, which will contribute to the adoption of more effective responses when the former is not forthcoming. One way of doing this is by appreciating that political willingness is a matter of degree. Peacebuilding efforts might be undermined when some political willingness for change exists, but not to a sufficient

[6] Bell (n 1) ch 7.

[7] Open Society Justice Initiative, *From Rights to Remedies: Structures and Strategies for Implementing International Human Rights Decisions* (New York, Open Society Foundation, 2013) 25; Daniel Bar-Tal, 'From Intractable Conflict through Conflict Resolution to Reconciliation: Psychological Analysis' (2000) 21 *Political Psychology* 351, 361.

[8] William Burke-White, 'Human Rights and National Security: The Strategic Correlation' (2004) 17 *Harvard Human Rights Journal* 249.

[9] Tonya L Putnam, 'Human Rights and Sustainable Peace' in Stephen Stedman, Donald Rothchild and Elizabeth Cousens (eds), *Ending Civil Wars: The Implementation of Peace Agreements* (Boulder, Lynne Rienner, 2002).

[10] ibid 255.

[11] Makau W Mutua, 'The Transformation of Africa: A Critique of Rights in Transitional Justice' in Ruth Buchanan and Peer Zumbansen (eds), *Law in Transition: Human Rights, Development and Transitional Justice* (Oxford, Hart Publishing, 2016) 92. See also Committee on Legal Affairs and Human Rights, *Draft Resolution on the Implementation of Judgments of the European Court of Human Rights*, Doc 13864 (Strasbourg, Parliamentary Assembly of the Council of Europe, 9 September 2015) [7] and [46]; Open Society Justice Initiative (n 7) 16.

[12] The UN Secretary-General ((n 2) [20]) notes that 'the international community has frequently underestimated the extent of political will necessary to support effective rule of law reform in post-conflict States', pointing to the need to pay closer attention to this factor.

degree to induce comprehensive reforms. Another is by acknowledging that political willingness to implement human rights is only one of the factors that lead to the promotion of peace. Equally important is the specific way in which the human rights-inspired laws have been drafted and the extent to which their provisions can effectively address the conflicts in question. A third consideration is that the public bodies that oversee the enforcement of human rights laws have the independence, power, resources and expertise to undertake this task successfully.

Peacebuilders have already started identifying these considerations as important. Consequently, over the years, they have shifted their attention from vague human rights pronouncements to robust mechanisms that ensure their enforcement in practice.[13] However, in addition to pinpointing the factors that affect the peacebuilding potential of human rights, it is also essential to understand *how* the absence of each specifically affects conflict resolution efforts. Undertaking this exercise is necessary because the lack of political willingness, problematic legislative drafting and the establishment of an ill-equipped implementing body are distinct challenges, with each calling for a different peacebuilding response. The chapter concludes by examining two such responses, namely the involvement of the international community and the strengthening of civil society. The two responses can address the problem of political unwillingness to induce positive change by exerting international or grassroots pressure for the enforcement of human rights in a way that will promote peacebuilding objectives. Concurrently, they can help tackle some of the more technical difficulties by offering expertise and through the sharing of good practices, both in terms of drafting new laws and creating the appropriate institutions for their successful implementation. Yet, while the two responses can encourage human rights enforcement and contribute to successful conflict resolution, they should be used with caution because they also risk having detrimental effects on peacebuilding efforts.

II. THE IMPORTANCE OF POLITICAL WILLINGNESS TO IMPLEMENT HUMAN RIGHTS

The most commonly cited reason as to why states do not comply with their human rights obligations is that they do not want to. Assertions that 'political will remains the most important factor for the successful implementation of human rights judgments',[14] that human rights abuse 'is almost always caused by purposeful disobedience by actors who choose defection from the rules'[15] or that human rights implementation takes place because of the 'government's

[13] Bell (n 3).

[14] Open Society Justice Initiative (n 7) 16.

[15] Emilie M Hafner-Burton, *Forced to Be Good: Why Trade Agreements Boost Human Rights* (Ithaca, Cornell University Press, 2005) 597.

willingness to respect the human rights of citizens' are commonplace in the literature.[16] These arguments are largely persuasive and examples abound where the non-implementation of a human rights decision or law was due to the lack of political willingness to act, which, in turn, resulted in negative peacebuilding effects.[17] Thus, Bar-Tav is right that political elites play an important role in this respect, both because they can get things done and because their endorsement of human rights initiatives can encourage in-group members' support for the peacebuilding process.[18] At the same time, however, the relationship between willingness to implement human rights and their ability to promote peace is not a binary one. Rather, it is a matter of degree and in instances where there is some willingness to enforce human rights, but only to a limited extent, partial compliance with the post-violence society's legal obligations might result in no (or even negative) peacebuilding effects.

Illustrative of the simple observation that political will to implement human rights can have positive peacebuilding effects, while its absence might result in negative outcomes, are two ECtHR cases, one against the RoC and the other against BiH, concerning violations of the right to vote and freedom from discrimination. In the first case, *Aziz v Cyprus*, a TC applicant complained that he was prevented from participating in the 2001 RoC parliamentary election on the grounds of his ethnicity.[19] Finding a violation of Article 3 of Protocol No 1 (Article 3-1) of the European Convention, the ECtHR ordered the RoC authorities 'to implement such measures as they consider appropriate to fulfil their obligations to secure the right to vote in compliance with this judgment'.[20] Since Article 3-1 only safeguards 'the free expression of the opinion of the people in the choice of the legislature', the RoC could have complied with its human rights obligations under the Convention by merely amending the law concerning parliamentary elections. Yet, despite the existence of internal nationalist voices, the RoC went further than the strict requirements of the right and passed legislation that allowed TCs residing in the RoC-controlled areas to vote in the presidential, parliamentary and municipal elections.[21] The electoral law also allows TCs to run as candidates in the parliamentary and municipal elections,

[16] David Cingranelli and David Richards, 'Respect for Human Rights after the End of the Cold War' (1999) 36 *Journal of Peace Research* 511, 511.

[17] Michelle Parlevliet, *Rethinking Conflict Transformation from a Human Rights Perspective* (Berghof Handbook Dialogue Series No 9, Berlin, Berghof Research Centre for Constructive Conflict Management, 2009) 14, arguing that: 'Those in power may be reluctant to accommodate demands for change … even if those have been formally agreed upon in a peace settlement, or even if the state is formally obliged to abide by international human rights treaties and instruments it has ratified.'

[18] Bar-Tal (n 7) 362.

[19] *Aziz v Cyprus* App No 69949/01 (ECtHR, 22 September 2004) [15]. The case is discussed in more detail in section II.B in ch 4.

[20] ibid [43].

[21] The Law Concerning the Right to Vote and Be Elected of the Members of the Turkish Community that Permanently Reside in the Unoccupied Areas of the Republic of 2006 (2(I)/2006).

but not the presidential election.[22] These developments were further bolstered in 2014 when a new legislative amendment allowed all TCs with an RoC identity card – whether residing in the Republic-controlled areas or not – to participate in the elections of the European Parliament.[23] The 2019 elections marked the first time ever that a TC was elected to the European Parliament and the first time since 1963 that a TC was elected into an official post of the Republic.[24]

In best-case scenarios, the implementation of human rights is likely to result in amendments to laws, practices and institutions, all of which are necessary to promote objective peace in the post-violence society. Additionally, these can be the first step towards changing the living conditions and perceptions of the people and therefore also developing feelings of subjective peace. For example, *Aziz* led to the amendment of the electoral law, which allowed TCs residing in the RoC-controlled areas to become involved in the democratic process for the first time in decades and sent the message that they are equal citizens of the Republic. In practical terms, this was significant because it enfranchised TCs, who, by voting in RoC elections, impliedly rejected Turkey's rhetoric that only an independent 'TRNC' can protect their interests, and promoted feelings of reconciliation.[25] Moreover, as a result of the amendment, TCs who are politically active in the RoC have an incentive, and are given the opportunity, to communicate with the GC public directly and explain their community's concerns. It is only through discussions such as these that each side can understand the other's point of view and reconciliation can start being promoted on the island. TCs who decide to run for elections in the RoC do so because they imagine and work towards a united Cyprus. They are among the most vocal supporters of peace between the two communities and their empowerment can show to GCs and TCs alike that there is an alternative to the more dominant nationalist views expressed within both communities.[26]

Contrasting the positive peacebuilding effects of *Aziz*'s implementation in Cyprus is the inaction of the BiH government following *Sejdić and Finci v BiH*,[27] which more than 10 years after the ECtHR's decision remains unenforced.[28] The international community's response to *Sejdić* has been momentous: reports

[22] ibid art 2.

[23] Election of Members of the European Parliament Law of 2014 (10(I)/2004), as amended by 35(I)2014.

[24] Euronews, 'EU Elections 2019: Country-by-Country Full Results' 28 May 2019, available at https://www.euronews.com/2019/05/25/eu-elections-2019-country-by-country-guide-on-what-to-look-out-for.

[25] Ibrahim Aziz, *Ibrahim Aziz v Republic of Cyprus*, Series of Lectures 'The People Behind Judicial Decisions' (Nicosia, University of Cyprus, 26 November 2016).

[26] Yiannis Papadakis, 'Nation, Narrative and Commemoration: Political Ritual in Divided Cyprus' (2003) 13 *History and Anthropology* 253.

[27] *Sejdić and Finci v Bosnia and Herzegovina* App No 27996/06 (ECtHR, 22 December 2009). For a detailed discussion of this case, see section IV.B in ch 4.

[28] Ministry for Human Rights and Refugees, *Communication from Bosnia and Herzegovina Concerning the Case of Sejdic and Finci v Bosnia and Herzegovina (Application No 27996/06) for the 1288th Meeting of the Committee of Ministers of the Council of Europe*, DH-DD(2017)380 (Sarajevo, BiH Ministry of Human Rights and Refugees, 2017).

and suggestions for its implementation have been published by the UN Human Rights Council,[29] the Venice Commission,[30] the Parliamentary Assembly of the Council of Europe,[31] non-governmental organisations[32] and academics.[33] Additionally, its implementation has been made a condition for BiH's EU accession process, something repeated frequently by European officials.[34] They sometimes cajole the BiH elite by promising that implementing the decision and joining the EU will have concrete positive economic consequences for the country.[35] On other occasions, they have issued warnings that non-enforcement can 'potentially undermine the legitimacy and credibility of the country's future elected bodies'[36] and that continued non-compliance with the ECtHR judgment will be financially detrimental to BiH.[37]

As a result of this international pressure, BiH elites have been involved in a series of negotiations with the ultimate objective of amending the Constitution. In fact, since the discriminatory effects of the electoral provisions were identified by the Venice Commission in 2005, these negotiations had been underway even before *Sejdić* was decided.[38] So far, three sets of suggestions – the April Package in 2006, the Prud Process in 2008 and the Butmir Process in 2009 – have been debated by BiH politicians, although without resulting in any concrete results.[39] While Bosniacs, who make up the largest of the three ethnic groups, are pushing for the reduction of minority protections and the creation of liberal institutions,[40] Serbs and Croats are keen to preserve, and even increase, their

[29] UN Human Rights Council, *National Report Submitted in Accordance with Paragraph 5 of the Annex to Human Rights Council Resolution 16/21: Bosnia and Herzegovina,* A/HRC/WG6/20/BIH/1 (New York, UN General Assembly, 8 August 2014).

[30] Venice Commission, *Opinion on the Constitutional Situation in Bosnia and Herzegovina and the Powers of the High Representative*, CDL-AD(2005)004 (Strasbourg, Council of Europe, 2005); Venice Commission, *Opinion on Different Proposals for the Election of the Presidency of Bosnia and Herzegovina*, CDL-AD(2006)004 (Strasbourg, Council of Europe, 2006).

[31] Parliamentary Assembly, *The Functioning of Democratic Institutions in Bosnia and Herzegovina*, Doc 12112 (Strasbourg, Council of Europe, 11 January 2010).

[32] International Crisis Group, *Bosnia's Future,* Europe Report N° 232 (Sarajevo/Brussels, International Crisis Group, 2012); International Crisis Group, *Bosnia's Gordian Knot: Constitutional Reform,* Europe Briefing N° 68 (Sarajevo/Instanbul/Brussels, International Crisis Group, 2012).

[33] Edin Hodzic and Nenad Stojanović, *New/Old Constitutional Engineering? Challenges and Implications of the European Court of Human Rights Decision in the Case of Sejdić and Finci v BiH* (Sarajevo, Analitika Centre for Social Research, 2011).

[34] European Commission, *Bosnia and Herzegovina 2013 Progress Report,* SWD(2013) 415 final (Brussels, European Commission, 16 October 2013).

[35] European Commission, *Bosnia-Herzegovina – EU: Deep Disappointment on Sejdić-Finci Implementation* (Brussels, Council of Europe, 18 February 2014).

[36] Committee of Ministers, *Interim Resolution,* CM/ResDH(2013)259 (Strasbourg, Council of Europe, 22 December 2009).

[37] In 2013, and as a result of *Sejdić*'s non-implementation, the EU launched a procedure that would reduce the funding received by BiH through the Instrument for Pre-accession Assistance by 54 per cent (i.e. €47 million); European Commission (n 35).

[38] Venice Commission, Opinion on the constitutional situation (n 30) [80].

[39] Parliamentary Assembly (n 31).

[40] Christopher McCrudden and Brendan O'Leary, *Courts and Consociations: Human Rights versus Power-Sharing* (Oxford, Oxford University Press, 2013) 132.

ethnic group representation in federal structures.[41] These diametrically opposed positions have not changed since the delivery of the *Sejdić* judgment. Thus, in 2013, BiH politicians agreed on the 'principles for finding an agreement' to this constitutional conundrum, but subsequent negotiations fizzled out due to the inability of the parties to compromise.[42] In 2016, political parties sought to postpone the local elections until an agreement could be reached on *Sejdić*'s implementation and the relevant laws could be amended, but with no consensus among them, these were ultimately held on schedule.[43]

The prolonged non-compliance with the ECtHR's decision, despite the international community's pressure for implementation, reflects the 'absence of political will among the key actors to seriously address the issue'.[44] Problematically, this lack of political will for reform extends far beyond the electoral system. The international community was faced with similarly uncooperative actors, when, for instance, political elites demoted local officers who worked towards the reform of the police and replaced them with others who were more willing to serve their own agendas.[45] Highlighting the importance of political willingness in this respect, the US Department of Justice noted that 'the success of foreign assistance in promoting democratic policing is directly proportional to the country's enthusiasm for it'.[46] Undoubtedly, the lack of enthusiasm to implement human rights and reform problematic institutions has undermined peacebuilding efforts in the country. The parties' inability to reach a commonly agreed-upon compromise confirms (and further cements) the chasm between them and the sense of insecurity that one creates towards the other.[47] Moreover, the nationalist rhetoric that accompanies every failed attempt to negotiate constitutional amendments or implement police reform damages efforts to promote reconciliation. At the same time, and more specifically in relation to *Sejdić*'s non-enforcement, the ongoing disenfranchisement of a portion of the BiH population undermines justice. Finally, the maintenance of the current

[41] International Crisis Group, *Bosnia's Gordian Knot* (n 32) 7.

[42] European Stability Initiative, *Lost in the Bosnian Labyrinth: Why the Sejdić-Finci Case Should Not Block an EU Application* (Berlin/Brussels/Instanbul, European Stability Initiative, 2013) 2.

[43] Freedom House, 'Nations in Transit – Bosnia and Herzegovina Country Profile', available at freedomhouse.org/report/nations-transit/2017/bosnia-and-herzegovina.

[44] Hodzic and Stojanović (n 33) 33. For a similar conclusion reached half a decade later, see Valery Perry, 'Constitutional Reform Processes in Bosnia and Herzegovina: Top-down Failure, Bottom-up Potential, Continued Stalemate' in Soeren Keil and Valery Perry (eds), *State Building Democratization in Bosnia and Herzegovina* (Farnham, Ashgate, 2015) 15.

[45] Thomas Muehlmann, 'International Policing in Bosnia and Herzegovina: The Issue of Behavioural Reforms Lagging behind Structural Reforms, Including the Issue of Reengaging the Political Elite in a New System' (2007) 16 *European Security* 357, 384.

[46] David H Bayley, *Democratizing the Police Abroad: What to Do and How to Do it* (Washington DC, US Department of Justice, 2001) 35.

[47] Maria Ioannou, Nicolas Jarraud and Alexandros Lordos, 'The Bosnia SCORE: Measuring Peace in a Multi-ethnic Society' in Tabitha Morgan (ed), *Predicting Peace: The Social Cohesion and Reconciliation Index as a Tool for Conflict Transformation* (Cyprus, UNDP-Action for Cooperation and Trust, 2015).

electoral provisions, which guarantee reserved seats to specific ethnic groups at the expense of others, and the insistence among political elites that this 'pluralisation of ethnocracy'[48] is necessary for 'the establishment of peace and dialogue',[49] has an additional negative impact on reconciliation. It sends the divisive message that a constructive and safe political debate can only take place when people are represented by members of their ethnic group and ignores the detrimental effects that separating a population into pre-determined categories can have on efforts to develop a common national identity.[50]

The Cypriot and Bosnian voting cases confirm expectations that political willingness to implement human rights can promote peace, while its absence can have the opposite effect. Yet, the relationship between the two is more complex than this binary schema suggests, since it is not the case that the implementation of every human rights policy or decision leads to the promotion of peace. At times, human rights might be implemented, without this resulting in successful conflict resolution, while on other occasions, their enforcement can even impact peacebuilding efforts in a negative way. These instances are usually characterised by *some* political willingness to implement human rights that is not, however, sufficient to induce a sense of security, justice and reconciliation. Ultimately, therefore, political willingness is a matter of degree and if there is some, but not enough of it, this can hamper rather than promote conflict resolution.

An example of where the enforcement of human rights did not promote justice and reconciliation concerns the half-hearted efforts to protect the TCs right to property in the RoC-controlled part of Cyprus.[51] GCs and TCs had been living scattered around the island of Cyprus until the outbreak of the 1974 Turkish invasion, which resulted in a forcible population transfer and the geographical segregation of the two communities.[52] While under the 'TRNC' Constitution, GC displaced persons abandoned their properties in the north and therefore have no legal title to them,[53] the RoC claims that TCs who left their properties in the south of the island remain the rightful owners.[54] However, the claim continues, it is necessary for the 'Custodian', who is the RoC Minister of the Interior, to manage and protect these properties on behalf of TCs until 'the end of the abnormal situation in Cyprus'.[55] Despite the seemingly altruistic

[48] Hodzic and Stojanović (n 33) 15.

[49] *Sejdić* (n 27) [34].

[50] Avingail Eisenberg, 'Identity and Liberal Politics: The Problem of Minorities within Minorities' in Avigail Eisenberg and Jeff Spinner-Halev (eds), *Minorities within Minorities: Equality, Rights and Diversity* (Cambridge, Cambridge University Press, 2005).

[51] For background information on the property conflict in Cyprus, see section II.C in ch 4.

[52] International Crisis Group, *Cyprus: Bridging the Property Divide*, Europe Report N° 210 (Nicosia/Instanbul/Brussels, International Crisis Group, 2009) i.

[53] 'TRNC' Constitution, enacted on 15 May 1985, art 159.

[54] The Law Concerning Turkish-Cypriot Properties (Administration and Other Matters) (Temporary Provisions) of 1991 (Law 139/1991).

[55] ibid s 2. For more information on the Custodianship, see Nasia Hadjigeorgiou and Nikolas Kyriakou, 'Entrenching Hegemony in Cyprus: The Doctrine of Necessity and the Principle

motives of the RoC legislation, the legal impossibility of opting out of this system of protection meant that, in practice, TCs were prevented from accessing and controlling their properties, which resulted in possibly rights-violating situations. Thus, in 2010, the RoC introduced a series of amendments to the law that made it possible for TCs to apply for the return of their properties and opt out of the Custodianship regime.[56] These amendments were the result of a case, *Sofi v Cyprus*, that had been submitted to the ECtHR by a TC complaining about a violation of her right to property.[57] Recognising the vulnerability of its own legislation and presumably afraid that *Sofi* would be detrimental to its international reputation, the Republic settled and committed to amend the Custodianship provisions.[58] *Kazali v Cyprus*, a TC attempt to challenge this amended state of affairs as still being in violation of the right to property, was found to be inadmissible by the Court.[59]

Despite the ECtHR refusing to find that the amended Custodianship regime violates human rights, the current legal framework is unlikely to promote feelings of peace among the TC population. Since 2010, all TCs can technically apply to acquire control of their properties, but in fact, very few have been successful.[60] When the Custodian considers lifting his or her powers from a specific property, he takes a number of factors into account that, in practice, restrict access to justice for TCs. For instance, it is extremely unlikely that a TC who permanently lives in the non-RoC controlled area of the island will be successful in his or her application.[61] Moreover, in most situations where the Custodianship has been lifted, this was done on the condition that the property would be immediately sold, either to a GC buyer or to the RoC itself, thus preventing TCs from using their properties as they see fit and feeling truly remedied.[62] A sense of injustice is further heightened by the fact that even in situations where the property has been returned, no applicant has so far received any compensation for loss of use of his or her property since 1974.[63] However, a remedy that only applies to a

of Bi-communality' in Y Roznai and R Albert (eds), *Constitutionalism under Extreme Conditions: Law, Emergency, Exception* (New York, Springer, 2020 forthcoming).

[56] The Law Concerning Turkish-Cypriot Properties (Administration and Other Matters) (Temporary Provisions) (Amendment) of 2010 (Law 39(I)/2010), s 2.

[57] *Sofi v Cyprus* App No 18163/04 (ECtHR, 14 January 2010).

[58] Nasia Hadjigeorgiou, 'Case Note on *Kazali and Others v Cyprus*' (2013) 2 *Cyprus Human Rights Law Review* 103.

[59] *Kazali v Cyprus* App No 49247/08 (ECtHR, 6 March 2012).

[60] The government does not make statistics on this issue publicly available. According to statistics it disclosed to the Court in *Kazali* ((n 59) [88]), 32 applications were lodged between May 2010 and August 2011 and were put before the Custodian for decision. From these, inquiries were continuing in respect of 21. In the 11 concluded cases, the Custodianship was lifted in three and maintained in eight.

[61] Law 139/1991 (n 54), s 3.

[62] *Kazali* (n 59) [86], [87] and [137].

[63] This has been confirmed by the Office of the Custodian as standard practice; comments have also been made that there is no intention of changing this in the future (personal communication with the Ministry of the Interior on 5 June 2014).

small minority of potential applicants and is provided under such strict conditions, even if it has in principle been approved by the ECtHR, cannot contribute to successful conflict resolution. These limitations of the Custodianship legislation, and its consequent failure to promote peace, are not accidental; rather, they stem from the fact that the RoC government is unwilling to allow TCs to return to their houses, while the properties of GCs in the occupied areas are still unavailable to them.[64] Thus, despite some willingness on behalf of the RoC to comply with human rights in order to safeguard its international reputation, this was not present to a sufficient degree to make a real difference to feelings of justice among TCs.

An additional way in which human rights may negatively affect conflict resolution efforts is when states comply with them only partially, a phenomenon that has not received the attention it deserves among peacebuilders. States partially comply with a human rights decision if they unduly delay its implementation, adopt measures that do not address the essence of the violation or respond to some part, rather than the whole, of the court's judgment.[65] One explanation for this is that they might be prepared to take some action in redressing human rights violations, such as pay the financial award required by the judgment, but lack sufficient political willingness to engage in comprehensive reform,[66] like adopt any general measures.[67] Since the payment of compensation to a single applicant is less politically controversial than adopting far-reaching legislative or institutional changes, political willingness for the former is likely to be greater than for the latter. Yet, if comprehensive reform does not accompany the payment of compensation, this is unlikely to be an effective conflict resolution strategy.[68] Thus, although partial compliance is usually seen as a positive development since the respondent state has taken at least some steps in the correct direction,[69] it does not always follow that this also promotes peacebuilding efforts.

[64] In *Senay Mehmet v Republic of Cyprus* (Case No 713/2011) (RoC Supreme Court, 31 January 2013), the Court acknowledged that the Custodianship legislation resulted in injustice for the TC applicant, but justified this by referring to the consequences of the Turkish invasion and the importance of addressing the needs of displaced GCs.

[65] Darren Hawkins and Wade Jacoby, 'Partial Compliance: A Comparison of the European and Inter-American Courts of Human Rights' (2010) 6 *Journal of International Law and International Relations* 35, 38; Dia Anagnostou and Alina Mungiu-Pippidi, 'Domestic Implementation of Human Rights Judgments in Europe: Legal Infrastructure and Government Effectiveness Matter' (2014) 25 *European Journal of International Law* 205, 210; Philip Leach and Alice Donald, *Parliaments and the European Court of Human Rights* (Oxford, Oxford University Press, 2016) ch 3.

[66] Open Society Justice Initiative (n 7) 108, noting that: 'While implementation is virtually impossible without political will, degrees of political will often translate into degrees of implementation.'

[67] Leach and Donald (n 65) 102–03.

[68] Brandon Hamber, *Dealing with Painful Memories and Violent Pasts: Towards a Framework for Contextual Understanding* (Berghof Handbook Dialogue Series No 11, Berlin, Berghof Foundation, 2015).

[69] Hawkins and Jacoby (n 65).

An example of a state's partial compliance with a human rights decision, and the detrimental peacebuilding effects that followed, is Turkey's response to *Loizidou*, in which the ECtHR held that the presence of Turkish troops and the legislative framework in the occupied part of Cyprus prevented the applicant from using her property and constituted a violation of Article 1 of Protocol No 1 (the right to property).[70] While in 1998 the ECtHR ordered the payment of compensation amounting to approximately 450,000 Cypriot pounds within three months,[71] Turkey refused to comply with the judgment for years, until this was finally paid at the end of 2003.[72] Equally problematic was the fact that Turkey compensated Ms Loizidou at the same time as maintaining that the Court's decision was mistaken.[73] Considering that the payment of compensation generally signifies an apology on behalf of the respondent state,[74] the delay and Turkey's public statements possibly undermined feelings of justice, both of the applicant herself and the thousands of GCs who identified with her plight. Moreover, this has been made worse by the fact that although *Loizidou* is the first of a number of identical cases where the Court found a violation of the right to property, Turkey explicitly stated that the payment of compensation in this case did not set a precedent for all subsequent cases.[75] As a result, most victims whose case was heard and in which a violation was found by the ECtHR after *Loizidou* remain unremedied to this day.[76]

Finally, Turkey complied with the specific measures ordered by the Court in *Loizidou*, but is still ignoring its obligations in relation to more comprehensive reforms. This point has been made by the Committee of Ministers of the Council of Europe, which noted that 'payment of just satisfaction, although it is a great step forward in the implementation of the judgment of 1998, still does not, in fact, implement the basic context of the decision'.[77] Ms Loizidou's complaint was that the presence of Turkish troops in the non-RoC-controlled areas of

[70] *Loizidou v Turkey (Merits)* App No 15318/89 (ECtHR, 18 December 1996) [63] and [64].

[71] *Loizidou v Turkey (Article 50)* App No 15318/89 (ECtHR, 28 July 1998).

[72] Committee of Ministers, *Resolution Concerning the Judgment of the European Court of Human Rights of 28 July 1998 in the Loizidou Case against Turkey*, ResDH(2003)190 (Strasbourg, Council of Europe, 2 December 2003).

[73] BBC News, 'Turkey Compensates Cyprus Refugee' 2 December 2003.

[74] Dinah Shelton, *Remedies in International Human Rights Law*, 2nd edn (Oxford, Oxford University Press, 2006) 16–17.

[75] BBC News (n 73).

[76] See, eg, *Strati v Turkey* App No 16082/90 (ECtHR, 22 September 2009); and Committee of Ministers, *Interim Resolution: Execution of the Judgments of the European Court of Human Rights in the Cases Varnava, Xenides-Arestis and 32 Other Cases against Turkey*, CM/ResDH (2014)185 (Strasbourg, Council of Europe, 25 September 2014).

[77] Parliamentary Assembly, *Implementation of Decisions of the European Court of Human Rights by Turkey*, Resolution 1381 (Strasbourg, Council of Europe, 22 June 2004) [5]. The Court also implicitly acknowledged the fact that Turkey implemented only part of the judgment when it stated in a subsequent case that 'individuals claiming to own property in the north may, in theory, come to the Court periodically and indefinitely to claim loss of rents until a political solution to the Cyprus problem is reached'; *Demopoulos and Others v Turkey* App No 46113/99 (ECtHR, 1 March 2010) [111].

Cyprus prevented her from using and enjoying her property. Since this state of affairs continues, despite the payment of compensation, partially complying with the decision has not promoted security, justice or reconciliation within the GC community.[78] Turkey's political willingness to implement at least part of the judgment related to its efforts to push its EU accession process forward[79] and had little to do with building peace in Cyprus. Thus, while there was some willingness to protect human rights, this was not present to a sufficient degree to also lead to conflict resolution within the post-violence society.

Partial compliance with human rights does not only take place when decisions are delivered by international courts. Delays, for instance, have also been observed when BiH authorities were expected to implement domestic legislation and remedy victims for harm they suffered during the war.[80] The BiH legislature has passed a series of laws in this respect, such as the 2004 Law on Missing Persons, which establishes a fund for support of the families of missing persons,[81] and the 1999 Law on Principles on Social Protection, which includes provisions that seek to remedy 'civilian war victims' and those who were made disabled during, and by, the war.[82] However, despite the existence of these legal provisions, few of them have been implemented so far, which has resulted in a 'dismaying contrast between the advancements that have been achieved on paper … and what has actually changed for war victims on the ground'.[83] The ECtHR made note of these delays in a 2014 judgment when it referred to the Missing Persons Fund and the Central Record of Missing Persons, which had still not been established, some 10 years after the passing of the relevant law.[84] Yet, ignoring the demands of such a symbolically powerful category of stakeholders for a long period of time and delaying the remedying of past injustices has undoubtedly had detrimental effects on peacebuilding efforts, in that it has prevented the intended beneficiaries from leaving the conflict behind them.[85]

[78] Supportive of this are the Pinheiro Principles, which expressly provide that: 'States shall demonstrably prioritize the right to restitution as the preferred remedy for displacement and as a key element of restorative justice' (UN Sub-Commission on the Promotion and Protection of Human Rights, *Housing and Property Restitution in the Context of the Return of Refugees and Internally Displaced Persons*, E/CN4/Sub2/2005/17 (Geneva, United Nations, 28 June 2005), Principle 2.2).

[79] Ioannis Grigoriades, *The Trials of Europeanization: Turkish Political Cutlure and the European Union* (Basingstoke, Palgrave Macmillan, 2009) 80.

[80] There is no well-accepted definition of war victims in BiH. They include, inter alia, victims of international crimes and their families, relatives of missing persons and victims of sexual violence, with their numbers calculated to be in the tens of thousands. See Kate Clark, *War Reparations and Litigations: The Case of Bosnia,* International Litigation Series No 1 (Amsterdam, Nuhanovic Foundation Center for War Reparations, 2014) 11.

[81] Law on Missing Persons (Official Gazette of Bosnia and Herzegovina Law No 50/2004), art 15.

[82] Law on Principles of Social Protection, Protection of Civil Victims of War and Protection of Families with Children (Official Gazette of Bosnia and Herzegovina Law No. 36/1999), art 54.

[83] Clark (n 80) 53.

[84] *Mujkanović et al v Bosnia and Herzegovina* App No47063/08 (ECtHR, 3 June 2014) [41]. Notably in this case, the ECtHR refused to find a violation because although the state authorities had delayed setting up the relevant institutions, they had not been completely inactive.

[85] Peter van der Auweraert, *Reparations for Wartime Victims in the Former Yugoslavia: In Search of the Way Forward* (Geneva, International Organization for Migration, 2013) 13.

III. THE DEVIL IS IN THE DETAIL: THE IMPORTANCE OF CAREFUL DRAFTING

Since political willingness to implement human rights and political willingness to promote peace often coexist, but are not identical, it is best that when peacebuilders draft human rights legislation, they connect its provisions to the specific objectives of security, justice or reconciliation they are trying to achieve. This strategy of ensuring that human rights contribute to the building of peace by explicitly linking the two is so obvious that is almost tautological, yet it has often been ignored by peacebuilders, with detrimental effects for the post-violence society. Two examples, one from BiH and the other from SA, serve to illustrate this point. In the first example, the drafters of the BiH legislation did not articulate its objectives clearly, which sent confused messages to intended beneficiaries about the promotion of justice. Conversely, the objectives of the SA law were well-defined, but the specific legislative provisions intended to give effect to them were such that they could not achieve the intended goals, even if these were perfectly implemented. Both examples contrast with section 75 of the NI Act 1998, which is more likely to contribute to conflict resolution, since it both clearly articulates its intended peacebuilding objectives and creates specific duties on public authorities that can make them a reality. These examples suggest that in order for a human-rights inspired law to become an effective peacebuilding tool, it cannot only consist of vague standards and principles; rather, its provisions should be precise and tailored to achieve the peacebuilding goals that shaped it in the first place.[86]

Reference has already been made to the BiH legislature's attempts to remedy war victims through the establishment of the Missing Persons Fund. The previous section argued that the Fund has not contributed to peacebuilding efforts because of delays in its establishment. Yet, even if the Fund had been set up on time, it might still have been ineffective in promoting a sense of justice because of the legal requirements that war victims would have to satisfy in order to benefit from it. For instance, the 1999 Law on Principles of Social Protection that makes war victims entitled to social benefits applies not only to them, but also to other categories of recipients, such as the elderly, the unemployed, orphans and disabled people who are unable to work.[87] In addition to applying to a wide range of beneficiaries, a series of provisions limit the right of war victims to claim compensation by making its payment conditional on factors that are not related to their victim status per se. So, the compensation received by the spouse of a person who died as a result of the war is conditional on her not marrying again,[88] and the payment made to a family member caring for someone who was

[86] Urban Jonsson, 'A Human Rights-Based Approach to Programming' in Paul Gready and Jonathan Ensor (eds), *Reinventing Development? Translating Rights-Based Approaches from Theory into Practice* (London, Zed Books, 2005) 52.

[87] Clark (n 80) 27.

[88] Law No 36/1999 (n 82), art 76.

made disabled by the war is stopped whenever the person is temporarily placed in institutional care.[89]

These provisions send the message that the objective of the 1999 Law is not really to remedy war victims and therefore undo as much as possible the injustices of the past; rather, its objective seems to be the establishment of a social safety net for all categories of vulnerable people in the country, irrespective of whether their vulnerability is causally linked to the war. However, while both are valuable causes, the two should not be conflated. If post-violence justice is to be promoted, the response of the state must directly connect to, and address, those injustices that were caused by the violence itself, and not consider the victim's circumstances since then.[90] A widow whose husband was killed during the war and who remarried at a later stage is no less of a victim than someone who has decided not to do so. Likewise, a war victim should be entitled to a remedy for the harm he or she has suffered, regardless of whether that person has prospered financially since these injustices took place. It might be the case that a poor war victim, or a single parent, is in need of greater assistance from the state, and this should indeed be provided, but not by stripping a more affluent beneficiary from his or her victim status. A remedy, in the form of compensation or otherwise, is not just a way of providing material assistance from the state, but has symbolic significance since it acknowledges the harm suffered by the recipient.[91] Precisely because that harm is distinct from the difficulties faced by other vulnerable groups in the society, if the objective of the state is to promote post-violence justice, the provisions of the law should reflect this.[92] Thus, by merging its different responsibilities – remedying war victims on the one hand and protecting members of vulnerable groups on the other – the state failed to send a clear message that the necessary steps have been taken to promote *post-violence* justice rather than social justice in a more general sense.

In addition to making sure that the aims of a law are clear, one must also ensure that the content of specific legislative provisions is such that their implementation will lead to the achievement of these goals. In other words, it is necessary that the aims of the Act that are often expressed in its preamble or policy papers that preceded it accurately translate into, and are reflected by, the nitty-gritty of the law itself. If this does not happen, even the perfect implementation of the law will not contribute to the resolution of the conflict, which it claims to address. This has been the case with the Broad-Based Black Economic Empowerment (B-BBEE) programme in SA, whose stated objective is

[89] ibid art 74.

[90] Linda Popić and Belma Panjeta, *Compensation, Transitional Justice and Conditional Credit in Bosnia and Herzegovina: Attempts to Reform Government Payments to Victims and Veterans of the 1992–1995 War* (Amsterdam, Nuhanovic Foundation, 2010).

[91] Brandon Hamber and Richard A Wilson, 'Symbolic Closure through Memory, Reparation and Revenge in Post-conflict Societies' (2002) 1 *Journal of Human Rights* 35, 44.

[92] Clark (n 80) 29.

to empower those whose race had prevented them from accessing the country's productive resources and developing their skills during apartheid.[93] The scheme was implemented 'in order to promote the achievement of the constitutional right to equality',[94] an objective which was expected to contribute to the development of all three elements of peace. Such a programme was necessary for the promotion of security, the Department of Trade and Industry argued when launching B-BBEE, because wealth disparities, especially when coupled with a history of racism, resulted in socially and politically unstable societies and could pose a threat to democracy.[95] B-BBEE was also associated with the promotion of justice, since its adoption was a direct response to the injustices stemming from apartheid policies,[96] and reconciliation, which would be enhanced by empowering those who had been marginalised in the past.[97]

B-BBEE was first introduced with the passing of the B-BBEE Act 53 of 2003, which requires that all public bodies comply with Codes of Good Practice issued by the Minister of Trade and Industry.[98] The Codes have to be followed when public bodies issue licences, are involved in the sale of state-owned enterprises or enter into partnerships with the private sector,[99] and essentially provide that 'black enterprises' and 'black empowered enterprises' are given preferential treatment.[100] 'Black enterprises' are those that are 50.1 per cent owned by black individuals, while 'black-empowered enterprises' are 25.1 per cent-owned by blacks.[101] A 'black person', according to the Act, 'is a generic term which means Africans, Coloureds and Indians'.[102] The objective of these provisions is to create government-supported incentives for the empowerment of black individuals in a country, where all positions of power had historically been held by whites. Thus, the B-BBEE Act theoretically promotes equality among

[93] President Mbeki declared that the B-BBEE Act would 'promote the interests of the disadvantaged black community through job creation and skills development' (quoted in Roger Tangri and Roger Southall, 'The Politics of Black Economic Empowerment in South Africa' (2008) 34 *Journal of Southern African Studies* 699, 713–14).

[94] B-BBEE Act 53 of 2003, Preamble.

[95] Department of Trade and Industry, *South Africa's Economic Transformation: A Strategy for Broad-Based Black Economic Empowerment* (Pretoria, Department of Trade and Industry, 2003) [1.6]–[1.7].

[96] Department of Trade and Industry, *The National Broad-Based Black Economic Empowerment Summit: A Decade of Economic Empowerment*, 2003–13 Summit Report (Pretoria, Department of Trade and Industry, 2013) 7.

[97] B-BBEE Commission, *Strategy of the Broad-Based Black Economic Empowerment Commission, 2017–2021* (Pretoria, Department of Trade and Industry, 2017).

[98] B-BBEE Act (n 94), s 10. The 2003 Act has since then been amended by the B-BBEE Amendement Act 46 of 2013, which has retained the basic provisions and processes of its predecessor.

[99] B-BBEE Act (n 94), s 10.

[100] Elizabeth A Hoffman, 'A Wolf in Sheep's Clothing: Discrimination against the Majority Undermines Equality, While Continuing to Benefit Few under the Guise of Black Economic Empowerment' (2008–09) 36 *Syracuse Journal of International Law and Commerce* 87, 94.

[101] (n 95), Appendix B – Definitions of Black Empowerment Entities, paras 1 and 2 respectively.

[102] B-BBEE Act (n 94), s 1.

racial groups and contributes to each of the elements of peace by ensuring that a sizeable proportion of managerial positions in companies that comply with the scheme is held by blacks.[103] In turn, this racialised understanding of trickle-down economics is expected to accommodate 'the needs of the masses' by involving blacks in the wealth-generation process.[104]

This scheme has, by and large, been a failure. While in principle, its objective is to promote equality, which, in turn, will help build peace in the country, more than 15 years since the passing of the B-BBEE Act, and despite the country's considerable wealth, SA has a Gini coefficient of 0.69, one of the highest in the world.[105] This failure is not because the Act has not been properly implemented; rather, it is because despite pronouncements to the contrary, its legislative provisions are not, in fact, concerned with the promotion of security, justice or reconciliation. The rhetoric of B-BBEE might claim that all SAs are equal, but the detail of the law suggests that those select few who have the skills and connections to be appointed to the management boards of large corporations, are more equal than others. In a country with more than 27 per cent unemployment,[106] what would have empowered the masses and allowed them to overcome the economic injustices of apartheid is the creation of new jobs and the provision of proper training to the unemployed.[107] Yet, B-BBEE did not create – and was not designed to create – *any* new jobs. Instead, it produced a tiny group of 'black diamonds', mega-rich black people sitting as directors or holding shares in multiple black or black-empowered companies, while doing nothing to address the injustices faced by the general public.[108] As Tangri and Southall put it, it is difficult to see 'how deals involving extremely wealthy and well-connected persons can possibly be called empowerment deals'.[109] Therefore, no matter how successfully the provisions of the Act are implemented, their content will always make them unable to promote any of the elements of peace.

The BiH and SA statutes contrast with the equality legislation in NI, which both clearly articulates its peacebuilding objectives and includes provisions that, when implemented, can successfully promote these. This is partly because the relevant provisions of the NI Act are the development of previous equality laws,

[103] The scheme is not legally binding and, as a result, companies that are not relying on government contracts, such as those in the tourism and retail industries, have not complied with it; Tangri and Southall (n 93) 707. Moreover, the Act's provisions do not apply to smaller companies that are excluded from these obligations by automatically being labelled as 'Level Four Contributors' with a B-BBEE recognition of 100 per cent in order to allow their owners to focus on making them profitable; see Department of Trade and Industry, *Code of Good Practice 2013, Issued under Section 9 of the Broad-Based Black Economic Empowerment Act of 2003,* No 36928 (Pretoria, Department of Trade and Industry, 2013) [4.1] and [4.2].

[104] African National Congress leader Saki Macozoma, quoted in Tangri and Southall (n 93) 714.

[105] B-BBEE Commission (n 97) 5. A Gini-coefficient is an indicator of inequality within countries, with the lowest value being 0 and the highest 1.

[106] South Africa Statistics Official Website, available at www.statssa.gov.za/?page_id=735&id=1.

[107] Hoffman (n 100) 103.

[108] ibid 101.

[109] Tangri and Southall (n 93) 709.

the rationale and drafting of which, politicians have revisited over the years in order to make them more effective. The first attempt to promote equality was the passing of the NI Constitution Act 1973, which made it unlawful for public authorities to discriminate, or aid someone in discriminating, against another person on the grounds of religious belief or political opinion.[110] This Act had done little to enhance security, justice or reconciliation among the population, as evidenced by the continuation of the violence until the end of the 1990s. Among its deficiencies was the fact that it was largely confined to direct discrimination in the religio-political context and therefore only applied to a very limited number of cases.[111]

Since then, there has been a growing appreciation that what is needed to build peace in NI is the adoption of broader policies of equality.[112] Thus, although the provisions of the 1973 Act have been included, almost unchanged, in the NI Act 1998,[113] they have also been substantially reinforced through the addition of legal duties that seek to mainstream equality. In particular, section 75 of the 1998 Act has two broad objectives, both of which are clearly articulated and directly connect to peacebuilding efforts. Section 75(1) seeks to promote justice by creating an obligation on public authorities 'to have due regard to the need to promote equality of opportunity' and section 75(2) enhances reconciliation through the duty to promote 'good relations between persons of different religious belief, political opinion or racial group'. It is encouraging that over the years, there has been an increasingly nuanced understanding of how these duties connect to each other and to peacebuilding efforts more generally. While originally an assumption existed that the promotion of equality of opportunity was almost synonymous with the promotion of good relations,[114] it has now been appreciated that the two might also contradict each other.[115] This insight, which suggests that sometimes distinct measures will have to be adopted for the promotion of each objective, directly mirrors the mechanics of the proposed definition of peace.

Also important is the fact that the law has been drafted in such a way that, when implemented, its provisions can indeed contribute to these articulated

[110] NI Constitution Act 1973, art 19(1).

[111] Christopher McCrudden, 'Mainstreaming Equality in the Governance of Northern Ireland' (1998–99) 22 *Fordham International Law Journal* 1696, 1705.

[112] Colin Harvey, 'Contextualised Equality and the Politics of Legal Mobilisation: Affirmative Action in Northern Ireland' (2012) 21 *Social & Legal Studies* 23, 27.

[113] NI Act 1998, s 76.

[114] The inter-dependence of equality and good relations was articulated in the NI Programme of Government, quoted in Joanne Hughes and Caitlin Donnelly, 'Community Relations in Northern Ireland: A Shift in Attitudes?' (2003) 29 *Journal of Ethnic and Migration Studies* 643, 659. It states that: 'The protection of human rights and the provision of equality are central to the Agreement. These policies are prerequisites for improving community relations and building community capacity, particularly in areas of greatest need.'

[115] Roz Goldie, 'Law and the Politics of Promoting Equality and Good Relations in the Northern Ireland Peace Process' (Quest Proceedings of the Queen's University Belfast AHSS Conference, June 2008) 233.

objectives. Schedule 9, which includes detailed guidelines for the enforcement of section 75, requires that all public bodies adopt equality schemes that explain, using timelines and numerical goals, how they will promote equality through their operations.[116] The consultation procedure that should precede the drafting of each equality scheme requires input from non-governmental organisations, such as community groups, pressure groups and unions.[117] It is, of course, not the case that the mere existence of the objectives under section 75 and the clearly drafted procedure in Schedule 9 will in themselves help build peace. As the following section suggests, in order for that to happen, it is also necessary that the Equality Commission for Northern Ireland (hereinafter ECNI or Commission), which has been tasked with reviewing the public bodies' actions under section 75, has, among other things, the power to properly respond to cases of non-compliance with the Act.[118] In this respect, the drafting of the 1998 Act can be improved further, since although Schedule 9 creates an obligation on public authorities to review their equality schemes within five years of their first submission and inform the ECNI of the outcome of this review,[119] it is not clear what, if anything, the Commission must do with this information.[120] By and large, however, section 75 has been drafted in such a way that when enforced, its peacebuilding contribution is likely to be a positive one.

IV. LOOKING BEYOND THE WORDING OF THE STATUTE: HUMAN RIGHTS BODIES AND THEIR POWERS

Additional factors that influence the implementation and peacebuilding potential of human rights are the independence, powers, expertise and resources of the institutions responsible for their enforcement.[121] The importance of human rights institutions in the peacebuilding process has already been acknowledged both in the theoretical literature and seminal UN reports. Bell, for instance, explains the failure of the Dayton Agreement to promote peace in BiH by highlighting the fact that negotiators 'gave little thought to institutional questions

[116] NI Act (n 113), sched 9, s 2.

[117] ibid sched 9, s 9(2); McCrudden (n 111) 1771.

[118] NI Act (n 113), sched 9, s 1(a).

[119] ibid sched 9, s 8(3).

[120] Brice Dickson and Colin Harvey, *Assessing the Role of the Equality Commission in the Effectiveness of Section 75 of the Northern Ireland Act 1998* (Belfast, Human Rights Centre, School of Law, Queen's University Belfast, 2006) 84.

[121] See UN General Assembly Resolution 48/134 (20 December 1993), 'National Institutions for the Promotion and Protection of Human Rights', art 2, which '[r]eaffirms the importance of developing, in accordance with national legislation, effective national institutions for the promotion and protection of human rights'. The bureaucratic weaknesses of the state that make change in post-violence societies difficult to achieve are also explored in Padraig McAuliffe, *Transformative Transitional Justice and the Malleability of Post-conflict States* (Cheltenham, Edward Elgar, 2017) 202–05 and 216–17.

of implementation' of human rights.[122] Even more explicit is Parlevliet, who concludes that 'if human rights are to have meaning beyond the paper they are written on, conflict transformation must involve the development of legitimate, independent and capable institutions'.[123] Similarly, the UN notes that: 'Effective strategies for building domestic justice systems will give due attention to laws, processes (both formal and informal) and institutions (both official and non-official).'[124] This section confirms these findings, suggesting that two post-violence societies may adopt laws with similar objectives and wording, but the different characteristics of human rights institutions in each will affect the level of compliance with these provisions. Moreover, it makes the point that the inability of an institution to comply with its mandate can result in non-compliance, but more often tends to manifest as partial compliance. After all, '[l]ow capacity state bureaucracies struggling to understand and comply with international rules are unlikely to be utterly incompetent and devoid of resources'.[125] This conclusion deserves attention because, as was argued in section II above, partial compliance can be as detrimental to peacebuilding efforts as the complete lack of implementation.

Supporting the argument that the characteristics of human rights institutions play an important role in conflict resolution is the contrast between the implementation of similar policies adopted in SA and NI. In both instances, past injustices had resulted in inequalities in the workplace among different religious and racial groups, with the two policies being attempts by the respective governments to respond to these.[126] Both laws impose positive duties on employers to promote equality in the workplace and task a specific institution to ensure that these duties are properly enforced. In SA, the Employment Equity Act No 55 of 1998 applies to designated employers, who are defined as those who employ more than 50 people or are a public authority.[127] It creates an obligation on them to implement affirmative action measures,[128] ensuring that suitably qualified

[122] Bell (n 1) 228.

[123] Parlevliet (n 17) 9.

[124] UN Secretary-General (n 2) [35].

[125] Hawkins and Jacoby (n 65) 42. See also Alice Donald and Elizabeth Mottershaw, 'Evaluating the Impact of Human Rights Litigation on Policy and Practice: A Case Study of the UK' (2009) 1 *Journal of Human Rights Practice* 339, 354, noting that: 'It is rarely as straightforward as a public authority saying it cannot afford to implement case law; rather, limitations on resources and capacity create different dynamics in relation to how case law affects policy and practice.'

[126] The preamble of the SA Act makes explicit reference to apartheid and to the need to address the inequalities that were created because of past discriminatory practices. Moreover, the ANC expressly linked the promotion of equality with the element of justice when it declared that one of its policy objectives was 'to overcome the legacy of *inequality and injustice* created by colonialism and apartheid' (African National Congress, *Ready to Govern: ANC Policy Guidelines for a Democratic South Africa* (National Conference 28–31 May 1992, African National Congress), emphasis added). In relation to the objectives of the NI affirmative action legislation, see Harvey (n 112).

[127] Employment Equity Act No 55 of 1998, s 1.

[128] ibid s 13.

members of the designated groups[129] have equal opportunities and are equitably represented in high-ranking occupational categories in the workforce.[130] Employers must describe these affirmative action measures in Employment Equity Plans,[131] which are reported to the Department of Labour either on an annual or bi-annual basis, depending on the employer's size.[132] Similarly, in NI, the Fair Employment and Treatment Order (FETO or Order) 1998 creates an obligation on entities employing more than 10 individuals[133] to report to the ECNI the 'community' of their employees[134] and, in cases where the numbers suggest that members of one community are not enjoying 'fair participation' in employment, suggest the adoption of affirmative action as a response to this problem.[135] In both societies, the enforcement bodies – the SA Department of Labour and the ECNI – have powers to ensure that employers comply with their obligations and impose penalties if they do not. The main substantive difference between the two schemes is that, while the SA law allows for the adoption of quotas in order to encourage the employment of those who fall within the designated groups,[136] the NI Order explicitly prohibits the use of this method and relies on softer measures.[137]

Despite the similarities in the two pieces of legislation, they have in fact resulted in very different outcomes. On the one hand, the (SA) Employment Equity Act has mostly been unsuccessful in achieving its objective to 'promote the constitutional right to equality'.[138] Between 1997, the year before the Act came into operation, and 2006, the only designated race group whose employment rate increased was African,[139] yet this was also the only group that had a negative growth rate in its salary during the same period.[140] By 2016, the percentages of whites in managerial and skilled positions continued decreasing slightly compared to previous years,[141] but the labour market remained segmented, with the majority of blacks and coloureds* being employed by the

[129] ibid s 1. The designated groups covered by the Act are 'black people, women and people with disabilities'. The Act clarifies that 'black people' is 'a generic term which means Africans, Coloureds and Indians'.

[130] ibid s 15.

[131] ibid s 20.

[132] ibid s 21(1) and 21(2).

[133] FETO 1998, art 48(2).

[134] ibid art 53. In other words, if they are Protestant or Roman Catholic.

[135] ibid art 55.

[136] Employment Equity Act (n 127), ss 13 and 15.

[137] ECNI, *Fair Employment in Northern Ireland: Code of Practice* (Belfast, Equality Commission for Northern Ireland, date unknown).

[138] Employment Equity Act (n 127), Preamble.

[139] Rulof Burger and Rachel Jafta, 'Affirmative Action in South Africa: An Empirical Assessment of the Impact on Labour Market Outcomes', CRISE Working Paper No 76 (Oxford, Centre for Research on Inequality, Human Security and Ethnicity, University of Oxford, 2010) 13.

[140] ibid 15.

[141] The decrease is between 0.7 per cent (at the skilled technical level) and 3.9 per cent (at the professionally qualified level). See Commission for Employment Equity, *Annual Report 2015–2016* (Pretoria, Department of Labour, 2016) 78.

* See footnote (*), p 12.

government, and most private company skilled positions being retained for whites and Indians.[142] Conversely, the (NI) FETO has had positive results, with the gap between Catholics in monitored employment and those available for work consistently dropping year after year.[143] Employment equity has been promoted in all industries, with cases of near-total segregation becoming much rarer.[144] Most impressively, while in 2000 the majority of firms in the services sector were highly segregated, by the end of the decade, a near-majority had mixed workforces.[145] It therefore appears that the NI Order has promoted an objective sense of justice to a greater extent than the SA Act. These differences are arguably not the result of disparities in political willingness to protect human rights and cannot be explained by differences in the drafting of the two pieces of legislation; rather, they have to do with the independence, powers and strategies adopted by the enforcement body in each society.

Both the SA Department of Labour and the ECNI have been tasked with ensuring that employers adopt measures that encourage the occupation of under-represented groups, and in both instances, 'employers' include not only larger private companies, but also governmental departments. In order for a body to monitor whether this is in fact happening and to take action against those who are not complying with their statutory duties, it is necessary that it is itself independent from those it supervises.[146] The UN has argued that such 'institutional independence' requires legal and operational autonomy from other governmental bodies,[147] independence in terms of the institution's funding[148] and the appointment and dismissal of its members.[149] On the one hand, the ECNI enjoys such independence, since it is itself a 'non-departmental public body',[150] its funding is regulated by the statute that established it[151] and its members, who are directly appointed by the Secretary of State, have tenure.[152]

[142] ibid 79.

[143] ECNI, *Fair Employment Monitoring: Compositon of Employment – Trends over Time* (Belfast, Equality Commission for Northern Ireland, 2013) 13. The reference to Catholics here is because, in most cases, they are the underrepresented group in employment. See Secretary of State for Northern Ireland, *White Paper – Partnership for Equality: The Government's Proposals for Future Legislation and Policies on Employment Equality in Northern Ireland*, Cm 3890 (London, Secretary of State for Northern Ireland, 1998) [1.5].

[144] Christopher McCrudden, Robert Ford and Anthony Heath, 'Legal Regulation of Affirmative Action in Northern Ireland' (2004) 24 *Oxford Journal of Legal Studies* 363, 389.

[145] ibid.

[146] Linda C Reif, 'Building Democratic Institutions: The Role of National Human Rights Institutions in Good Governance and Human Rights Protection' (2000) 13 *Harvard Human Rights Journal* 1.

[147] UN Centre for Human Rights, *National Human Rights Institutions: A Handbook on the Establishment and Strengthening of National Institutions for the Promotion and Protection of Human Rights*, Professional Training Series No 4 (New York, United Nations, 1995) [70].

[148] ibid [74].

[149] ibid [78] and [80].

[150] ECNI Official Website, 'About Us', www.equalityni.org/AboutUs.

[151] NI Act (n 113), ss 3, 6 and 7 of sched 8.

[152] ibid s 73(2) and s 2 of sched 8.

Conversely, while an independent Commission for Employment Equity has been established by the (SA) Employment Equity Act,[153] this has a more limited role than the ECNI, since its functions are restricted to advising the Minister of Labour on the drafting of Codes, regulations and policies on matters concerning the Act.[154] The more day-to-day implementation of the equality legislation is left to labour inspectors,[155] who are employees of the Ministry of Labour and therefore do not enjoy any of the independence that is necessary for them to fulfil their functions.[156] In this regard, it may be unsurprising that in 2005, it was reported that 25 municipalities, 13 provincial government departments, nine national government departments, the SA Parliament and the Director of Public Prosecutions did not submit their Employment Equity reports to the Department of Labour.[157] This failure to comply with reporting obligations does not necessarily provide evidence of high-level political unwillingness to implement the law; rather, it could stem from underfunding of these institutions, which prevents them from carrying out all their statutory duties or, alternatively, from resistance to comply with the Act by individual (mid-level) spoilers. However, the fact remains that the lack of independence of the Department of Labour from some of the very institutions it is tasked to review, as they are all parts of the executive, results in possible conflicts of interest. In turn, this makes it less likely that the Department will push for the protection of the right to equality and contribute to the promotion of justice in the process.

The second factor that affects an institution's ability to successfully implement human rights is whether it has been given sufficient powers to undertake its task – and understands itself as being in possession of these. 'Power', according to the UN's guidance, 'refers to the ability of a national institution to perform a certain act or to compel such performance by an individual or other entity' and includes 'the imposition of legal and administrative sanctions when the free exercise of a national institution's powers is obstructed'.[158] Whether such power is adequate depends on the functions that the institution has to perform,[159] which in this case are quite comparable between the two jurisdictions. In SA, the Department of Labour has to ensure that employers are 'implementing affirmative action measures to redress the disadvantages in employment experienced by designated groups, in order to ensure their equitable representation in all occupational categories and levels in the workforce'.[160] Similarly, the ECNI

[153] Employment Equity Act (n 127), s 26.

[154] ibid s 30.

[155] ibid s 36.

[156] Basic Conditions of Employment Act No 75 of 1997, s 63.

[157] Andries Bezuidenhout et al, *Tracking Progress on the Implementation and Impact of the Employment Equity Act since Its Inception*, Research Consortium: Human Science Research Council, Development Policy Research Unit, Sociology of Work Unit (Johannesburg, Research Commissioned by Department of Labour South Africa, 2008) 24.

[158] UN Centre for Human Rights (n 147) [95].

[159] ibid [96].

[160] Employment Equity Act (n 127), s 2(b).

is responsible for 'eliminating discrimination based on religion or political opinion, and promoting greater equality [in the workplace] between all sections of the population in Northern Ireland'.[161] Arguably, however, neither the powers given to the SA Ministry of Labour nor the way it has interpreted these are sufficient to meet the Act's objectives and 'promote equality in the workplace'.[162] Since the duties listed in the Employment Equity Act only apply to public bodies and private companies that employ more than 50 people,[163] the vast majority of employers – 88 per cent of companies, which contribute 33 per cent to the gross domestic product – do not have to report to the Department of Labour at all, or adopt any affirmative action measures.[164] As a result, both the Department's powers of obtaining an accurate picture of the levels of employment equity in the country and the impact of the Act, through seemingly far-reaching positive obligations, are curtailed. This is in contrast to the powers of the ECNI, which can monitor the employment practices of all companies that employ 10 people or more, and has even encouraged smaller entities that do not officially have to comply with the FETO to follow its recommendations.[165]

Also problematic in this respect is the fact that the SA Ministry of Labour has interpreted its powers narrowly to include only the collection of information about the measures adopted by the designated companies rather than also engaging with this information in a productive manner. As a result, it has failed to offer guidance to individual designated employers on the best way to promote equality in the workplace, has missed the opportunity to facilitate the sharing of good practices and has left employers guessing what steps they should be adopting in order to comply with their statutory obligations. Thus, companies have received no help from the authorities when being called upon to draft and implement their Employment Equity Plans,[166] which has arguably resulted in the adoption of inadequate or inappropriate affirmative action measures.[167] Similarly lacking is the guidance from Ministry officials to designated employers on a one-to-one basis. Although Ministry officials are empowered under the Act to carry out inspections of designated employers,[168] very few of these have actually taken place in practice.[169] Even in one case where such an inspection had taken place, the Labour Court held that the Department's recommendation with regard to the filling of the Equality Employment Plan was 'cryptic' and did not offer the employer in question any meaningful guidance.[170]

[161] Secretary of State for Northern Ireland (n 143) [1.1].
[162] Employment Equity Act (n 127), s 2(b).
[163] ibid s 1.
[164] Burger and Jafta (n 139) 8.
[165] ECNI (n 137) [5.2.2].
[166] Bezuidenhout et al (n 157) 21.
[167] Lize Booysen, 'Barriers to Employment Equity Implementation and Retention of Blacks on Management in South Africa' (2007) 31 *South African Journal of Labour Relations* 47.
[168] Employment Equity Act (n 127), s 35.
[169] Bezuidenhout et al (n 157) 18.
[170] *Director General of the Department of Labour and Another v Comair Ltd* (J 2326/07) (SA Labour Court, 11 August 2009) [42].

An equally narrow interpretation of its powers has been adopted by the (SA) Commission for Employment Equity. While the 1998 Act created a responsibility on the Commission to draft Codes of Good Practice that would provide guidance to employers,[171] the first 'Draft Code of Good Practice on the Preparation and Implementation of Employment Equity Plan' was only published in 2016.[172] This provides broad recommendations that could be useful to employers when drafting their Plans,[173] but many of these had already been included in the Act itself,[174] other parts are excessively general,[175] and no mention is made of affirmative action examples that have already proven effective and could be adopted by employers. Finally, little guidance seems to exist as to the specific goals that employers should be working towards. The Commission has the power to report to the Minister of Labour 'well-researched norms and benchmarks for the setting of numerical goals in various sectors', yet no such benchmarks or goals are included in the Code of Good Practice.[176] Instead, the Commission's Annual Reports rely on statistics, divided by gender and race, of the economically active population of SA and merely state that employers should use these as guides as to what they should strive towards.[177] No acknowledgement is made of the fact that because of past injustices, members of certain groups may be better trained for highly skilled positions than others, which shifts the responsibility to the employers to attract and retain those few sought-after individuals who have both the expertise to do the job and the racial profile to meet the Act's demands.[178] However, the authorities' neglect in providing any practical guidance on how best to comply with the Act makes it more likely that employers will either ignore their obligations altogether or adopt little thought-out affirmative action measures in order to get this exercise over and done with.

In contrast, the ECNI interpreted its powers very differently and has, as a result, produced detailed recommendations on the best ways of promoting

[171] Employment Equity Act (n 127), s 30(1)(a).

[172] Department of Labour, *Employment Equity Act 1988 (Act 55 of 1998 as Amended) Draft Code of Good Practice on the Preparation and Implementation of Employment Equity Plan* (Pretoria, Department of Labour, 2016).

[173] Such as factors that should be considered when identifying barriers that impede designated groups from being equitably represented in the workplace (ibid [6.1.3.3]).

[174] eg, the requirement that a manager should be assigned for the implementation of the Equity Employment Plan (included in s 24 of the Employment Equity Act and Department of Labour, (n 172) [6.1.1]) or that the Plan must be preceded by a consultation exercise with employees (included in ss 16 and 17 of the Employment Equity Act and Department of Labour, (n 172) [6.1.2.2] and [6.1.2.5]).

[175] The only reference made to the resources needed for the implementation of the Plan is that '[r]esources must be appropriately allocated, including human resources, financial resources and material resources' (Department of Labour, *Employment Equity Act 1988 Draft Code of Good Practice* [7.7]).

[176] Employment Equity Act (n 127), s 30.

[177] Commission for Employment Equity (n 141) 12.

[178] Booysen (n 167) 50.

equality in the workplace. In turn, this has made it easier for employers to meet their obligations and promote greater employment equity, and therefore justice, in the country. Thus, the Commission encourages employers to consult with it if they have any questions about the monitoring process or the types of affirmative action measures they can adopt.[179] This one-to-one consultation is additional to the already detailed guidance that is provided in the ECNI's Code of Practice, which includes information both about the employer's monitoring obligations and the adoption of affirmative action measures if these are deemed necessary. For instance, the Code explains who is to be considered an employee of a company,[180] how employers are to collect information about their employees' 'community background' and what they should be careful about when undertaking this task,[181] while also offering examples of affirmative action measures that employers can consider.[182] Finally, compared to the methodology adopted in the SA Annual Reports, the NI Code of Practice relies on a more nuanced understanding of what employers should be striving towards. It notes that:

> What is not required is that the proportionate distribution of Protestants and Roman Catholics in the population as a whole should be automatically reflected in every job category, occupation or position in each undertaking throughout the province. That is quite unrealistic; and obviously it is accepted that the realities of each specific location need to be addressed in framing appropriate affirmative action measures.[183]

In addition to guiding employers, attention should be paid to the powers of enforcement bodies to ensure that their decisions are complied with. In both countries, the respective institutions can impose fines on those that do not respect their statutory obligations[184] and also resort to courts when employers ignore their recommendations.[185] In NI, an employer's failure to respect his or her reporting obligations or follow the ECNI's guidance are criminal offences, which carry heavy fines that increase for each day the non-compliance continues.[186] Moreover, in the event that a public authority does not follow the law, the ECNI has the power to send a report to the Minister the authority reports to, who in turn must ensure that it fulfils its statutory obligations.[187] At the same time, the ECNI can enter into voluntary but legally binding agreements

[179] ECNI (n 137) [1.2.3].
[180] ibid [6.1.10].
[181] ibid [6.2.10] and [6.2.27]–[6.2.39].
[182] ibid [6.5].
[183] ibid [6.5.7].
[184] For SA, see Employment Equity Act (n 127), sched 1 (listing the maximum amount an employer can be fined). For NI, see ECNI (n 137) Appendix (listing the criminal offences that non-compliance with the FETO can give rise to and their respective fines).
[185] The Labour Court in the case of SA (Employment Equity Act (n 127), s 37(7)) and the Employment Tribunal for NI (ECNI (n 137) [4.3.3]).
[186] ECNI (n 137) Appendix.
[187] ibid.

concerning the affirmative action measures that will be adopted by individual employers.[188] These agreements, which avoid the inconvenience, cost and delay of formal investigations and the need to apply to the Employment Tribunal in the event of non-compliance,[189] have been taken seriously by employers and have resulted in the adoption of effective strategies promoting fair participation in the workplace.[190] Conversely, the Ministry of Labour in SA, which until recently had exclusively relied on fines in order to encourage implementation, commands more limited enforcement powers. Before the adoption of a 2013 amendment, these fines were insubstantial and, unlike those imposed by the Competition Commission in the country, did not reflect the employer's turnover and could not be gradually increased.[191] As a result, especially large companies were not deterred by the threat of a fine and some even budgeted for such a possibility,[192] which reflected the lack of seriousness with which they viewed their statutory obligations. It remains to be seen whether the 2013 amendments (that increased the maximum fine for an offence and altered the method of calculation to take into account the employer's turnover) will contribute to the effective implementation of the Act and the promotion of justice in the country.[193]

The final factor that affects human rights enforcement is the overall strategy that the relevant institution adopts. For instance, affirmative action, particularly where this includes the use of quotas, as in the case of SA, is controversial and likely to result in pushback from middle-management employees, who are usually both the ones asked to implement such policies and who have the most to lose by empowering the competition.[194] Thus, especially when strong enforcement powers are absent, it makes more sense to convince rather than coerce employers and employees to comply with their statutory obligations. This was the approach adopted from the outset by the ECNI, which argued that: 'Equality of opportunity in employment makes good business sense. It broadens the recruitment base and widens the choice of personnel; it also enhances the probity of a company's personnel practices and improves corporate image.'[195] Conversely, the original approach adopted by the Commission of Employment Equity was to coerce employers in carrying out their duties under the Act,[196]

[188] ibid [6.3.17].
[189] ibid [6.3.18].
[190] McCrudden, Ford and Heath (n 144).
[191] Bezuidenhout et al (n 157) 25.
[192] ibid.
[193] Employment Equity Amendment Act 37 of 2013, sched 1.
[194] Booysen (n 167)56.
[195] ECNI (n 137) [5.2.1].
[196] See, eg, Commission for Employment Equity, *Annual Report 2005–2006* (Pretoria, Department of Labour, 2006) 59, where the Department of Labour, adopting a strict implementation approach, argues that 'the unwillingness of corporate South Africa to embrace the transformation agenda leaves very little room to introduce some sort of deregulation in the employment equity environment, which leaves little or no sympathy for the outcry by organised business for the EE targets in the BBBEE Codes being too aggressive'.

disregarding the fact that it did not have the necessary powers or financial resources to police them into action.[197] Perhaps acknowledging the failure of its strategy, the Commission has more recently started emphasising the fact that 'Transformation Makes Business Sense'[198] and has opted to award employers that excel in capturing the true spirit of the Act's objectives rather than merely punishing those that ignore it.[199] Notably, this reflects a change in the strategy rather than the powers of the Commission, which could 'make awards recognising achievements of employers in furthering the purpose of this Act' from its inception, but chose not to.[200]

The ability to devise and carry out an effective implementation strategy depends both on the expertise of those staffing the relevant institution and on the resources that are available to them.[201] For example, choosing to monitor only procedural compliance with statutory obligations could reflect a lack of resources and adequate expertise to ensure substantive implementation of the law rather than disinterest in the protection of human rights and promotion of the objectives of the Act. After all, it is no coincidence that the biggest and most successful human rights institutions in the world have been established in the developed countries of Europe, North America and Australiasia.[202] Governments experiencing severe economic difficulties, a situation that is often the case in post-violence societies, are likely to opt for less ambitious implementation strategies because these may be the only ones they can afford. As McAuliffe put it when exploring the limitations of certain institutions in inducing socio-economic change in post-violence societies: 'However willing may be the spirit, the flesh interpreted in terms of power, organizational capacity and know-how, is weak.'[203] In this respect, the ECNI is unique since its location in Europe and constitutional status as a UK public body have provided it with considerable funding and expertise.[204] As a result, it has been able to adopt an in-depth assessment of each employer's affirmative action plan and substantively engage with it. It has also stressed the importance of employers liaising with it when reviewing their recruitment, training and promotion practices,

[197] Emma Fergus and Debbie Collier, 'Equality at Work: The Role of the Judiciary in Promoting Transformation' (2014) 30 *South African Journal on Human Rights* 484, 499 makes reference to two cases where, although the Labour Court confirmed the Department of Labour's recommendations to the designated employers, neither organisation complied with its statutory obligations.

[198] Commission for Employment Equity (n 141) 1.

[199] ibid 7.

[200] Employment Equity Act (n 127), s 30(2)(a).

[201] UN Centre for Human Rights (n 147) [119]–[123].

[202] ibid [123].

[203] McAuliffe (n 121) 54.

[204] Nevin T Aiken, 'Learning to Live Together: Transitional Justice and Intergroup Reconciliation in Northern Ireland' (2010) 4 *International Journal of Transitional Justice* 166; John D Brewer, *Peace Processes: A Sociological Approach* (Cambridge, Polity Press, 2010) 169.

and informed them of its duty to assist and offer advice to them during this process.[205] This contrasts with the approach adopted in SA, where Ministry officials have expressly cited strict budgetary restraints as the reason for their strategic decision to focus on procedural rather than substantive compliance.[206]

V. STRATEGIES FOR BETTER HUMAN RIGHTS IMPLEMENTATION

The conditions outlined in sections II, III and IV above are significant because the *reason* that a human rights law or policy is unable to help build objective peace – in other words, whether its non-implementation is due to lack of political willingness, bad legislative drafting or limited institutional capacity – affects the response that peacebuilders should adopt.[207] Two of the most popular responses in such situations are the involvement of the international community[208] and the strengthening of civil society,[209] with one imposing outside pressure for the implementation of human rights and the other pushing from the grassroots up. This section examines both strategies and argues that each can assist peacebuilders in distinct ways, depending on the challenge being addressed. If the problem is a lack of political willingness, the international community can exert pressure on unwilling politicians to support the human rights policy. In such instances, civil society organisations can also push for human rights implementation through lobbying or mass demonstrations, thus increasing political costs for actors who refuse to support peacebuilding initiatives. Alternatively, if the problem is a practical one, such as deficient drafting of the law or limited capacity of domestic institutions, both the international community and civil society organisations can help by providing technocratic expertise to policy makers or by supporting the enforcement body itself.[210] The lens through which the involvement of the international community and strengthening of civil society organisations are examined here should not be taken to mean that these can only be understood as responses to failures to adequately implement human rights.

[205] ECNI (n 137) [6.3.10].

[206] Bezuidenhout et al (n 157) 18.

[207] Cole M Wade, 'Mind the Gap: State Capacity and Implementation of Human Rights Treaties' (2015) 69 *International Organization* 405, 409.

[208] There is a vast literature on the involvement of the international community in peacebuilding operations. See, eg, Roland Paris, *At War's End: Building Peace after Civil Conflict* (Cambridge, Cambridge University Press, 2004); Kristoffer Liden, 'Building Peace between Global and Local Politics: The Cosmopolitical Ethics of Liberal Peacebuilding" (2009) 16 *International Peacekeeping* 616; Oliver Richmond, 'UN Peacebuilding Operations and the Dilemma of the Peacebuilding Consensus' (2004) 11 *International Peacekeeping* 83; Severine Autesserre, *Peaceland: Conflict Resolution and the Everyday Politics of International Intervention* (Cambridge, Cambridge University Press, 2014).

[209] Thania Paffenholz, 'Civil Society' in Roger Mac Ginty (ed), *Routledge Handbook of Peacebuilding* (London, Routledge, 2014); Raffaele Marchetti and Nathalie Tocci (eds), *Civil Society, Conflicts and the Politicization of Human Rights* (Tokyo, United Nations University Press, 2011).

[210] Perry (n 44).

In fact, both strategies are valuable in their own right, with international actors, for instance, contributing more generally to peacebuilding efforts by providing financial assistance,[211] and civil society organisations promoting conflict resolution through the creation of safe spaces where members of different groups can interact.[212] Such peacebuilding effects notwithstanding, this section assesses the contributions of each strategy *only* in terms of offering support for the implementation of human rights.

The term 'civil society' encapsulates several stakeholders that are not directly operating within the political process, such as activist non-governmental organisations, lobbying groups, religious movements, the media, and research institutions like think tanks and universities.[213] Conversely, it is less clear what is meant by 'international community', since the term incorrectly implies the existence of a unified group of actors. In fact, the 'international community' consists of states and organisations with often conflicting interests and different agendas,[214] which might even be at odds with the best interests of the post-violence society itself.[215] The distinction between the two strategies – involving the international community and strengthening civil society – is also not always clear-cut.[216] Over the years, there has been an emergence of a 'global civil society',[217] which includes local civil society with connections to international organisations, such as the UN, the EU, NATO and the Organization for Security and Co-operation in Europe (OSCE).[218] Through this process of 'glocalisation', well-organised and well-funded civil society groups act as a medium between the local and the national, but also the national and the global, which suggests that often the two responses explored here go hand in hand.[219] This is a valuable

[211] Paul Collier et al, *Breaking the Conflict Trap: Civil War and Development Policy* (Washington DC, World Bank and Oxford University Press, 2003).

[212] Huma Haider, '(Re)Imagining Coexistence: Striving for Sustainable Return, Reintegration and Reconciliation in Bosnia and Herzegovina' (2009) 3 *International Journal of Transitional Justice* 91.

[213] Raffaele Marchetti and Nathalie Tocci, 'Conflict Society and Human Rights: An Analytical Framework' in Marchetti and Tocci (eds) (n 209).

[214] Roland Kostić, 'Shadow Peacebuilders and Diplomatic Counterinsurgencies: Informal Networks, Knowledge Production and the Art of Policy-Shaping' (2017) 11 *Journal of Intervention and Statebuilding* 120.

[215] Oliver Ramsbotham, Tom Woodhouse and Hugh Miall, *Contemporary Conflict Resolution: The Prevention, Management and Transformation of Deadly Conflicts* (Cambridge, Polity Press, 2016).

[216] Kostić (n 214).

[217] Mary Kaldor, *Global Civil Society* (Cambridge, Polity Press, 2003).

[218] Brewer (n 204) 47.

[219] Robert Robertson, 'Glocalization: Time-Space and Homogeneity-Heterogeneity' in Mike Featherstone, Scott Lash and Roland Robertson (eds), *Global Modernitites* (London, SAGE, 1995). The problem with this phenomenon is that it tends to favour large and well-connected organisations over less professionalised agencies, thus excluding a part of the local population, mostly found in rural areas. See Stefanie Kappler, 'Liberal Peacebuilding's Presentation of "the Local": The Case of Bosnia and Herzegovina' in Oliver Richmond and Audra Mitchell (eds), *Hybrid Forms of Peace: From Everyday Agency to Post-liberalism* (Basingstoke, Palgrave Macmillan, 2016).

insight because purely citizen-driven civil society organisations that have no support from the state or the international community rarely have an impact beyond the local level.[220]

The extent of the international community's involvement in assisting peacebuilding efforts ranges from context to context. While, for instance, its presence in BiH was (and remains) keenly felt by the people, the transition in NI has been almost exclusively powered by domestic peacebuilders.[221] However, even countries with mostly local peacebuilding initiatives have been indirectly influenced by the agendas of international organisations, such as the World Bank, which make their funding conditional on this.[222] It should be acknowledged from the outset that it is not the case that the greater the international community's intervention, the more likely the promotion of security, justice and reconciliation.[223] On the contrary, international involvement, especially when it is as direct and intrusive as in BiH, should be a measure of last resort or should not be used at all, since it risks stifling local peacebuilding initiatives or making them forever dependent on international aid.[224] Both dangers have arguably materialised in BiH, where fears that nationalist politicians would obstruct peacebuilding efforts, including 'the promotion and respect of human rights',[225] led to the creation of the Office of the High Representative.[226] The High Representative is an international official who was made responsible for the civilian implementation of the Dayton Agreement, a mandate that he is still operating under today. While in theory, the High Representative's primary objective is to render his Office obsolete by ensuring that the Agreement is being enforced without his assistance, his powers were considerably expanded a mere few months after he started operating. From 1996 onwards, this appointed (and unaccountable) international official has been empowered to pass any legislation he considers necessary at both the entity and federal levels, and dismiss elected officials whose actions he considers to be contrary to peacebuilding efforts.[227] The High Representative has used these powers extensively, especially in the early years after the war.[228] This was often necessary, precisely because of the unwillingness on behalf of politicians or technocrats to implement human

[220] McAuliffe (n 121) 31.

[221] Bell (n 1) chs 4 and 3 respectively.

[222] Bezuidenhout et al (n 157) 6.

[223] Roger Mac Ginty, 'Indigenous Peace-Making versus the Liberal Peace' (2008) 43 *Cooperation and Conflict* 139.

[224] David Chandler, 'Bosnia: The Democracy Paradox' (2001) 100 *Current History* 114.

[225] General Framework Agreement for Peace in BiH, Annex 10, art I(1).

[226] Venice Commission, Opinion on the constitutional situation (n 30) 8.

[227] The changes in the High Representative's powers were authorised by the Peace Implementation Council in Bonn in December 1996. For a summary of the Bonn Conference's conclusions, see Office of the High Representative, 'Peace Implementation Council Bonn Conclusions: Bosnia and Herzegovina 1998: Self-Sustaining Structures' (Sarajevo, Office of the High Representative, 10 December 1997), available at www.ohr.int/?p=54133&print=pdf.

[228] Venice Commission, Opinion on the constitutional situation (n 30) [92].

rights policies, but overreliance on these powers has arguably undermined the peacebuilding process. Although it was easier in the short term for international peacebuilders to override the elected representatives and take decisions themselves, this has had negative long-term consequences.[229] Bosnian politicians quickly learned that if the situation got dire or urgent enough, the High Representative would intervene, while they could act as onlookers, criticising any necessary action he took, without engaging in inter-ethnic cooperation or suffering any political cost themselves.[230] This has arguably created a vicious cycle whereby the international community has locked itself in BiH, since the continuous intervention of the High Representative in everyday politics has stopped political elites from developing the skills and incentives to run the country on their own in an effective and responsible manner.[231]

Additionally, while good intentioned, the practices of the High Representative have on certain occasions themselves been in violation of human rights, thus compromising a sense of justice among the population. For instance, after avoiding becoming involved in the adjudication of this conflict for years, the BiH Constitutional Court held in *AP-953/05* that the High Representative's practice of dismissing officials from their positions without providing them with an opportunity to explain their actions, or compensating them in any way, was in violation of the right to an effective remedy.[232] In a move that resembled more dictatorial regimes than the democratic and peaceful state that the international community was trying to build in BiH, the High Representative issued a statement threatening that:

> [A]ny step taken by any institution or authority in Bosnia and Herzegovina to establish any domestic mechanism to review the Decisions of the High Representative will be considered an attempt to undermine implementation of the civilian aspects of the Dayton Peace Accords and treated accordingly.[233]

Arguably, this response has given nationalist voices a legitimate reason to complain about international intervention and delegitimised other peacebuilding initiatives that the High Representative had supported in the country.[234]

Despite the dangers of excessive international intervention, it has also proven to be an invaluable aid in the enforcement of human rights and the building of

[229] Muehlmann (n 45) 391–92.

[230] Gergana Dimitrova, 'Democracy and International Intervention in Bosnia and Herzegovina' (2005) 6 *Central European Political Studies Review* 45.

[231] Richard Caplan, 'Who Guards the Guardians? International Accountability in Bosnia' in David Chandler (ed), *Peace without Politics? Ten Years of International State Building in Bosnia* (London, Routledge, 2006).

[232] *AP-953/05* (BiH Constitutional Court, 8 July 2006).

[233] Office of the High Representative, *Order on the Implementation of the Decision of the Constitutional Court of Bosnia and Herzegovina in the Appeal of Milorad Bilbija et al, No AP-953/05*, Doc 37/07 (Sarajevo, Office of the High Representative, 23 March 2007).

[234] Constance Grewe and Michael Riegner, 'Internationalized Constitutionalism in Ethnically Divided Societies: Bosnia-Herzegovina and Kosovo Compared' (2011) 15 *Max Planck Yearbook of United Nations Law* 1, 58.

peace in BiH. Perhaps no other instance exemplifies this better than attempts to protect the right to property, which remained unsuccessful for years because of both the political unwillingness and technocratic challenges that surrounded its implementation. The eventual success of this human rights initiative becomes even more obvious because of a change in strategy that took place in 1999, which resulted in a clear 'before and after' picture.[235] With this in mind, the 'before' picture is a rather bleak one: in the early stages after Dayton, the international community's strategy was to encourage returns of displaced persons in areas where this was considered safe, but actively discourage them in others, where it was believed that the conditions were not yet ripe.[236] The strategy relied on the political right to return and the belief that peacebuilders could encourage ethnic groups to accept minority returnees in their areas of effective control through political pressure and economic incentives.[237] Its implementation, which essentially prioritised the element of security over justice, was largely a failure because all three ethnic groups proved unwilling to cooperate. Despite encouraging promises, they adopted discriminatory laws against minorities, prioritised restitution applications by their own community members and were slow to stop any nationalist violence that took place upon the return of the displaced.[238] The political unwillingness to implement this strategy was easily camouflaged under the complexity of, and contradictions between, the laws that existed at the time.[239] Consequently, between 1996 and 2000, the first time that the international community started systematically collecting statistics, only 12 per cent of applications by displaced people had been dealt with.[240]

The huge contrast between the 'before' and 'after' pictures is largely attributed to the abandonment of the *political* right to return and the implementation

[235] The 'success' that will be described here concerns only the building of objective peace; the limitations of this strategy in promoting subjective security, justice and reconciliation are explored in section III in ch 6.

[236] Marcus Cox and Madeline Garlick, 'Musical Chairs: Property Repossession and Return Strategies in Bosnia and Herzegovina' in Scott Leckie (ed), *Returning Home: Housing and Property Restituiton Rights of Refugees and Displaced Persons* (New York, Transnational Publishers, 2003).

[237] See Peace Implementation Council, *PIC Sintra Declaration: Political Declaration from Ministerial Meeting of the Steering Board of the Peace Implementation Council* (Sarajevo, Office of the High Representative, 30 May 1997) [46], which states that 'assistance for housing and local infrastructure should be dependent on the acceptance of return'. The term 'minority returnees' refers to displaced people returning to areas where they are not in the majority ethnic group.

[238] Ayaki Ito, 'Politicisation of Minority Return in Bosnia-Herzegovina: The First Five Years Examined' (2001) 13 *International Journal of Refugee Law* 98.

[239] Shortly after the war, different and often contradictory sets of laws existed and were selectively applied: laws passed by the ex-Yugoslav state, pre-war laws that only applied to BiH, wartime legislation (which was different according to the ethnic group that controlled each area), the Constitution, post-war legislation and international instruments that were directly applicable at the national level. For an excellent background to the property laws in BiH, see Charles Philpott, 'Though the Dog is Dead, the Pig Must Be Killed: Finishing with Property Restitution to Bosnia Herzegovina's IDPs and Refugees' (2005) 18 *Journal of Refugee Studies* 1.

[240] Office of the High Representative, *Statistics: Implementation of the Property Laws in Bosnia and Herzegovina* (Sarajevo, Office of the High Representative, 31 May 2000).

of the *legal* right to property instead. The change took place in 1999 when the international community introduced the Property Law Implementation Plan (PLIP). This relied on a series of legislative amendments, pushed through by the High Representative, and the active involvement of international peacebuilders for their enforcement in practice.[241] On the one hand, the PLIP's objectives were both clearly and explicitly articulated: to implement the right to property of all displaced persons, which would in turn promote each of the elements of peace.[242] On the other hand, the way in which specific amendments to the law were drafted ensured that their enforcement would indeed contribute to the promotion of these objectives. Thus, the PLIP retrospectively put out of force the discriminatory property laws that had been passed during and before the war, harmonised the claim procedures in both entities and created a process that was heavily weighted in favour of the claimants.[243] In particular, under the new law, displaced people only had to show that they had pre-war rights to the property and the responsible authority had 30 days to investigate the claim.[244] If the current occupant had no right to occupy the property or had access to other housing, he or she had to vacate it within 15 days.[245] If he or she was in need of alternative accommodation, the authorities had 90 days to secure it for him or her and he or she had to be evicted, even if no such accommodation had been provided.[246] Although these deadlines were often exceeded by several months, the new legislation jump-started the process and prevented uncooperative politicians and public officials from using excuses.[247]

It is estimated that if restitution continued with the same rate as it did before 1999, the process would have taken another 40 years to complete.[248] Rather, the

[241] Charles Philpott, 'From the Right to Return to the Return of Rights: Completing Post-war Property Restitution in Bosnia Herzegovina' (2006) 18 *International Journal of Refugee Law* 30.

[242] Office of the High Representative, *PLIP Inter-agency Framework Document* (Sarajevo, Office of the High Representative, 15 October 2000).

[243] Philpott (n 239).

[244] Law on Cessation of the Application of the Law on Temporarily Abandoned Real Property Owned by Citizens (Official Gazette of Federation of BiH, No 11/98), art 12; Law on the Cessation of the Application of the Law on Abandoned Apartments (Official Gazette of BiH Law No 11/98), art 6; Law on the Cessation of the Application of the Law on the Use of Abandoned Property (Official Gazette of Republika Srpska Law No 38/98), art 9.

[245] Law on Cessation of the Application of the Law on Temporarily Abandoned Real Property Owned by Citizens (Official Gazette of Federation of BiH, No 11/98), art 7; Law on the Cessation of the Application of the Law on Abandoned Apartments (Official Gazette of BiH Law No. 11/98), art 3; Law on the Cessation of the Application of the Law on the Use of Abandoned property (Official Gazette of Republika Srpska Law No 38/98), art 11a.

[246] Law on Cessation of the Application of the Law on Temporarily Abandoned Real Property Owned by Citizens (Official Gazette of Federation of BiH, No 11/98), art 12a; Law on the Cessation of the Application of the Law on Abandoned Apartments (Official Gazette of BiH Law No 11/98), art 7a; Law on the Cessation of the Application of the Law on the Use of Abandoned Property (Official Gazette of Republika Srpska Law No 38/98), art 11a.

[247] Philpott (n 239).

[248] Office of the High Representative, *PLIP – Non-negotiable Principles in the Context of the Property Law Implementation* (Sarajevo, Office of the High Representative, 7 March 2000).

international community's implementation of the right to property meant that by December 2003, when the PLIP came to an end, 93 per cent of the property claims had been handled and the few remaining cases were handed over to the local authorities to complete.[249] Ultimately, '[t]he restoration of property rights and the return of refugees and displaced persons to their homes must rank as the most dramatic success of the peace process in Bosnia and Herzegovina'.[250] At the most basic level, the legislative amendments adopted by the international community, resulting in almost all displaced people being empowered to return to their houses, promoted security by sending the message that the war was truly over and the conflict was being left behind. As the UN High Commissioner for Refugees (UNHRC) put it: 'When they choose voluntarily to go back to their homeland, refugees are, quite literally, voting with their feet and expressing confidence in the future of their country.'[251] It is arguably for this reason that the nationalist leaders in BiH were keen to prevent minority returns and why it is considered such a big success of the international community that this was prevented.

Perhaps more importantly, the implementation programme promoted peace by contributing to a sense of objective justice in three ways. First, the PLIP moved beyond empty political promises and put in place clear laws and procedures, which displaced people could rely on in practice. This empowered applicants since it clarified the process through which they could demand – rather than merely wait at the discretion of the uncooperative state – for the return of their properties.[252] Second, the clear legal provisions made it easy to identify state officials who refused to protect the right to property and impose strict penalties on them. As a result, in November 1999 the High Representative removed 22 officials from office for failing to comply with the PLIP and sent the message that the return of displaced people was a peacebuilding priority.[253] Third, the PLIP's singular and clear objective – the implementation of the right to property – helped coordinate different international organisations that were operating in BiH. Thus, OSCE and UNHCR officials were sent in every municipality in the country, where they collected statistics and delivered PLIP guidelines to the local authorities, which, in turn, assisted the implementation process.[254] These measures resulted in a speedier and more professional response by the authorities by, for example, stopping the popular practice of prioritising 'easy applications' (usually returns where the applicant was in the majority or

[249] Office of the High Representative (n 240).

[250] Cox and Garlick (n 236) 65.

[251] UNHCR, *The State of the World's Refugees: In Search of Solidarity* (New York, UN High Commissioner for Refugees, 2012) 162.

[252] Wade (n 207) 414.

[253] Lisa D'Onofrio, *Welcome Home? Minority Return in South-East Rebublika Srpska*, Sussex Migration Working Paper No 19 (Sussex Centre for Migration Research, University of Sussex, 2004) 9.

[254] Philpott (n 239).

there was no secondary occupier in the property). Instead, all applications were treated in the chronological order they had been submitted, hence preventing the privileging of applicants because of their personal connections or ethnic group membership.[255] The process also gave a rough indication to people as to when their claim would be dealt with, therefore allowing them to better prepare, financially and psychologically, for their return.

An assessment of the impact of implementing the right to property in BiH suggests that the international community can play a seminal role in encouraging human rights implementation. Importantly, its involvement in this instance was multifaceted, addressing the problem of political unwillingness by circumventing uncooperative politicians, avoiding the challenges of bad legislative drafting by undertaking this task itself, and responding to the difficulties of limited enforcement capacity by offering more hands-on assistance. Had only one of these strategies been preferred, the intervention of the international community would not have been as effective. At the same time, however, the positive effects of these policies in relation to the right to property should be assessed by bearing in mind the detrimental consequences of excessive international intervention. This suggests that peacebuilders should prefer, where possible, more light-touch interventions, which seek to guide rather than replace local actors,[256] who will after all remain in the country long after the international personnel has left.[257] In other words, they should shape their actions and policies by bearing in mind that '[t]he international community is, at best, the facilitator of peace, but certainly not the engineer of it'.[258] If such light-touch interventions fail to promote human rights implementation, strengthening civil society organisations may be a more organic and sustainable response to the problem than sidestepping local political actors altogether. In fact, the more time passes from the signing of the peace agreement and as the post-violence society moves from a phase of intervention through to stabilisation and finally to normalisation, the more appropriate the adoption of this alternative strategy becomes.[259]

The involvement of civil society is already a popular peacebuilding strategy in post-violence societies.[260] However, arguably, to the extent that local initiatives and civil society organisations have played a role in conflict resolution

[255] ibid. One of the few exceptions to this strict chronological order was the prioritisation of policemen, with the rationale being that they could make minority returnees feel more secure. This is an example of a conscious policy decision to prioritise security over justice in a post-violence society.

[256] Such as the interventions of the Venice Commission, which makes recommendations on the best way to improve democratic institutions and human rights practices in specific countries; see Leach and Donald (n 65) 55.

[257] Autesserre (n 208) 64.

[258] McAuliffe (n 121) 29.

[259] Ramsbotham, Woodhouse and Miall (n 215) 253.

[260] Oliver Richmond and Audra Mitchell, 'Introduction – Towards a Post-liberal Peace: Exploring Hybridity via Everyday Forms of Resistance, Agency and Autonomy' in Richmond and Mitchell (n 219) 7–8.

efforts, these have mostly been as afterthought reactions to the limitations of the liberal peacebuilding agenda.[261] What is being proposed here is the opposite: peacebuilders should appreciate the limitations of their existing strategies and *planning ahead*, empower the types of local actors that can address these. The first contribution that civil society can make in this respect is to bring into the spotlight, and add to the public agenda, the private grievances of individuals,[262] and therefore put the government under increasing pressure to respond to them.[263] In other words, civil society organisations can identify an injustice, frame it in human rights terms and encourage the grassroots to demand from officials the adoption of a policy that will address it.[264] Arguably, one of the reasons the international community has not been as successful in its efforts to reform key institutions in BiH, such as the police force, is precisely because of the absence of public participation and civil society involvement in the process, which could have motivated unwilling politicians to act.[265]

Conversely, in NI it was the good cooperation between civil society actors and the government that contributed to the reform of the Historical Enquiries Team (HET), which resulted in the more effective protection of the right to life and the consequent promotion of justice. The HET was established in 2005 as part of a 'package of measures' announced by the UK government following the findings of the ECtHR that the investigation processes that took place after the deaths of members or sympathisers of the Irish Republican Army (IRA) were so defective that they constituted violations of the procedural aspect of the right to life.[266] In light of these deficiencies, the UK committed to re-examine, through the HET, 3,268 conflict-related deaths that occurred between 1968 and 1998.[267] In 2009, Dr (now Professor) Patricia Lundy, an academic at the University of Ulster, approached the then Chief Constable of the Police Service of Northern Ireland and secured access to the HET in order to undertake research on how it operated.[268] Her findings were damning: among other things, she identified problems with the procedures that were being followed, showed that the HET was not always operating in a consistent manner, since it distinguished between

[261] ibid 5.

[262] Brewer (n 204) 55.

[263] Marchetti and Tocci (n 213).

[264] Thania Paffenholz and Christoph Spurk, *Civil Society, Civic Engagement and Peacebuilding*, Social Development Papers, Conflict Prevention and Reconstruction Paper No 36 (Washington DC, World Bank, 2006); Thania Paffenholz and Christoph Spurk, 'A Comprehensive Analytical Framework' in Thania Paffenholz (ed), *Civil Society and Peacebuilding: A Critical Assessment* (Boulder, Lynne Rienner, 2010).

[265] Muehlmann (n 45) 391.

[266] HMIC, *Inspection of the Police Service of Northern Ireland Historical Enquiries Team* (United Kingdom, Her Majesty's Inspectorate of Constabulary, 2013) 7.

[267] Patricia Lundy and Bill Rolston, 'Redress for Past Harms? Official Apologies in Northern Ireland' (2016) 20 *International Journal of Human Rights* 104, 110.

[268] HMIC (n 266) 31.

suspects who were state actors and those who were not, and raised questions about the lack of independence of some of the HET's staff.[269] The identification of these problems by a civil society actor transformed the personal complaints of the victims' families into issues of public concern and put pressure on the government to respond to them. Thus, a formal inspection of the HET was instituted in order to assess whether Professor Lundy's findings were indeed accurate.[270] When these were confirmed by Her Majesty's Inspectorate of Constabulary in 2013, the HET undertook changes to its procedures with the express objective of ensuring that it was complying with the judgments of the European Court 'in a way that commands the confidence of the wider community'.[271]

The HET's reform offers an example where a civil society actor was able to push for the implementation of a human rights judgment in a way that promoted justice and reconciliation. At the same time, it suggests that the effectiveness of civil society largely depends on the context in which it is operating[272] and the extent to which the state is willing to cooperate with it.[273] Professor Lundy's contribution to the improvement of the HET became possible due to the UK's culture of valuing expert opinions and because it took place in a context where human rights are usually taken seriously, factors that enhance the effectiveness of civil society organisations.[274] Had these not been present, her request to secure access to the HET, which after all dealt with some very sensitive information, would have been denied or her recommendations would have simply been ignored. This is supported by the experiences of BiH civil society organisations, which failed to make any positive peacebuilding contributions in the early stages after Dayton because they were used to operating within a context where free speech, especially when this did not align with of the interests of political elites, was curtailed.[275]

The second peacebuilding contribution that civil society organisations can make is that they can push for the resolution of a conflict by lobbying to amend problematic legislation or adopt new human rights initiatives.[276] For instance, when the TRC in SA was being set up, civil society organisations successfully lobbied against the idea that was being considered at the time of holding hearings

[269] Patricia Lundy, 'Can the Past Be Policed? Lessons from the Historical Enquiries Team Northern Ireland' (2009) 11 *Journal of Law and Social Challenges* 109.

[270] The findings of this process are summarised in HMIC (n 266).

[271] HET, 'Standard Operating Procedure' (2005), Section 2.2, quoted in ibid 7.

[272] Paffenholz and Spurk (n 264); Marchetti and Tocci (n 213); Camilla Orjuela, 'Building Peace in Sri Lanka: A Role for Civil Society?' (2003) 40 *Journal of Peace Research* 195.

[273] McAuliffe (n 121) 578.

[274] Courtney Hillebrecht, 'Implementing International Human Rights Law at Home: Domestic Politics and the European Court of Human Rights' (2012) 13 *Human Rights Review* 279.

[275] Giulio Marcon and Sergio Andreis, 'Human Rights, Civil Society and Conflict in Bosnia-Herzegovina' in Marchetti and Tocci (eds) (n 213).

[276] Lucja Miara and Victoria Prais, 'The Role of Civil Society in the Execution of Judgments of the European Court of Human Rights' (2012) 5 *European Human Rights Law Review* 528.

behind closed doors.[277] By using human rights language and changing the state's preferred policy, civil society contributed towards making the TRC's findings more well-known among SA, helped dispel any myths about the actions of the apartheid government and started the reconciliation process.[278] Moreover, at the end of the TRC's proceedings, civil society came to the forefront again when, following delays in the payment of compensation to the victims, it successfully pushed the government to fulfil its obligations.[279] The final contribution of civil society organisations is that they can provide practical guidance and support to public bodies, which, in turn, can enhance their capacity, make it easier for them to enforce human rights and promote peace. Thus, the database that the TRC relied on in order to collect evidence about past human rights abuses, which formed the basis of its operations, was developed by representatives of six human rights organisations with experience in the design of human rights information systems.[280]

Like with the involvement of the international community, the strengthening of civil society can assist peacebuilding efforts, both in instances where the problem concerns a lack of political willingness to see change and when human rights institutions would benefit from greater practical support. However, at the same time, indiscriminately empowering these organisations without having a better understanding of their profile and objectives is not always conductive to peace. Despite simplistic assumptions that all civil society actors encourage the protection of human rights[281] and that this will, in turn, lead to peace,[282] they can, in fact, also have the reverse effect, especially if they do not enjoy the trust of the general public. Thus, while there are some organisations that do not accept any external funding in order to preserve their independence,[283] most receive either direct or indirect support from the international community.[284] If this is, for any reason, discredited among the population, civil society organisations that are supported by it are also likely to be dismissed as biased.[285] At the same time, whether an organisation is associated with the international community or not, it is possible that its offices are populated by members of local elites that might be using its neutrality veneer in order to further their own agendas. This can potentially put civil society actors in a lose-lose

[277] TRC, *Report of the Truth and Reconciliation Commission* (Pretoria, TRC, 1998), vol 1, ch 4 [23].

[278] ibid vol 1, ch 1 [79]; ibid, vol 1, ch 12 [45]–[46].

[279] Ereshnee Naidu, 'Symbolic Reparations and Reconciliation: Lessons from South Africa' (2012–13) 19 *Buffalo Human Rights Law Review* 251, 262.

[280] TRC, *Report of the Truth and Reconciliation Commission*, vol 1, ch 6, Appendix 1 [9].

[281] See, eg, Miara and Prais (n 276).

[282] John Paul Lederach, *Building Peace: Sustainable Reconciliation in Divided Societies* (Washington DC, United States Institute of Peace Press, 1997).

[283] Marcon and Andreis (n 275).

[284] Orjuela (n 272); Kappler (n 219) 263.

[285] Maria Hadjipavlou and Bülent Kanol, *Cumulative Impact Case Study: The Impacts of Peace-building Work on the Cyprus Conflict* (Nicosia, CDA Collaborative Learning Projects, 2008).

situation: although attracting attention from local elites for the wrong reasons can be dangerous, being ignored by them is also counterproductive in terms of making any real impact on the ground.[286] Also important in terms of an organisation's profile is its staff composition and, in particular, whether it is run by professionals or volunteers.[287] Those that are operating almost exclusively in urban centres and are staffed by professional peacebuilders are less likely to represent, and properly communicate with, the grassroots throughout the post-violence society, a factor that can undermine both their effectiveness and credibility.[288] These observations suggest that the strengthening of civil society organisations has to mean more than simply throwing money at them. Doing so runs the risk of 'taming' and turning them into urban-focused 'service deliverers', or even empowering actors that, in fact, seek to undermine the peacebuilding agenda.[289]

In order to identify which civil society actors should be empowered, peacebuilders must pay attention to each organisation's objectives and, consequently, the way in which it utilises human rights language in order to achieve these. If it represents a single ethnic group or has a more nationalist agenda, it is likely to use human rights as a way of justifying maximalist demands, thus polarising the public and further fuelling the conflict.[290] This is, for example, the case with many civil society organisations in Cyprus, which receive either exclusively GC or TC support.[291] These bodies have over the years been organising events commemorating the suffering of their ethnic group's members (while ignoring similar experiences of the other side) and pushing for laws and a peace agreement that will fully safeguard their interests, despite the fact that the other ethnic group considers these unacceptable. Even when their intention is to protect the interests of their members rather than undermine peacebuilding efforts per se, they might inadvertently have this effect when they conceptualise human rights in communal rather than universal terms.[292] For instance, GC displaced peoples' organisations have played a key role in interpreting *Loizidou* in a very specific light, which in turn has discouraged GCs from accepting a solution that does not fully safeguard the restitution of their properties.[293] Being aware of these dangers should not automatically give rise to 'defensive formalism', where only

[286] McAuliffe (n 121) 264.
[287] Paffenholz (n 209) 353.
[288] Marcon and Andreis (n 275).
[289] Paffenholz (n 209) 353.
[290] Ramsbotham, Woodhouse and Miall (n 215) 285.
[291] Olga Demetriou and Ayla Gürel, 'Human Rights, Civil Society and Conflict in Cyprus' in Marchetti and Tocci (eds) (n 213) 100.
[292] ibid 108.
[293] Nicos Trimikliniotis and Corina Demetriou, *Displacement in Cyprus: Consequences of Civil and Military Strife: Legal Framework in the Republic of Cyprus*, 3/2012 (Nicosia, PRIO Cyprus Centre, 2012) 19.

state institutions are trusted to participate in the peacebuilding process;[294] rather, they should act as a warning, especially to international peacebuilders who are not as familiar with the local context, to be careful when distinguishing between civil society organisations that can help promote peace and others that might have the reverse effect.[295]

VI. CONCLUSION

Human rights implementation can indeed resolve outstanding conflicts and promote security, justice and reconciliation. Conversely, when the state does not comply with its human rights obligations, or when it only partially complies with them, this can have detrimental peacebuilding effects. While often accurate, this binary schema of the relationship between human rights and peace fails to explain situations where human rights have technically been implemented, but have nevertheless not contributed to conflict resolution. Moreover, it offers little guidance to peacebuilders about the conditions that must be in place for the implementation of the former to assist in the building of the latter and what strategies should be adopted when these are not present. This chapter has argued that three factors affect the peacebuilding potential of enforcing human rights and that distinguishing between them is important because the absence of each merits a different peacebuilding response.

Successful conflict resolution depends on sufficient political willingness to induce comprehensive change, the human rights policy being guided by clear peacebuilding objectives and it being drafted in a way that reflects these. Finally, it is necessary that the body that has been tasked with the implementation of human rights has the institutional independence, powers, resources and expertise to achieve its objectives. If these conditions are not present, two strategies that peacebuilders can adopt are to involve the international community and strengthen civil society. These strategies respond to the absence of each of the three conditions in distinct ways, such as by imposing international or grassroots pressure on politicians who are unwilling to take action, offering practical assistance in the drafting of human rights provisions, or strengthening the capacities of enforcement bodies to undertake their task. However, at the same time, while capable of aiding peacebuilding efforts, both the involvement of the international community and the strengthening of civil society organisations can be dangerous when the former completely takes over the functions of domestic actors, or in cases where peacebuilders fail to distinguish between 'civil' and 'uncivil society'.[296]

[294] Brian Gormally and Kieran McEvoy, *Dealing with the Past in Northern Ireland 'from Below': An Evaluation* (Belfast, Community Foundation for Northern Ireland, 2009) 12.

[295] Paris (n 208) ch 9.

[296] Christoph Spurk, 'Understanding Civil Society' in Thania Paffenholz (ed), *Civil Society and Peacebuilding: A Critical Assessment* (Boulder, Lynne Rienner, 2010).

6

Protecting Human Rights and Promoting Subjective Peace

I. INTRODUCTION

THE PREVIOUS CHAPTERS focused on the adjudication and implementation of human rights and argued that under the right conditions, these can directly lead to institutional and legal reforms that contribute to the objective improvement of security, justice and reconciliation. This chapter is concerned with the way in which human rights can help resolve conflicts as psychological states of affairs and induce the socio-economic and psychological changes that are necessary for the promotion of subjective feelings of peace.[1] The impact of law on social change has been the subject of scholarly debate for decades, with academics disagreeing on whether, and in what ways, the former can effectively promote the latter.[2] On the one hand, some argue that a change in the law, especially when this comes from the bench rather than an elected body, is unlikely to affect social perceptions[3] and could even result in negative outcomes.[4] Others have contended that public interest litigation can induce positive social change, but have disagreed on the reasons why. McCann, for instance, believes that rights allow activists to put specific issues on the public agenda and threaten to impose litigation costs, unless legislative – and subsequently social – change takes place.[5] Alternatively, Scheingold proposes

[1] Social and psychological change relate to each other since '[w]hat is happening at the social level, such as the destruction of social ties, is integrally connected to individual well-being, and vice versa' (Brandon Hamber, *Dealing with Painful Memories and Violent Pasts: Towards a Framework for Contextual Understanding* (Berghof Handbook Dialogue Series No 11, Berlin, Berghof Foundation, 2015) 4). See also Nadim N Rouhana, 'Identity and Power in the Reconciliation of National Conflict' in Alice H Eagly, Reuben M Baron and Lee V Hamilton (eds), *The Social Psychology of Group Identity and Social Conflict* (Washington DC, American Psychological Association, 2004) 180; Patrick Bracken and Petty Celia (eds), *Rethinking the Trauma of War* (London, Save the Children/Free Association Books, 1998).

[2] Sharyn L Roach-Anleu, *Law and Social Change*, 2nd edn (Los Angeles, SAGE, 2010).

[3] Gerarld N Rosenberg, *The Hollow Hope: Can Courts Bring about Social Change?*, 2nd edn (Chicago, University of Chicago Press, 2008).

[4] Jeremy Rabikin, 'Racial Progress and Constitutional Roadblocks' (1992) 34 *William & Mary Law Review* 75.

[5] Michael McCann, 'How Does Law Matter for Social Movements' in Bryant G Garth and Austin Sarat (eds), *How Does Law Matter? Fundamental Issues in Law and Society Research* (Evanston, Northwestern University Press, 1998) 92.

that the main contribution of rights is that their ethical connotations help mobilise the masses, who, in turn, can push legislators into action.[6] However, while fruitful, these debates have mostly focused on seminal cases of the US Supreme Court, such as *Brown v Board of Education of Topeka*[7] and *Roe v Wade*,[8] and have only been applied to post-violence contexts sparingly.

Although the peacebuilding literature lacks a detailed analysis of the relationship between human rights and social change, especially in relation to feelings of reconciliation, it is filled with brief assertions that this very relationship is a positive one. Yet, the absence of a well-developed theoretical framework has left decision-makers unclear as to how one leads to the other. The chapter addresses this gap by applying the conclusions of the socio-legal literature to post-violence societies. Section II outlines specific ways in which human rights can contribute to the resolution of conflicts as psychological states of affairs, namely by providing a vocabulary that allows victims to articulate their plight and incentivising state institutions to officially acknowledge and ultimately respond to it. It further asserts that subjective feelings of peace do not automatically follow when such a vocabulary is utilised, or even when a technically flawless implementation of the law has taken place, but can only materialise in the presence of at least two sets of conditions. The first, outlined in section III, is that human rights institutions must deliver on their promises and induce *meaningful* change in the lives of the people, since a failure to do so can result in disillusionment and loss of confidence in the peacebuilding process. The second set of conditions, discussed in section IV, relate to the idea that human rights must not only promote security, justice and reconciliation, but they must be *perceived* by the population at large as also having this effect. What must be done for these conditions to develop depends on the context, needs and demands of each post-violence society. Nonetheless, there are strategies that peacebuilders can consider, which when adopted together with the protection of human rights can help induce subjective change. Section V elaborates on two of these, namely rethinking the composition of the peacebuilding teams and establishing effective communication channels between them and their target audience.

II. PROTECTING HUMAN RIGHTS AND INDUCING SOCIAL AND PSYCHOLOGICAL CHANGE

An explicit expectation that human rights can induce social and psychological change within the post-violence society is articulated by the Brahimi Report,

[6] Stuart A Scheingold, *The Politics of Rights: Lawyers, Public Policy, and Political Change*, 2nd edn (Ann Arbor, University of Michigan Press, 2004).

[7] *Brown v Board of Education of Topeka* 47 US 483 (1954) (US Supreme Court, 31 May 1955).

[8] *Roe v Wade* 410 US 113 (1973) (US Supreme Court, 22 January 1973).

which confidently declares that 'the human rights component of a peace operation is indeed critical to effective peace-building. United Nations human rights personnel can play a leading role, for example, in helping to implement a comprehensive programme for national reconciliation'.[9] Similarly, legislation in SA often draws a connecting line between the protection of human rights and the promotion of reconciliation in the country. Section 3 of the Promotion of National Unity and Reconciliation Act No 34 of 1995 states that its main objective is 'to promote national unity and reconciliation in a spirit of understanding which transcends the conflicts and divisions of the past' by 'establishing as complete a picture as possible of the causes, nature and extent of the gross violations of human rights'. Likewise, the preamble of the Promotion of Equality and Unfair Discrimination Act No 4 of 2000 refers to SA's international and constitutional human rights obligations and declares that these can result, through the adoption of 'special legal and other measures', in the transformation of society into a democracy 'united in its diversity, marked by human relations that are caring and compassionate'.

However, despite these proclamations, arguments have also been made that the language of reconciliation can be, and has been, used in order to prevent the protection of human rights, thus resulting in a reverse relationship than the expected one.[10] Moreover, critical scholars have contended that legal tools are ill-suited and are in fact unable to induce social and psychological changes within the post-violence society.[11] Ultimately, they continue, this inability leads to a 'hollow peace', to the promotion of security, justice and reconciliation in the eyes of the outside observer, but to the lack of any meaningful change as experienced by the population itself.[12] Rejecting these pessimistic views, the chapter argues that human rights can contribute to – although not wholly achieve – the resolution of conflicts as psychological states of affairs in three distinct steps. As a first step, they can provide victims with a vocabulary to articulate their grievances, communicate 'their awareness of the discrepancy between the actual and the possible',[13] evaluate the state's performance in closing this gap and lay the

[9] Panel on United Nations Peace Operations, *Report of the Panel on United Nations Peace Operations,* A/55/305–S/2000/809 (New York, United Nations, 2000) (hereinafter 'Brahimi Report') [41]; see also [24].

[10] Lesley McEvoy, Kieran McEvoy and Kirsten McConnachie, 'Reconciliation as a Dirty Word: Conflict, Community Relations and Education in Northern Ireland' (2006) 60 *Journal of International Affairs* 81; Christine Bell and Johanna Keenan, 'Lost on the Way Home? The Right to Life in Northern Ireland' (2005) 32 *Journal of Law and Society* 68; Nevin T Aiken, 'Learning to Live Together: Transitional Justice and Intergroup Reconciliation in Northern Ireland' (2010) 4 *International Journal of Transitional Justice* 166.

[11] John D Brewer, *Peace Processes: A Sociological Approach* (Cambridge, Polity Press, 2010).

[12] Roger Mac Ginty, 'Indigenous Peace-Making versus the Liberal Peace' (2008) 43 *Cooperation and Conflict* 139, 158.

[13] David Elkind, 'Adolescent Cognitive Development' in James F Adams (ed), *Understanding Adolsence: Current Developments in Adolsescent Psychology* (Boston, Allyn & Bacon, 1968), as quoted in Judith Gallatin and Joseph Adelson, 'Legal Guarantees of Individual Freedom: A Cross-national Study of the Development of Political Thought' (1971) 27 *Journal of Social Issues* 93, 104.

foundations for protest.[14] While there have been claims that requiring victims to articulate their grievance in a formal setting, such as a court of law, risks leaving them feeling dismayed,[15] most references in the literature suggest that being given the opportunity to voice one's indignation does contribute to a sense of justice.[16] This is supported by claims that the assertion of one's entitlement to fair treatment results in a feeling of being recognised by the state[17] and causes victims to identify more strongly with the dignity and self-respect that their claim assumes.[18] Notably, these positive feelings that can help promote justice and reconciliation are not wholly dependent on the provision of a remedy at the end of the process; rather, the articulation of the grievance is in itself a positive first step towards peace.[19]

Relying on human rights is an especially effective way of asserting a political or social demand because they ground one's expectations in law, on which most governments base their own legitimacy.[20] In practice, making such a demand either requires the victims to resort to adjudication or rely on human rights in order to mobilise a movement that will lobby and push for change through legislative amendments.[21] An example of the former is when TCs residing in the areas controlled by the RoC challenged the fact that they had been disenfranchised for 50 years on the ground of their ethnicity by taking a case to the ECtHR.[22] Conversely, an instance of the latter is when GC and TC relatives of missing persons exerted pressure on their respective leaders to locate and identify the remains of their family members.[23] It is also possible that the two strategies can be used simultaneously. Lawyers can raise public awareness,

[14] Frances Kahn Zemans, 'Legal Mobilization: The Neglected Role of the Law in the Political System' (1983) 77 *American Political Science Review* 690, 700; Patricia Ewick and Susan Silbey, *The Common Place of Law: Stories from Everyday Life: Language and Legal Discourse* (Chicago, Chicago University Press, 1998) 43.

[15] Eric Stover, *The Witnesses: War Crimes and the Promise of Justice in the Hague* (Philadelpia, University of Pennsylvania Press, 2005).

[16] Kathryn Abrams, 'Emotions in the Mobilization of Rights' (2011) 46 *Harvard Civil Rights-Civil Liberties Law Review* 551.

[17] David M Engel and Frank W Munger, *Rights of Inclusion: Law and Identity in the Life Stories of Americans with Disabilities* (Chicago, University of Chicago Press, 2003) 4, noting that: 'Although relatively few [interviewees] have actually asserted their rights by using … legal mechanisms … many have found their lives and careers changed by the indirect, symbolic, constitutive effects of rights.'

[18] Patricia Williams, 'Alchemical Notes: Reconstructing Ideals from Deconstructed Rights' (1987) 22 *Harvard Civil Rights-Civil Liberties Law Review* 401.

[19] Abrams (n 16) 580.

[20] Beth Simmons, *Mobilizing for Human Rights: International Law in Domestic Politics* (Cambridge, Cambridge University Press, 2009) 139.

[21] Pieter Bouwen and Margaret McCown, 'Lobbying versus Litigation: Political and Legal Strategies of Interest Representation in the European Union' (2007) 14 *Journal of European Public Policy* 422.

[22] *Aziz v Cyprus* App No 69949/01 (ECtHR, 22 September 2004).

[23] Iosif Kovras and Neophytos Loizides, 'Delaying Truth Recovery for Missing Persons' (2010) 17 *Nations and Nationalism* 520.

reveal the vulnerability of structural arrangements that result in the violation of the right, and encourage mass mobilisation,[24] at the same time as lobbyists are threatening with increased litigation costs if change does not materialise.[25] This is the approach adopted in relation to the property rights of GC displaced persons, who rely both on litigation at the ECtHR and the lobbying of governments and international organisations in order to address the injustice they have been suffering from.[26]

An additional advantage of articulating a grievance under the banner of human rights is that this can foster a new political identity among the divided population and further contribute to the development of reconciliation.[27] Human rights aid in this identity transformation process by challenging dominant narratives that present one group's interests and concerns as diametrically opposed to those of the other.[28] In this respect, Abrams argues that human rights can be particularly effective in facilitating connections among victims from different groups, since they highlight the similar affronts or losses they have experienced.[29] This view is supported by statements made by a missing person's relative in Cyprus, who described how the joint experience of victimhood created 'interpersonal bonds' between GC and TC family members and encouraged them 'to come forward and speak out instead of leaving the nationalists to use our problem to further their own interests … because nobody has experienced what we [relatives] have gone through'.[30] It should be noted that identity transformation in this context only took place after family members started relying on human rights to express their grievances; before that, the victimhood language had been hijacked by each community and even mentioning the existence of a missing person from a different ethnic group was considered a national betrayal.[31] Given that in a recent survey, more than 20 per cent of Cypriot respondents claimed that a close family member was a missing person,[32] the coming together of different communities'

[24] Scott L Cummings and Deborah L Rhode, 'Public Interest Litigation: Insights from Theory and Practice' (2009) 36 *Fordham Urban Law Journal* 603.

[25] McCann (n 5) 92.

[26] Nasia Hadjigeorgiou, 'A One-Sided Coin: A Critical Analysis of the Legal Accounts of the Cypriot Conflicts' in Berber Bevernage and Nico Wouters (eds), *The Palgrave Handbook of State-Sponsored History after 1945* (London, Palgrave Macmillan, 2018).

[27] Aileen Kavanagh, 'The Role of a Bill of Rights in Reconstructing Northern Ireland' (2004) 26 *Human Rights Quarterly* 956, 973.

[28] Scheingold (n 6) 138, noting that: 'To the extent that litigation can demonstrate that individuals are not isolated in their discontents and that these discontents have a status in the law, legal tactics can help to establish a collective political identity.'

[29] Abrams (n 16) 564.

[30] Quoted in Iosif Kovras, *Grassroots Activism and the Evolution of Transitional Justice: The Families of the Disappeared* (Cambridge, Cambridge University Press, 2017) 162.

[31] ibid 163–64.

[32] Djordje Stefanovic, Neophytos Loizides and Charis Psaltis, 'Attitudes of Victims towards Transitional Justice: The Case of Cyprus', Conference on 'Referendums and Peace Processes' (Nicosia, University of Cyprus, 26 and 27 October 2016).

members under the single banner of 'human rights victims' could have a significant impact on reconciliation on the island.[33]

The second step that can lead to conflict resolution and subjective feelings of peace flows from the official acknowledgement that the human rights violation deserves a response. The acts of formally recognising that the victims have suffered an injustice and naming the perpetrator further promote justice and can enhance efforts for reconciliation.[34] Commenting on *Brown v Board of Education*, Schiengold rightly points out that the victims of the discriminatory strategy did not have to be told by the US Supreme Court that their schools were inferior – they were perfectly aware of this already.[35] Rather, the case's significance lies in the fact that it affected American culture because it was 'read as a signal that changes were on the way, and surely it gave rise to anticipations which set the tone, established the direction, and influenced the outcome of a political controversy'.[36] In other words, it was the *official* acknowledgement of the injustices, which the victims already knew they were experiencing, that was seen as a victory by them. This is further supported by Ms Loizidou's statement that she felt vindicated and respected following the ECtHR's decision, which recognised and confirmed the violation of her right to property, despite the fact that this did not result for another five years in the provision of a remedy.[37] Reliance on human rights is particularly likely to lead to the official acknowledgement that a harm has been committed because human rights provide standards against which both the demands of the populace and the actions of the government can be assessed. When applicants articulate their complaint as a failure of the state to meet these benchmarks, the latter will more readily admit the harm that it has caused rather than if this were expressed as an abstract complaint that an injustice has taken place.[38] On the other side of the coin, a failure of the victims to label, or an unwillingness or inability of the authorities to acknowledge, an injustice as a human rights violation can have the reverse effect and undermine efforts to induce social and psychological change.

The final contribution of human rights to subjective feelings of peace stems from the provision of remedies, a step that most effectively communicates that an injustice is coming to an end.[39] In order for this to happen, it is not necessary that each single victim turns to the law, since one human rights case or initiative can inspire rule revision with a broad impact.[40] In addition to having a direct

[33] Kovras (n 30) 155, arguing that the vibrant bi-communal group of relatives has used the problem of missing persons as a symbol of rapprochement and reconciliation.

[34] Roach-Anleu (n 2).

[35] Scheingold (n 6).

[36] ibid 137.

[37] Titina Loizidou, 'Titina Loizidou v Turkey', series of lectures 'The People behind Judicial Decisions' (Nicosia, University of Cyprus, 14 October 2013).

[38] Simmons (n 20).

[39] Scheingold (n 6).

[40] Simmons (n 20).

effect on the victims, the provision of a remedy can promote feelings of peace among the general population in three ways. First, if the remedy includes measures to punish past human rights violations or ensure that they are not repeated again, this can contribute to a general sense of security.[41] Second, while violations are targeted against specific individuals, in cases where they are triggered by the victims' ethnic or racial identities, they are experienced as an affront by members of the group as a whole.[42] In such instances, remedying the violation empowers the victim, but also sends a broader message that the society remembers, regrets and condemns the injustice, while looking towards the future. The effect of addressing past injustices on feelings of reconciliation is illustrated by the implementation of the Fair Employment and Treatment Order (FETO) in NI, a response to discriminatory practices in the employment sphere, which had left Catholics economically worse off than Protestants.[43] While there are differences among sectors, the FETO has resulted in an improvement in overall employment, with segregated occupations between the two communities declining and integrated firms growing in number.[44] In turn, this has improved socio-economic conditions among disempowered members of the population and NI more generally,[45] and has resulted in greater willingness for peaceful co-existence.[46] Admittedly, there are some indications that the empowerment and increasing confidence among Catholics has caused Protestants to feel marginalised,[47] but other studies suggest that legal and political changes post-1998, including in the employment sphere, have encouraged members of the Protestant community to critically examine their identities and have helped 'mellow' their perception of the other.[48]

Third, the provision of a human rights remedy can help break down identity barriers by providing a reference point, which reminds people of the things they have in common and the ideals they all value, despite their distinct ethnic or racial identities.[49] Such ideals, like inclusivity, dignity and respect of the

[41] Otto Kirchheimer, *Political Justice: The Use of Legal Procedure for Political Ends* (Westport, Greenwood Press, 1961) 352, arguing that the provision of a remedy enables 'the construction of a permanent, unmistakable wall between the new beginnings and the old tyranny'.

[42] Brewer (n 11) 107. See also Kovras (n 30) 123, who argues that finding the disappeared is both an individual and a societal concern.

[43] The FETO's provisions are discussed in detail in section IV in ch 5.

[44] Christopher McCrudden, Robert Ford and Anthony Heath, 'Legal Regulation of Affirmative Action in Northern Ireland' (2004) 24 *Oxford Journal of Legal Studies* 363.

[45] Colin Harvey, 'Contextualised Equality and the Politics of Legal Mobilisation: Affirmative Action in Northern Ireland' (2012) 21 *Social & Legal Studies* 23, 34.

[46] In the period from 1989 to 1996, there was a 25 per cent increase in the number of Catholics and Protestants who believed that relations had improved. After 1996, the increasing tendency continued, albeit at a much lower rate (Joanne Hughes and Caitlin Donnelly, 'Community Relations in Northern Ireland: A Shift in Attitudes?' (2003) 29 *Journal of Ethnic and Migration Studies* 643, 650).

[47] ibid.

[48] Jennifer Todd et al, 'Does Being Protestant Matter? Protestants, Minorities and the Remaking of Ethno-religious Identity after the Good Friday Agreement' (2009) 11 *National Identities* 87.

[49] Kavanagh (n 27) 973.

person that are popularly associated with human rights, could help promote reconciliation.[50] In this respect, human rights can be used as educational and communicative tools by a range of different legal actors.[51] Academics have already raised the possibility of the judiciary utilising human rights in this way[52] and the SA Constitutional Court has often linked their protection to the need to introduce social and psychological changes that will overcome the country's apartheid history.[53] For instance, making specific reference to the educational potential of human rights, the Court has held that the state has an obligation to educate the public through the use of, inter alia, 'road shows, regional workshops, radio programs and publications'.[54] The objective of such educational activities is to facilitate an informed and continuous dialogue between the public and policy makers, which will encourage the latter to be more responsive to the former's needs, and therefore promote feelings of justice and reconciliation in the post-violence society.[55] Additionally, (legal) human rights can contribute to educating the citizenry and inducing social and psychological changes when they are being used by bodies other than the judiciary, such as the Human Rights Ombudsman in BiH,[56] the Independent Commission on Policing for NI[57] and the SA Human Rights Commission.[58]

Notably, the three ways in which human rights can lead to change – articulation of the harm, its acknowledgement, and the provision of a remedy – are inter-related. If, for instance, the victim is given the opportunity to communicate the injustice he or she has suffered, but this injustice is not then recognised as a violation by the state or is not effectively remedied, this is likely to result in

[50] Bertrand Ramcharan, 'Human Rights and Human Security' (2004) 3 *Disarmament Forum* 39, 45.

[51] Sara Clarke-Habibi, 'Transforming Worldviews: The Case of Education for Peace in Bosnia and Herzegovina' (2005) 3 *Journal of Transformative Education* 33.

[52] James L Gibson, 'Truth, Reconciliation and the Creation of a Human Rights Culture in South Africa' (2004) 38 *Law and Society Review* 5.

[53] See, eg, *August v Electoral Commission* (CCT 8/99) (SA Constitutional Court, 1 April 1999) [17] (per Sacchs J).

[54] *Doctors for Life International v Speaker of the National Assembly and Others* (CCT 12/05) (SA Constitutional Court, 17 August 2006) [132].

[55] ibid [97] and [111].

[56] General Framework Agreement for Peace in BiH, Annex 6, arts 4–6. Although the Ombusdman does not have a specific mandate to educate the public, he appears frequently in the media, provides assistance to citizens on how to use the most adequate legal remedies and advises them on which institution to address. See the Institution of Human Rights Ombudsman of Bosnia and Herzegovina Official Website, 'Role and Function', available at www.ombudsmen.gov.ba/Default.aspx?id=10&lang=EN.

[57] The Northern Ireland Peace Agreement, Agreement Reached in the Multi-party Negotiations, signed on 10 April 1998, Annex 1 (hereinafter 'Belfast Agreement'). Under its terms of reference, the Patten Commission should provide recommendations on a range of issues, including education, that are required in the transition to a peaceful society. Note also that the NI Equality Commission has educational functions (FETO, art 8).

[58] One of the tasks of the Commission, under s 184(2)(d) of the SA Constitution, is to educate the public about human rights. For more information about how the Commission has approached this task, see Claudia Lohrenscheit, 'International Approaches in Human Rights Education' (2002) 48 *International Review of Education* 173, 181.

'too much law and too little justice' and have a negative effect on peacebuilding efforts.[59] The importance of combining the three types of human rights contributions is illustrated through the workings and impact of the TRC in SA. The way in which the TRC received information about gross human rights violations from victims and perpetrators and then, based on these testimonies, published its report and findings[60] provided an effective medium for the articulation and formal acknowledgement of grievances, and also contributed to feelings of security, justice and reconciliation in the short and medium term. However, the Commission's inability to push the government to provide victims with the remedies it considered most appropriate in a timely fashion ultimately undermined efforts to resolve conflicts in the long term. A total of 38 per cent of those who testified before the TRC requested financial assistance to improve the quality of their lives and nine out of 10 asked for a range of services which could be purchased if money had been made available (for example, education, medical care and housing).[61] The need to provide such remedies to the victims was also recognised by the SA Constitutional Court, which recommended the payment of compensation, bursaries and scholarships, the provision of occupational training, complex surgical interventions and medical help, and subsidies to prevent evictions.[62] In its report, the TRC adopted some of these recommendations, such as the payment of reparations and the establishment of skills training, and further added as proposed remedies the resettlement of those who had been displaced by political violence and the provision of mental health services.[63] However, despite these promising recommendations, the SA government decided to award only monetary compensation to the victims (and for a significantly lower compensation amount than that suggested by the Commission), considerably delayed the process and acted in a way that failed to treat the victims with respect. For instance, after refusing to engage in a dialogue with them and civil society organisations about the payment of reparations, government officials justified their actions and dismissed criticisms by noting that they were under no legal obligation to consult with stakeholders at any point in the process.[64] Ultimately, the ability of the applicants to articulate their grievances, and the

[59] Cummings and Rhode (n 24) 604.

[60] This process is discussed in more detail below in section V.B.

[61] Rebecca Saunders, 'Lost in Translation: Expressions of Human Suffering, the Language of Human Rights, and the South African Truth and Reconciliation Commission' (2008) 9 *International Journal on Human Rights* 51. This was further confirmed in a study by the human rights group Khulumani, which found that the most pressing needs of the families of the missing in SA are material, including employment (71 per cent), housing (22 per cent) and skills training (17 per cent) (Kovras (n 30) 205).

[62] *The Azarian Peoples Organisation (AZAPO) and Others v President of the Republic of South Africa* (CCT 17/96) (SA Constitutional Court, 25 July 1996) [45].

[63] TRC, *Report of the Truth and Reconciliation Commission* (Pretoria, TRC, 1998), vol 6, s 2, ch 1 [16].

[64] Ereshnee Naidu, 'Symbolic Reparations and Reconciliation: Lessons from South Africa' (2012–13) 19 *Buffalo Human Rights Law Review* 251, 262.

state's formal recognition of these through the TRC's report, contributed to subjective feelings of peace only temporarily. These were eventually undermined by the inadequate remedies received by the victims and the way in which the whole process was managed by the government.

The preceding analysis suggests that the protection of human rights can indeed contribute to socio-economic and psychological changes, which are necessary for the promotion of subjective feelings of peace. However, as the following sections suggest, these contributions do not follow automatically from the articulation and acknowledgement of the human rights violation, or even from the provision of the remedy. Rather, the ability of human rights to resolve conflicts as psychological states of affairs is dependent on *at least* two sets of conditions that must also be present in the post-violence society. The first is that human rights remedies must actually deliver what they promised to achieve, namely make a meaningful change in people's lives, lest they result in disappointment among the population. The second is based on the notion that what is important is not only the protection of human rights itself, but also ensuring that this happens in a way that people *perceive* as being conducive to the promotion of peace.

III. THE GAP BETWEEN THE LEGAL AND THE REAL: MAKING A MEANINGFUL CHANGE IN PEOPLE'S LIVES

One of the strengths of human rights and the reason many see them as powerful peacebuilding tools is that they are legally binding and their use sends the message that any promises made in the peace agreement will be kept. However, in addition to the implementation challenges explored in Chapter 5, there is a danger that even when human rights have been enforced, the remedy they give rise to may not result in *meaningful* changes in practice.[65] In turn, this can undermine efforts to build subjective peace because if the state makes a promise to improve people's lives, which the intended beneficiaries do not experience as having been fulfilled, they are likely to feel cheated or betrayed, and lose their confidence in the new state of affairs.[66] Conversely, ensuring that the provision of a legal remedy makes a real impact in the lives of the people allows them, to the extent that is possible, to leave the experiences of the past behind them, and becomes one of the most effective ways of resolving conflicts as psychological states of affairs. Since subjective peace depends on the perceptions and beliefs of the population within the post-violence society, what is important

[65] Luc Reychler, 'Peace Architecture: The Prevention of Violence' Eagly, Baron, Reuben and Hamilton (eds) (n 1).

[66] Jennifer Widner, 'Courts and Democracy in Postconflict Transitions: A Social Scientist's Perspective on the African Case' (2001) 95 *American Journal of International Law* 64, 66.

in this respect is not that a human rights institution is set up, but that the public – the victims and the general population alike[67] – is satisfied with the results it delivers. In order for this to happen, it is necessary that peacebuilders take the context in which they operate into account and tailor their strategies accordingly. As McAuliffe put it, such strategies:

> [M]ust understand and relate to the power relations at play in the distinct post-conflict context. Without grounding theory in the realities of post-conflict states, [peacebuilding strategies can result in] a form of ideological support devoid of any realistic or pragmatic [plan] to actually address the deprivations identified and with little regard for what can reasonably be accomplished.[68]

Perhaps the importance of making meaningful changes to people's lives is most clearly illustrated through an analysis of the Property Law Implementation Plan (PLIP) in BiH.[69] As a result of PLIP, four years after its inception, 93 per cent of displaced persons had been given the title to their properties and told they could return back to their homes.[70] Yet, this statistical success has not been translated in the physical return of the victims: although it is unclear how many displaced persons resettled back to their properties, the anecdotal evidence is disappointing.[71] For instance, in the Republika Srpska (one of the two entities in BiH), only 20–30 per cent of those to whom property was returned actually live in it, since the remaining applicants obtained their property titles and sold them on so that they could buy a house in areas where they were in the majority.[72]

In order for the remedy of restitution to be a meaningful one, it was necessary that the return of the displaced population to their houses was a real option that people could use if they wished to. Important factors influencing this outcome, in addition to making it legally possible, include the extent to which the social climate around return is welcoming and whether people have the economic resources for this move.[73] In BiH, the disproportionate emphasis on the legal

[67] Paying attention to the general public and not only those who were most directly affected by the violence is necessary because '[r]econciliation in the psychological framework refers to a societal-cultural process that encompasses the majority of society's members' (Daniel Bar-Tal, 'From Intractable Conflict through Conflict Resolution to Reconciliation: Psychological Analysis' (2000) 21 *Political Psychology* 351, 356).

[68] Padraig McAuliffe, *Transformative Transitional Justice and the Malleability of Post-conflict States* (Cheltenham, Edward Elgar, 2017) xiii.

[69] The legal framework of the PLIP is discussed in more detail in section V in ch 5.

[70] Office of the High Representative, *Statistics: Implementation of the Property Laws in Bosnia and Herzegovina* (Sarajevo, Office of the High Representative, 31 May 2000).

[71] International Crisis Group, *The Continuing Challenge of Refugee Return in Bosnia & Herzegovina*, Balkans Report N° 137 (Sarajevo, International Crisis Group, 2002) 11.

[72] European Commission against Racism and Intolerance, *First Report on Bosnia and Herzegovina*, CRI(2005)2 (Strasbourg, Council of Europe, 25 June 2004) [22].

[73] Amnesty International, *Bosnia and Herzegovina: Behind Closed Gates: Ethnic Discrimination in Employment*, EUR 63/001/2006 (Sarajevo, Amnesty International, 2006) notes that ethnic segregation in the provision of education, health and social security services has prevented a welcoming climate from materialising.

protection of the right to property to the detriment of these additional considerations often made the option to return merely imaginary. Especially in the early days after Dayton, there was an endemic problem of discrimination in all areas of life: a minority returnee found it difficult, if not impossible, to get a job, be served without discrimination by public officials or socialise with the majority of the community, which was of a different ethnic group.[74] Lack of legal access to property was not the only barrier to return, something confirmed by the fact that 20 per cent of Bosnians who were unwilling to return to their houses would reconsider their decision if the job market improved.[75] This raises questions as to whether displaced people who sold their returned properties and moved to areas where they were in the majority did so voluntarily or because they lacked the support to remain there. However, if the low number of returnees is due to socio-economic difficulties to resettle rather than a voluntary decision on their behalf, it is unlikely that they felt that justice had truly been done.

The insight that law is only one variable in the efforts to achieve social change is a well-rehearsed theme in the general socio-legal literature[76] and has also been shared by peacebuilders themselves.[77] In theory, the need to supplement legal protections with other peacebuilding strategies in order to achieve the multidimensional objective of refugee return was accepted by the international community in BiH, which stated just before closing down PLIP that:

> While property law implementation is the fundamental first step, it is only one among many of the elements underpinning sustainable return. *Full implementation of Annex VII means that not only can people return to their homes but that they can do so safely with equal expectations of employment, education and social services.*[78] (Emphasis in original)

In practice, however, there was a continuous overreliance on law as a tool for social change that failed to take these insights into account. Despite appreciating the limitations of a purely legal solution to the problem of forced displacement, no other approach was seriously adopted to supplement it and therefore the PLIP's potentially transformative message was lost in translation. The emphasis that was put on the legal protection of the right dwarfed any attention to issues of social justice, which in turn made the possibility of return an illusory one.

[74] European Commission against Racism and Intolerance (n 72) [40]–[45].

[75] Commission for Real Property Claims of Displaced Persons and Refugees, *Return, Local Integration and Property Rights in Bosnia Herzegovina* (Sarajevo, Commission for Real Property Claims of Displaced Persons and Refugees, 1999).

[76] Alice Donald and Elizabeth Mottershaw, 'Evaluating the Impact of Human Rights Litigation on Policy and Practice: A Case Study of the UK' (2009) 1 *Journal of Human Rights Practice* 339, 352.

[77] UN Secretary-General, *In Larger Freedom: Towards Security, Development and Human Rights of All*, A/59/2005 (New York, United Nations, 2005) [156].

[78] Office of the High Representative, PLIP Press Release, 'Property Law Implementation is Just One Element of Annex VII' (Sarajevo, Office of the High Representative, 27 February 2003), emphasis in original.

In 2011, the unemployment rate in BiH was more than 40 per cent[79] and, in 2009, approximately half of the population in both entities lived below the poverty line or were at risk of falling below it at any time.[80] In this difficult economic climate, minority returnees 'face[d] discrimination in all areas of daily life'[81] and found it even harder than the rest of the population to get a job,[82] send their children to school[83] or enjoy an adequate level of healthcare.[84] None of these problems were addressed by the PLIP. However, if returnees cannot secure their employment, if their children do not feel safe going to school or if they find it difficult to enjoy social services – in other words, if the socio-economic conditions that make their return possible are absent – then being legally allowed to take such a step on paper fails to provide a real option to them and does little to promote justice in their eyes.[85] It seems that peacebuilders in BiH ignored the basic truths that restitution is not the same as return, that human rights do not in themselves guarantee justice and that '[r]ecognition of title in a vacuum, where the conditions for return do not exist, will at best result in a mass sell-off of property'.[86] In essence, their excessive focus on the law hid the 'messiness and tough choices that characterize the lives of many' and was thus unable to help peacebuilders navigate these very choices.[87]

The emphasis on the law has not only prevented real change in BiH in terms of promoting subjective feelings of justice, but also reconciliation. Even in cases where people did return permanently to their old houses, this resulted in some co-existence and interaction between ethnic groups, but no genuine improvement in inter-ethnic relations. Stefansson vividly makes this point through his analysis of the 'big' and the 'small home'.[88] The right to property can successfully protect the latter – the return to the actual structure – but it cannot on its own promote the former – the feeling of a shared community between the ethnic

[79] 'Index Mundi: Bosnia and Herzegovina Unemployment Rate', available at www.indexmundi.com/bosnia_and_herzegovina/unemployment_rate.html.

[80] Huma Haider, '(Re)Imagining Coexistence: Striving for Sustainable Return, Reintegration and Reconciliation in Bosnia and Herzegovina' (2009) 3 *International Journal of Transitional Justice* 91, 97.

[81] European Commission against Racism and Intolerance, *Second Report on Bosnia and Herzegovina,* CRI(2011)2 (Strasbourg, Council of Europe, 7 December 2010) [96].

[82] ibid [79]–[80].

[83] ibid [63].

[84] ibid [85].

[85] See Clare Magill, Alan Smith and Brandon Hamber, *The Role of Education in Reconciliation: The Perspectives of Children and Young People in Bosnia and Herzegovina and Northern Ireland* (Ulster, Special EU Programmes Body, University of Ulster, 2009), who argue that economic insecurity is seen by young people in BiH and NI as an impediment to building a lasting peace and reconciliation.

[86] Charles Philpott, 'Though the Dog is Dead, the Pig Must Be Killed: Finishing with Property Restitution to Bosnia Herzegovina's IDPs and Refugees' (2005) 18 *Journal of Refugee Studies* 1, 21.

[87] Kieran McEvoy, 'Beyond Legalism: Towards a Thicker Understanding of Transitional Justice' (2007) 34 *Journal of Law and Society* 411, 418.

[88] Anders H Stefansson, 'Homes in the Making: Property Restitution, Refugee Return and Senses of Belonging in a Post-war Bosnian Town' (2006) 44 *International Migration* 115.

groups. Indicative in this is his example of minority returnees of Muslim origin, who avoided wearing green, a colour associated with their religion, in public places so that they did not provoke reactions.[89] This is not to argue that changing a state's formal practices cannot influence the politicians' and public's opinions and eventually make a positive impact on reconciliation. There are suggestions, for instance, that as human rights are implemented, they become institutionalised, which, in turn, makes state actors and subsequently the people more receptive to the peacebuilding messages communicated through the language they use.[90] Moreover, Gibson and Gouws provide evidence that a human rights decision by the SA Constitutional Court to allow an unpopular party to protest is likely to increase levels of 'grudging tolerance' in the population.[91] However, it is unclear what the long-term impact of legal decisions is on people's feelings and whether tolerant attitudes usually take root or are ephemeral, especially when these are not accompanied by additional reconciliation-promoting measures. Ultimately, in BiH, the implementation of the right to property happened to the detriment of such measures. Partly due to this lack of legal humility, people from different ethnic groups live parallel lives side by side, but they do not interact meaningfully.[92] This might be an improvement from being actively hostile to others, but it is a far cry from having achieved reconciliation or subjective peace more generally.

Similar conclusions concerning the importance of inducing real change in the lives of the people arise from an assessment of the SA Commission on Restitution of Land Rights (hereinafter CRLR or Commission), a body tasked with remedying those who had been forcibly displaced during apartheid, by providing either restitution or compensation to them.[93] The Commission failed to make an impact in people's lives because it sought to legally protect the right to property, without considering the context in which this was happening and the possibility that socio-economic support structures would be needed to render its protection effective. Essentially, the CRLR assumed that the implementation of the law and the remedying of victims marked the end rather than the beginning of the state's efforts to promote justice. As a result of this assumption, large areas of land were returned to communities that had been displaced decades ago, but had no rural life experience. Left to their own devices and with

[89] ibid.

[90] Open Society Justice Initiative, *From Rights to Remedies: Structures and Strategies for Implementing International Human Rights Decisions* (New York, Open Society Foundation, 2013) 25 and 108.

[91] James L Gibson and Amanda Gouws, *Overcoming Intolerance in South Africa: Experiments in Democratic Persuasion* (Cambridge, Cambridge University Press, 2003) 171, arguing that a positive judgment from the Court could boost tolerance from 27.7 per cent to 56.8 per cent of the population, an increase of 29.1 per cent.

[92] McEvoy (n 87) 425. The argument here is not that the absence of legal humility and the over-reliance on human rights are wholly responsible for the failure of the PLIP to resolve conflicts as psychological states of affairs; rather, they provide one explanation among many.

[93] Restitution of Land Rights Act No 22 of 1994.

no post-restitution support from the state, the new owners were expected to make a living by competing with commercial farmers.[94] The outcome of this policy has often been the dismantling of successful farming enterprises – and the consequent loss of jobs – in order to replace them with the inexperienced running of properties and barren fields.[95] A confirmation of this is provided by a study in which the majority of the 179 projects examined were dysfunctional, in that little, if any, production was being pursued.[96] Responding to this, the government has started making restitution conditional on the existence of strategic partnerships between the displaced communities and commercial farmers. Nevertheless, because the interests of the two parties are not always aligned, these partnerships do not necessarily improve the lives of displaced persons.[97] For example, in an attempt to maximise yield, the agreements usually prevent communities from residing on the restituted land or growing crops for their own personal use.[98] As a result, community members become landlords of large estates on paper and remain homeless and destitute in practice.[99] Considering that two of the four objectives of the restitution process in SA were 'to redress the injustices of apartheid; [and] to foster national reconciliation and stability',[100] the failure of the Commission to deliver, is likely to have undermined subjective feelings of peace.

The limitations of the CRLR's legalistic approach in making meaningful changes in people's lives have also become apparent when providing the remedy of compensation. In theory, compensation promotes reconciliation by creating a feeling of closure to the victims and empowering them to leave the past behind them.[101] However, in order for this to happen, it is necessary not only to compensate them with an adequate amount, but also to explain to the victims

[94] Lungisile Ntsebeza and Ruth Hall, *The Land Question in South Africa: The Challenge of Transformation and Redistribution* (Cape Town, HSRC Press, 2007).

[95] Community Agency for Social Enquiry, *Assessment of the Status Quo of Settled Land Restitution Claims with a Developmental Component Nationally* (Pretoria, Department of Land Affairs, 2006).

[96] Ruth Hall, 'Reconciling the Past, Present and Future: The Parameters and Practices of Land Restitution in South Africa' in Cherryl Walker et al (eds), *Land, Memory, Reconstruction and Justice: Perspectives on Land Claims in South Africa* (Athens, OH, Ohio University Press, 2010).

[97] Edward Lahiff, *State, Market or Worst of Both? Experimenting with Market-Based Land Reform in South Africa*, Occasional Paper No 30 (Bellville, Programme for Land and Agrarian Studies, University of the Western Cape, 2007).

[98] Bill Derman, Edward Lahiff and Espen Sjaastad, 'Strategic Questions about Strategic Partners' in Walker et al (n 96).

[99] Deborah James, *Gaining Ground? 'Rights' and 'Property' in South African Land Reform* (New York, Routledge-Cavendish, 2007) 74; Wouter Veraart, 'Redressing the Past with an Eye to the Future: The Impact of the Passage of Time on Property Rights Restitution in Post-apartheid South Africa' (2009) 27 *Netherlands Quarterly of Human Rights* 45.

[100] Department of Land Affairs, *White Paper on South African Land Policy* (Pretoria, Department of Land Affairs, 1997) 7.

[101] Naomi Roht-Arriaza, 'Reparations and Development' in Rugh Buchanan and Peer Zumbansen (eds), *Law in Transition: Human Rights, Development and Transitional Justice* (Oxford, Hart Publishing, 2016) 194.

why compensation was paid in the first place.[102] Problematically, neither of the two conditions was satisfied in SA. During apartheid, a single property was often occupied by several families, whose members have multiplied since their dispossession. By the time the compensation award was shared between them, there was very little money left and was usually used to buy everyday supplies or pay off debts rather than in a way that could make a long-term difference in people's welfare.[103] This likely undermined feelings of justice and reconciliation among the different communities in the country because the continuing inequality had the effect of reinforcing the marginalisation of the displaced from the rest of the population.[104]

Therefore, what is needed in order to address feelings of injustice is the payment of an amount that empowers the recipients to take steps to integrate themselves back into society. Reparations cannot, and should not, replace long-term development strategies, which should also be part of the peacebuilding process[105] and can more effectively respond to socio-economic inequalities.[106] However, at the same time, the compensation amount must be such that it can convey an intention to develop a more equitable relationship between the state and its citizens and among the citizens themselves. This has not been the result of payment of compensation in SA, where:

> The disparity between the promise of the constitution and the material progress 'on the ground' is striking. The symbolic break with the past does not correspond with the actual distribution of property rights in South Africa, which is still based, in many ways on the Apartheid era.[107]

Yet, perhaps more problematic than the actual amount has been the fact that some of the displaced people did not even understand *why* they received money in the first place. They perceived the compensation as another piece of financial help from the haves (including the state) to the have-nots rather than as a unique payment reflecting an acknowledgement of the injustices they had suffered.[108] However, if victims did not understand the purpose of the compensation,

[102] Brandon Hamber, 'Narrowing the Micro and Macro: A Psychological Perspective on Reparations in Societies in Transition' in Pablo de Greiff (ed), *The Handbook of Reparations* (Oxford, Oxford University Press, 2006), arguing that genuine reparation and the process of healing does not occur only, or primarily, through the delivery of an object or acts of reparations, but also through the process that takes place around the object or act.

[103] Bernadette Atuahene, 'Paying for the Past: Redressing the Legacy of Land Dispossession in South Africa' (2011) 45 *Law and Society Review* 955.

[104] Kaushik Basu, 'Participatory Equity and Economic Development: Policy Implications for a Globalized World' World Bank Conference 'New Frontiers of Social Policy: Development in a Globalizing World' (Arusha, 12–15 December 2005) 2. See also Hamber (n 1) 13.

[105] ibid.

[106] Roht-Arriaza (n 101) 201.

[107] Veraart (n 99) 59.

[108] Anna Bohlin, 'A Price on the Past: Cash Compensation in South African Land Restitution' (2004) 38 *Canadian Journal of African Studies* 672.

the remedy is unlikely to help them feel reconciled.[109] Evidence suggests that when state officials apologise using appropriate language alongside suitable remedies,[110] they contribute to psychological and social change.[111] Conversely, if no apologies are made, or are perceived as inauthentic, they can have the reverse effect.[112] In the absence of a communication strategy accompanying the right to property, its protection produced legal changes, but not the psychological changes that were crucial for the building of subjective peace. Moreover, this legalistic response to the problem has not only prevented the victims from feeling reconciled, but has arguably also had similar consequences for the perpetrators. The lack of an apology that should have preceded the compensation awards has allowed most of those who benefited from the displacement to go on with their lives and pretend that the geography and wealth distribution in the country are unrelated to its apartheid past. To the extent that land restitution is discussed among white SAs, debates tend to focus on how much compensation has been paid and whether displaced persons have used that money wisely rather than on what the remedy signifies.[113] Consequently, 'land issues are terribly important to black South Africans, and they are practically invisible to white South Africans',[114] with 77 per cent of the former considering apartheid to be a factor that has influenced land inequality and only 34 per cent of the latter agreeing.[115] This points to a lingering perception, which is detrimental to reconciliation efforts, and which the current human rights strategy has been unable to address – that economic inequalities are better explained by the laziness of the majority rather than the history of the country.

The final illustration of the need to look beyond the law and assess the social consequences of a human rights initiative stems from the experience of the relatives of missing persons with the SA TRC. The Commission has been the subject of a vast literature, much of which has applauded its achievements.[116] However, relatively absent from this – albeit with notable exceptions[117] – is an

[109] Bar-Tal (n 67) 354.

[110] Hamber (n 1) 15.

[111] Raymond Cohen, 'Apology and Reconciliation in International Relations' in Yaacov Bar-Siman-Tov (ed), *From Conflict Resolution to Reconciliation* (Oxford, Oxford University Press, 2004).

[112] Jennifer Lind, *Sorry States: Apologies in International Relations* (Ithaca, Cornell University Press, 2010).

[113] Bohlin (n 108).

[114] James L Gibson, *Overcoming Historical Injustices: Land Reconciliation in South Africa* (Cambridge, Cambridge University Press, 2009) 84.

[115] ibid 46.

[116] James L Gibson, *Overcoming Apartheid: Can Truth Reconcile a Divided Nation?* (New York, Russell Sage Foundation, 2004); Martha Minow, 'Breaking the Cycles of Hatred' in Martha Minow (ed), *Breaking the Cycles of Hatred: Memory, Law and Repair* (Princeton, Princeton University Press, 2002). For a more critical view of the TRC, see Audrey R Chapman and Patrick Ball, 'The Truth of Truth Commissions: Comparative Lessons from Haiti, South Africa and Guatemala' (2001) 23 *Human Rights Quarterly* 1; Richard A Wilson, *The Politics of Truth and Reconciliation in South Africa: Legitimzing the Post-apartheid State* (Cambridge, Cambridge University Press, 2001).

[117] Jay D Aronson, 'The Strengths and Limitations of South Africa's Search for Apartheid-Era Missing Persons' (2011) 5 *International Journal of Transitional Justice* 262.

examination of the TRC's efforts to uncover the truth about those who went missing during apartheid. The academic disinterest in this aspect of the TRC's mandate is, on the one hand, understandable, considering the relatively small number of missing persons. To put it in perspective, of the 38,000 allegations of gross violations of human rights made to the Commission, nearly 10,000 were killings[118] and only 2,000 concerned disappearances.[119] Nonetheless, the lack of greater attention to this issue has also been surprising in light of the TRC's stark self-admission that '[t]he resolution of these disappearance cases is perhaps the most significant piece of unfinished business for the Commission'.[120]

As a result of political support and generous funding, the TRC was able to set up an impressive network of investigations in order to uncover the truth about human rights violations that took place during apartheid. The work of the 17 Commissioners was supported by some 400 members of staff and a separate research department, the operations of which were geographically dispersed in six offices around the country.[121] Over its three years of operations, the TRC held several hundred public hearings (during which over 1,800 victims were heard), concluded more than 21,000 victim interviews and processed approximately 7,000 amnesty applications.[122] Through these efforts, the Commission made it impossible 'for the average South African to suffer from selective amnesia or to deny the nature and extent of the gross human rights violations'.[123] Its impressive operations notwithstanding, the TRC has been unable to contribute to feelings of justice and reconciliation among the relatives of the missing for two reasons: first, it has not returned the bodies of the missing to their families; and, second, it has not made the perpetrators in any way accountable. In short, despite its compliance with the law, the TRC produced no results that could have made a real difference in the lives of those most directly affected by the violations. Consequently, family members of the disappeared have complained bitterly that the Commission deprived them of closure and dignity, not least because they have perceived the nominal compensation amount they received as 'blood money';[124] as payment for their silence and the exertion of unwanted pressure to stop them from expressing their ongoing sense of injustice.

The TRC's inability to return the bodies of missing persons to their families stems from two limitations in the way in which it operated. First, although the Commission had heard approximately 1,500 testimonies about disappearances, it decided to rely on an exceptionally narrow definition of a 'missing person',

[118] TRC (n 63) vol 1, Appendix 2 [21].

[119] Kovras (n 30) 185.

[120] TRC (n 63) vol 6, s 4, ch 1 [96].

[121] Chapman and Ball (n 116).

[122] ibid 8.

[123] Dorothy C Shea, *The South African Truth Commission: The Politics of Reconciliation* (Washington DC, Institute of Peace Press, 2000) 6.

[124] Quoted in Kovras (n 30) 182.

which reduced the number of cases under its mandate to 477.[125] In particular, in order for someone to be considered a disappeared person for the purposes of the TRC, his or her disappearance had to have been politically motivated,[126] a requirement that was difficult to prove at a time when many opposed apartheid without necessarily being members of a political organisation. This narrow definition meant that many families that experienced the detrimental effects of a relative's disappearance, whether these were economic or psychological, could not benefit from the Commission's investigative powers or the provision of a remedy at the end of the process. Second, the practices of the Missing Persons Task Team, a follow-up to the TRC established in 2005, also resulted in disappointing outcomes. Its decision not to rely on DNA testing (at a time when the technology was available and used, for example, in BiH) resulted in just 89 identifications, of which only 60 per cent were accurate.[127] In instances of misidentification, families had to return the body they had been given, thus causing their retraumatisation and inhibiting the process of reconciliation.

In terms of its second limitation, the TRC could not issue blanket amnesties, but it did provide individual amnesties to those perpetrators who came forward and admitted their crimes.[128] While this was a bitter pill to swallow for family members,[129] the expectation was that finding out the truth would have a more positive peacebuilding impact for the society at large than making the perpetrators legally accountable for their past crimes.[130] This assumption has been challenged as being principally flawed, since it does not necessarily follow that truth leads to feelings of justice or reconciliation.[131] Even more problematically on a practical level, no prosecutions took place, even when it became clear that perpetrators had not told the truth during the TRC hearings. For example, in the 'Pebco Three' case in Eastern Cape, the perpetrators testified before the Commission that they had burned the bodies and thrown the ashes in a nearby river to destroy incriminating evidence. More than a decade after their testimony, forensic evidence from exhumations contradicted their original statement, since parts of the victims' bodies were found in a nearby septic tank.[132]

[125] Aronson (n 117) 271.

[126] Promotion of National Unity and Reconciliation Act No 34 of 1995, s 1.

[127] Kovras (n 30) 185.

[128] TRC (n 63) vol 1, ch 1 [29].

[129] Hamber (n 102) 4.

[130] *The Azarian Peoples Organisation (AZAPO)* [17].

[131] Oliver Ramsbotham, Tom Woodhouse and Hugh Miall, *Contemporary Conflict Resolution: The Prevention, Management and Transformation of Deadly Conflicts* (Cambridge, Polity Press, 2016) 294, arguing that from the point of the ANC, the main objective of the TRC was to be a Truth Commission; reconciliation was mostly an afterthought, pushed by Archbishop Desmond Tutu. See also Robert Rotberg, 'Truth Commissions and the Provision of Truth, Justice and Reconciliation' in Robert Rotberg and Dennis Thompson (eds), *Truth v Justice: The Morality of Truth Commissions* (Princeton, Princeton University Press, 2000).

[132] Kovras (n 30) 200.

This forensic evidence could have been used as a legal basis to overturn the perpetrators' amnesty, yet this did not happen, thus further compromising feelings of justice and reconciliation among the family members.

Like PLIP and the CRLR, the TRC offers a stark example of a body which technically complied with its mandate of responding to human rights violations, without meeting the expectations of some of the victims, thus failing to resolve the conflict as a psychological state of affairs. Part of the reason for this failure is the excessive reliance of all three institutions on legal provisions and strategies that did not – and could not – fully address the needs and concerns of the intended beneficiaries. This critique should not be taken to mean that human rights must not be protected at all, or that they are altogether ineffective peacebuilding tools. Rather, it is making the more nuanced point that legal humility is necessary because while human rights might be able to contribute to some socio-economic and psychological changes, they cannot complete this process on their own. Building subjective peace also requires the adoption of a range of other peacebuilding strategies that will supplement the protection of human rights, such as initiatives that will promote community-building in BiH and provide better social services in SA.

IV. PEACE MUST BE BUILT AND BE SEEN TO BE BUILT

In addition to ensuring that real change takes place in post-violence societies, subjective peace requires that the public *perceives* that change in a positive light.[133] Human rights can help achieve this goal and shape public perceptions when at least four conditions are met. These are that human rights are implemented in a climate that is conducive to social change; the public is made aware of human rights-inspired policies and the way they connect to peacebuilding objectives; these policies are understood by people as genuine attempts to promote peace; and they are implemented by a body that the public considers legitimate. Of course, whether a peacebuilding strategy will affect the perceptions of a given individual also depends on factors that are wholly outside the peacebuilders' control, such as the psychology of each person. However, paying attention to the four conditions can at least improve the possibility of resolving conflicts as psychological states of affairs. Importantly, these are neither exhaustive nor to be seen in isolation from each other. For instance, making the public aware of human rights-inspired policies and their peacebuilding objectives becomes more difficult if they are implemented in a climate that is not conducive

[133] Tomas Amparo, 'Reforms that Benefit Poor People – Practical Solutions and Dilemmas of Rights-Based Approaches to Legal and Justice Reform' in Paul Gready and Jonathan Ensor (eds), *Reinventing Development? Translating Rights-Based Approaches from Theory into Practice* (London, Zed Books, 2005) 172, arguing that 'the question is not only whether particular laws or institutions exist or how they appear, but rather how laws and institutions relate to people and how people perceive, use, change and develop them'.

to peace. Therefore, it is only by considering the different conditions in tandem that human rights can start contributing to social and psychological, in addition to legal and institutional, changes for peace.

Since human rights do not operate in a vacuum, the first and perhaps most difficult condition to satisfy is that they are protected within a context that is already somewhat supportive of peacebuilding efforts.[134] If this does not happen, human rights institutions will, at best, become marginalised and ineffective and, at worst, be hijacked by spoilers and used in a way that undermines the conflict resolution process.[135] Illustrative of this danger are the effects of *Selimović and Others v Republika Srpska*, in which relatives of people who had gone missing during the Srebrenica massacre, argued before the Human Rights Chamber of BiH that the continuous lack of effective investigation constituted violations of Articles 3, 8 and 14 of the European Convention.[136] While the Republika Srpska (RS) had already published a report about what had allegedly happened in Srebrenica, this was one-sided since it only included details about violations that had been perpetrated against the Serbs, sought to excuse and justify any violations against Bosniacs, and its description of the events was in contrast to the ICTY's findings in *Krstić*,[137] which had dealt with the same issue.[138] The Human Rights Chamber, reasoning that the authorities had failed to locate, discover and disclose accurate information about the fate of the missing, found in the applicants' favour and ordered a number of remedies.[139] Taking into account that more than 1,800 family members had filed related motions with the Chamber between November 2001 and March 2002,[140] it ordered that the payment of compensation should be made not to the individual applicants, but to the Srebrenica-Potocari Memorial and Cemetery Foundation, which would use it for the benefit of all the families and victims.[141] Moreover, the RS was ordered to adopt a number of measures which had the objective of directly challenging social perceptions about what had happened in Srebrenica and making the applicants feel properly remedied. For instance, the authorities were asked to release any information they had about the fate of the missing persons,[142] conduct an effective investigation into the events in question[143] and disseminate

[134] Roland Paris, *At War's End: Building Peace after Civil Conflict* (Cambridge, Cambridge University Press, 2004).

[135] Marko Milanovic, 'The Impact of the ICTY on the Former Yugoslavia: An Anticipatory Post-mortem' (2016) 110 *American Journal of International Law* 233.

[136] *Selimović and Others v Republika Srpska* (CH/01/8365) (BiH Human Rights Chamber, 7 March 2003). These are the right to be free from torture, inhuman and degrading treatment, the right to private and family life, and freedom from discrimination respectively.

[137] *Krstić* (IT-98-33) (ICTY, 2 August 2001).

[138] *Selimović* (n 136) [179].

[139] ibid [178].

[140] ibid [1].

[141] ibid [217].

[142] ibid [211].

[143] ibid [212].

the information included in the Chamber's decision as widely as possible within their territory.[144]

At the insistence of the High Representative, the RS authorities implemented the decision and formed a new 'Commission for the Investigation of the Events in and around Srebrenica between 10 and 19 July 1995'.[145] This Commission, involving RS government members, representatives of survivor groups and international observers, concluded that large-scale massacres, mostly against Bosniacs, had taken place in July 1995, disclosed the location of more than 30 mass graves and provided additional information that assisted in locating the missing.[146] While the Commission's findings were also followed by an apology from RS President Dragan Čavić,[147] the implementation of this case has not resulted in any notable social or psychological changes in BiH or the promotion of reconciliation among the ethnic groups. In a 2011 survey, some seven years after the publication of the Commission's findings, only 71.6 per cent of Bosnian Serbs had heard of the events in Srebrenica and less than a third believed that these were true.[148] The ineffectiveness of the human rights judgment to induce those changes that were necessary for subjective peace, despite its successful implementation, is arguably because this took place within a social and political climate where nationalism and denialism were the norm.[149] Yet, if the context itself is hostile to change, solely relying on the law is most likely to have a superficial or no impact on people's perceptions and practices.[150] In Osiel's words: 'When collective memory has already become comfortably entrenched, the law's efforts to excavate and scrutinize it are only likely to discredit the law and its professional spokesmen.'[151] In such instances, peacebuilders are advised to rely on alternative strategies, such as reforming the educational system or launching an information campaign, that will more effectively reach and have an impact on the masses.

The second condition is that people must be made aware of the existence of human rights-inspired policies or case law and the ways in which these connect to peacebuilding objectives. Referring to the judiciary, Rosenberg argues that: 'It is naïve to expect an institution seen as distant and unfamiliar, shrouded in mystery, and using arcane language and procedures to change people's views.'[152]

[144] ibid [213].

[145] Jeremy Sarkin et al, *Bosnia i Herzegovina Missing Persons from the Armed Conflicts of the 1990s: A Stocktaking* (Sarajevo, International Commission on Missing Persons, 2014) 111.

[146] ibid.

[147] Denis Dzidic, 'Bosnian Serb Leader Urges Srebrenica "Truth Commission"' *Balkan Transitional Justice*, 25 March 2015.

[148] Milanovic (n 135).

[149] ibid.

[150] Gerarld N Rosenberg, 'The Irrelevant Court: The Supreme Court's Inability to Influence Popular Beliefs about Equality (or Anything Else)' in Neal Devins and Dave Douglas (eds), *Redefining Equality* (Oxford, Oxford University Press, 1998) 174.

[151] Mark J Osiel, *Mass Atrocity, Collective Memory, and the Law* (New York, Routledge, 2017) 113.

[152] Rosenberg (n 150) 187.

To put it simply, if the average person does not know or understand what human rights institutions are doing, then their actions and decisions, no matter how well-reasoned or intentioned, will be unable to contribute to subjective feelings of peace.[153] This makes it necessary that specific efforts are made to inform the public about human rights initiatives and the rationale behind them.

One example in which this was done successfully was during the proceedings of the Patten Commission in NI, a body that was tasked with making recommendations for the reform of the police following the signing of the Belfast Agreement.[154] The Commission's terms of reference explicitly stated that what was important was not only that the police service was reformed, but that it was also perceived as being reformed, so that it 'can enjoy widespread support from, and is seen as an integral part of, the community as a whole'.[155] Operating under this mandate, the Commission put human rights at the centre of its recommendations, but did not stop at that.[156] Further, it relied on a methodology, which had the express objective of challenging social perceptions and building 'reconciliation, tolerance and mutual trust' among its target audience.[157] For instance, it recommended that police stations have, as far as possible, the appearance of ordinary buildings;[158] the composition of the police staff should be broadly reflective of the population of NI as a whole;[159] and community leaders should encourage their members to apply to join the force.[160] In making these recommendations, the Commission took into account findings about the perception of the police service among the Protestant and Catholic communities, and stressed that efforts needed to be made to ensure that the differences between the two were eliminated.[161] Moreover, it worked towards operating in a manner that was as inclusive as possible, for example, by inviting the views of the public about the police service, both through a press conference and newspaper advertisements.[162] In addition, it directly contacted about 130 stakeholders, such as political parties, churches, non-governmental organisations and others known to have a particular interest in policing, and asked them to participate in the consultation exercise.[163] As a result of this effort, more than 10,000 people attended public meetings that were organised by

[153] Simmons (n 20) 132, referring to the importance of establishing some degree of 'legal literacy' among individuals.

[154] Independent Commission on Policing for Northern Ireland, *A New Beginning: Policing in Northern Ireland* (Belfast, Northern Ireland Office, 1999) (hereinafter 'Patten Report').

[155] Belfast Agreement (n 57), Annex 1 ('Terms of Reference for the Commission of Policing for Northern Ireland').

[156] Patten Report (n 154) [4.1] and [4.6]–[4.12].

[157] From the preamble of the Belfast Agreement (n 57), quoted in Patten Report (n 154) [1.1].

[158] ibid [8.5].

[159] ibid [14.17].

[160] ibid [15.2].

[161] ibid [3.6] and [3.7].

[162] ibid [2.3].

[163] ibid [2.3].

the Commission and approximately 2,500 written submissions were received.[164] This community-centred approach and the subsequent implementation of the Commission's recommendations has arguably had a positive impact on improving social perceptions of the police and promoting subjective feelings of security among the two communities. Thus, while in 2016 Protestants were still more satisfied with the performance of the police service compared to Catholics,[165] the difference between the two groups had decreased considerably since 1996.[166]

The condition that people must be informed about human rights-inspired policies and their peacebuilding objectives sounds almost tautological, yet examples where conflicts remained unresolved because this was taken for granted abound in almost all post-violence societies. Such was, for instance, the case with the efforts of the international community to locate the remains of missing persons in BiH. This peacebuilding initiative could have resulted in important social and psychological changes among the population, because the suffering of missing persons' relatives, and the need to address it, is almost universally perceived as transcending ethnic divisions.[167] Although attempts to locate the disappeared were originally framed in humanitarian terms, over time, and as a result of case law from Bosnian and European courts, they started being understood as a human rights issue.[168] In turn, this has had a significant positive impact on efforts to locate missing persons, confirming the previous chapter's conclusions that the enforcement of human rights can result in reforms that are instrumental to the building of objective peace. Thus, in 2004 and with the help of the International Commission on Missing Persons, BiH passed the Law on Missing Persons, the first of its kind in a post-violence society, and established the Missing Persons Institute.[169] The Institute has been responsible for locating grave sites and identifying bodies, a task that has been progressing successfully, with more than 70 per cent of missing persons having been found.[170] Over the last few years, laboratories set up by the International Commission on Missing Persons in BiH have amassed such expertise that they are now providing

[164] ibid [2.3].

[165] A total of 73 per cent of Protestant respondents indicated that they thought the police were doing a very/fairly good job in their area, as compared with 64 per cent of Catholics (Northern Ireland Statistics and Research Agency, *Public Perceptions of the Police, PCSPs and the Northern Ireland Policing Board* (Belfast, Northern Ireland Policing Board, 2016) 7). Jonny Byrne and Neil Jarman, 'Ten Years after Patten: Young People and Policing in Northern Ireland' (2011) 43 *Youth & Society* 433, 443 argue that trust in the police force among Protestant and Catholic young people is roughly equal.

[166] Before 1998, over 80 per cent of Protestant respondents indicated that they thought the police were doing a very/fairly good job, compared to less than 50 per cent of Catholics (Patten Report (n 154) [3.4]).

[167] Sarkin et al (n 145) 115.

[168] ibid 129.

[169] Law on Missing Persons (Official Gazette of Bosnia and Herzegovina Law No 50/2004) art 7.

[170] Sarkin et al (n 145) 11.

technical assistance to other post-violence societies facing similar problems, such as Cyprus.[171]

However, despite the objective success of the process, this has not been conveyed effectively to the population itself. Bosnians seem to have underappreciated what the Commission has achieved, at the same time as entertaining excessive expectations about what it should accomplish. Specifically, in a 2014 study, only 17 per cent of the people asked about the number of missing persons that had been located gave the correct answer, which, at the time, was approximately two-thirds.[172] Simultaneously, almost 60 per cent of survey respondents believed that justice would only be achieved when every single person had been identified, an objective that, in light of the large numbers of victims involved and the passage of time since their disappearance, is practically impossible to meet.[173] In addition to being misinformed about how much the relevant human rights bodies have accomplished, the general population also harbours negative perceptions about the procedures followed by key peacebuilding actors, with more than half of the people asked believing that the Institute's attempts to locate missing persons favour one ethnic group over the others.[174] Importantly, this percentage is lower among family members – 42 per cent of them share the same belief – thus suggesting that those who are closer to its work and better informed about it have a more positive view of the Institute.[175]

This more positive perception among family members is arguably partly due to the conscious efforts made by the BiH Ministry of Human Rights and Refugees to involve key stakeholders, including family associations, the International Commission of Missing Persons and the International Commission of the Red Cross, in a consultation exercise regarding the passing of the Law on Missing Persons.[176] Moreover, it has possibly also been enhanced by the fact that the Institute has a mandate to help family members, even after the remains of the missing person have been identified, by, for example, providing financial assistance for the funeral costs.[177] Conversely, the more negative perceptions among the general population could be due to public allegations from mostly the Serb members of the Institute, which were made even before it began its operations, that it was acting in an ethnically biased manner.[178] These observations suggest that while important, implementing human rights might not be a sufficient peacebuilding measure in itself; it will also be necessary to accurately inform the

[171] Fiona Hill, 'How Bosnia is Helping Identify Cypriots Murdered 50 Years Ago' *BBC News*, 1 October 2014.
[172] Sarkin et al (n 145) 116.
[173] ibid 117.
[174] ibid 115–16.
[175] ibid 115–16.
[176] ibid 36.
[177] Law on Missing Persons (Official Gazette of Bosnia and Herzegovina Law No 50/2004) art 18.
[178] Sarkin et al (n 145) 41–42.

general public about what peacebuilders are trying to achieve and how specific steps taken by them contribute to these objectives. Unsurprisingly, the more powerful and vocal the opposition to peace within the post-violence society, the more it can delegitimise the reconciliation process and the greater the emphasis that must be paid to this condition.[179] Although peacebuilders are already diligent and well-versed in communicating the success of their projects to external funders, it is necessary that they use these skills towards a different audience as well. Rather than seeking to convince outsiders of the need for and achievements of human rights institutions, they should explain to the victims and general population within the post-violence society how these promote their interests and can address their concerns. In doing so, peacebuilders should be able to respond to spoilers' allegations and find ways of effectively conveying messages of justice and reconciliation to potentially negatively predisposed audiences.

The third condition for inducing psychological changes requires that people perceive the protection of human rights as a genuine attempt to build peace rather than something the state does because it has a legal obligation to do so.[180] Such authenticity can be conveyed through unilateral gestures of goodwill, reciprocal acts of concession and joint ventures among previously warring parties.[181] When these are absent and if the belief is that the government is doing as little as possible to comply with its human rights obligations rather than as much as possible to resolve the conflict, even when technically implemented, a human rights strategy will fail to induce feelings of peace among the population.[182] In order for this condition to be satisfied, peacebuilders must pay attention to 'how things are done – that is whether the discussion and delivery of [the remedy] is set up in a way that makes the goals of acknowledgement, respect, the restoration of dignity and civic interest in the betterment of lives a felt reality for the survivors'.[183] Illustrative of this are the (disappointing) peacebuilding effects of the HET, a body that had been tasked with re-examining conflict-related deaths that had taken place in NI.[184] At a first glance, the HET was a successful attempt by the UK government to comply with the ECtHR judgments that flagged up the absence of an effective and impartial investigation into these deaths.[185] Yet, despite its technical compliance with human rights, both the HET's mandate

[179] Bar-Tal (n 67) 361.

[180] Brewer (n 11) 110–11; John Braithwaite, *Restorative Justice and Responsive Regulation* (Oxford, Oxford University Press, 2002) 203.

[181] Bar-Tal (n 67) 362.

[182] Roht-Arriaza (n 101) 201; Hamber (n 1) 13.

[183] Roht-Arriaza (n 101) 201.

[184] Patricia Lundy and Bill Rolston, 'Redress for Past Harms? Official Apologies in Northern Ireland' (2016) 20 *International Journal of Human Rights* 104, 110.

[185] Committee of Ministers, *Interim Resolution on Action of the Security Forces in Northern Ireland (Case of McKerr against the United Kingdom and Five Similar Cases)*, ResDH(2005)20 (Strasbourg, Council of Europe, 23 February 2005); Committee of Ministers, *Interim Resolution on the Action of the Security Forces in Northern Ireland (Case of McKerr against the United Kingdom and Five Similar Cases)*, CM/ResDH(2007)73 (Strasbourg, Council of Europe, 17 October 2007).

(what it was trying to achieve) and its practices (how this would happen) left much to be desired. The HET's failure to appreciate the importance of these factors undermined its efforts to be perceived as a genuine peacebuilding institution and to contribute to feelings of justice and reconciliation to the extent that it could have.

In terms of what it sought to achieve, the HET's objective was:

> [T]o reexamine all deaths attributable to 'the troubles' and ensure that all investigative and evidential opportunities are subject to thorough and exhaustive examination in a manner that satisfies the Police Service of Northern Ireland's obligation of an effective investigation.[186]

The HET had interpreted this as requiring the review of previous investigations and assessing whether they had left any 'evidential opportunities' unexplored. If such evidential opportunities existed, it was its responsibility to investigate them internally and subsequently report them to the Police Service of Northern Ireland.[187] This review process, which was intended to bring 'a measure of resolution' to the families of the victims,[188] was 'designed to be exhaustive and include[d] the re-examination of all documentation'.[189] Yet, at the same time, it was clear that the HET was part of a 'package of measures' and these procedures were not intended to fully comply with the UK's human rights obligations on their own.[190] This, as was pointed out during an official review of the HET's practices in 2013, resulted in 'confusion, both internally and externally about whether the HET is a body which investigates crimes; reviews previous investigated cases; conducts "cold case" reviews; or gathers information for families'.[191] Due to this confusion, family members often believed that the HET's mandate was to re-investigate their loved ones' deaths and were disappointed, leading to renewed feelings of injustice when this did not happen.[192] The lack of clarity was addressed following the official review of the HET and its terms of reference were revised to state the organisation's objectives, values and purpose more clearly.[193] This improvement notwithstanding, the line between review and re-investigation is a thin one and is still likely to lead to misunderstandings and disappointment among family members.

In addition to the lack of clarity about the HET's mandate, its practices also left much to be desired. Perhaps the most problematic of its procedures

[186] HMIC, *Inspection of the Police Service of Northern Ireland Historical Enquiries Team* (United Kingdom, Her Majesty's Inspectorate of Constabulary, 2013) 7.

[187] ibid 8.

[188] HET Operational Guide – 'A document that provides an overview of the work of the HET', quoted in ibid 57.

[189] Committee of Ministers, *Interim Resolution CM/ResDH(2007)73* (n 185).

[190] ibid.

[191] HMIC (n 186) 55.

[192] ibid 57.

[193] HMIC, *A Follow-up Inspection of the Police Service of Northern Ireland Historical Enquiries Team* (United Kingdom, Her Majesty's Inspectorate of Constabulary, 2015) [2.12].

was the fact that it distinguished between cases based on whether the alleged perpetrator was a state official or not, and investigated the latter much more vigorously.[194] This distinction was based on the reasoning that 'it is not appropriate to compare the review process in military cases with reviews of murders committed by terrorists'.[195] The practice was considered to be so problematic during the official review of the HET that all investigations of state involvement cases were suspended until the review's recommendations for improvement were implemented.[196] This preferential treatment of state agents also permeated the HET's 'pragmatic approach', a practice where HET agents dispensed with the caution before an interview with a potential suspect in order to encourage him to provide as much evidence as possible.[197] Under the pragmatic approach, the suspect was essentially treated as a witness, his testimony was not recorded and no notes were taken, thus making the evidence that he was providing inadmissible in potential criminal proceedings.[198] Considering the HET's distinction between state agents and 'terrorists', this practice is likely to have been favoured when interviewing the former, something confirmed by the fact that of the 39 cases that had been referred to the Police Service of Northern Ireland for further investigation by the time the official review took place, not one involved a state agent as a suspect.[199] However, if the victims' families resorted to the ECtHR because they felt that the original investigations into their relatives' deaths lacked independence, the HET practices failed to change their perceptions and, in fact, reinforced them. The 'measure of resolution' that the HET was intended to bring – in other words, those psychological changes that would contribute to feelings of peace – could only be achieved if it was clear that the deaths had been investigated in a non-biased manner, a goal that such practices undermined.

Attempts to promote subjective peace were arguably undercut, even in cases where the HET had found evidence of problematic practices in the original investigation and sent a letter of apology to the families. According to the official review report, by 2013, at least five individual families had received an apology, but no information is provided on what exactly these letters consisted of.[200] Other sources indicate that in many cases, the language used by the HET in its letters was distant and sought to excuse, instead of properly apologise for, the death of the victim.[201] For instance, some of the letters sent out to the families stated that the soldier 'honestly and genuinely believed' that he was shooting at a

[194] HMIC (n 186) 74.
[195] HET Operational Guide [6.19], quoted in ibid 57.
[196] Lundy and Rolston (n 184) 110.
[197] HMIC (n 186) 81.
[198] ibid 83.
[199] ibid 82.
[200] ibid 57.
[201] For a distinction between apology as an excuse and apology as a justification, see Susan Marks, 'Apologising for Torture' (2004) 73 *Nordic Journal of International Law* 365.

dangerous person, that he had 'no recollection' of the incident or that he would 'never have intentionally fired'.[202] On other occasions, the letters contained inaccuracies concerning the steps that were taken by the HET during the review process, the health of the alleged perpetrator and the extent to which he had expressed any remorse.[203] Considering that many families had been waiting for years for a *genuine apology* that would help them overcome the injustices they had suffered, it is unlikely that these 'formalistic' responses from the state, or those that tried to 'explain' rather than show remorse for the death, actually had this effect.[204]

The HET's failure to properly engage with and change the perceptions of its target audience, despite its technical compliance with human rights obligations, is reflected through several satisfaction surveys that had been carried out on its behalf. While the survey results appear promising at first glance – with 64 per cent of respondents being satisfied with the organisation's performance and only three per cent expressly disagreeing with this statement – these numbers do not cover all of the intended beneficiaries.[205] Specifically, they exclude the categories of people who were most likely to be dissatisfied with the HET, like families who refused to engage with it from the beginning of the review process, others who disengaged along the way and those who were still waiting for a report. The bias in these results is also confirmed by independent research, which suggests that the percentage of those who were glad that they had engaged with the HET only reached 12 per cent, with four in 10 definitely not being glad that they had done so.[206] Perhaps more worrying is the fact that even when the HET's disappointing performance was highlighted during its official review and it was recommended that satisfaction surveys were used more regularly, this proposal was among the few that was ignored.[207] When faced with the HET's unsatisfactory practices and reluctance to hear from those who are directly affected by them, one could be excused for thinking that it was established only as a way of complying with the UK's ECHR obligations rather than as a genuine peacebuilding body. In turn, this perceived unwillingness to honestly and effectively address the injustices of the past, despite the presence of institutions suggesting otherwise, made it less likely that social and psychological change would be induced.

The HET had not completed its mandate when in January 2015 its tasks were taken over by the newly established Legacy Investigation Branch, which,

[202] From letters sent to the families by the HET, quoted in Lundy and Rolston (n 184) 113.

[203] ibid.

[204] This accusation has been made not only against the state authorities, but Sinn Fein as well (Lauren Dempster, 'The Republican Movement, "Disappearing" and Framing the Past in Northern Ireland' (2016) 10 *International Journal of Transitional Justice* 250).

[205] HMIC (n 186) 71.

[206] Bill Rolston, *Satisfaction with the Historical Enquiries Team: Relatives' Views,* Research Paper 14-06 (Ulster, Transitional Justice Institute, 2014).

[207] HMIC (n 193) 31.

unlike its predecessor, which was institutionally independent, is part of the Police Service of Northern Ireland.[208] In theory, the change should not affect the public's perceptions of the peacebuilding initiative, since the new body's mandate and practices have remained the same.[209] Ultimately, it has been argued, what is important is not the title of the body, but 'the confidence of the families and the public at large'.[210] However, especially in post-violence contexts, symbolism matters. It makes a difference that the Legacy Investigation Branch is much smaller and commands far fewer resources than the HET, not only because this is likely to further delay ongoing investigations, but also due to the importance that the government is seen as ascribing to this matter.[211] Moreover, considering that the main problem with the original investigations was one of partiality, asking the Police Service of Northern Ireland, which currently employs former long-serving Royal Ulster Constabulary officers, to review past actions of their old colleagues seems counter-intuitive.[212] Finally, it is expected that, also due to limited resources, the Legacy Investigation Branch will engage less directly than the HET with the families of the victims.[213] Yet, this decision will do little to convey a genuine interest in promoting feelings of peace. Since one of the hurdles for reconciliation is the lack of trust between family members and the state authorities, a close relationship between the two during the review process could help address this. Reducing communication between the key stakeholders and the investigating officers undermines both transparency and the possibility that this trust will develop.

The final condition for human rights to successfully induce subjective psychological changes among the population is that they are protected by an institution that the public trusts and does not consider to be biased or illegitimate.[214] If the institution does not possess these characteristics, the victims and the general population observing its proceedings are unlikely to feel that rights have been adequately protected and risk becoming disillusioned with the peace process.[215] Allegations of illegitimacy or bias are usually spread by those who oppose

[208] ibid 6.

[209] ibid Annex D 59.

[210] ibid 49.

[211] At the start of the initial inspection, it was estimated that the HET would review 40 cases per month. This was revised to 30 cases shortly thereafter and by the end of the second inspection, it was estimated that with the reduced number of staff of the Legacy Investigation Unit, the number would drop to 10 cases per month (ibid 25–26).

[212] Patricia Lundy, 'Exploring Home-Grown Transitional Justice and Its Dilemmas: A Case Study of the Historical Enquiries Team, Northern Ireland' (2009) 3 *International Journal of Transitional Justice* 321, 331. The Royal Ulster Constabulary changed its name to the Police Service of Northern Ireland following the recommendations of the Patten Commission.

[213] HMIC (n 193) 17.

[214] Brewer (n 11) 120; Richard Moorhead, Mark Sefton and Lesley Scanlan, *Just Satisfaction? What Drives Public and Participant Satisfaction with Courts and Tribunals*, Ministry of Justice Research Series 5/08 (London, Ministry of Justice, 2008).

[215] Eva Brems and Laurens Lavrysen, 'Procedural Justice in Human Rights Adjudication: The European Court of Human Rights' (2013) 35 *Human Rights Quarterly* 176.

the human rights policy and can take root especially in instances where the public does not know or understand much about the institution's operations.[216] Moreover, such allegations are generally more pronounced and effective if the decision of the human rights body is controversial or unpopular, or if it rests on a complicated or nuanced point of law that non-lawyers might not be able to follow easily.[217] In such cases, suspicious audiences might view human rights as tools through which policy makers are trying to trick or manipulate them, and therefore become even more resistant to social or psychological changes associated with their protection.

This was, for instance, the case with *Demopoulos v Turkey*, in which it was held that GC displaced persons had an obligation to apply to the Immovably Property Commission (IPC) and exhaust domestic remedies before they resorted to the ECtHR.[218] Until *Demopoulos*, the argument made by the applicants and accepted by the Court was that the legal and factual situation in the occupied area of Cyprus was such that it was futile applying to the 'TRNC' courts for a remedy, since the outcome of that application was a forgone conclusion.[219] This was primarily because of two reasons. First, as a matter of law, under Article 159 of the 'TRNC' Constitution, GCs were considered as having voluntarily abandoned their properties in 1974, which subsequently became ownership of the 'TRNC'.[220] Second, as a matter of fact, the effects of Article 159 were that GCs were prevented from using, accessing or benefiting from their properties in any way.[221] In *Demopoulos*, the Court completely reversed this position and held that the newly established IPC, which had been set up by Turkey in occupied Cyprus in order to remedy GC displaced persons, was an effective domestic remedy that applicants should use. This is despite the fact that both Article 159 and the factual situation on the ground remained unchanged. The ECtHR theoretically addressed the applicants' concerns with regard to the IPC's (lack of) legality, legitimacy and effectiveness by arguing, for instance, that since they could sue Turkey for its actions in the areas not under the control of the Republic, it was Turkey's right, and indeed responsibility, to respond in some way to their allegations.[222] The IPC was simply Turkey's response to these allegations and should not be seen as legitimising the illegal invasion or the 'TRNC' in any way.[223]

Yet, in its reasoning, the Court failed to pay adequate attention to the fact that the IPC was in no way an organ that the target audience trusted or

[216] Marko Milanovic, 'Establishing the Facts about Mass Atrocities: Accounting for the Failure of the ICTY to Persuade Target Audiences' (2016) 47 *Georgetown Journal of International Law* 1321.
[217] ibid.
[218] *Demopoulos and Others v Turkey* App No 46113/99 (ECtHR, 1 March 2010).
[219] *Cyprus v Turkey* App No 25781/94 (ECtHR, 10 May 2001) [82]–[102].
[220] ibid [186].
[221] ibid [187].
[222] ibid [98].
[223] *Demopoulos* (n 218) [96].

considered legitimate. GCs had been displaced from their properties and forced to stay away by an occupying power. Now the only remedy that was available to them for this injustice was to turn to the very same occupying power and, starting from the premise established by Article 159 of the 'TRNC' Constitution (which remains in place and on which the IPC Law is based),[224] receive compensation for the loss of their property. The IPC can offer no apology for the forced displacement, cannot order the withdrawal of the Turkish troops from the occupied area of Cyprus (in fact, its very existence is premised on Turkey maintaining effective control over that part of the island) and, in the vast majority of cases, cannot offer restitution to the displaced persons.[225] Moreover, in practice, the IPC is almost designed to make applicants distrustful of it: it imposes unreasonable obligations in terms of the documents that they are expected to produce (such as a complete list of all the movable properties they had left behind in their homes more than 40 years ago),[226] uses the criminal standard of proof of beyond reasonable doubt,[227] and its language of operation is Turkish, which almost none of the applicants (nor the two international members that lend credibility to it) speak.[228] Perhaps most problematically, both its composition and procedures are designed to protect the interests of Turkey and the 'TRNC' and not the GC applicants, who tend to resort to it because they have lost hope that there will be a comprehensive settlement to the Cyprus problem or are financially desperate.[229] As a result, since 2005, when the IPC was established, only 6,539 of the 165,000 eligible displaced persons have applied to it.[230] Consequently, both the ECtHR and the IPC have been delegitimised in the eyes of GCs, a phenomenon that has further aggravated efforts for reconciliation on the island.[231] In the absence of a body that the public trusts and considers legitimate, even when human rights are technically protected, conflicts as psychological states of affairs are likely to linger rather than be properly resolved.

V. STRATEGIES FOR PROMOTING SUBJECTIVE FEELINGS OF PEACE

At first glance, the conditions for ensuring that human rights contribute to subjective feelings of peace might sound abstract and unable to shape peacebuilding

[224] ('TRNC') Law for the Compensation, Exchange and Restitution of Immovable Properties which are within the scope of sub-para (B) of para 1 of art 159 of the Constitution (No 67/2005).

[225] Nasia Hadjigeorgiou, 'Remedying Displacement in Frozen Conflicts: Lessons from the Case of Cyprus' (2016) 18 *Cambridge Yearbook of European Legal Studies* 152.

[226] No 67/2005, art 6.

[227] ibid.

[228] *Demopoulos* (n 218) [60].

[229] Hadjigeorgiou (n 225).

[230] Presidency of Immovable Property Commission, *Monthly Bulletin* (Nicosia, Immovable Property Commission, April 2019).

[231] Rhodri C Williams and Ayla Gürel, *The European Court of Human Rights and the Cyprus Property Issue: Charting a Way Forward*, 1/2011 (Nicosia, PRIO Cyprus Centre, 2011).

policies on the ground. This section addresses the criticism by outlining two practical proposals that can help with their materialisation. The first recommends that peacebuilding responses to complex and multidimensional conflicts are tailored to the needs of the specific post-violence society and are themselves equally multifaceted.[232] In turn, this necessitates a partial shift in the staffing of peacebuilding operations along two axes: from international to local experts on the one hand, and from lawyers to a range of other professionals on the other. The second proposal focuses on the adoption of a two-way communication strategy between the peacebuilders and the population within the post-violence society.

A. Rethinking the Composition of the Peacebuilding Team

Perhaps one of the most insightful scholarly works on the limitations of liberal peacebuilding is *Peaceland* by Severine Autesserre, an academic with previous experience as a peacebuilder.[233] Autesserre notes that there are two types of knowledge that could be helpful to the conflict resolution process, namely thematic or technical expertise on the one hand and local or country expertise on the other. Over the years, the international peacebuilding community has been consistently favouring the former because locating local and reliable experts can be difficult when trying to intervene in a post-violence society at short notice. Thus, international policy makers and the peacebuilders they employ on the ground have tended to operate on the assumption that thematic expertise is easily transferable from one post-violence society to the next, and that programmes that have been successful in one place can be implemented in another with relatively little knowledge of the context. This favouring of thematic experts (who are almost always non-local) has been further promoted by several competitive advantages they enjoy over domestic actors. International peacebuilders do not have any connections to the post-violence society to which they are deployed, which makes it easier for them to avoid pressures from family members or friends to secure jobs, money or other services for them, and minimises the possibility that they will be coerced in any way.[234] Moreover, their detachment from the context means that they can avoid the perception of a group bias and that, unlike some local elites, they have no vested interest in the status quo.[235] Due to these practical advantages, international peacebuilders have been discouraged from mingling with the locals or spending too much time in the same post-violence society, which has in turn resulted in their even more

[232] Roht-Arriaza (n 101) 190.

[233] Severine Autesserre, *Peaceland: Conflict Resolution and the Everyday Politics of International Intervention* (Cambridge, Cambridge University Press, 2014).

[234] ibid 64–65.

[235] ibid.

sanitised understanding of the context, glimpsed mainly through reports and executive summaries.[236]

While to some extent understandable, the remoteness of international peacebuilders risks undermining the effectiveness of their strategies because even in rare occasions when they are stationed in the same post-violence society for several years, they lack the network, reputation, legitimacy and credibility that is often enjoyed by their local counterparts.[237] Furthermore, since international actors do not have a deep insight of the post-violence society, they have to rely on dominant narratives rather than more complex analyses of what specific conflicts are about and how their resolution may be hindered by customs, taboos, history and politics.[238] However, a peacebuilding strategy can only address the conflicts that its designers know about and understand. A superficial knowledge of the context of a specific dispute will necessarily result in an equally superficial response. If this response fails to address the most divisive conflicts, its impact in terms of building peace will be a limited one. An illustration of this is the fact that between 1996 and 1999, the international community in BiH spent approximately four times as much on rebuilding houses as it did on social support of displaced persons,[239] a strategy that was most likely based on the (faulty) assumption that people would return if only they had somewhere to stay. This shows little appreciation of the more layered reasons for the displaced persons' reluctance to move, such as their socio-economic insecurity and the fact that they might not have been made to feel welcome by their old neighbours, and goes to explain why ultimately relatively few people chose to go back to their old homes.

While international actors with exclusively thematic expertise generally find it harder to make meaningful changes to people's lives, the sole involvement of local peacebuilders should also be avoided. Locals have vested personal interests in the post-violence society, which can encourage them to act as spoilers or make them more interested in increasing their personal or political power rather than contributing to peace.[240] Consequently, the best strategy forward is to shift power from international to local peacebuilders only to a certain extent. The two should participate in the same working groups and the expertise of each – thematic or contextual – should be valued equally. Such a step is not only essential for the design and implementation of effective peacebuilding strategies, but

[236] ibid.

[237] David Marshall and Shelley Inglis, 'Human Rights in Transition: The Disempowerment of Human Rights-Based Justice in the United Nations Mission in Kosovo' (2003) 16 *Harvard Human Rights Journal* 95.

[238] Michael Pugh, 'The Social-Civil Dimension' in Michael Pugh (ed), *Regeneration of War-Torn Societies* (Basingstoke, Macmillan Press, 2000) 123.

[239] Rhodri C Williams, 'The Significance of Property Restitution to Sustainable Return in Bosnia and Herzegovina' (2006) 44 *International Migration* 39.

[240] Autesserre (n 233) 106.

is also in line with the UN's pronounced commitment to self-determination[241] and necessary for avoiding allegations that exclusively international teams are operating as neo-colonialists.[242] Furthermore, hybrid staff operations are crucial because international peacebuilders report and are accountable to a different audience from local ones.[243] While the latter are concerned with the responses of people within the post-violence society – their friends, families or political supporters – for the former, their bosses in different capitals around the world and journalists from the *New York Times* or the *Washington Post* are potentially more influential in setting the mission's agenda.[244] Thus, it is only by combining the strengths of the two sets of professionals that peacebuilding strategies will start making real, and not only legal, changes to the society in which they are operating. However, while for the moment, the UN has acknowledged the importance of such an integrated approach on paper,[245] in practice, initiatives to empower the grassroots have tended to only be adopted in an ad hoc and haphazard manner.[246]

If one of the reasons that some peacebuilding strategies have failed to address the real concerns of people in post-violence societies is the international peacebuilders' more superficial knowledge of the context, another is the significant attention that has been paid to protecting human rights by reforming the law as opposed to inducing social change through other mediums.[247] While support is gradually being built in favour of more multidisciplinary teams, this trend should not be exaggerated as peacebuilding 'still remains legalistic in orientation and rooted in a civil and political rights-based framework at a policy level'.[248] This is, at least partly, because many of the peacebuilders are themselves lawyers.[249]

[241] UN Secretary-General, *An Agenda for Peace: Preventive Diplomacy, Peacemaking and Peace-Keeping: Report of the Secretary-General Pursuant to the Statement Adopted by the Summit Meeting of the Security Council on 31 January 1992*, A/47/277 – S/24111 (New York, United Nations, 1992) [19].

[242] Gerald Knaus and Felix Martin, 'Lessons from Bosnia and Herzegovina: Travails of the European Raj' (2003) 14 *Journal of Democracy* 64.

[243] Roland Kostić, 'Shadow Peacebuilders and Diplomatic Counterinsurgencies: Informal Networks, Knowledge Production and the Art of Policy-Shaping' (2017) 11 *Journal of Intervention and Statebuilding* 120.

[244] Quote from a peacebuilder based in Congo, in Autesserre (n 233) 210.

[245] UN Secretary-General, *The Rule of Law and Transitional Justice in Conflict and Post-conflict Societies*, S/2004/616 (New York, United Nations, 2004) [15]–[17].

[246] Patricia Lundy and Mark McGovern, 'The Role of Community in Participatory Transitional Justice' in Kieran McEvoy and Lorna McGregor (eds), *Transitional Justice from Below: Grassroots Activism and the Struggle for Change* (Oxford, Hart Publishing, 2008) 107; McAuliffe (n 68) 49; Oliver Richmond and Audra Mitchell, 'Introduction – Towards a Post-liberal Peace: Exploring Hybridity via Everyday Forms of Resistance, Agency and Autonomy' in Oliver Richmond and Audra Mitchell (eds), *Hybrid Forms of Peace: From Everyday Agency to Post-liberalism* (Basingstoke, Palgrave Macmillan, 2016).

[247] McEvoy (n 87).

[248] McAuliffe (n 68) 4.

[249] See Kjetil Mujezinovic Larsen, 'United Nations Peace Operations and International Law: What Kind of Law Promotes What Kind of Peace?' in Cecillia Marcela Baillet and Kjetil Mujezinovic Larsen (eds), *Promoting Peace through International Law* (Oxford, Oxford University Press, 2015)

Arguably, lawyers have been favoured over other professionals within peacebuilding operations because among the key challenges in post-violence societies is the absence of the rule of law. In such contexts, law is a useful tool, since its association with values like justice, objectivity, uniformity, universality and rationality lends legitimacy to the new state of affairs and helps make the post-violence society a member of the international community.[250] A second reason for the emphasis on the 'legal' components of a peacebuilding operation is that (especially international) decision makers tend to favour short-term, technical projects that are easy to measure and justify to their funders rather than taking action to address soft issues, such as building community relations and responding to subjective feelings of insecurity or mistrust of the locals.[251] Focusing on legal outcomes, with their emphasis on the volume of cases that have been litigated, the amount of properties that have been returned or the number of bodies that have been retrieved, is convenient because their effects are quantifiable and easy to put on a chart.[252]

They say that to the hammer, the world looks like a nail. Similarly, there is a risk that to a lawyer, a complex conflict – with political, social, economic, cultural, psychological and some legal dimensions – looks like a legal puzzle. As a result, when a peacebuilding operation is mainly staffed by lawyers, it is almost natural for them to emphasise the protection of (legal) human rights because their training and background fuels their existing tendencies to search for the resolution of a conflict in law.[253] In light of their composition, it is therefore unsurprising that, by and large, peacebuilding teams have 'prioritised justice issues and [are] financing and supporting the implementation of a plethora of legal initiatives'.[254] However, while lawyers are well-suited to drafting complex pieces of legislation, they are generally not trained in identifying and developing the conditions that must be in place in order for a peacebuilding strategy, including the implementation of a human rights law, to function effectively.

299–320, who notes that 'the tendency is to focus ever more on the articulation of human rights as legal entitlements and on the possibility of pursuing human rights ambitions through legal mechanisms. Earlier, one spoke exclusively about the human rights *functions* of peace obligations, but now it becomes ever more common to speak about human rights *obligations*' (emphasis in original). Lawyers have a predominant role, even in expressly interdisciplinary institutions like the SA TRC; see Nicky Rousseau and Madeleine Fullard, 'Accounting and Reconciling in the Balance Sheet of the South African Truth and Reconciliation Commission' (2009) 4 *Journal of Multicultural Discourses* 123, 131.

[250] McEvoy (n 87) 417.

[251] Christine Bell, 'Human Rights and the Struggle for Change: A Study in Self-Critical Legal Thought' in Rob Dickinson et al (eds), *Examining Critical Perspectives on Human Rights* (Cambridge, Cambridge University Press, 2012).

[252] Erik G Jensen, 'Justice and the Rule of Law' in Charles T Call (ed), *Building States to Build Peace* (Boulder, Lynne Rienner, 2008).

[253] Tom Gerard Daly, *The Alchemists: Questioning Our Faith in Courts as Democracy-Builders* (Cambridge, Cambridge University Press, 2017) 104.

[254] Lundy and McGovern (n 246) 99.

Thus, although focusing on these conditions is crucial for the promotion of subjective peace, they have tended to receive relatively limited attention.

In light of this problem, if we want to achieve 'embedded' rather than just 'distant justice',[255] we should use legal tools, yet also be wary of the 'seduction of legalism'.[256] Achieving this balance requires that peacebuilding operations are staffed by a range of professionals in addition to lawyers, such as psychologists, economists, social workers, educators, people working within the media, representatives of victim groups, politicians and political analysts. If 'change is driven by multiple factors', then the composition of peacebuilding teams should give the opportunity to different thematic and country experts to identify these and promote them.[257] Of course, involving such a wide range of professionals in the planning and implementation stages of a peacebuilding strategy may be difficult, both in terms of cost and the time it would take for them to reach a decision. One way of addressing the cost problem is to engage with local experts, whose services are almost always cheaper than those of international peacebuilders. This might not be an option in all post-violence societies due to the possible lack of sufficient expertise among the locals, but it can work well in some contexts, such as Cyprus, which boasts of high educational levels[258] and an engaged civil society within both communities.[259] On the other hand, the coordination problem can be addressed by making a conscious effort to build a multidisciplinary core team of peacebuilders, who are then regularly consulted by a range of other professionals. Admittedly, this is likely to result in much more complex, expensive and long-term peace operations. These are indeed significant hurdles, but if they are used as excuses to prevent much-needed changes in the composition of peacebuilding teams, we run the risk that 'symbolic victories may be mistaken for substantive ones, covering a reality that is distasteful'.[260] Empowering different types of peacebuilders – both in terms of their nationality

[255] Paul Gready, 'Reconceptualising Transitional Justice: Embedded and Distanced Justice' (2005) 5 *Conflict, Security and Development* 2.

[256] Kieran McEvoy, 'Letting Go of Legalism: Developing a "Thicker" Version of Transitional Justice' in McEvoy and McGregor (eds) (n 246) 19.

[257] Donald and Mottershaw (n 76) 352. See also Yehezkel Dror, 'Law and Social Change' (1958–59) 33 *Tulane Law Review* 787, 801, who argues that 'changes in law have more impact on emotionally neutral and instrumental areas of activity than on expressive and evaluative areas of activity' and that in the case of the latter, other tools, such as education and economic development, may be more effective than legal changes.

[258] Cyprus ranks among the first countries in the EU in terms of numbers of university graduates (Eurostat, 'Educational Attainment Statistics', June 2018, available at www.ec.europa.eu/eurostat/statistics-explained/index.php/Educational_attainment_statistics).

[259] For more information on civil society actors involved in peacebuilding in Cyprus, see the UNDP's website, available at www.cy.undp.org/content/cyprus/en/home/operations/projects/action_for_cooperation_and_trust.html.

[260] Rosenberg (n 3) 424. See also Scheingold (n 6) 6, who argues that the myth of rights can cause one to 'mistakenly identify isolated courtroom victories with real progress'.

and professional qualifications – might make peacebuilding more challenging, but it will also make its effects more real.

B. Adopting a Two-Way Communication Strategy

Peacebuilders often expect that human rights initiatives might be opposed by those actively trying to undermine the peace process, but there is little appreciation that they may also be unpopular with the general population at large.[261] In other words, they sometimes fail to realise that while the public might *in principle* support efforts to promote peace, what this means in each context and for different individuals may vary. Especially in post-violence societies, where people have shaped their lives and identities around community-tailored perceptions of what is just, 'what might be obvious conclusions to human rights groups and advocates, as well as victim organizations, is not necessarily so for other sectors of society'.[262] It is for this reason that often one or more of the conditions discussed in section IV may be absent and why human rights, while adequately protected in a technical sense, will be unable to induce subjective feelings of peace. One way of addressing this problem is by developing effective channels of communication between peacebuilders and their target audience.

Notably, what is meant by 'target audience' must be carefully defined, as local leaders and the general population of a post-violence society are not always one and the same. If the two are not distinguished, there is a danger that peacebuilders will solely communicate with one and assume – often wrongly – that their messages will be accurately communicated to the other as well. The outcome of the GC referendum on the Annan Plan in Cyprus, which was a complete surprise to the international community, illustrates this danger. While GC political leaders had been negotiating a peace agreement under the auspices of the UN for decades and reassuring the international community that the basis of this agreement was understood and accepted by the GC public, they had made no effort to prepare their constituents for the compromises that would be required of them. On the contrary, the polemic language that was used within – but never outside of – Cyprus[263] and the nationalist focus of the educational system[264] were completely at odds with what GC politicians were declaring in

[261] Jemima Garcia-Godos, 'It's about Trust: Transitional Justice and Accountability in the Search for Peace' in Baillet and Larsen (eds) (n 249).

[262] ibid 329.

[263] Yiannis Papadakis, 'Nation, Narrative and Commemoration: Political Ritual in Divided Cyprus' (2003) 13 *History and Anthropology* 253.

[264] Yiannis Papadakis, *History Education in Divided Cyprus: A Comparison of Greek Cypriot and Turkish Cypriot Schoolbooks on the 'History of Cyprus'*, 2/2008 (Nicosia, PRIO Cyprus Centre, 2008); Michalinos Zembylas et al, 'Human Rights and the Ethno-Nationalist Problematic through the Eyes of Greek-Cypriot Teachers' (2016) 11 *Education Citizenship and Social Justice* 19.

international fora. As a result, when the Annan Plan was presented to the GC public and was rejected by a staggering 75.8 per cent of the population,[265] both the international community and most GCs felt cheated: the former because GCs swiftly dismissed Kofi Annan's brainchild – the outcome of years of negotiations – as unacceptable, and the latter because the international community had dared to propose such a peace agreement in the first place. It seems that what was needed (and lacking) in Cyprus in 2004 was the adoption of a communication strategy that directly linked peacebuilders and their *real* target audience, the public, without having to depend on potentially unreliable political messengers. The importance of this strategy was appreciated early on by the Inter-American Court of Human Rights, which noted in a case concerned with investigations into enforced disappearances that 'society has the right to know the truth regarding such crimes, so as to be capable of preventing them in the future'.[266] As a result, it created a duty on the state to investigate the forced disappearances and 'publicly divulge the results of said investigation',[267] both in the Official Gazette and also a daily newspaper with 'national circulation'.[268]

It is often the case, especially in the twenty-first century, that a communication strategy has been understood as engagement with the media, essentially outsourcing to journalists the responsibility of filtering for, explaining to and convincing the public that they should change their war-held perceptions.[269] This is arguably what Lynch and Galtung had in mind when they coined the term 'peace journalism'.[270] However, the 'communication strategy' proposed here requires more than this for two reasons. First, individuals are 'neither passive subjects nor non-reflexive in their interactions' with the state, which makes it necessary to convey messages *to* them (such as explaining the objectives of a given peacebuilding strategy) but also receive feedback *from* them (like whether they find this strategy necessary, legitimate or effective).[271] While the media, and especially local and national news outlets, are particularly effective in talking to the people,[272] just relying on this strategy results in one-way traffic, which leaves the public with no way of communicating their views and concerns back to the peacebuilders. Second, the media might make positive contributions to peace,

[265] UN Secretary-General, *Report of the Secretary-General on His Mission of Good Offices in Cyprus*, S/2004/437 (New York, United Nations, 28 May 2004) [72].

[266] *Bámaca-Velásquez v Guatemala* (Inter-American Court of Human Rights, 25 November 2000) [77].

[267] ibid [78].

[268] ibid [106(3)].

[269] Brewer (n 11) 154.

[270] Jake Lynch and Johan Galtung, *Reporting Conflict: New Directions in Peace Research Journalism* (Brisbane, University of Queensland Press, 2010).

[271] Scott Barclay, Lynn C Jones and Anna-Maria Marshall, 'Two Spinning Wheels: Studying Law and Social Movements' in Austin Sarat (ed), *Special Issue: Social Movements/Legal Possibilities* (Bingley, Emerald, 2011) 3.

[272] Eytan Gilboa, 'Media and Conflict Resolution: A Framework for Analysis' (2009) 93 *Marquette Law Review* 87.

but it is also possible that, by disseminating nationalist messages, they can have the opposite effect.[273] Thus, what is needed is a *two-way* communication strategy that is *comprehensive* in that it actively considers both the types of messages it is sending to the general population and the best way of disseminating these.

Perhaps it is the SA TRC, among all peacebuilding institutions covered by this study, that has adopted the most effective and multifaceted communication strategy and was therefore able to assist SA to 'come to terms with their past on a morally accepted basis and to advance the cause of reconciliation'.[274] One of the reasons why the TRC's communication strategy was so effective was that it satisfied all three requirements – paying attention to the content, listening to victims and ensuring the effective dissemination of its message – that are essential for maximising the reach and impact of a peacebuilding institution's work. The content of the TRC's message was a five-volume (subsequently seven-volume) account of the human rights violations that had taken place between 1960 and 1994 in the country.[275] This took care to describe atrocities in the country's history in an accurate, comprehensive and sensitive manner, while at the same time communicating a message that was both nuanced and simple. On the one hand, by allowing individual victim stories to become integrated into the broader national narrative, the TRC emphasised the human consequences of apartheid. In turn, this made its message universal in its reach and easy to comprehend and accept, even by those who kept track of the Commission's proceedings only intermittently.[276] On the other hand, it was careful to nuance its conclusions, such as that there are different categories of perpetrators, with varying degrees of culpability.[277] Furthermore, while the TRC could have chosen to document only human rights violations that had taken place against blacks – which, after all, constituted the overwhelming majority of violations during this period[278] – it also referred to those that had been committed by blacks themselves.[279] This strategy, coupled with the Commission's acknowledgement that someone could be both a victim and a perpetrator, showed that it did not try to sell an obvious message[280] and pre-empted the sort of defensive alarms that often stop new information from inducing social and psychological change.[281]

[273] Christophoros Christophorou, Sanem Sahin and Synthia Pavlou, *Media Narratives, Politics and the Cyprus Problem*, 1/2010 (Nicosia, PRIO Cyprus Centre, 2010); Mikro Klarin, 'The Impact of the ICTY Trials on Public Opinion in the Former Yugoslavia' (2009) 7 *Journal of International Criminal Justice* 89.

[274] Mr Dullah Omar, former Minister of Justice of SA, cited on the official TRC website, www.justice.gov.za/Trc.

[275] The report is accessible at www.justice.gov.za/Trc.

[276] Naidu (n 64).

[277] Tristan Anne Borer, 'A Taxonomy of Victims and Perpetrators: Human Rights and Reconciliation in South Africa' (2003) 25 *Human Rights Quarterly* 1088.

[278] TRC (n 63) vol 1, ch 6, Appendix 2 [29].

[279] ibid vol 2, ch 4 [78].

[280] Borer (n 277).

[281] James L Gibson, 'On Legitimacy Theory and the Effectiveness of Truth Commissions' (2009) 72 *Law and Contemporary Problems* 123.

In many instances, for example, during judicial proceedings, listening to the experience of the victims is an integral and unchanging part of the process, thus leaving relatively little flexibility to peacebuilding actors to improve this part of their communication strategy. However, in other cases, it is possible to rely on different methods that will allow the institution in question to listen to the victims, such as by relying on consultation procedures[282] or satisfaction surveys,[283] or talking to the victims directly.[284] Over the years, the TRC used several of these methods, thus allowing itself to fine-tune its communication with the victims in a way that balanced its different objectives and achieved them to the greatest possible extent. Its procedures originally involved detailed interviews of the victims with statement-takers who had been trained by psychologists to function as supportive counsellors and respond to the participants' psychological needs.[285] While this arguably had positive effects in inducing psychological changes among the victims, it was such a slow and expensive process that the Commission could only have continued with it if it radically reduced the number of testimonies that it was willing to hear. As a result, this was replaced by a questionnaire consisting of closed-ended questions that was faster to go through, but resulted in a drop in the quality of the interviews and evidence received.[286] Compromising between the two processes, the Commission settled on the use of semi-structured interviews that tried to combine the strengths while avoiding the weaknesses of the two previous approaches.[287] While this has been criticised as detracting from the victims' testimonial experience and therefore undermining the possibility that it would result in psychological change,[288] it allowed the Commission to obtain information from a wider range of witnesses.[289] In turn, this had the advantage of compensating more victims – since only those who had given testimony to the TRC were eligible for an individual remedy[290] – and produced better-supported conclusions than the Commission would have arrived at had it limited the number of testimonies it heard. It is through processes such as these that the TRC ensured not only that it *was* heard, but also that *it* heard what the public had to say.

Equally well thought-out was the dissemination strategy of the TRC, which was based on a realisation early on that if a society-wide change was to be made, it had to also address the bystanders – the average SAs – rather than solely focus on the victims. This resulted in a decision that all of the Commission's proceedings would be broadcast live on radio, while their launch and some high-profile

[282] This was the process followed by the Patten Commission (Patten Report (n 154) [2.3]).
[283] This was recommended in HMIC, (n 186) 15.
[284] This is the approach adopted by the Missing Persons Institute in BiH (Sarkin et al (n 145) 39).
[285] Saunders (n 61).
[286] Chapman and Ball (n 116) 26.
[287] ibid.
[288] Saunders (n 61).
[289] Chapman and Ball (n 116) 27.
[290] TRC (n 63) vol 6, s 2, ch 1 [11].

hearings would also be televised.[291] Moreover, the hearings took place in town halls, civic centres and churches around the country, thus giving members of the public the opportunity to watch the Commission's proceedings in person.[292] It is a matter of contention whether what the TRC had to say was conducive to reconciliation in the country.[293] However, what is undisputed is that its methods of communicating with the SA population worked; the Commission's message might not always have been agreeable, but it was always heard.[294] This approach of the TRC is in sharp contrast to the workings of the (SA) CRLR, which, although had a similar mandate of providing 'support to the process of reconciliation and development', perceived its role in a much more technical way and did not attempt to communicate with its target audience beyond the minimum of providing the displaced victims with the necessary remedy.[295] This contrast in approaches resulted in very different levels of impact from each institution, thus confirming the importance of taking communication with the target audience seriously.[296]

VI. CONCLUSION

One limitation of liberal peacebuilding is that it assumes that the protection of human rights can induce the socio-economic and psychological changes that are necessary for subjective peace, but it does not explain how or why these will take place. At the same time, critiques of liberal peacebuilding have identified this limitation, but have made only general recommendations, if any, on how it can be addressed.[297] This chapter has navigated a course between the two positions by arguing that the protection of human rights can contribute to subjective feelings of peace in three distinct but compounded ways: by empowering victims to articulate their grievances, pushing the state to formally acknowledge these and resulting in the provision of a remedy. However, in order for these steps to achieve the successful resolution of conflicts as psychological states of affairs,

[291] ibid, vol 1, ch 1 [78].

[292] ibid, vol 1, ch 12 ('Regional Office Reports: Durban Office') [41]; ibid vol 1, ch 12 ('Regional Office Reports: Johannesburg Office') [43].

[293] Mahmood Mamdani, 'Amnesty or Impunity? A Preliminary Critique of the Report of the Truth and Reconciliation Commission of South Africa (TRC)' (2002) 32 *Diacritics* 32; Rosemary Nagy, 'Reconciliation in Post-Commission South Africa: Thick and Thin Accounts of Solidarity' (2002) 35 *Canadian Journal of Political Science* 323.

[294] One example of the TRC's least popular conclusions was its finding that 'the ANC and its organs … committed gross violations of human rights in the course of their political activities and armed struggles, for which they are morally and politically accountable' (TRC (n 63) vol 5, ch 6 [132]).

[295] Department of Land Affairs (n 100) 14.

[296] Theunis Roux, 'Land Restitution and Reconciliation in South Africa' in Francois du Bois and Antje du Bois-Pedain (eds), *Justice and Reconciliation in Post-apartheid South Africa* (Cambridge, Cambridge University Press, 2008).

[297] Mac Ginty (n 12) 159.

at least two conditions must be in place. On the one hand, it is necessary that peacebuilding strategies induce social and economic improvements and therefore make a real impact in the lives of the people within the post-violence society. On the other hand, they must be perceived by the target audience as having this effect, which will in turn result in psychological changes that are conducive to peace.

While these conditions might appear to be fairly abstract, two concrete peacebuilding strategies have been suggested in order to contribute to their materialisation. The first involves the shifting of power within peacebuilding teams from international to local and from legal to non-legal actors. This will encourage the team to devise and implement strategies that will complement the protection of human rights, thus addressing the real needs of the public in the post-violence society in a more holistic manner. The second calls for the adoption of a two-way strategy that will allow the local population to communicate its needs and concerns, and peacebuilders to respond to them, in a way that resembles a dialogue between the two. This strategy should be comprehensive in that it is concerned not only with the content of the message that is being communicated, but also the most effective ways of reaching the intended recipients of the message in each instance.

7

Conclusion

I. INTRODUCTION

CRITIQUES OF LIBERAL peacebuilding can generally be divided into two camps: those that involve a fundamental appraisal of the concept, and the rest that adopt a practical problem-solving approach.[1] The first take issue with the theoretical foundations that shape peacebuilding operations by questioning the power of democratic institutions to build peace,[2] or the ability of market liberalisation policies to promote socio-economically equitable relations within the post-violence society.[3] The second are concerned with identifying ways of making existing peacebuilding structures more effective by, for example, strengthening local actors,[4] raising concerns about the lack of legitimacy of different institutions[5] or making recommendations about what powers should be afforded to different peacebuilding bodies within the society.[6] This dichotomy between the two camps has created a lacuna in terms of producing research that is *both* theoretically informed *and* results in proposals about how peacebuilding operations can become more effective. It is this gap that the book has sought to fill in relation to one peacebuilding strategy, namely the protection of human rights. To this end, the book was broadly divided between the first part, which devised the theoretical framework, and the second, which developed and applied it in relation to specific case studies. This chapter brings the two analytical strands together, explaining how the conclusions of

[1] Michael Pugh, 'The Problem-Solving and Critical Paradigms' in Roger Mac Ginty (ed), *Routledge Handbook of Peacebuilding* (New York, Routledge, 2013).

[2] Luc Reychler, *Democratic Peace-Building and Conflict Prevention: The Devil is in the Transition* (Leuven, Leuven University Press, 1999).

[3] Jan Selby, 'The Political Economy of Peace Processes' in Michael Pugh, Neil Cooper and Mandy Turner (eds), *Whose Peace? Critical Perspectives on the Political Economy of Peacebuilding* (Basingstoke, Palgrave Macmillan, 2011).

[4] Oliver Richmond and Audra Mitchell (eds), *Hybrid Forms of Peace: From Everyday Agency to Post-liberalism* (Basingstoke, Palgrave Macmillan, 2016).

[5] Rebecca Everly, 'Assessing the Accountability of the High Representative' in Dina Francesca Haynes (ed), *Deconstructing the Reconstruction: Human Rights and Rule of Law in Postwar Bosnia and Herzegovina* (Farnham, Ashgate, 2008).

[6] Richard H Pildes, 'Ethnic Identity and Democratic Institutions: A Dynamic Perspective' in Sujit Choudhry (ed), *Constitutional Design for Divided Societies: Integration or Accommodation?* (Oxford, Oxford University Press, 2008).

both inform the fundamental critique on the one hand and result in practical recommendations on the other.

II. INFORMING THE LIBERAL PEACEBUILDING CRITIQUE

Theoretical appraisals of liberal peacebuilding over the last two decades have generally been scathing of the model currently applied in post-violence societies. Thus, Ignatieff has argued that liberal peace operations are essentially types of 'empire[s] lite',[7] which, according to Richmond, can only build 'virtual peace'.[8] Thiessen has lamented the fact that even when properly implemented, such strategies result in 'a shell of a state'[9] and Autessere has explained the relatively disappointing record of peacebuilding operations by pointing to the 'practice of number worship' when measuring social change.[10] Related to this are Mac Ginty's criticisms that the international community's inability or unwillingness to shape its practices by taking into account the unique context of each society have resulted in 'off the shelf peace interventions' and a 'peace from IKEA'.[11]

Rather paradoxically, considering the vigour with which such criticisms are made, they rarely result in specific recommendations about what needs to change in order to avoid the pitfalls they identify. Most theoretical critiques either produce no practical recommendations at all[12] or give rise to broad, vaguely articulated suggestions that are a far cry from being implementable on the ground. For instance, despite Mac Ginty stressing the need to move beyond a solely negative critique,[13] his recommendations for improving the liberal peace model are unduly open-ended. His first suggestion – that we work towards an 'everyday peace' – is 'highly context-, location- and time-specific and relies on well-honed interpersonal skills', characteristics that make it difficult to understand what this would look like in a post-violence society.[14] Alternatively, his

[7] Michael Ignatieff, *Empire Lite: Nation-Building in Bosnia, Kosovo and Afghanistan* (London, Vintage, 2003).

[8] Oliver Richmond, 'UN Peacebuilding Operations and the Dilemma of the Peacebuilding Consensus' (2004) 11 *International Peacekeeping* 83, 96.

[9] Charles Thiessen, 'Emancipatory Peacebuilding: Critical Responses to (Neo)Liberal Trends' in Thomas Matyok, Jessica Senehi and Sean Byrne (eds), *Critical Issues in Peace and Conflict Studies: Theory, Practice and Pedagogy* (Lanham, Lexington Books, 2011) 118.

[10] Severine Autesserre, *Peaceland: Conflict Resolution and the Everyday Politics of International Intervention* (Cambridge, Cambridge University Press, 2014) 241.

[11] Roger Mac Ginty, 'Indigenous Peace-Making versus the Liberal Peace' (2008) 43 *Cooperation and Conflict* 139, 145.

[12] See, eg, Chandra Lekha Sriram, 'Justice as Peace? Liberal Peacebuilding and Strategies of Transnational Justice' (2007) 21 *Global Society* 579.

[13] Mac Ginty (n 11) 159, arguing that: 'The radical research agenda now needs to move beyond merely criticizing the failings of the liberal peace to scoping the extent to which alternatives … are possible.'

[14] Roger Mac Ginty, 'Everyday Peace: Bottom-up and Local Agency in Conflict Affected Societies' (2014) 45 *Security Dialogue* 548, 555.

proposal to adopt 'indigenous peace-making' over liberal peacebuilding strategies lacks content, beyond the obvious observation that local actors should be empowered.[15] Similarly, Richmond's proposal to work towards 'eirinism' – a revision of liberal peace that makes social rather than institutional change a priority – is intuitively persuasive, but even clarificatory statements, such as that this depends on 'acceptance of peacebuilding as an empathetic, emancipatory process, focused on everyday care, human security and a social contract that provides care as well as security', remain excessively vague.[16] Finally, Paris' suggestion to address the limitations of the existing peacebuilding model through 'institutionalization before liberalization' is sufficiently specific, but its increased emphasis on institutions and processes, to the almost total disregard of social change, is at odds with the needs of subjective peace.[17]

This study is unique in adopting exactly the opposite approach to the existing literature: it delivers a mixed, instead of a wholly negative, review of human rights as one instrument in the liberal peace toolbox and makes practical recommendations for their continuing improvement, rather than merely focusing on their theoretical limitations. On the one hand, an assessment of their peacebuilding potential in the four case studies suggests that human rights can almost always have positive effects, whether these are symbolic, result in institutional and legal amendments or, most ambitiously, induce social and psychological changes among the population. *All* of these changes are essential in post-violence societies: if institutional and legal amendments are adopted in the absence of broader social initiatives, then only a superficial type of peace is likely to be built. Alternatively, if attempts are made to induce social, but not legal change, then the results of peacebuilding efforts are likely to be ephemeral. In practice, human rights language has made symbolic inroads even in relation to fundamental conflicts, such as those concerning missing persons in Cyprus, resulted in legal amendments (for example, in relation to the right to life in NI), and contributed to social and psychological changes when being used by the TRC in SA. At the same time, the picture is not all rosy: despite some positive developments in Cyprus, the most divisive fundamental conflicts, such as those relating to remedying the displaced, have largely remained unresolved. Similarly, institutional and legal amendments in NI, and even more so in BiH, have not been transformed to social and psychological changes among the population, while in SA, this has only happened to a limited extent and is mostly due to the efforts of a single institution.

[15] Mac Ginty (n 11).

[16] Oliver Richmond, 'A Post-liberal Peace: Eirinism and the Everyday' (2009) 35 *Review of International Studies* 557, 578.

[17] Roland Paris, *At War's End: Building Peace after Civil Conflict* (Cambridge, Cambridge University Press, 2004).

This mixed review suggests that more can and needs to be done in order to enhance the peacebuilding potential of human rights. On the most abstract level, peacebuilders must be clear from the outset on what they are working towards rather than merely having a vague idea of what peace looks like. Taking into account the specific needs of each society, they must strike a balance between security, justice and reconciliation considerations, and explicitly rely on these in order to shape peacebuilding policies on the ground. More practically, when using human rights to adjudicate disputes, peacebuilders should acknowledge the strengths of the judiciary in resolving minor conflicts and its limitations in addressing their fundamental counterparts. With these in mind, they must seek to resolve as many zero-sum conflicts as possible during the negotiation of the comprehensive peace agreement and take advantage of the peace momentum rather than push differences under the carpet by opting for constructive ambiguity. At the same time, since minor disagreements are often successfully resolved in the courtroom, the judiciary should be strengthened through the training of legal actors, the creation of specialised courts, the simplification of legal procedures and the better cooperation between domestic and international institutions. Finally, peacebuilders should decide whether, and when, to rely on human rights adjudication by considering the effect that the passage of time can have on a court's reasoning, ability and willingness to resolve the conflict.

When using human rights with the expectation that they will result in the adoption and implementation of peacebuilding policies, the political willingness of the decision makers to induce change must be a primary consideration. However, even when this is present, challenges might arise in relation to the drafting of the relevant legislation, or when it is being implemented by a body that lacks the capacity, expertise, institutional independence or resources to undertake the task successfully. These hurdles can be overcome by involving, where needed, international actors and civil society organisations. Such involvement can give rise to political pressure to build peace or to the provision of technical expertise that will address the other two challenges. Further, the analysis suggests that the composition of the peacebuilding team should be reconsidered and shifted along two axes: from international to also domestic actors and from legal to non-legal experts as well. This will provide the team with the local knowledge and multidisciplinary perspectives needed to induce socio-economic and psychological changes within the post-violence society. Finally, since peace must not only be built, but must also be seen to be built, it is important that any initiatives are accompanied by a comprehensive communication strategy that speaks to, and also receives information from, the local population about its needs and concerns.

These recommendations do not form an exhaustive list of steps that necessarily lead to the building of peace. They should also not be endorsed by detracting attention from additional challenges of peacebuilding operations that have been identified by the UN, such as insufficient funding or lack of coordination among different actors.[18] Rather, their adoption, alongside other proposals for improvement, can be one way of enhancing the effectiveness of peacebuilding operations. Thus, the aforementioned recommendations seek to achieve this not by overhauling the liberal peace agenda, but by merely making tweaks to it. For example, they take for granted that the international community will have an interest, and continue being involved, in peacebuilding initiatives within post-violence societies, but urge that such involvement does not overshadow the importance of local ownership of the process. Similarly, the study accepts that there is an international trend, both in post-violence societies and elsewhere, of the judiciary being asked to adjudicate and resolve political disagreements.[19] Taking this as a given, the recommendations focus on ensuring that increased judicial involvement in the resolution of conflicts will be such that it produces positive results.

Nevertheless, the difficulty of adopting and internalising (even small) changes to the liberal peace agenda should not be underestimated. In an ideal scenario, these will not only shape local practices, but will also have an impact on those who fund peace operations, such as international organisations, governments and large non-governmental bodies. In such a case, the recommendations could reshape from within how peacebuilders present, justify and assess their work. As a result, if they are taken seriously, they can lead to a shift in the balance of power among existing actors and, as such, are likely to be resisted by some, while being endorsed by others. At the same time, hurdles in the adoption of such proposals are not insurmountable. For instance, the emphasis on subjective security, justice and reconciliation is indeed likely to make any peacebuilding operation longer, as socio-economic and psychological changes need several years before they can take root. While this risks making the operation unaffordable, the empowerment of local peacebuilders and the strengthening of civil society organisations can reduce costs and give a different kind of momentum to the process, thus ensuring its longevity.

III. GETTING FROM PEACE IN THE BOOKS TO PEACE ON THE GROUND

In three out of the four case studies – BiH, NI and SA – the peacebuilding operation has been in place for more than 20 years and, as a result, it is too late to implement all of the recommendations that have been made here. However, in

[18] For a discussion of these challenges, see Roland Paris, 'Understanding the "Coordination Problem" in Postwar Statebuilding' in Roland Paris and Timothy D Sisk (eds), *The Dilemmas of Statebuilding: Confronting the Contradictions of Postwar Peace Operations* (London, Routledge, 2009).

[19] There is an extensive literature discussing this phenomenon. See, eg, Tom Gerard Daly, *The Alchemists: Questioning Our Faith in Courts as Democracy-Builders* (Cambridge, Cambridge

all of them, it is still possible to make at least some changes that draw inspiration from the preceding analysis. For instance, an assessment of the provisions of the (SA) Employment Equality Act No 55 of 1998 that seeks to address the problem of discrimination in the workplace suggests that these should be amended. While the Act creates specialised bodies that applicants can theoretically resort to, procedural hurdles make both the Commission of Conciliation, Mediation and Arbitration, and the Labour Courts, on which the Act relies, inaccessible. As a result, relatively minor conflicts that could have been successfully addressed in these forums remain unresolved and perpetuate a sense of injustice in the country. Taking into account the continuing inequalities and discrimination in SA, such amendments could, even today, have a positive peacebuilding effect.

Similarly, the proposals point to overdue changes that must take place to the BiH peace architecture and, in particular, the need to shift power from international to local actors. Significant improvements on this front have already been made, as evidenced by a comparison between the existing situation and the days when the High Representative was responsible for each single major legislative change in the country.[20] Even so, it is arguably high time that the international community starts considering how best to dissolve the Office of the High Representative and create the space for local politicians to come to the fore. This is not to suggest that the transition will be seamless or that all local actors will resist the temptation to continue acting as spoilers. However, it is a necessary step, not only because the Office of the High Representative's lack of accountability has festered and allegedly resulted in shady backroom politics over the years,[21] but because at some point, BiH must start being run like a truly democratic state. In this endeavour, the strengthening of civil society organisations to counterbalance the gradual withdrawal of the international community will also be helpful, but insights which warn against a simplistic and overly positive depiction of such actors should be taken into account as well.

Finally, lessons can be learned about the improvement of the peacebuilding process in NI. This has aptly been characterised as 'piecemeal', since it lacks a central commitment among the parties to address fundamental questions as to who is a victim and a perpetrator, and what are appropriate responses for each type of actor.[22] The limitations of this fragmented process notwithstanding, the

University Press, 2017); Ran Hirschl, *Towards Juristocracy: The Origins and Consequences of the New Constitutionalism* (Cambridge, MA, Harvard University Press, 2004); Samuel Issacharoff and Richard H Pildes, 'Politics as Markets: Partisan Lockups of the Democratic Process' (1998) 50 *Stanford Law Review* 643.

[20] Gergana Dimitrova, 'Democracy and International Intervention in Bosnia and Herzegovina' (2005) 6 *Central European Political Studies Review* 45.

[21] Roland Kostić, 'Shadow Peacebuilders and Diplomatic Counterinsurgencies: Informal Networks, Knowledge Production and the Art of Policy-Shaping' (2017) 11 *Journal of Intervention and Statebuilding* 120.

[22] Nevin T Aiken, 'Learning to Live Together: Transitional Justice and Intergroup Reconciliation in Northern Ireland' (2010) 4 *International Journal of Transitional Justice* 166, 167.

many initiatives within it give peacebuilders a greater opportunity to strike a balance between the different elements of peace that each promotes. This makes it even more important for them to have a clear understanding of what peace means and, considering this together with the needs of the NI society, make decisions about what should be prioritised and when. A more practical observation is that the replacement of the Historical Enquiries Team, which investigated conflict-related deaths, by the Legacy Investigation Branch provides authorities with the opportunity to change policies and adopt a much more effective communication strategy with the public. This will ensure that its investigations do not merely comply with the UK's human rights obligations, but are also perceived by the parties as a genuine effort to promote reconciliation among the victims' families.

However, it is Cyprus that has the most to gain from a careful consideration of this study's recommendations. Although some peacebuilding initiatives on the island are already underway, the lack of a comprehensive peace agreement gives Cypriots the opportunity to take such proposals into account (almost) from the outset. For example, peacebuilders should consider during the negotiations what is meant by 'justice' in the context of Cyprus and how this is best promoted in the eyes of both communities. At the same time, they should determine the powers of a newly formed constitutional court and other specialised bodies by bearing in mind the preceding analysis of the judiciary's mixed ability to resolve different types of conflicts. Perhaps most importantly in light of the island's history and their past mistakes, negotiators should take meaningful steps to establish a communication strategy between them and the general population. If they do not, they leave the public uninformed about what is being discussed on its behalf, with the risk that when the peace settlement is put to a referendum, it will (again) be rejected. The way in which the idea of the 'communication strategy' is understood here, as one that talks to but also receives feedback from the public, acquires increased importance because it is only by engaging in this two-way process that negotiators can become both effective *and* legitimate peacebuilders. In this respect, the empowerment of local actors and strengthening of civil society organisations, who should act not as assistants to the international community, but as equal partners, are also important considerations to take into account. The international community should learn from past experiences in Cyprus and acknowledge that peacebuilding policies that are devised and implemented by those actually experiencing the challenges such policies seek to address are much more likely to speak to the local population and be effective in achieving their objectives.

Finally, the lessons drawn from the four case studies can be usefully applied to other societies that have recently emerged from, or are in the process of ending, violent conflict. With various levels of violence raging in Syria, Yemen, Mozambique and Haiti, growing instability in Tunisia, the Democratic Republic of Congo and Sri Lanka, and frozen conflicts being maintained or becoming hotter in Kashmir, Nagorno-Karabakh and Ukraine, to name but a few, the stakes for the success of peacebuilding operations could not be higher. Especially in societies where the security situation on the ground makes academic research difficult, a theoretical framework and practical recommendations derived from a comparison of other post-violence contexts could offer a useful starting point for action.

IV. THE NEED FOR FURTHER RESEARCH

The theoretical analysis undertaken in relation to the potential of human rights to resolve conflicts and the practical recommendations that have been drawn from this, concern only one component of the peacebuilding agenda. A similar exercise, where existing assumptions are unpacked and examined, must take place in relation to its other components, such as the rule of law and the rapid push towards democratisation and market liberalisation.[23] More directly connected to the subject matter of this study is also the need to conduct further research on the peacebuilding effects of socio-economic[24] and group rights.[25] Additionally, a frequent feature in the literature is the assumption that human rights, this time understood more broadly as social values and not only as legal tools, have an untapped educative potential.[26] Whether this is indeed the case, the conditions under and ways in which they can educate the public should also be explored. Finally, an application of the theoretical framework that has been proposed here to different post-violence societies could shed light on other conditions, the presence of which can further enhance the peacebuilding potential of human rights.

[23] This further research has already started taking place. See, eg, Erik G. Jensen, 'Justice and the Rule of Law' in Charles T Call (ed), *Building States to Build Peace* (Boulder, Lynne Rienner, 2008).

[24] See, eg, Padraig McAuliffe, *Transformative Transitional Justice and the Malleability of Post-conflict States* (Cheltenham, Edward Elgar, 2017).

[25] See, eg, Raffaele Marchetti and Nathalie Tocci (eds), *Civil Society, Conflicts and the Politicization of Human Rights* (Tokyo, United Nations University Press, 2011).

[26] Claudia Lohrenscheit, 'International Approaches in Human Rights Education' (2002) 48 *International Review of Education* 173; George J. Andreopoulos and Richard Pierre Claude (eds), *Human Rights Education for the Twenty-First Century* (Philadelphia, University of Pennsylvania Press, 1997); Felisa Tibbits, 'Understanding What We Do: Emerging Models for Human Rights Education' (2002) 48 *International Review of Education* 159.

Bibliography

Abrams K, 'Emotions in the Mobilization of Rights' (2011) 46 *Harvard Civil Rights-Civil Liberties Law Review* 551

African National Congress, *Ready to Govern: ANC Policy Guidelines for a Democratic South Africa* (National Conference 28–31 May 1992, African National Congress)

Aiken NT, 'Learning to Live Together: Transitional Justice and Intergroup Reconciliation in Northern Ireland' (2010) 4 *International Journal of Transitional Justice* 166

Albin C, 'Peace vs Justice – and Beyond' in Kremenyuk J, Bercovitch V and Zartman W (eds), *The SAGE Handbook of Conflict Resolution* (London, SAGE, 2008) 580–94

Allan P, 'Measuring International Ethics: A Moral Scale of War, Peace, Justice and Global Care' in Allan P and Keller A (eds), *What is Just Peace?* (Oxford, Oxford University Press, 2006) 90–129

Allan P and Keller A, 'The Concept of Just Peace, or Achieving Peace through Recognition, Renouncement and Rule' in Allan P and Keller A (eds), *What is Just Peace?* (Oxford, Oxford University Press, 2006) 195–215

——. (eds), *What is Just Peace?* (Oxford, Oxford University Press, 2006)

Allen T, 'Restitution and Transitional Justice in the European Court of Human Rights' (2007) 13 *Columbia Journal of European Law* 1

Allen T and Douglas B, 'Closing the Door on Restitution: The European Court of Human Rights' in Buyse A and Hamilton M (eds), *Transitional Jurisprudence and the ECHR: Justice, Politics and Rights* (Cambridge, Cambridge University Press, 2011) 208–38

Amnesty International, *Bosnia and Herzegovina: Behind Closed Gates: Ethnic Discrimination in Employment* (EUR 63/001/2006, Sarajevo, Amnesty International, 2006)

Amparo T, 'Reforms that Benefit Poor People – Practical Solutions and Dilemmas of Rights-Based Approaches to Legal and Justice Reform' in Gready P and Ensor J (eds), *Reinventing Development? Translating Rights-Based Approaches from Theory into Practice* (London, Zed Books, 2005) 171–84

Anagnostou D and Mungiu-Pippidi A, 'Domestic Implementation of Human Rights Judgments in Europe: Legal Infrastructure and Government Effectiveness Matter' (2014) 25 *European Journal of International Law* 205

Anastasiou H, 'Communication across Conflict Lines: The Case of Ethnically Divided Cyprus' (2002) 39 *Journal of Peace Research* 581

——. *Nationalism, Ethnic Conflict, and the Quest for Peace in Cyprus: Volume One: The Impasse of Ethnonationalism* (Syracuse, Syracuse University Press, 2008)

Andreopoulos GJ and Claude RP (eds), *Human Rights Education for the Twenty-First Century* (Philadelphia, University of Pennsylvania Press, 1997)

Annan K, 'The Quiet Revolution' (1998) 4 *Global Governance* 123

Anonymous, 'Human Rights in Peace Negotiations' (1996) 18 *Human Rights Quarterly* 249

Anthony G, 'Judicial Review in Northern Ireland: A Guide to the "Real" Devolution Issues' (2009) 14 *Judicial Review* 230

Archer R, "Introduction to the Special Issue: Where is the Evidence?" (2009) 1 *Journal of Human Rights Practice* 333

Aron R, *Peace and War: A Theory of International Relations* (London, Weidenfeld & Nicolson, 1962)

Aronson JD, 'The Strengths and Limitations of South Africa's Search for Apartheid-Era Missing Persons' (2011) 5 *International Journal of Transitional Justice* 262

Atuahene B, 'From Reparation to Restoration: Moving Beyond Restoring Property Rights to Restoring Political and Economic Visibility' (2007) 60 *Southern Methodist University Law Review* 1419
——. 'Paying for the Past: Redressing the Legacy of Land Dispossession in South Africa' (2011) 45 *Law and Society Review* 955
Aubert V, 'Competition and Dissensus: Two Types of Conflict and of Conflict Resolution' (1963) 7 *The Journal of Conflict Resolution* 26
Aunger EA, 'Religion and Occupational Class in Northern Ireland' (1975) 7 *Economic and Social Review* 1
Autesserre S, *Peaceland: Conflict Resolution and the Everyday Politics of International Intervention* (Cambridge, Cambridge University Press, 2014)
Aziz I, *Ibrahim Aziz v Republic of Cyprus* (Series of Lectures 'The People Behind Judicial Decisions', Nicosia, University of Cyprus, 26 November 2016)
Bailliet CM, 'Normative Foundation of the International Law of Peace' in Baillet CM and Mujezinovic Larsen K (eds), *Promoting Peace through International Law* (Oxford, Oxford University Press, 2015) 43–65
Baillet CM and Mujezinovic Larsen K, 'Introduction' in Baillet CM and Mujezinovic Larsen K (eds), *Promoting Peace through International Law* (Oxford, Oxford University Press, 2015) 1–18
Baker P, 'Conflict Resolution versus Democratic Governance: Divergent Paths to Peace?' in Crocker C, Hampson FO, Aall P (eds), *Managing Global Chaos: Sources of and Responses to International Conflict* (Washington DC, United States Institute of Peace, 1996) 37–50
Baldwin D, 'The Concept of Security' (1997) 23 *Review of International Studies* 5
Ball P, Tabeau E and Verwimp P, *The Bosnian Book of Dead: Assessment of the Database* (Brighton, Households in Conflict Network, 2007)
Bar-Siman-Tov Y, 'Dialectics between Stable Peace and Reconciliation' in Bar-Siman-Tov Y (ed), *From Conflict Resolution to Reconciliation* (Oxford, Oxford University Press, 2004) 61–80
Bar-Tal D, 'From Intractable Conflict through Conflict Resolution to Reconciliation: Psychological Analysis' (2000) 21 *Political Psychology* 351
Bar-Tal D and Bennink G, 'The Nature of Reconciliation as an Outcome and as a Process' in Bar-Siman-Tov Y (ed), *From Conflict Resolution to Reconciliation* (Oxford, Oxford University Press, 2004) 11–38
Barash DP and Webel CP, *Peace and Conflict Studies*, 2nd edn (Berkeley, SAGE, 2009)
Barclay S, Jones LC and Marshall A-M, 'Two Spinning Wheels: Studying Law and Social Movements' in Sarat A (ed), *Special Issue: Social Movements/Legal Possibilities* (Bingley, Emerald, 2011) 1–16
Barnett M and Zurcher C, 'The Peacebuilder's Contract: How External Statebuilding Reinforces Weak Statehood' in Paris R and Sisk TD (eds), *The Dilemmas of Statebuilding: Confronting the Contradictions of Postwar Peace Operations* (London, Routledge, 2009) 23–52
Basu K, 'Participatory Equity and Economic Development: Policy Implications for a Globalized World' (World Bank Conference 'New Frontiers of Social Policy: Development in a Globalizing World', Arusha, 12–15 December 2005)
Baum L, *Judges and Their Audiences: A Perspective on Judicial Behavior* (Princeton, Princeton University Press, 2006)
Bayley DH, *Democratizing the Police Abroad: What to Do and How to Do it* (Washington DC, US Department of Justice, 2001)
BBC News, 'Turkey Compensates Cyprus Refugee' (2 December 2003)
Beetham D, *The Legitimation of Power* (London, Macmillan, 1991)
Beilin Y, 'Just Peace: A Dangerous Objective' in Allan P and Keller A (eds), *What is Just Peace?* (Oxford, Oxford University Press, 2006) 130–48
Beirne M and Knox C, 'Reconciliation and Human Rights in Northern Ireland: A False Dichotomy?' (2014) 6 *Journal of Human Rights Practice* 26
Beitz CR, *The Idea of Human Rights* (Oxford, Oxford University Press, 2009)
Bell C, *Peace Agreements and Human Rights* (Oxford, Oxford University Press, 2000)
——. 'Dealing with the Past in Northern Ireland' (2003) 26 *Fordham International Law Journal* 1095

——. 'Human Rights, Peace Agreements and Conflict Resolution: Negotiating Justice in Northern Ireland' in Mertus J and Helsing JW (eds), *Human Rights and Conflict: Exploring the Links between Rights, Law and Peacebuilding* (Washington DC, United States Institute of Peace Press, 2006) 345–74

——. *Negotiating Justice? Human Rights and Peace Agreements* (Geneva, International Council of Human Rights Policy, 2006)

——. 'Human Rights and the Struggle for Change: A Study in Self-Critical Legal Thought' in Dickinson R, Katselli E, Murray C and Pdersen OW (eds), *Examining Critical Perspectives on Human Rights* (Cambridge, Cambridge University Press, 2012) 217–46

Bell C and Keenan J, 'Lost on the Way Home? The Right to Life in Northern Ireland' (2005) 32 *Journal of Law and Society* 68

Bellamy AJ, 'The "Next Stage" in Peace Operations Theory?' (2004) 11 *International Peacekeeping* 17

Bellamy R, 'The Democratic Qualities of Courts: A Critical Analysis of Three Arguments' (2013) 49 *Representation* 333

Benvenisti E and Harel A, 'Embracing the Tension between National and International Human Rights Law: The Case for Discordant Parity' (2017) 15 *International Journal of Constitutional Law* 36

Bezuidenhout A, Bischoff C, Buhlungu S and Lewins K, *Tracking Progress on the Implementation and Impact of the Employment Equity Act since its Inception* (Research Consortium: Human Science Research Council, Development Policy Research Unit, Sociology of Work Unit, Johannesburg, Research Commissioned by Department of Labour South Africa, 2008)

Bickel AM, *The Least Dangerous Branch* (New Haven, Yale University Press, 1986)

Biggar N, 'Making Peace or Doing Justice: Must We Choose?' in Biggar N (ed), *Burying the Past: Making Peace and Doing Justice after Civil Conflict* (Washington DC, Georgetown University Press, 2003) 3–24

Bisogno M and Chong A, 'Poverty and Inequality in Bosnia and Herzegovina after the Civil War' (2002) 30 *World Development* 61

Blumenstock T, 'Legal Protection of the Missing and Their Relatives: The Example of Bosnia and Herzegovina' (2006) 19 *Leiden Journal of International Law* 773

Bohlin A, 'A Price on the Past: Cash Compensation in South African Land Restitution' (2004) 38 *Canadian Journal of African Studies* 672

Bonacker T, Diez T, Gnomes T, Groth A and Pia E, 'Human Rights and the (De)Securitization of Conflict' in Marchetti R and Tocci N (eds), *Civil Society, Conflicts and the Politicization of Human Rights* (Tokyo, UN University Press, 2001) 13–46

Booysen L, 'Barriers to Employment Equity Implementation and Retention of Blacks on Management in South Africa' (2007) 31 *South African Journal of Labour Relations* 47

Borer TA, 'A Taxonomy of Victims and Perpetrators: Human Rights and Reconciliation in South Africa' (2003) 25 *Human Rights Quarterly* 1088

Bose S, *Contested Lands: Israel-Palestine, Kashmir, Bosnia, Cyprus and Sri Lanka* (Cambridge, MA, Harvard University Press, 2007)

Boulding KE, *Stable Peace* (Austin, University of Texas Press, 1978)

Bouwen P and McCown M, 'Lobbying versus Litigation: Political and Legal Strategies of Interest Representation in the European Union' (2007) 14 *Journal of European Public Policy* 422

Boyle K, 'Linking Human Rights and Other Goals' in Morison J, McEvoy K and Anthony G (eds), *Judges, Transition, and Human Rights* (Oxford, Oxford University Press, 2007) 401–422

Bracken P and Celia P (eds), *Rethinking the Trauma of War* (London, Save the Children/Free Association Books, 1998)

Braithwaite J, *Restorative Justice and Responsive Regulation* (Oxford, Oxford University Press, 2002)

Brems E and Lavrysen L, 'Procedural Justice in Human Rights Adjudication: The European Court of Human Rights' (2013) 35 *Human Rights Quarterly* 176

Brewer JD, 'The Public Value of the Sociology of Peace Processes' ('Innovation and Engagement' public lecture series, Cardiff University, 2 December 2014)

Brewer JD, *Peace Processes: A Sociological Approach* (Cambridge, Polity Press, 2010)

Broad-Based Black Economic Empowerment Commission, *Strategy of the Broad-Based Black Economic Empowerment Commission, 2017–2021* (Pretoria, Department of Trade and Industry, 2017)

Buchanan A, *Human Rights, Legitimacy, and the Use of Force* (Oxford, Oxford University Press, 2010)

——. *The Heart of Human Rights* (New York, Oxford University Press, 2014)

Burger R and Jafta R, 'Affirmative Action in South Africa: An Empirical Assessment of the Impact on Labour Market Outcomes' (CRISE Working Paper No 76, Oxford, Centre for Research on Inequality, Human Security and Ethnicity, University of Oxford, 2010)

Burke-White W, 'Human Rights and National Security: The Strategic Correlation' (2004) 17 *Harvard Human Rights Journal* 249

Burton J, *Resolving Deep-Rooted Conflict: A Handbook* (Lanham, University Press of America, 1987)

——. *Conflict: Resolution and Prevention* (Basingstoke, Macmillan, 1990)

——. *Conflict: Resolution and Provention* (New York, St Martin's Press, 1990)

Byrne J and Jarman N, 'Ten Years after Patten: Young People and Policing in Northern Ireland' (2011) 43 *Youth & Society* 433

Call CT and Stanley W, 'Civilian Security' in Stedman S, Rothschild D and Cousens E (eds), *Ending Civil Wars: The Implemntation of Peace Agreements* (Boulder, Lynne Rienner, 2002) 303–26

Campbell C, Ni Aolain F and Harvey C, 'The Frontiers of Legal Analysis: Reframing the Transition in Northern Ireland' (2003) 66 *Modern Law Review* 317

Caplan R, 'Who Guards the Guardians? International Accountability in Bosnia' in Chandler D (ed), *Peace without Politics? Ten Years of International State Building in Bosnia* (London, Taylor & Francis, 2006) 157–169

Cassia PS, *Bodies of Evidence: Burial, Memory and the Recovery of Missing Persons in Cyprus* (New York, Berghahn Books, 2005)

Chandler D, 'Bosnia: The Democracy Paradox' (2001) 100 *Current History* 114

Chapman AR and Ball P, 'The Truth of Truth Commissions: Comparative Lessons from Haiti, South Africa and Guatemala' (2001) 23 *Human Rights Quarterly* 1

Choudhry S, 'After the Rights Revolution: Bills of Rights in the Post-conflict State' (2010) 6 *Annual Review of Law and Social Science* 301

Christophorou C, Sahin S and Pavlou S, *Media Narratives, Politics and the Cyprus Problem* (1/2010, Nicosia) (PRIO Cyprus Centre, 2010)

Cingranelli D and Richards D, 'Respect for Human Rights after the End of the Cold War' (1999) 36 *Journal of Peace Research* 511

Clark K, *War Reparations and Litigations: The Case of Bosnia* (International Litigation Series No 1, Amsterdam, Nuhanovic Foundation Center for War Reparations, 2014)

Clarke-Habibi S, 'Transforming Worldviews: The Case of Education for Peace in Bosnia and Herzegovina' (2005) 3 *Journal of Transformative Education* 33

Cohen M, 'South Africa's Racial Income Inequality Persists, Census Shows' (*Bloomberg*, 30 October 2012)

Cohen R, 'Apology and Reconciliation in International Relations' in Bar-Siman-Tov Y (ed), *From Conflict Resolution to Reconciliation* (Oxford, Oxford University Press, 2004) 177–196

Collier P, 'Demobilization and Insecurity: A Study in the Economics of the Transitions from War to Peace' (1994) 6 *Journal of International Development* 349

Collier P, Elliott VL, Hegre H, Hoeffler A, Reynal-Querol M and Sambanis N, *Breaking the Conflict Trap: Civil War and Development Policy* (Washington DC, World Bank and Oxford University Press, 2003)

Commission for Employment Equity, *Annual Report 2005–2006* (Pretoria, Department of Labour, 2006)

——. *Annual Report 2015–2016* (Pretoria, Department of Labour, 2016)

Commission for Real Property Claims of Displaced Persons and Refugees, *Return, Local Integration and Property Rights in Bosnia Herzegovina* (Sarajevo, Commission for Real Property Claims of Displaced Persons and Refugees, 1999)

Committee of Ministers, *Resolution Concerning the Judgment of the European Court of Human Rights of 28 July 1998 in the Loizidou Case against Turkey* (ResDH(2003)190, Strasbourg, Council of Europe, 2 December 2003)

——. *Interim Resolution on Action of the Security Forces in Northern Ireland (Case of McKerr against the United Kingdom and Five Similar Cases)* (ResDH(2005)20, Strasbourg, Council of Europe, 23 February 2005)

——. *Interim Resolution on the Action of the Security Forces in Northern Ireland (Case of McKerr against the United Kingdom and Five Similar Cases)* (CM/ResDH(2007)73, Strasbourg, Council of Europe, 17 October 2007)

——. *Interim Resolution* (CM/ResDH(2013)259, Strasbourg, Council of Europe, 22 December 2009)

——. *Interim Resolution: Execution of the Judgments of the European Court of Human Rights in the Cases Varnava, Xenides-Arestis and 32 Other Cases against Turkey* (CM/ResDH (2014)185, Strasbourg, Council of Europe, 25 September 2014)

Committee on Legal Affairs and Human Rights, *Draft Resolution on the Implementation of Judgments of the European Court of Human Rights* (Doc 13864, Strasbourg, Parliamentary Assembly of the Council of Europe, 9 September 2015)

Committee on Missing Persons in Cyprus, *Figures and Statistics of Missing Persons up to 31 March 2019* (Nicosia, Committee of Missing Persons, 2019)

Community Agency for Social Enquiry, *Assessment of the Status Quo of Settled Land Restitution Claims with a Developmental Component Nationally* (Pretoria, Department of Land Affairs, 2006)

Corkalo D, Ajdukovic D, Weinstein HM, Stover E, Djipa D and Biro M, 'Neighbors Again? Intercommunity Relations after Ethnic Cleansing' in Stover E and Weinstein HM (eds), *My Neighbor, My Enemy: Justice and Community in the Aftermath of Mass Atrocity* (Cambridge, Cambridge University Press, 2004) 143–61

Cornell S and Hartmann D, *Ethnicity and Race: Making Identities in a Changing World* (Thousand Oaks, Pine Forge Press, 2007)

Cowen T, 'How Far Back Should We Go? Why Restitution Should Be Small' in Elster J (ed), *Retribution and Reparation in the Transition to Democracy* (Cambridge, Cambridge University Press, 2006) 17–32

Cox M and Garlick M, 'Musical Chairs: Property Repossession and Return Strategies in Bosnia and Herzegovina' in Leckie S (ed), *Returning Home: Housing and Property Restituiton Rights of Refugees and Displaced Persons* (New York, Transnational Publishers, 2003) 65–83

Cryer R, Friman H, Robinson D and Wilmshurst E, *An Introduction to International Criminal Law and Procedure*, 2nd edn (Cambridge, Cambridge University Press, 2012)

Cummings SL and Rhode DL, 'Public Interest Litigation: Insights from Theory and Practice' (2009) 36 *Fordham Urban Law Journal* 603

D'Onofrio L, *Welcome Home? Minority Return in South-East Rebublika Srpska* (Sussex Migration Working Paper No 19, Sussex Centre for Migration Research, University of Sussex, 2004)

Daly TG, 'The Alchemists: Courts as Democracy-Builders in Contemporary Thought' (2017) 6 *Global Constitutionalism* 101

——. *The Alchemists: Questioning Our Faith in Courts as Democracy-Builders* (Cambridge, Cambridge University Press, 2017)

Daye R, *Political Forgiveness: Lessons from South Africa* (Maryknoll, Orbis Books, 2004)

Demetriou O and Gürel A, 'Human Rights, Civil Society and Conflict in Cyprus' in Marchetti R and Tocci N (eds), *Civil Society, Conflicts and the Politicization of Human Rights* (Tokyo, United Nations University Press, 2011) 100–22

Dempster L, 'The Republican Movement, "Disappearing" and Framing the Past in Northern Ireland' (2016) 10 *International Journal of Transitional Justice* 250

Department of Foreign Affairs and International Trade, *Human Security: Safety for People in a Changing World* (Ottawa, Government of Canada, 1999)

Department of Labour, *Employment Equity Act 1988 (Act 55 of 1998 as Amended) Draft Code of Good Practice on the Preparation and Implementation of Employment Equity Plan* (Pretoria, Department of Labour, 2016)

Department of Land Affairs, *White Paper on South African Land Policy* (Pretoria, Government of South Africa, 1997)

Department of Statistics and Research, *Census of Population and Agriculture 1960 (Volume III – Demographic Characteristics)* (Nicosia, Department of Statistics and Research, 1963)

Department of Trade and Industry, *South Africa's Economic Transformation: A Strategy for Broad-Based Black Economic Empowerment* (Pretoria, Department of Trade and Industry, 2003)

——. *Code of Good Practice 2013, Issued under Section 9 of the Broad-Based Black Economic Empowerment Act of 2003* (Pretoria, Department of Trade and Industry, 2013)

——. *The National Broad-Based Black Economic Empowerment Summit: A Decade of Economic Empowerment* (2003–13 Summit Report, Pretoria, Department of Trade and Industry, 2013)

Derman B, Lahiff E and Sjaastad E, 'Strategic Questions about Strategic Partners' in Walker C, Bohlin A, Hall R and Kepe T (eds), *Land, Memory, Reconstruction and Justice: Perspectives on Land Claims in South Africa* (Athens, OH, Ohio University Press, 2010) 306–24

Deutsch M, 'A Theory of Cooperation and Conflict' (1949) 2 *Human Relations* 149

——. *The Resolution of Conflict: Constructive and Destructive Processes* (New Haven, Yale University Press, 1973)

Dickson B, 'The House of Lords and the Northern Ireland Conflict: A Sequel' (2006) 69 *Modern Law Review* 383

——. 'Policing and Human Rights after the Conflict' in Cox M, Guelke A and Stephen F (eds), *A Farewell to Arms? From 'Long War' to Long Peace in Northern Ireland* (Manchester, Manchester University Press, 2006) 104–15

Dickson B and Harvey C, *Assessing the Role of the Equality Commission in the Effectiveness of Section 75 of the Northern Ireland Act 1998* (Human Rights Centre, School of Law, Queen's University Belfast, 2006)

Dimitrova G, 'Democracy and International Intervention in Bosnia and Herzegovina' (2005) 6 *Central European Political Studies Review* 45

Donald A and Mottershaw E, 'Evaluating the Impact of Human Rights Litigation on Policy and Practice: A Case Study of the UK' (2009) 1 *Journal of Human Rights Practice* 339

Donnelly J, 'Peace as a Human Right: Commentary' in Mertus J and Helsing JW (eds), *Human Rights and Conflict: Exploring the Links between Rights, Law and Peacebuilding* (Washington DC, United States Institute of Peace Press, 2006) 151–57

Downs G and Stedman SJ, 'Evaluation Issues in Peace Implementation' in Stedman S, Rothschild D and Cousens E (eds), *Ending Civil Wars: The Implementation of Peace Agreements* (Boulder, Lynne Rienner, 2002) 43–69

Doyle MW and Sambanis N, *Making War and Building Peace* (Princeton, Princeton University Press, 2006)

Dror Y, 'Law and Social Change' (1958–59) 33 *Tulane Law Review* 787

Du Toit P, *South Africa's Brittle Peace: The Problem of Post-settlement Violence* (Basingstoke, Palgrave, 2001)

Dudouet V, *Transitions from Violence to Peace: Revisiting Analysis and Intervention in Conflict Tranformation* (Berghof Handbook Dialogue Series No 15, Berlin, Berghof Research Centre, 2006)

Dunne T and Wheeler NJ, '"We the Peoples": Contending Discourses of Security in Human Rights Theory and Practice' (2004) 18 *International Relations* 9

Dzidic D, 'Bosnian Serb Leader Urges Srebrenica "Truth Commission"' (Balkan Transitional Justice, 25 March 2015)

Eide K, 'Note on Galtung's Concept of "Violence"' (1971) 8 *Journal of Peace Research* 71

Eisenberg A, 'Identity and Liberal Politics: The Problem of Minorities within Minorities' in Eisenberg A and Spinner-Halev J (eds), *Minorities within Minorities: Equality, Rights and Diversity* (Cambridge, Cambridge University Press, 2005) 249–70

Elkind D, 'Adolescent Cognitive Development' in Adams JF (ed), *Understanding Adolsence: Current Developments in Adolsescent Psychology* (Boston, Allyn & Bacon, 1968) 125–58

Ellison G, Pino NW and Shirlow P, 'Assessing the Determinants of Public Confidence in the Police: A Case Study of a Post-conflict Community in Northern Ireland' (2010) 13 *Criminology and Criminal Justice* 552

Engel DM and Munger FW, *Rights of Inclusion: Law and Identity in the Life Stories of Americans with Disabilities* (Chicago, University of Chicago Press, 2003)

Equallity Commission for Northern Ireland, *Fair Employment Monitoring: Composiiton of Employment – Trends over Time* (Belfast, Equality Commission for Northern Ireland, 2013)

Equallity Commission for Northern Ireland, *Fair Employment in Northern Ireland: Code of Practice* (Belfast, Equality Commission for Northern Ireland, date unknown)

Ergas Y, 'Human Rights Impact: Developing an Agenda for Interdisciplinary, International Research' (2009) 1 *Journal of Human Rights Practice* 459

Eriksson M and Wallensteen P, 'Armed Conflict, 1989–2003' (2004) 41 *Journal of Peace* Research 625

Euronews, 'EU Elections 2019: Country-by-Country Full Results' (28 May 2009)

European Commission, *Bosnia and Herzegovina 2013 Progress Report* (SWD(2013) 415 final, Brussels, European Commission, 16 October 2013)

——. *Bosnia-Herzegovina – EU: Deep Disappointment on Sejdić-Finci Implementation* (Brussels, Council of Europe, 18 February 2014)

——. *Instrument for Pre-Accession Assistance (IPA II) 2014–2020 – Bosnia and Herzegovina: Enhanced Justice Sector and Cooperation in Rule of Law* (Brussels, European Commission, 2014)

European Commission against Racism and Intolerance, *First Report on Bosnia and Herzegovina* (CRI(2005)2, Strasbourg, Council of Europe, 25 June 2004)

——. *Second Report on Bosnia and Herzegovina* (CRI(2011)2, Strasbourg, Council of Europe, 7 December 2010)

——. *ECRI Report on Bosnia and Herzegovina (Fifth Monitoring Cycle)* (CRI(2017)2, Strasbourg, Council of Europe, 6 December 2016)

European Stability Initiative, *Lost in the Bosnian Labyrinth: Why the Sejdić-Finci Case Should Not Block an EU Application* (Berlin/Brussels/Instanbul, European Stability Initiative, 2013)

Everly R, 'Assessing the Accountability of the High Representative' in Haynes DF (ed), *Deconstructing the Reconstruction: Human Rights and Rule of Law in Postwar Bosnia and Herzegovina* (Farnham, Ashgate, 2008) 79–113

Ewick P and Silbey S, *The Common Place of Law: Stories from Everyday Life: Language and Legal Discourse* (Chicago, University of Chicago Press, 1998)

Ferejohn J, 'Judicializing Politics, Politicizing Law' (2002) 65 *Law and Contemporary Problems* 41

Fergus E and Collier D, 'Equality at Work: The Role of the Judiciary in Promoting Transformation' (2014) 30 *South African Journal on Human Rights* 484

Ferrers Comella V, 'The Consequences of Centralizing Constitutional Review in a Special Court: Some Thoughts on Judicial Activism' (2003–04) 82 *Texas Law Review* 1705

Fetherston B, 'Peacekeeping, Conflict Resolution and Peacebuilding: A Reconsideration of Theoretical Frameworks' (2000) 7 *International Peacekeeping* 190

Fiol MC and O'Connor EJ, 'Managing Intractable Identity Conflicts' in Christie DJ (ed), *The Encyclopedia of Peace Psychology* (New York, Wiley-Blackwell, 2012) 937–40

Fiss OM, 'Human Rights as Social Ideals' in Hesse C and Post R (eds), *Human Rights in Political Transitions: Gettysburg to Bosnia* (New York, Zone Books, 1999) 263–76

Follesdal A, 'The Legitimacy Deficits of the Human Rights Judiciary: Elements and Implications of a Normative Theory' (2013) 14 *Theoretical Inquiries in Law* 339

——. 'Much Ado about Nothing? International Judicial Review of Human Rights in Well Functioning Democracies' in Follesdal A, Schaffer JK and Ulfstein G (eds), *The Legitimacy of International Human Rights Regimes* (Cambridge, Cambridge University Press, 2014) 272–99

Freeman M, *Truth Commissions and Procedural Fairness* (New York, Cambridge University Press, 2006)

Friedman B, 'Mediated Popular Constitutionalism' (2003) 101 *Michigan Law Review* 2595

Fuller L, 'The Forms and Limits of Adjudication' (1978–79) 92 *Harvard Law Review* 353

Galanter M, 'Why the "Haves" Come out Ahead: Speculations on the Limits of Legal Change' (1974) 9 *Law and Society Review* 95

Galenkamp M, 'The Rationale of Minority Rights: Wishes Rather than Needs?' in Räikkä J (ed), *Do We Need Minority Rights? Conceptual Issues* (The Hague, Martinus Nijhoff Publishers, 1996) 41–57

Gallatin J and Adelson J, 'Legal Guarantees of Individual Freedom: A Cross-national Study of the Development of Political Thought' (1971) 27 *Journal of Social Issues* 93

Galtung J, 'An Editorial' (1964) 1 *Journal of Peace Research* 1

——. 'Violence, Peace and Peace Research' (1969) 6 *Journal of Peace Research* 167

——. 'Twenty-Five Years of Peace Research' (1985) 22 *Journal of Peace Research* 141

——. 'Cultural Violence' (1990) 27 *Journal of Peace Research* 291

——. *Peace by Peaceful Means: Peace and Conflict, Development and Civilization* (London, SAGE, 1996)

——. 'Introduction: Peace by Peaceful Conflict Transformation: The Transcend Approach' in Webel C and Galtung J (eds), *The Handbook of Peace and Conflict Studies* (London, Routledge, 2007) 14–32

——. 'Peace, Positive and Negative' in Christie DJ (ed), *The Encyclopedia of Peace Psychology* (Chichester, Wiley-Blackwell, 2012) 758–65

Garcia-Godos J, 'It's about Trust: Transitional Justice and Accountability in the Search for Peace' in Baillet CM and Mujezinovic Larsen K (eds), *Promoting Peace through International Law* (Oxford, Oxford University Press, 2015) 331–44

Gaze B and Hunter R, 'Access to Justice for Discrimination Complaints: Courts and Legal Representation' (2009) 32 *University of New South Wales Law Journal* 699

Geneva Declaration Secretariat, *Global Burden of Armed Violence* ((Geneva, Geneva Declaration on Armed Violence and Development, 2008)

Ghai Y (ed), *Autonomy and Ethnicity: Negotiating Competing Claims in Multi-ethnic States* (Cambridge, Cambridge University Press, 2000)

Gibson JL, *Overcoming Apartheid: Can Truth Reconcile a Divided Nation?* (New York, Russell SAGE Foundation, 2004)

——. 'Truth, Reconciliation and the Creation of a Human Rights Culture in South Africa' (2004) 38 *Law and Society Review* 5

——. 'On Legitimacy Theory and the Effectiveness of Truth Commissions' (2009) 72 *Law and Contemporary Problems* 123

——. *Overcoming Historical Injustices: Land Reconciliation in South Africa* (Cambridge, Cambridge University Press, 2009)

Gibson JL and Gouws A, *Overcoming Intolerance in South Africa: Experiments in Democratic Persuasion* (Cambridge, Cambridge University Press, 2003)

Gilad S, 'Why the Haves Do Not Necessarily Come out Ahead in Informal Dispute Resolution' (2010) 32 *Law and Policy* 283

Gilboa E, 'Media and Conflict Resolution: A Framework for Analysis' (2009) 93 *Marquette Law Review* 87

Global IDP Database, *Profile of Internal Displacement: Cyprus* (Geneva, Norwegian Refugee Council/Global IDP Project, 2003)
Goetschel L and Hagmann T, 'Civilian Peacebuilding: Peace by Bureaucratic Means?' (2009) 9 *Conflict, Security and Development* 55
Goldie R, 'Law and the Politics of Promoting Equality and Good Relations in the Northern Ireland Peace Process' (Quest Proceedings of the Queen's University Belfast AHSS Conference, Belfast, June 2008)
Gormally B and McEvoy K, *Dealing with the Past in Northern Ireland 'from Below': An Evaluation* (Belfast, Community Foundation for Northern Ireland, 2009)
Gorvin I, 'Producing the Evidence that Human Rights Advocacy Works: First Steps towards Systematized Evaluation at Human Rights Watch' (2009) 1 *Journal of Human Rights Practice* 477
Govier T and Verwoerd W, 'Trust and the Problem of National Reconciliation' (2002) 32 *Philosophy of the Social Sciences* 178
Gready P, 'Reconceptualising Transitional Justice: Embedded and Distanced Justice' (2005) 5 *Conflict, Security and Development* 2
——. 'Reasons to Be Cautious about Evidence and Evaluation: Rights-Based Approaches to Development and the Emerging Culture of Evaluation' (2009) 1 *Journal of Human Rights Practice* 380
Greener BK, 'Revisiting the Politics of Post-conflict Peacebuilding: Reconciling the Liberal Agenda?' (2011) 23 *Global Change, Peace and Security* 357
Grewe C and Riegner M, 'Internationalized Constitutionalism in Ethnically Divided Societies: Bosnia-Herzegovina and Kosovo Compared' (2011) 15 *Max Planck Yearbook of United Nations Law* 1
Griffin J, 'Discrepancies between the Best Philosophical Account of Human Rights and the International Law of Human Rights' (2001) 101 *Proceedings of the Aristotelian Society,* New Series 1
Griffith JAG, *The Politics of the Judiciary*, 5th edn (London, Fontana Press, 1997)
Grigoriades I, *The Trials of Europeanization: Turkish Political Cutlure and the European Union* (Basingstoke, Palgrave Macmillan, 2009)
Guarnieri C and Pederzoli P, *The Power of Judges: A Comparative Study of Courts and Democracy* (Oxford, Oxford University Press, 2002)
Guelke A, *South Africa in Transition: The Misunderstood Miracle* (London, IB Tauris, 1999)
——. 'South Africa: The Long View on Political Transition' (2009) 15 *Nationalism & Ethnic Politics* 417
Gürel A, Hatay M and Yakinthou C, *Displacement in Cyprus: Consequences of Civil and Military Strife: An Overview of Events and Perceptions* (2012/5, Nicosia, PRIO Cyprus Centre, 2012)
Gürel A, Mullen F and Tzimitras H, *The Cyprus Hydrocarbons Issue: Context, Positions and Future Scenarios* (1/2013, Nicosia, PRIO Cyprus Centre, 2012)
Gürel A and Özersay K, *The Politics of Property in Cyprus: Conflicting Appeals to 'Bizonality' and 'Human Rights' by the Two Cypriot Communities* (3/2006, Nicosia, PRIO Cyprus Centre, 2006)
Hadjigeorgiou N, 'Case Note on *Kazali and Others v Cyprus*' (2013) 2 *Cyprus Human Rights Law Review* 103
——. 'Remedying Displacement in Frozen Conflicts: Lessons from the Case of Cyprus' (2016) 18 *Cambridge Yearbook of European Legal Studies* 152
——. 'Conflict Resolution in Post-violence Societies: Some Guidance for the Judiciary' (ICON·S 2017 Conference on 'Courts, Powers, Public Law', Copenhagen, July 2017)
——. 'Promoting Reconciliation and Protecting Human Rights: An Underexplored Relationship' in Chainoglou K, Collins B, Phillips M and Strawson J (eds), *Injustice, Memory and Faith in Human Rights* (London, Routledge, 2017) 106–21
——. '*Joannou v Turkey*: An Important Legal Development and a Missed Opportunity' (2018) 2 *European Human Rights Law Review* 168

——. 'A One-Sided Coin: A Critical Analysis of the Legal Accounts of the Cypriot Conflicts' in Bevernage B and Wouters N (eds), *The Palgrave Handbook of State-Sponsored History after 1945* (London, Palgrave Macmillan, 2018) 583–95

Hadjigeorgiou N and Kyriakou N, 'Entrenching Hegemony in Cyprus: The Doctrine of Necessity and the Principle of Bi-communality' in Roznai Y and Albert R (eds), *Constitutionalism under Extreme Conditions: Law, Emergency, Exception* (New York, Springer, forthcoming, 2020)

Hadjipavlou M and Kanol B, *Cumulative Impact Case Study: The Impacts of Peacebuilding Work on the Cyprus Conflict* (Nicosia, CDA Collaborative Learning Projects, 2008)

Hafner-Burton EM, *Forced to Be Good: Why Trade Agreements Boost Human Rights* (Ithaca, Cornell University Press, 2005)

Haider H, '(Re)Imagining Coexistence: Striving for Sustainable Return, Reintegration and Reconciliation in Bosnia and Herzegovina' (2009) 3 *International Journal of Transitional Justice* 91

Hall R, 'Reconciling the Past, Present and Future: The Parameters and Practices of Land Restitution in South Africa' in Walker C, Bohlin A, Hall R and Kepe T (eds), *Land, Memory, Reconstruction and Justice: Perspectives on Land Claims in South Africa* (Athens, OH, Ohio University Press, 2010) 17–40

Halpern J and Weinstein HM, 'Empathy and Rehumanization after Mass Violence' in Stover E and Weinstein HM (eds), *My Neighbor, My Enemy: Justice and Community in the Aftermath of Mass Atrocity* (Cambridge, Cambridge University Press, 2004) 303–22

Hamber B, 'Narrowing the Micro and Macro: A Psychological Perspective on Reparations in Societies in Transition' in De Greiff P (ed), *The Handbook of Reparations* (Oxford, Oxford University Press, 2006) 560–88

——. *Dealing with Painful Memories and Violent Pasts: Towards a Framework for Contextual Understanding* (Berghof Handbook Dialogue Series No 11, Berlin, Berghof Foundation, 2015)

Hamber B, Ševčenko L and Naidu E, 'Utopian Dreams or Practical Possibilities? The Challenges of Evaluating the Impact of Memorialization in Societies in Transition' (2010) 4 *International Journal of Transitional Justice* 397

Hamber B and Wilson RA, 'Symbolic Closure through Memory, Reparation and Revenge in Post-conflict Societies' (2002) 1 *Journal of Human Rights* 35

Hannum H, 'Human Rights in Conflict Resolution: The Role of the Office of High Commissioner for Human Rights in UN Peacemaking and Peacebuilding' (2006) 28 *Human Rights Quarterly* 36

Harris D, O'Boyle M, Bates E and Buckley C, *Harris, Boyle and Warbrick: Law of the European Convention on Human Rights*, 3rd edn (Oxford, Oxford University Press, 2014)

Harris P and Reilly B, *Democracy and Deep-Rooted Conflict: Options for Negotiators* (Stockholm, International Institute for Democracy and Electoral Assistance, 1998)

Harvey C, 'Contextualised Equality and the Politics of Legal Mobilisation: Affirmative Action in Northern Ireland' (2012) 21 *Social & Legal Studies* 23

——. 'Power-Sharing, Communal Contestation, and Equality: Affirmative Action, Identity and Conflict in Northern Ireland' in Terence GE and Ralph P (eds), *Affirmative Action, Ethnicity and Conflict* (London, Routdledge, 2013) 154–82

Hawkins D and Jacoby W, 'Partial Compliance: A Comparison of the European and Inter-American Courts of Human Rights' (2010) 6 *Journal of International Law and International Relations* 35

Hayner PB, *Unspeakable Truths: Transitional Justice and the Challenge of Truth Commissions* (London, Routledge, 2011)

Hearn J, *Foreign Aid, Democratisation and Civil Society in Africa: A Study of South Africa, Ghana and Uganda* (Brighton, Institute of Development Studies, 1999)

Hill F, 'How Bosnia is Helping Identify Cypriots Murdered 50 Years Ago' (*BBC News*, 1 October 2014)

Hillebrecht C, 'Implementing International Human Rights Law at Home: Domestic Politics and the European Court of Human Rights' (2012) 13 *Human Rights Review* 279

Hirschl R, *Towards Juristocracy: The Origins and Consequences of the New Constitutionalism* (Cambridge, MA, Harvard University Press, 2004)
——. 'The Question of Case Selection in Comparative Constitutional Law' (2005) 53 *American Journal of Comparative Law* 125
——. 'Editorial: From Comparative Constitutional Law to Comparative Constitutional Studies' (2013) 11 *International Journal of Constitutional Law* 1
Hirschman AO, 'Social Conflicts as Pillars of Democratic Market Society' (1994) 22 *Political Theory* 203
HMIC, *Inspection of the Police Service of Northern Ireland Historical Enquiries Team* (UK, Her Majesty's Inspectorate of Constabulary, 2013)
HMIC, *A Follow-up Inspection of the Police Service of Northern Ireland Historical Enquiries Team* (UK, Her Majesty's Inspectorate of Constabulary, 2015)
Hodzic E and Stojanović N, *New/Old Constitutional Engineering? Challenges and Implications of the European Court of Human Rights Decision in the Case of Sejdić and Finci v BiH* (Sarajevo, Analitika Centre for Social Research, 2011)
Hoffman EA, 'A Wolf in Sheep's Clothing: Discrimination against the Majority Undermines Equality, While Continuing to Benefit Few under the Guise of Black Economic Empowerment' (2008–2009) 36 *Syracuse Journal of International Law and Commerce* 87
Holbrooke R, *To End a War* (New York, The Modern Library, 1999)
Horowitz D, *Ethnic Groups in Conflict*, 2nd edn (Berkeley, University of California Press, 1985)
Horowitz DL, 'Constitutional Courts: A Primer for Decision Makers' (2006) 17 *Journal of Democracy* 125
Hughes J and Donnelly C, 'Community Relations in Northern Ireland: A Shift in Attitudes?' (2003) 29 *Journal of Ethnic and Migration Studies* 643
Ife J, 'Human Rights and Peace' in Webel C and Galtung J (eds), *The Handbook of Peace and Conflict Studies* (London, Routledge, 2007) 160–72
Ignatieff M, 'Articles of Faith' (1996) 5 *Index of Censorship* 110
——. 'Human Rights' in Hesse C and Post R (eds), *Human Rights in Political Transitions: Gettysburg to Bosnia* (New York, Zone Books, 1999) 313–24
——. *Empire Lite: Nation-Building in Bosnia, Kosovo and Afghanistan* (London, Vintage, 2003)
Independent Commission on Policing for Northern Ireland, *A New Beginning: Policing in Northern Ireland* (Belfast, Northern Ireland Office, 1999)
International Crisis Group, *The Continuing Challenge of Refugee Return in Bosnia & Herzegovina* (Balkans Report N° 137, Sarajevo, International Crisis Group, 2002)
——. *Bosnia's Stalled Police Reform: No Progress, No EU* (Europe Report N° 164, Sarajevo/Brussels, International Crisis Group, 2005)
——. *Cyprus: Bridging the Property Divide* (Europe Report N° 210, Nicosia/Instanbul/Brussels, International Crisis Group, 2009)
——. *Bosnia's Future* (Europe Report N° 232, Sarajevo/Brussels, International Crisis Group, 2012)
——. *Bosnia's Gordian Knot: Constitutional Reform* (Europe Briefing N° 68, Sarajevo/Instanbul/Brussels, International Crisis Group, 2012)
——. *Divided Cyprus: Coming to Terms on an Imperfect Reality* (Europe Report N° 229, Nicosia/Instanbul/Brussels, International Crisis Group, 2014)
Ioannou M, Filippou G and Lordos A, 'The Cyprus SCORE: Finding New Ways to Resolve a Frozen Conflict' in Morgan T (ed), *Predicting Peace: The Social Cohesion and Reconciliation Index as a Tool for Conflict Transformation*, 2nd edn (Cyprus, UNDP-Action for Cooperation and Trust, 2015) 100–40
Ioannou M, Jarraud N and Lordos A, 'The Bosnia SCORE: Measuring Peace in a Multi-ethnic Society' in Morgan T (ed), *Predicting Peace: The Social Cohesion and Reconciliation Index as a Tool for Conflict Transformation* (Cyprus, UNDP-Action for Cooperation and Trust, 2015) 141–75

Issacharoff S and Pildes RH, 'Politics as Markets: Partisan Lockups of the Democratic Process' (1998) 50 *Stanford Law Review* 643

Ito A, 'Politicisation of Minority Return in Bosnia-Herzegovina: The First Five Years Examined' (2001) 13 *International Journal of Refugee Law* 98

James D, *Gaining Ground? 'Rights' and 'Property' in South African Land Reform* (New York, Routledge-Cavendish, 2007)

James DA, 'A Formal Interpretation of the Theory of Relative Deprivation' (1959) 22 *Sociometry* 280

Jensen EG, 'The Rule of Law and Judicial Reform: The Political Economy of Diverse Institutional Patterns and Reformers' Responses' in Jensen EG and Heller TC (eds), *Beyond Common Knowledge: Empirical Approaches to the Rule of Law* (Stanford, Stanford University Press, 2003) 336–81

——. 'Justice and the Rule of Law' in Call CT (ed), *Building States to Build Peace* (Boulder, Lynne Rienner, 2008)

Jonsson U, 'A Human Rights-Based Approach to Programming' in Gready P and Ensor J (eds), *Reinventing Development? Translating Rights-Based Approaches from Theory into Practice* (London, Zed Books, 2005) 47–62

Jukic EM, 'EU Censures Bosnia for Missing Reform Deadline' (*Balkan Insight*, 4 September 2012)

——. 'EU "Losing Patience with Bosnia", Official Says' (*Balkan Insight*, 4 February 2013)

Kalb J, 'The Judicial Role in New Democracies: A Strategic Account of Comparative Citation' (2013) 38 *Yale Journal of International Law* 423

Kaldor M, *Global Civil Society* (Cambridge, Polity Press, 2003)

Kappler S, 'Liberal Peacebuilding's Presentation of "the Local": The Case of Bosnia and Herzegovina' in Richmond O and Mitchell A (eds), *Hybrid Forms of Peace: From Everyday Agency to Post-liberalism* (Basingstoke, Palgrave Macmillan, 2016) 260–76

Katselli-Proukaki E, 'The Right of Displaced Persons to Property and to Return Home after Demopoulos' (2014) 14 *Human Rights Law Review* 701

Kaufmann CD, 'When All Else Fails: Ethnic Population Transfers and Partitions in the Twentieth Century' (1998) 23 *International Security* 120

Kavanagh A, 'The Role of a Bill of Rights in Reconstructing Northern Ireland' (2004) 26 *Human Rights Quartrerly* 956

Keenan A, 'Building a Democratic Middle Ground: Professional Civil Society and the Politics of Human Rights in Sri Lanka's Peace Process' in Mertus J and Helsing JW (eds), *Human Rights and Conflict: Exploring the Links between Rights, Law and Peacebuilding* (Washington DC, United States Institute of Peace Press, 2006) 459–508

Kelman H, *International Behaviour: A Social Psychological Analysis* (New York, Holt, Rinehart & Winston, 1965)

Kennedy D, 'The International Human Rights Movement: Part of the Problem?' (2002) 15 *Harvard Human Rights Journal* 101

Ker-Lindsay J, *Resolving Cyprus: New Approaches to Conflict Resolution* (London, IB Tauris, 2014)

Kirchheimer O, *Political Justice: The Use of Legal Procedure for Political Ends* (Westport, Greenwood Press, 1961)

Klarin M, 'The Impact of the ICTY Trials on Public Opinion in the Former Yugoslavia' (2009) 7 *Journal of International Criminal Justice* 89

Knaus G and Martin F, 'Lessons from Bosnia and Herzegovina: Travails of the European Raj' (2003) 14 *Journal of Democracy* 64

Kok A, 'The Promotion of Equality and Prevention of Unfair Discrimination Act 4 of 2000: Proposals for Legislative Reform' (2008) 24 *South African Journal on Human Rights* 445

Koskenniemi M, 'Legitimacy, Rights and Ideology: Notes towards a Critique of the New Moral Internationalism' (2003) 7 *Associations* 349

Kostić R, 'Shadow Peacebuilders and Diplomatic Counterinsurgencies: Informal Networks, Knowledge Production and the Art of Policy-Shaping' (2017) 11 *Journal of Intervention and Statebuilding* 120–139

Kostiner I, 'Evaluating Legality: Toward a Cultural Approach to the Study of Law and Social Change' (2003) 37 *Law and Society Review* 323

Kovras I, *Grassroots Activism and the Evolution of Transitional Justice: The Families of the Disappeared* (Cambridge, Cambridge University Press, 2017)

Kovras I and Loizides N, 'Delaying Truth Recovery for Missing Persons' (2010) 17 *Nations and Nationalism* 520

Krause K, 'The Key to a Powerful Agenda, if Properly Delimited' (2004) 35 *Security Dialogue* 367

Krause K and Jütersonke O, 'Peace, Security and Development in Post-conflict Environments' (2005) 36 *Security Dialogue* 447

Kremenyuk J, Bercovitch V and Zartman W, 'Introduction: The Nature of Conflict and Conflict Resolution' in Kremenyuk J, Bercovitch V and Zartman W (eds), *The SAGE Handbook of Conflict Resolution* (London, SAGE, 2008) 1–12

Kriesbert L, *Social Conflict* (Englewood Cliffs, Prentice Hall, 1982)

Kyriakou N, 'Enforced Disappearances in Cyprus: Problems and Prospects of the Case Law of the European Court of Human Rights' (2011) 2 *European Human Rights Law Review* 190

Lahiff E, *State, Market or Worst of Both? Experimenting with Market-Based Land Reform in South Africa* (Occasional Paper No 30, Bellville, Programme for Land and Agrarian Studies, University of the Western Cape, 2007)

Landman T, *Issues & Methods in Comparative Politics: An Introduction* (New York, Routledge, 2000)

Laplante LJ and Phenicie K, 'Media, Trials and Truth Commissions: "Mediating" Reconciliation in Peru's Transitional Justice Process' (2010) 4 *International Journal of Transitional Justice* 207

Lawler P, *A Question of Values: Johan Galtung's Peace Research* (London, Lynne Rienner, 1995)

Leach P and Donald A, *Parliaments and the European Court of Human Rights* (Oxford, Oxford University Press, 2016)

Lederach JP, 'Beyond Violence: Building Sustainable Peace' in Williamson A (ed), *Beyond Violence: The Role of Voluntary and Community Action in Building a Sustainable Peace in Northern Ireland* (Belfast, Community Relations Council, 1995) 1–22

——. *Preparing for Peace: Conflict Transformation across Cultures* (Syracuse, Syracuse University Press, 1995)

——. *Building Peace: Sustainable Reconciliation in Divided Societies* (Washington DC, United States Institute of Peace Press, 1997)

Lederach JP, 'Conflict Transformation: Beyond Intractability' in Burgess G and Burgess H (eds), *Conflict Information Consortium* (Boulder, University of Colorado, 2003)

——. *The Little Book of Conflict Transformation* (New York, Good Books, 2003)

Lerner H, *Making Constitutions in Deeply Divided Societies* (Cambridge, Cambridge University Press, 2011)

Liden K, 'Building Peace between Global and Local Politics: The Cosmopolitical Ethics of Liberal Peacebuilding' (2009) 16 *International Peacekeeping* 616

Lijphart A, *Democracy in Plural Societies: A Comparative Exploration* (New Haven, Yale University Press, 1977)

Lind J, *Sorry States: Apologies in International Relations* (Ithaca, Cornell University Press, 2010)

Little D, 'Peace, Justice and Religion' in Allan P and Keller A (eds), *What is Just Peace?* (Oxford, Oxford University Press, 2006) 149–77

Livingstone S, 'The House of Lords and the Northern Ireland Conflict' (1994) 57 *Modern Law Review* 333

Lohrenscheit C, 'International Approaches in Human Rights Education' (2002) 48 *International Review of Education* 173

Loizides N, *Designing Peace: Cyprus and Institutional Innovations in Divided Societies* (Philadelphia, University of Pennsylvania Press, 2015)

Loizidou T, *Titina Loizidou v Turkey* (Series of Lectures 'The People behind Judicial Decisions', Nicosia, University of Cyprus, 14 October 2013)

Lordos A and Kaymak E, *Public Opinion and the Property Issue: Quantitative Findings* (Cyprus 2015: Research and Dialogue for a Sustainable Future, Cyprus, Interpeace, 2010)
Loucaides LG, 'Is the European Court of Human Rights Still a Principled Court of Human Rights after the Demopoulos Case?' (2011) 24 *Leiden Journal of International Law* 435
Lund M, *What Kind of Peace is Being Built? Taking Stock of Post-conflict Peacebuilding and Charting Future Directions* (Working Paper No 7, Ottawa, The Peacebuilding and Reconstruction Program Initiative, International Development Research Centre, 2003)
Lundy P, 'Can the Past Be Policed? Lessons from the Historical Enquiries Team Northern Ireland' (2009) 11 *Journal of Law and Social Challenges* 109
——. 'Exploring Home-Grown Transitional Justice and its Dilemmas: A Case Study of the Historical Enquiries Team, Northern Ireland' (2009) 3 *International Journal of Transitional Justice* 321
Lundy P and McGovern M, 'The Role of Community in Participatory Transitional Justice' in McEvoy K and McGregor L (eds), *Transitional Justice from Below: Grassroots Activism and the Struggle for Change* (Oxford, Hart Publishing, 2008) 99–120
Lundy P and Rolston B, 'Redress for Past Harms? Official Apologies in Northern Ireland' (2016) 20 *International Journal of Human Rights* 104
Lynch J and Galtung J, *Reporting Conflict: New Directions in Peace Research Journalism* (Brisbane, University of Queensland Press, 2010)
Mac Ginty R, 'Indigenous Peace-Making versus the Liberal Peace' (2008) 43 *Cooperation and Conflict* 139
——. 'Everyday Peace: Bottom-up and Local Agency in Conflict Affected Societies' (2014) 45 *Security Dialogue* 548
MacCormick N, 'Children's Rights: A Test-Case for Theories of Right' in MacCormick N (ed), *Legal Right and Social Democracy: Essays in Legal and Political Philosophy* (Oxford, Oxford University Press, 1984) 154–68
Mack R and Snyder R, 'The Analysis of Social Conflict: Toward an Overview and Synthesis' (1957) 1 *Journal of Conflict Resolution* 212
Magean P and O'Brien M, 'From the Margins to the Mainstream: Human Rights and the Good Friday Agreement' (1998–99) 22 *Fordham International Law Journal* 1499
Magill C, Smith A and Hamber B, *The Role of Education in Reconciliation: The Perspectives of Children and Young People in Bosnia and Herzegovina and Northern Ireland* (Ulster, Special EU Programmes Body, University of Ulster, 2009)
Maley W, 'Introduction: Peace Operations and Their Evaluation' in Druckman D and Diehl PF (eds), *Peace Operation Success: A Comparative Analysis* (Leiden, Martinus Nijhoff Publishers, 2013) 1–9
Mamdani M, 'Amnesty or Impunity? A Preliminary Critique of the Report of the Truth and Reconciliation Commission of South Africa (TRC)' (2002) 32 *Diacritics* 32
Mani R, *Beyond Retribution: Seeking Justice in the Shadows of War* (Cambridge, Polity Press, 2002)
Marchetti R and Tocci N, 'Conflict Society and Human Rights: An Analytical Framework' in Marchetti R and Tocci N (eds), *Civil Society, Conflicts and the Politicization of Human Rights* (Tokyo, United Nations University Press, 2011) 47–72
——. (eds), *Civil Society, Conflicts and the Politicization of Human Rights* (Tokyo, United Nations University Press, 2011)
Marcon G and Andreis S, 'Human Rights, Civil Society and Conflict in Bosnia-Herzegovina' in Marchetti R and Tocci N (eds), *Civil Society, Conflicts and the Politicization of Human Rights* (Tokyo, United Nations University Press, 2011) 123–38
Marks S, 'Apologising for Torture' (2004) 73 *Nordic Journal of International Law* 365
Marshall D and Inglis S, 'Human Rights in Transition: The Disempowerment of Human Rights-Based Justice in the United Nations Mission in Kosovo' (2003) 16 *Harvard Human Rights Journal* 95
McAuliffe P, 'Transitional Justice and the Rule of Law: The Perfect Couple or Awkward Bedfellows?' (2010) 2 *Hague Journal on the Rule of Law* 110

——. *Transformative Transitional Justice and the Malleability of Post-conflict States* (Cheltenham, Edward Elgar, 2017)

McCann M, 'How Does Law Matter for Social Movements' in Garth BG and Austin S (eds), *How Does Law Matter? Fundamental Issues in Law and Society Research* (Evanston, Northwestern University Press, 1998) 76–108

McCrudden C, 'Mainstreaming Equality in the Governance of Northern Ireland' (1998–99) 22 *Fordham International Law Journal* 1696

——. 'Common Law of Human Rights? Transitional Judicial Conversations on Constitutional Rights' (2000) 20 *Oxford Journal of Legal Studies* 499

——. 'Consociationalism, Equality and Minorities in the Northern Ireland Bill of Rights Debate: The Role of the OSCE High Commissioner on National Minorities' in Morison J, McEvoy K and Anthony G (eds), *Judges, Transition and Human Rights* (Oxford, Oxford University Press, 2007) 315–356

McCrudden C, Ford R and Heath A, 'Legal Regulation of Affirmative Action in Northern Ireland' (2004) 24 *Oxford Journal of Legal Studies* 363

McCrudden C and O'Leary B, 'Courts and Consociations, or How Human Rights Courts May De-Stabilise Power-Sharing Settlements' (2013) 24 *European Journal of International Law* 477

——., *Courts and Consociations: Human Rights versus Power-Sharing* (Oxford, Oxford University Press, 2013)

McEvoy K, 'Beyond Legalism: Towards a Thicker Understanding of Transitional Justice' (2007) 34 *Journal of Law and Society* 411

——. 'Letting Go of Legalism: Developing a "Thicker" Version of Transitional Justice' in McEvoy K and McGregor L (eds), *Transitional Justice from Below* (Oxford, Hart Publishing, 2008) 15–46

McEvoy K and Mallinder L, 'Amnesties in Transition: Punishment, Restoration and the Governance of Mercy' (2012) 39 *Journal of Law and Society* 410

McEvoy K and Schwartz A, 'Judges, Conflict and the Past' (2015) 42 *Journal of Law and Society* 528

McEvoy L and Lundy L, '"In the Small Places": Education and Human Rights Culture in Conflict-Affected Societies' in Morison J, McEvoy K and Anthony G (eds), *Judges, Transition, and Human Rights* (Oxford, Oxford University Press, 2007) 595–614

McEvoy L, McEvoy K and McConnachie K, 'Reconciliation as a Dirty Word: Conflict, Community Relations and Education in Northern Ireland' (2006) 60 *Journal of International Affairs* 81

McGarry J and O'Leary B, 'Consociation and its Critics: Northern Ireland after the Belfast Agreement' in Choudhry S (ed), *Constitutional Design for Divided Societies: Integration or Accommodation?* (Oxford, Oxford University Press, 2008) 369–408

McGregor L, 'International Law as a "Tiered Process": Transitional Justice at the Local, National and International Level' in McEvoy K and McGregor L (eds), *Transitional Justice from Below: Grassroots Activism and the Struggle for Change* (Oxford, Hart Publishing, 2008) 47–74

Mendeloff D, 'Truth-Seeking, Truth-Telling, and Postconflict Peacebuilding: Curb the Enthusiasm?' (2004) 6 *International Studies Review* 355

Mertus J and Helsing JW (eds), *Human Rights and Conflict: Exploring the Links between Rights, Law and Peacebuilding* (Washington DC, United States Institute of Peace Press, 2006)

Miara L and Prais V, 'The Role of Civil Society in the Execution of Judgments of the European Court of Human Rights' (2012) 5 *European Human Rights Law Review* 528

Michael MS, *Resolving the Cyprus Conflict: Negotiating History* (New York, Palgrave Macmillan, 2009)

Milanovic M, 'Establishing the Facts about Mass Atrocities: Accounting for the Failure of the ICTY to Persuade Target Audiences' (2016) 47 *Georgetown Journal of International Law* 1321

——. 'The Impact of the ICTY on the Former Yugoslavia: An Anticipatory Post-mortem' (2016) 110 *American Journal of International Law* 233

Miller D, 'Nationality in Divided Societies' in Gagnon AG and Tully J (eds), *Multinational Democracies* (Cambridge, Cambridge University Press, 2001) 299–318

Ministry for Human Rights and Refugees, *Communication from Bosnia and Herzegovina Concerning the Case of Sejdić and Finci v Bosnia and Herzegovina (Application No. 27996/06) for the 1288th Meeting of the Committee of Ministers of the Council of Europe* (DH-DD(2017)380, Sarajevo, Bosnia and Herzegovina Ministry of Human Rights and Refugees, 2017)

Minow M, 'Breaking the Cycles of Hatred' in Minow M (ed), *Breaking the Cycles of Hatred: Memory, Law and Repair* (Princeton, Princeton University Press, 2002) 14–76

Moore M, 'Globalization, Cosmopolitanism and Minority Nationalism' in Keating M and McGarry J (eds), *Minority Nationalism and the Changing International Order* (Oxford, Oxford University Press, 2001) 44–60

Moorhead R, Sefton M and Scanlan L, *Just Satisfaction? What Drives Public and Participant Satisfaction with Courts and Tribunals* (Ministry of Justice Research Series 5/08, UK, Ministry of Justice, 2008)

Morison J and Lynch M, 'Litigating the Agreement: Towards a New Judicial Constitutionalism for the UK from Northern Ireland' in Morison J, McEvoy K and Anthony G (eds), *Judges, Transition and Human Rights* (Oxford, Oxford University Press, 2007) 105–45

Muehlmann T, 'International Policing in Bosnia and Herzegovina: The Issue of Behavioural Reforms Lagging Behind Structural Reforms, Including the Issue of Reengaging the Political Elite in a New System' (2007) 16 *European Security* 357

Mujezinovic Larsen K, 'United Nations Peace Operations and International Law: What Kind of Law Promotes What Kind of Peace?' in Baillet CM and Mujezinovic Larsen K (eds), *Promoting Peace through International Law* (Oxford, Oxford University Press, 2015) 299–320

Mutua MW, 'The Transformation of Africa: A Critique of Rights in Transitional Justice' in Buchanan R and Zumbansen P (eds), *Law in Transition: Human Rights, Development and Transitional Justice* (Oxford, Hart Publishing, 2016) 91–102

Nadler A, 'Reconciliation: Instrumental and Socioemotional Aspects' in Christie DJ (ed), *The Encyclopedia of Peace Psychology* (New York, Wiley-Blackwell, 2012) 536–40

Nagy R, 'Reconciliation in Post-Commission South Africa: Thick and Thin Accounts of Solidarity' (2002) 35 *Canadian Journal of Political Science* 323

Naidu E, 'Symbolic Reparations and Reconciliation: Lessons from South Africa' (2012–2013) 19 *Buffalo Human Rights Law Review* 251

Nherere P and Kumi A-K, 'Human Rights and Conflict Resolution' in Nherere P, Lindgren G, Wallensteen P and Nordquist KA (eds), *Issues in Third World Conflict Resolution* (Uppsala, Uppsala University, 1990) 3–42

Nixon R, *Real Peace* (London, Sidgwick & Jackson, 1983)

Northern Ireland Statistics and Research Agency, *Census 2011: Key Statistics for Northern Ireland* (Belfast, Northern Ireland Statistics and Research Agency, 2012)

——. *Public Perceptions of the Police, PCSPs and the Northern Ireland Policing Board* (Belfast, Northern Ireland Policing Board, 2016)

Ntsebeza L and Hall R, *The Land Question in South Africa: The Challenge of Transformation and Redistribution* (Cape Town, HSRC Press, 2007)

Nystuen G, *Achieving Peace or Protecting Human Rights? Conflicts between Norms Regarding Ethnic Discrimination in the Dayton Peace Agreement* (Leiden, Martinus Nijhoff Publishers, 2005)

Office of the High Representative, *Peace Implementation Council Bonn Conclusions: Bosnia and Herzegovina 1998: Self-Sustaining Structures* (Sarajevo, Office of the High Representative, 10 December 1997)

——. *PLIP – Non-negotiable Principles in the Context of the Property Law Implementation* (Sarajevo, Office of the High Representative, 7 March 2000)

——. *Statistics: Implementation of the Property Laws in Bosnia and Herzegovina* (Sarajevo, Office of the High Representative, 31 May 2000)

——. *PLIP Inter-Agency Framework Document* (Sarajevo, Office of the High Representative, 15 October 2000)

——. PLIP Press Release, 'Property Law Implementation is Just One Element of Annex VII' (Sarajevo, Office of the High Representative, 27 February 2003)

——. *Order on the Implementation of the Decision of the Constitutional Court of Bosnia and Herzegovina in the Appeal of Milorad Bilbija et al, No AP-953/05* (Doc 37/07, Sarajevo, Office of the High Representative, 23 March 2007)

Open Society Justice Initiative, *From Rights to Remedies: Structures and Strategies for Implementing International Human Rights Decisions* (New York, Open Society Foundation, 2013)

Orentlicher DF, 'Setting Accounts: The Duty to Prosecute Human Rights Violations of a Prior Regime' (1991) 100 *Yale Law Journal* 2537

Orjuela C, 'Building Peace in Sri Lanka: A Role for Civil Society?' (2003) 40 *Journal of Peace Research* 195

OSCE, *Security Sector Governance and Reform: Guidelines for OSCE Staff* (Vienna, Organization for Security and Cooperation in Europe, 2016)

OSCE Mission to Bosnia and Herzegovina, *Special Report: Musical Chairs: Property Problems in Bosnia and Herzegovina* (Sarajevo, Organisation for Security and Cooperation in Europe, 1996)

Osiel MJ, 'Ever Again: Legal Remembrance of Administrative Massacre' (1995–96) 144 *University of Pennsylvania Law Review* 463

——. *Mass Atrocity, Collective Memory, and the Law* (New York, Routledge, 2017)

Packer J, 'On the Content of Minority Rights' in Raikka J (ed), *Do We Need Minority Rights? Conceptual Issues* (The Hague, Martinus Nijhoff Publishers, 1996) 223–73

Paffenholz T, 'Civil Society' in Mac Ginty R (ed), *Routledge Handbook of Peacebuilding* (London, Routledge, 2014) 347–59

Paffenholz T and Spurk C, *Civil Society, Civic Engagement and Peacebuilding* (Social Development Papers, Conflict Prevention and Reconstruction Paper No 36, Washington DC, World Bank, 2006)

——. 'A Comprehensive Analytical Framework' in Paffenholz T (ed), *Civil Society and Peacebuilding: A Critical Assessment* (Boulder, Lynne Rienner, 2010) 65–76

Panel on United Nations Peace Operations, *Report of the Panel on United Nations Peace Operations* (A/55/305–S/2000/809, New York, United Nations, 2000)

Papadakis Y, 'Nation, Narrative and Commemoration: Political Ritual in Divided Cyprus' (2003) 13 *History and Anthropology* 253

——. *History Education in Divided Cyprus: A Comparison of Greek Cypriot and Turkish Cypriot Schoolbooks on the 'History of Cyprus'* (2/2008, Nicosia, PRIO Cyprus Centre, 2008)

Paraskeva C and Meleagrou E, 'Homes from the Past: An Expiration Date for the Right to Respect for Home under Article 8 of the European Convention on Human Rights' (2012–13) VII *Annuaire International des Droits de l'homme* 845

Paris R, 'Wilson's Ghost: The Faulty Assumptions of Postconflict Peacebuilding' in Crocker C, Hampson FO and Aall P (eds), *Turbulent Peace: Conflict Resolution versus Democratic Governance: Divergent Paths to Peace?* (Washington DC, United States Institute of Peace Press, 2001) 765–784

——. *At War's End: Building Peace after Civil Conflict* (Cambridge, Cambridge University Press, 2004)

——. 'Understanding the "Coordination Problem" in Postwar Statebuilding' in Paris R and Sisk TD (eds), *The Dilemmas of Statebuilding: Confronting the Contradictions of Postwar Peace Operations* (London, Routledge, 2009) 53–78

Parlevliet M, *Bridging the Divide: Exploring the Relationship between Human Rights and Conflict Management* (Track Two Occasional Paper, Cape Town, Centre for Conflict Resolution, March 2002)

——. *Rethinking Conflict Transformation from a Human Rights Perspective* (Berghof Handbook Dialogue Series No 9, Berlin, Berghof Research Centre for Constructive Conflict Management, 2009)

Parliamentary Assembly, *Implementation of Decisions of the European Court of Human Rights by Turkey* (Resolution 1381, Strasbourg, Council of Europe, 22 June 2004)

——. *The Functioning of Democratic Institutions in Bosnia and Herzegovina* (Doc 12112, Strasbourg, Council of Europe, 11 January 2010)

Peace Implementation Council, *PIC Sintra Declaration: Political Declaration from Ministerial Meeting of the Steering Board of the Peace Implementation Council* (Sarajevo, Office of the High Representative, 30 May 1997)

Peck C, *Sustainable Peace: The Role of the UN and Regional Organizations in Preventing Conflict* (Lanham, Rowman & Littlefield, 1998)

Perry V, 'Constitutional Reform Processes in Bosnia and Herzegovina: Top-down Failure, Bottom-up Potential, Continued Stalemate' in Keil S and Perry V (eds), *State Building Democratization in Bosnia and Herzegovina* (Surrey, Ashgate, 2015) 15–40

Philpott C, 'Though the Dog is Dead, the Pig Must Be Killed: Finishing with Property Restitution to Bosnia Herzegovina's IDPs and Refugees' (2005) 18 *Journal of Refugee Studies* 1

——. 'From the Right to Return to the Return of Rights: Completing Post-war Property Restitution in Bosnia Herzegovina' (2006) 18 *International Journal of Refugee Law* 30

Philpott D, 'An Ethic of Political Reconciliation' (2009) 23 *Ethics and International Affairs* 389

Philpott D and Powers GF (eds), *Strategies of Peace: Transforming Conflict in a Violent World* (Oxford, Oxford University Press, 2010)

Pia E and Diez T, 'Human Rights Discourses and Conflict: Moving Towards Desecuritization' in Marchetti R and Tocci N (eds), *Civil Society, Conflicts and the Politicization of Human Rights* (Tokyo, United Nations University Press, 2011) 204–19

Pikis GM, *Constitutionalism – Human Rights – Separation of Powers: The Cyprus Precedent* (Leiden, Martinus Nijhoff Publishers, 2006)

Pildes RH, 'Ethnic Identity and Democratic Institutions: A Dynamic Perspective' in Choudhry S (ed), *Constitutional Design for Divided Societies: Integration or Accommodation?* (Oxford, Oxford University Press, 2008) 173–203

Popić L and Panjeta B, *Compensation, Transitional Justice and Conditional Credit in Bosnia and Herzegovina: Attempts to Reform Government Payments to Victims and Veterans of the 1992–1995 War* (Amsterdam, Nuhanovic Foundation, 2010)

Posner E and Vermeule A, 'Transitional Justice as Ordinary Justice' (2004) 117 *Harvard Law Review* 761

Powell EJ and Staton JK, 'Domestic Judicial Institutions and Human Rights Treaty Violation' (2009) 53 *International Studies Quarterly* 149

Presidency of Immovable Property Commission, *Monthly Bulletin* (Nicosia, Immovable Property Commission, April 2019)

Pugh M, 'The Social-Civil Dimension' in Pugh M (ed), *Regeneration of War-Torn Societies* (Basingstoke, Macmillan, 2000) 112–33

——. 'The Problem-Solving and Critical Paradigms' in Mac Ginty R (ed), *Routledge Handbook of Peacebuilding* (New York, Routledge, 2013) 11–24

Putnam TL, 'Human Rights and Sustainable Peace' in Stedman S, Rothschild D and Cousens E (eds), *Ending Civil Wars: The Implementation of Peace Agreements* (Boulder, Lynne Rienner, 2002) 237–72

Rabikin J, 'Racial Progress and Constitutional Roadblocks' (1992) 34 *William and Mary Law Review* 75

Rainey B, Wicks E and Ovey C, *Jacobs, White and Ovey: The European Convention on Human Rights*, 6th edn (Oxford, Oxford University Press, 2014)

Ramcharan B, 'Human Rights and Human Security' (2004) 3 *Disarmament Forum* 39

Ramet SP, *Balkan Babel: The Disintegration of Yugoslavia from the Death of Tito to the Fall of Milosević*, 4th edn (Boulder, Westview Press, 2002)

Ramsbotham O, Woodhouse T and Miall H, *Contemporary Conflict Resolution: The Prevention, Management and Transformation of Deadly Conflicts* (Cambridge, Polity Press, 2016)

Raz J, 'Legal Rights' (1984) 4 *Oxford Journal of Legal Studies* 1
——. *The Morality of Freedom* (Oxford, Oxford University Press, 1986)
——. 'Rights and Individual Well-Being' (1992) 5 *Ratio Juris* 127
Reardon BA, 'Human Rights as Education for Peace' in Andreopoulos GJ and Claude RP (eds), *Human Rights Education for the Twenty-First Century* (Philadelphia, University of Pennsylvania Press, 1997) 21–34
Reed L and Tehranian M, 'Evolving Security Regimes' in Tehranian M (ed), *Worlds Apart: Human Security and Global Governance* (London, IB Tauris, 1999) 23–47
Reif LC, 'Building Democratic Institutions: The Role of National Human Rights Institutions in Good Governance and Human Rights Protection' (2000) 13 *Harvard Human Rights Journal* 1
Reilly B, *Democracy in Divided Societies: Electoral Engineering for Conflict Management* (Cambridge, Cambridge University Press, 2001)
——. 'Electoral Systems for Divided Societies' (2002) 13 *Journal of Democracy* 156
Requa M, 'Keeping up with Strasbourg: Article 2 Obligations and Northern Ireland's Pending Inquests' [2012] *Public Law* 610
Requa M and Anthony G, 'Coroners, Controversial Deaths and Northern Ireland's Past Conflict' [2008] *Public Law* 443
Reychler L, *Democratic Peace-Building and Conflict Prevention: The Devil is in the Transition* (Leuven, Leuven University Press, 1999)
——. 'From Conflict to Sustainable Peacebuilding: Concepts and Analytical Tools' in Reychler L and Paffenholz T (eds), *Peace-Building: A Field Guide* (Boulder, Lynne Rienner, 2001) 3–15
——. 'Peace Architecture: The Prevention of Violence' in Eagly AH, Reuben BM and Hamilton LV (eds), *The Social Psychology of Group Identity and Social Conflict* (Washington DC, American Psychological Association, 2004) 133–46
Richmond O, 'UN Peacebuilding Operations and the Dilemma of the Peacebuilding Consensus' (2004) 11 *International Peacekeeping* 83
——. *The Transformation of Peace* (Basingstoke, Palgrave Macmillan, 2006)
——. 'The UN and Liberal Peacebuilding: Consensus and Challenges' in Darby J and Mac Ginty R (eds), *Contemporary Peacemaking: Conflict, Peace Processes and Post-war Reconstruction*, 2nd edn (New York, Palgrave Macmillan, 2008) 257–70
——. 'A Post-liberal Peace: Eirinism and the Everyday' (2009) 35 *Review of International Studies* 557
Richmond O and Mac Ginty R, 'Where Now for the Critique of the Liberal Peace?' (2015) 50 *Cooperation and Conflict* 171
Richmond O and Mitchell A, 'Introduction – Towards a Post-liberal Peace: Exploring Hybridity via Everyday Forms of Resistance, Agency and Autonomy' in Richmond O and Mitchell A (eds), *Hybrid Forms of Peace: From Everyday Agency to Post-liberalism* (Basingstoke, Palgrave Macmillan, 2016) 1–28
——. (eds), *Hybrid Forms of Peace: From Everyday Agency to Post-liberalism* (Basingstoke, Palgrave Macmillan, 2016)
Risse T and Sikkink K, 'The Socialisation of International Human Rights Norms and Domestic Practices: Introduction' in Risse T, Sikkink K and Ropp S (eds), *The Power of Human Rights: International Norms and Domestic Change* (Cambridge, Cambridge University Press, 1999) 1–38
Rittich K, 'Governing by Measuring: The Millennium Development Goals in Global Governance' in Buchanan R and Zumbansen P (eds), *Law in Transition: Human Rights, Development and Transitional Justice* (Oxford, Hart Publishing, 2016) 165–85
Roach-Anleu SL, *Law and Social Change*, 2nd edn (Los Angeles, SAGE, 2010)
Robertson D, *The Judge as Political Theorist: Contemporary Constitutional Review* (Princeton, Princeton University Press, 2010)
Robertson R, 'Glocalization: Time-Space and Homogeneity-Heterogeneity' in Featherstone M, Lash S and Robertson R (eds), *Global Modernitites* (London, SAGE, 1995) 25–44

Robinson D, 'The Identity Crisis of International Criminal Law' (2008) 21 *Leiden Journal of International Law* 952

Roht-Arriaza N, 'Reparations and Development' in Buchanan R and Zumbansen P (eds), *Law in Transition: Human Rights, Development and Transitional Justice* (Oxford, Hart Publishing, 2016) 189–202

Rolston B, *Satisfaction with the Historical Enquiries Team: Relatives' Views* (Research Paper 14-06, Ulster, Transitional Justice Institute, 2014)

Rosenberg GN, 'The Irrelevant Court: The Supreme Court's Inability to Influence Popular Beliefs about Equality (or Anything Else)' in Devins N and Douglas D (eds), *Redefining Equality* (Oxford, Oxford University Press, 1998) 172–90

——. *The Hollow Hope: Can Courts Bring about Social Change?*, 2nd edn (Chicago, University of Chicago Press, 2008)

Rosenberg SP, 'Equality after Genocide: Jurisprudence of the Legal Institutions Established in Dayton's Bosnia' in Haynes DF (ed), *Deconstructing the Reconstruction: Human Rights and the Rule of Law in Postwar Bosnia and Herzegovina* (Farnham, Ashgate, 2008) 115–48

——. 'Promoting Equality after Genocide' (2008) 16 *Tulane Journal of International and Comparative Law* 329

Rosenberg T, *The Haunted Land: Facing Europe's Ghosts after Communism* (London, Vintage, 1996)

Rotberg R, 'Truth Commissions and the Provision of Truth, Justice and Reconciliation' in Rotberg R and Thompson D (eds), *Truth v Justice: The Morality of Truth Commissions* (Princeton, Princeton University Press, 2000) 3–21

Rouhana NN, 'Identity and Power in the Reconciliation of National Conflict' in Eagly AH, Baron RM and Hamilton LV (eds), *The Social Psychology of Group Identity and Social Conflict* (Washington DC, American Psychological Association, 2004) 173–87

Rousseau N and Fullard M, 'Accounting and Reconciling in the Balance Sheet of the South African Truth and Reconciliation Commission' (2009) 4 *Journal of Multicultural Discourses* 123

Roux T, 'Land Restitution and Reconciliation in South Africa' in du Bois F and du Bois-Pedain A (eds), *Justice and Reconciliation in Post-apartheid South Africa* (Cambridge, Cambridge University Press, 2008) 144–71

——. *The Politics of Principle: The First South African Constitutional Court 1995–2005* (Cambridge, Cambridge University Press, 2013)

Said AA and Lerche CO, 'Peace as a Human Right: Toward an Integrated Understanding' in Mertus J and Helsing JW (eds), *Human Rights and Conflict: Exploring the Links between Rights, Law and Peacebuilding* (Washington DC, United States Institute of Peace Press, 2006) 129–150

Sapiano JM, 'Courting Peace: Judicial Review and Peace Jurisprudence' (2017) 6 *Global Constitutionalism* 131

——. 'Courting Peace: Peace Constitutions and Jurisprudence' (PhD thesis, University of St Andrews, 2017)

Sarkin J, Nettelfield L, Matthews M and Kosalka R, *Bosnia i Herzegovina Missing Persons from the Armed Conflicts of the 1990s: A Stocktaking* (Sarajevo, International Commission on Missing Persons, 2014)

Saunders R, 'Lost in Translation: Expressions of Human Suffering, the Language of Human Rights, and the South African Truth and Reconciliation Commission' (2008) 9 *International Journal on Human Rights* 51

Savelsberg JJ and King RD, 'Law and Collective Memory' (2007) 3 *Annual Review of Law and Social Science* 189

Scheingold SA, *The Politics of Rights: Lawyers, Public Policy, and Political Change*, 2nd edn (Ann Arbor, University of Michigan Press, 2004)

Schneckener U, 'Making Power-Sharing Work: Lessons from Successes and Failures in Ethnic Conflict Regulation' (2002) 39 *Journal of Peace Research* 203

Schuld M, 'The Prevalence of Violence in Post-conflict Societies: A Case Study of KwaZulu-Natal, South Africa' (2013) 8 *Journal of Peacebuilding and Development* 60

Schwartz A, 'International Judges on Constitutional Courts: Cautionary Evidence from Post-conflict Bosnia' (2017) *Law & Social Inquiry* 1

Secretary of State for Northern Ireland, *White Paper – Partnership for Equality: The Government's Proposals for Future Legislation and Policies on Employment Equality in Northern Ireland* (Cm 3890, London, Secretary of State for Northern Ireland, 1998)

Selby J, 'The Political Economy of Peace Processes' in Pugh M, Cooper N and Turner M (eds), *Whose Peace? Critical Perspectives on the Political Economy of Peacebuilding* (Basingstoke, Palgrave Macmillan, 2011) 11–29

Shea DC, *The South African Truth Commission: The Politics of Reconciliation* (Washington DC, Institute of Peace Press, 2000)

Shelton D, *Remedies in International Human Rights Law*, 2nd edn (Oxford, Oxford University Press, 2006)

Sikkink K, *The Justice Cascade: How Human Rights Prosecutions Are Changing World Politics* (New York, Norton & Company, 2011)

Simmons B, *Mobilizing for Human Rights: International Law in Domestic Politics* (Cambridge, Cambridge University Press, 2009)

Simpson G, Hodžić E and Bickford L, *Looking Back, Looking Forward: Promoting Dialogue through Truth-Seeking in Bosnia and Herzegovina* (Sarajevo, United Nations Development Programme, 2012)

Sisk TD, 'Pathways of the Political: Electoral Processes after Civil War' in Paris R and Sisk TD (eds), *The Dilemmas of Statebuilding: Confronting the Contradictions of Postwar Peace Operations* (London, Routledge, 2009) 196–224

Skarstad K, 'Human Rights Violations and Conflict Risk: A Theoretical and Empirical Assessment' in Baillet CM and Mujezinovic Larsen K (eds), *Promoting Peace through International Law* (Oxford, Oxford University Press, 2015) 133–147

Skorupski J, 'Human Rights' in Beeson S and Tasioulas J (eds), *The Philosophy of International Law* (Oxford, Oxford University Press, 2010) 357–75

Skoutaris N, 'Buidling Transitional Justice Mechanisms without a Peace Settlement: A Critical Appraisal of Recent Case Law of the Strasbourg Court on the Cyprus Issue' (2010) 35 *European Law Review* 720

Sluzki CE, 'The Process toward Reconciliation' in Chayes A and Minow M (eds), *Imagine Coexistence: Restoring Humanity after Violent Conflict* (San Francisco, Jossey-Bass, 2003) 22–26

Smit A, *The Property Rights of Refugees and Internally Displaced Persons: Beyond Restitution* (London, Routledge, 2012)

Smyth M, 'The Human Consequences of Armed Conflict: Constructing "Victimhood" in the Context of Northern Ireland's Troubles' in Cox M, Guelke A and Stephen F (eds), *A Farewell to Arms? From 'Long War' to Long Peace in Northern Ireland* (Manchester, Manchester University Press, 2000) 118–35

Spear J, 'Disarmament and Demobilisation' in Stedman S, Rothschild D and Cousens E (eds), *Ending Civil Wars: The Implementation of Peace Agreements* (Boulder, Lynne Rienner, 2002) 141–60

Spurk C, 'Understanding Civil Society' in Paffenholz T (ed), *Civil Society and Peacebuilding: A Critical Assessment* (Boulder, Lynne Rienner, 2010) 3–26

Sriram CL, *Confronting Past Human Rights Violations: Justice vs Peace in Times of Transition* (New York, Frank Cass, 2004)

——. 'Justice as Peace? Liberal Peacebuilding and Strategies of Transnational Justice' (2007) 21 *Global Society* 579

——. 'Post-conflict Justice and Hybridity in Peacebuilding: Resistance or Cooptation?' in Richmond OP and Mitchell A (eds), *Hybrid Forms of Peace: From Everyday Agency to Post-liberalism* (Basingstoke, Palgrave Macmillan, 2016) 58–72

Statistics South Africa, *Census 2011: Statistical Release (Revised)* (Pretoria, Statistics South Africa, 2012)

Stefanovic D, Loizides N and Psaltis C, *Attitudes of Victims Towards Transitional Justice: The Case of Cyprus* (Conference on 'Referendums and Peace Processes', Nicosia, University of Cyprus, 26 and 27 October 2016)

Stefansson AH, 'Homes in the Making: Property Restitution, Refugee Return and Senses of Belonging in a Post-war Bosnian Town' (2006) 44 *International Migration* 115

Steiner C and Ademović N, *Constitution of Bosnia and Herzegovina: Commentary*, 5th edn (Sarajevo, Konrad Adenauer, 2010)

Sternlight JR, 'In Search of the Best Procedure for Enforcing Employment Discrimination Laws: A Comparative Analysis' (2004) 78 *Tulane Law Review* 1401

Stover E, *The Witnesses: War Crimes and the Promise of Justice in the Hague* (Philadelpia, University of Pennsylvania Press, 2005)

Strazzari F, 'Between "Messy Aftermath" and "Frozen Conflicts": Chimeras and Realities of Sustainable Peace' (2008) 2 *Human Security Perspectives* 45

Sweeney J, 'Restorative Justice and Transitional Justice at the ECHR' (2012) 12 *International Criminal Law Review* 313

Tangri R and Southall R, 'The Politics of Black Economic Empowerment in South Africa' (2008) 34 *Journal of Southern African Studies* 699

Teitel R, *Transitional Justice* (Oxford, Oxford University Press, 2000)

——. 'Transitional Justice Genealogy' (2003) 16 *Harvard Human Rights Journal* 69

Thiessen C, 'Emancipatory Peacebuilding: Critical Responses to (Neo)Liberal Trends' in Matyok T, Senehi J and Byrne S (eds), *Critical Issues in Peace and Conflict Studies: Theory, Practice and Pedagogy* (Lanham, Lexington Books, 2011) 115–40

Thoms ON and Ron J, 'Do Human Rights Violations Cause Internal Conflict?' (2007) 29 *Human Rights Quarterly* 674

Tibbits F, 'Understanding What We Do: Emerging Models for Human Rights Education' (2002) 48 *International Review of Education* 159

Tierney S, *Constitutional Law and National Pluralism* (Oxford, Oxford University Press, 2004)

Todd J, Rougier N, O'Keefe T and Cañás Bottos L, 'Does Being Protestant Matter? Protestants, Minorities and the Remaking of Ethno-religious Identity after the Good Friday Agreement' (2009) 11 *National Identities* 87

Tremblay LB, 'The Legitimacy of Judicial Review: The Limits of Dialogue between Courts and Legislatures' (2005) 3 *International Journal of Constitutional Law* 617

Trimikliniotis N and Demetriou C, *Displacement in Cyprus: Consequences of Civil and Military Strife: Legal Framework in the Republic of Cyprus* (3/2012, Nicosia, PRIO Cyprus Centre, 2012)

Truth and Reconciliation Commission, *Truth and Reconciliation Commission South Africa Report* (Pretoria, Truth and Reconciliation Commission, 1998)

UN Centre for Human Rights, *National Human Rights Institutions: A Handbook on the Establishment and Strengthening of National Institutions for the Promotion and Protection of Human Rights* (Professional Training Series No 4, New York, United Nations, 1995)

UN Department of Public Information, *Prospects for Peace in the Middle East: An Israeli-Palestinian Dialogue: Proceedings of the United Nations Department of Public Information's International Encounter for European Journalists on the Question of Palestine* (New York, United Nations, 1992)

UN Human Rights Council, *National Report Submitted in Accordance with Paragraph 5 of the Annex to Human Rights Council Resolution 16/21: Bosnia and Herzegovina* (A/HRC/WG6/20/BIH/1, New York, United Nations General Assembly, 8 August 2014)

UN Secretary-General, *An Agenda for Peace: Preventive Diplomacy, Peacemaking and Peace-Keeping: Report of the Secretary-General Pursuant to the Statement Adopted by the Summit Meeting of the Security Council on 31 January 1992* (A/47/277 – S/24111, New York, United Nations, 1992)

——. *Report of the United Nations Secretary-General to the Security Council on the United Nations Operation in Cyprus* (S/1994/680, New York, United Nations, 7 June 1994)

——. *Supplement to an Agenda for Peace* (A/50/60 – S/1995/1, New York, United Nations, 1995)
——. *Press Release, Secretary General Expresses Hope for New Security Council Commitment to Place Justice, Rule of Law at Heart of Efforts to Rebuild War-Torn Countries* (SG/SM/8892, New York, United Nations, 2003)
——. *Report of the Secretary-General on His Mission of Good Offices in Cyprus* (S/2003/398, New York, United Nations, 1 April 2003)
——. *Report of the Secretary-General on His Mission of Good Offices in Cyprus* (S/2004/437, New York, United Nations, 28 May 2004)
——. *The Rule of Law and Transitional Justice in Conflict and Post-conflict Societies* (S/2004/616, New York, United Nations, 2004)
——. *Address by United Nations Secretary-General Kofi Annan to the Fifty-Sixth Session of the Executive Committee of the High Commissioner's Programme* (Geneva, United Nations, 6 October 2005)
——. *In Larger Freedom: Towards Security, Development and Human Rights of All* (A/59/2005, New York, United Nations, 2005)
——. *Report of the Secretary-General on the United Nations Operation in Cyprus* (S/2017/20, New York, United Nations, 9 January 2017)
UN Secretary-General's High-Level Panel on Threats Challenges and Change, *A More Secure World: Our Shared Responsibility* (A/59/565, New York, United Nations, 2004)
UN Security Council, *Report of the International Tribunal for the Prosecution of Persons Responsible for Serious Violations of International Humanitarian Law Committed in the Territory of the Former Yugoslavia since 1991* (S/1999/846, New York, United Nations, 25 August 1999)
UN Sub-Commission on the Promotion and Protection of Human Rights, *Housing and Property Restitution in the Context of the Return of Refugees and Internally Displaced Persons* (E/CN4/Sub2/2005/17, Geneva, United Nations, 28 June 2005)
UNDP, *Human Development Report: Annual Report* (New York, United Nations Development Programme, 1994)
——. *Governance for Peace: Securing the Social Contract* (New York, United Nations Development Programme, 2012)
UNHCR, *The State of the World's Refugees: In Search of Solidarity* (New York, United Nations High Commissioner for Refugees, 2012)
United Nations, *Proposal for the Comprhensive Settlement of the Cyprus Problem* (New York, United Nations, 2004)
Van der Auweraert P, *Reparations for Wartime Victims in the Former Yugoslavia: In Search of the Way Forward* (Geneva, International Organization for Migration, 2013)
Venice Commission, *Opinion on the Constitutional Situation in Bosnia and Herzegovina and the Powers of the High Representative* (CDL-AD(2005)004, Strasbourg, Council of Europe, 2005)
——. *Opinion on Different Proposals for the Election of the Presidency of Bosnia and Herzegovina* (CDL-AD(2006)004, Strasbourg, Council of Europe, 2006)
Veraart W, 'Redressing the Past with an Eye to the Future: The Impact of the Passage of Time on Property Rights Restitution in Post-apartheid South Africa' (2009) 27 *Netherlands Quarterly of Human Rights* 45
Verdirame G, 'Human Rights in Legal and Political Theory' in Rodley N and Sheeran S (eds), *Routledge Handbook of International Human Rights Law* (Abingdon, Routledge, 2013) 25–47
Villa-Vicencio C, 'Reconciliation' in Villa-Vicencio C and Doxtader E (eds), *Pieces of the Puzzle: Keywords on Reconciliation and Transitional Justice* (Cape Town, Institute of Justice and Reconciliation, 2004) 3–9
Von Tigerstrom B, *Human Security and International Law: Prospects and Problems* (Oxford, Hart Publishing, 2007)
Wade CM, 'Mind the Gap: State Capacity and Implementation of Human Rights Treaties' (2015) 69 *International Organization* 405

Waldron J, 'The Role of Rights in Practical Reasoning: "Rights" versus "Needs"' (2000) 4 *Journal of Ethics* 115

——. 'Redressing Historic Injustice' (2005) 52 *University of Toronto Law Journal* 135

——. 'Judges as Moral Reasoners' (2009) 7 *International Journal of Constitutional Law* 2

Wallensteen P, *Understanding Conflict Resolution: War, Peace and the Global System* (London, SAGE, 2002)

Welsh D, *The Rise and Fall of Apartheid* (Charlottesville, University of Virginia Press, 2009)

Widner J, 'Courts and Democracy in Postconflict Transitions: A Social Scientist's Perspective on the African Case' (2001) 95 *American Journal of International Law* 64

——. 'Constitution Writing in Post-conflict Settings: An Overview' (2008) 49 *William & Mary Law Review* 1513

Williams P, 'Alchemical Notes: Reconstructing Ideals from Deconstructed Rights' (1987) 22 *Harvard Civil Rights-Civil Liberties Law Review* 401

Williams RC, 'The Significance of Property Restitution to Sustainable Return in Bosnia and Herzegovina' (2006) 44 *International Migration* 39

Williams RC and Gürel A, *The European Court of Human Rights and the Cyprus Property Issue: Charting a Way Forward* (1/2011, Nicosia, PRIO Cyprus Centre, 2011)

Wilson RA, *The Politics of Truth and Reconciliation in South Africa: Legitimzing the Post-apartheid State* (Cambridge, Cambridge University Press, 2001)

Winter S, *Transitional Justice in Established Democracies: A Political Theory* (Basingstoke, Palgrave Macmillan, 2014)

Wippman D, 'Practical and Legal Constraints on Internal Power-Sharing' in Wippman D (ed), *International Law and Ethnic Conflict* (Ithaca, Cornell University Press, 1998) 211–41

Wolff S, 'Conceptualising Conflict Management and Settlement: Perspectives on Successes and Failures in Europe, Africa and Asia' in Schneckener U and Wolff S (eds), *Managing and Settling Ethnic Conflicts* (London, Hurst & Co Publishers, 2004) 1–17

Zartman W, 'Dynamics and Constraints in Negotiations in Internal Conflicts' in Zartman W (ed), *Elusive Peace: Negotiating an End to Civil Wars* (Washington DC, Brookings Institution, 1995) 3–27

——. 'Towards the Resolution of International Conflicts' in Zartman W and Rasmussen L (eds), *Peacemaking in International Conflict: Methods & Techniques*, 2nd edn (Washington DC, United States Institute of Peace Press, 2007) 3–24

Zemans FK, 'Legal Mobilization: The Neglected Role of the Law in the Political System' (1983) 77 *American Political Science Review* 690

Zembylas M, Charalambous P, Charalambous C and Lesta S, 'Human Rights and the Ethno-Nationalist Problematic through the Eyes of Greek-Cypriot Teachers' (2016) 11 *Education Citizenship and Social Justice* 19

Index

Page locators in *italics* refer to information in figures.